PASSPORT TO HOLLYWOOD

THE SUNY SERIES IN
POSTMODERN CULTURE
Joseph Natoli, editor

PASSPORT TO HOLLYWOOD

Hollywood Films, European Directors

James Morrison

State University of New York Press

Chapter 2 reprinted from *Modern Language Notes* 111.5 (December 1996), by permission of Johns Hopkins University Press.

Chapter 3 reprinted from *Arizona Quarterly* 52.1 (1996), by permission of the Regents of The University of Arizona.

Published by
State University of New York Press, Albany

For information, address State University of New York Press,
State University Plaza, Albany, N.Y., 12246

Production by Marilyn P. Semerad
Marketing by Fran Keneston

Library of Congress Cataloging-in-Publication Data

Morrison, James, 1960–
    Passport to Hollywood : Hollywood films, European directors / James Morrison.
       p.   cm. — (The SUNY series in postmodern culture)
    Includes bibliographical references and index.
    ISBN 0-7914-3937-2 (hardcover : alk. paper). — ISBN 0-7914-3938-0 (pbk. : alk. paper)
    1. Motion pictures—United States—History. 2. Motion pictures--United States—European influences. I. Title. II. Series.
PN1993.5.U6M656 1998
791.43'75'0973—dc21   98-13702
                                                 CIP

10 9 8 7 6 5 4 3 2 1

Contents

Illustrations

All stills reproduced courtesy of the Museum of Modern Art, New York.

Acknowledgments

During the five years of my work on this project, many friends and colleagues have helped me through the intellectual endgames and emotional downturns it has sometimes entailed. Mary Cappello and Jean Walton provided inspiration, challenge, and fun, and Karyn Sproles and Jon Thompson provided not only illuminating readings of the manuscript but crucial affection at key moments. Each of my colleagues in Film Studies at North Carolina State University has read parts of the project and offered encouraging suggestions: thanks to Joe Gomez, Andrea Mensch, Maria Pramaggiore and Tom Wallis. At large, Eyal Amiran, Charlie Baxter, Jim Caton, Suzanne Chester, Dante Harper, Elaine Orr, Rei Terada, and Deborah Wyrick have all eased me through various impasses, while Art Efron, Cynthia Erb, Brian Henderson, Kim Hunter, Irving Massey, Jim Mayes, Martin Pops, and Alan Spiegel helped to lay the groundwork. Thomas Schur provided me with an emotional and intellectual climate that enabled the completion of the project.

I thank the editors of *Arizona Quarterly* and *MLN*, in whose journals parts of this project first appeared, not only for their initial hospitality to the project but for their expert editorial work on those articles. I wish to thank as well Robert Burgoyne and Peter Lev for early readings of the manuscript that helped me to improve it. The readers for SUNY Press were similarly adroit, and Joseph Natoli and James Peltz of SUNY Press have been unstintingly professional throughout the project. Marilyn P. Semerad guided the project through production with great efficiency, and Terry Geesken of the Museum of Modern Art helped with the illustrations with unfailing good humor.

Introduction

Resident Aliens: Hollywood Films/ European Directors

When Salvador Dali and Cecil B. DeMille met in Hollywood, according to René Clair's wry report, the Spanish surrealist prostrated himself in an extravagant gesture of awe-stricken admiration as the famous American producer serenely welcomed his adulation.[1] Whether apocryphal or merely legendary, the meeting between these figures is difficult to imagine in part because of the vastly different cultural territories each inhabited. Dali's Euro-modernist pedigree defines him in the popular imagination—where despite that pedigree he surely retains a place—as clearly as DeMille's reputation as the doyen of American mass culture's commercialism, in turn, characterizes him. Yet on second thought, especially in the wake of the alternately joyous and terrorized deterritorialization of post-modern culture, their meeting not only makes sense, but it appears to be nothing less than inevitable.

The territories Dali and DeMille were instrumental in charting were those of a fantasy-Europe and a mythic-America, opposed cultural images that, confronting one another continually across variously projected lines of cultural demarcation, simultaneously defined themselves in relation to the other while defining the other in relation to themselves. Typically, such national/cultural self-definitions have been known to have a decidedly insular quality, producing the standard set of polarities that have long governed our conceptions of the relation of "Europe" and "America" as symbolic cultural spaces: European tradition versus American novelty, European high-seriousness

1

versus American free-spiritedness, European aristocratic elitism versus American democracy, European art versus American entertainment, European modernism versus American mass culture. While such polarities have always been subject to question, they were formerly sustained most often by a cultural complacency rooted in a fantasy of secure difference and separateness. When Sydney Smith asked his famous question in 1920—"In the four quarters of the globe, who reads an American book?"—he was merely expressing inversely the same contempt many American critics vented in responding to the Armory Show of 1914 (to take just one example) as an arrant display of European pretension and pomp. Though without the ethnic or racial dimension often characteristic of social demonologies, both responses nonetheless attribute demonized qualities—American intellectual vacancy, European intellectual elitism—to a projected "Other." In these cases, this rhetoric of alterity enforces its distinctions by appealing to established categories of nationality.

When Dali meets DeMille, that fantasy of separateness atomizes into a potentially liberatory confusion of realms, and the traditional polarities that have defined cultural territory must be redrawn, even assuming culture is any longer to be defined in territorial terms. By Clair's report, what defines the encounter between Dali and DeMille is not the high modernist's fear of the encroaching Philistines, nor is it the suspicion of the denizen of mass culture toward the elite artist; rather, their meeting is marked by a quality of mutual recognition. Even if DeMille did not know Dali's work or his reputation, he was apparently unsurprised by the flamboyance of his gesture; even if Dali's expression of awe was nothing more than a sly joke, it conjures nonetheless a hauntingly representative image of twentieth-century culture. In this image, Dali's adoption of a subordinate position, prostrate before DeMille, calls up traditional modernist conceptions of cultural hierarchy only to reverse them. The experimental modernist who adopts nontraditional modes of representation to ward off the taint of consumerism, who might be expected to express horror and loathing in relation to DeMille's crass commercialism, instead bows in reverence to it, while the successful businessman who might be expected to be repelled by the bohemian artist accepts his tribute graciously.

As a culturally symbolic scenario, the imaginary tableau of DeMille's meeting with Dali overturns conventional notions about the distinction between art and commerce and the related distinctions between "high" European culture and "popular" American culture that subtend the former. Though Clair's account of Dali's meeting with DeMille is crabbily sketchy, it is likely that the meeting occurred on the occasion of Dali's pilgrimage to Hollywood in 1945, to work on the climactic dream sequence of a Hollywood movie, *Spellbound* (Hitchcock, 1945). If Dali worried that his distinctive personal style would become commodified or contaminated through its unseemly trafficking with mass culture in that film, the fact of his having assented to work on the project at all (together with corroboration in biographies of Dali) suggests some recognition that art and commerce have always interrelated in complex ways, and that in the postindustrial age those interactions take on even more definitive force as pre-industrial cultural models come to seem ever less applicable. Such recognition hovers over the image of Dali's meeting with DeMille, who in turn worried about his own work's devaluation merely because it was popular.[2] The encounter between this representative of European high culture and his counterpart in American mass culture thus reveals not the expected opposition between cultural levels, but rather the overlapping territory that those levels share, even when they seek to close themselves off from one another.

The meeting between DeMille and Dali was regrettably not chronicled on film. Another unlikely encounter, however, between Alfred Hitchcock and Andy Warhol, was the subject of a 1974 photograph by Jill Krementz. In the photograph, Hitchcock sits with regal casualness in an uncomfortable-looking armchair, his hands linked before him with as much fey boyishness as his Olympian figure might be capable of expressing. Beside him, Warhol kneels, arms folded, in the attitude of a devotee. Again, as in the Dali-DeMille meeting Clair recounts, we are confronted with two embodied cultural icons, representative of cultural traditions seemingly remote from each other, facing one another with what appears in spite of this apparent remoteness to be a mutual admiration bordering, on Warhol's side at least, on worship. Again the encounter is worked out visually in the terms of an actual *physical* hierarchy, one figure above and one below, that appears as an analogue to a symbolic or cultural hierarchy that it suggestively illuminates. Yet the cultural levels in this tableau are, if anything, even less clearly determinate than those in the imagined meeting of DeMille and Dali as described by Clair. In the literal spatial terms of the picture, Hitchcock is ostensibly seated above the worshipful Warhol, who kneels at his feet, but in terms of scale, Warhol's height, because of the camera's angle, exceeds that of Hitchcock, whose physical aspect accordingly takes on a distinctly infantilized cast.

Given the undeniable proposition that Hitchcock and Warhol *are* cultural icons in any case, of what precisely are they, in the text of this photo or in the texts of reality, representative? Warhol's entire career, in its persistently affectless way, was dedicated to a prim assault on the mechanics and politics of cultural value in postmodern America. Experimenting with the effects of mechanical reproduction and the ramifications of commodified representation—the multiply cast silk-screens of Hollywood stars, the images of proliferated commodities such as cans of soup—Warhol pursued as a vanguard the now familiar effort to dismantle the twin cults of originality and individuality, and in turn the rhetoric of privileged self-expression, held over from previous centuries' aesthetics. Yet of what, paradoxically, is Warhol representative if not of that lingering effect of high culture, however modified, the "serious artist"? Hitchcock, on the other hand, made his career in the industry of the Hollywood film, nonetheless gaining a reputation certified by his status as *auteur* for, precisely, originality and individuality of expression, but an individuality and originality achieved within the inmost den of mass production and commercialism. A certain trade-off is thus effected between the two figures as cultural icons, with Warhol as the stand-in-by-default for the highbrow culture whose altered status his own work aspires to bring about, while Hitchcock comes to represent a popular culture reaching toward, and adopting, attitudes formerly harbored exclusively in the "high" mode of cultural discourse. Here once again, key issues of cultural valuation and cultural hierarchization find formulation in an image not of opposition and separation but of collusion and exchange, of shared ground rather than of distinct spheres, between Warhol, hipsterishly postmodern and blandly American, and Hitchcock, reticently modern and donnishly European.

These images may seem to be a roundabout route toward the introduction of the present book. But the subject of the book is precisely the juxtapositions of seemingly different, even opposed cultural frameworks—those of modernity and modernism, "high" culture and mass culture, the national cultures of Europe and America—that resulted when filmmakers from European cinemas came to Hollywood to make popular, mass-market films. Such emigrations have occurred from the beginning of cinema as a cultural form at the end of the nineteenth century until the present day, and have produced vital social, cultural, economic transactions that have given shape to fundamental aspects of cinema as a cultural form. Study of the emigration of European directors to Hollywood yields important implications, then, for many key issues of both history and theory in cinema studies, from the status of the "Classical Hollywood" paradigm to the construction of national ideologies or identities in film.

This study seeks to define the particular qualities of Hollywood cinematic representation that result from this phenomenon, and therefore to synthesize such issues of history and theory with methods of close psychocultural analysis of individual texts. Because of this ambition, I have defined the phenomenon in what may first appear to some readers to be a somewhat delimited way and have largely drawn upon examples that, though never atypical, may sometimes appear somewhat specialized. For instance, I have limited the frame of reference to the group of Hollywood emigrés who came to the institution of Hollywood with a body of work behind them in European cinemas. Thus, the work of Fritz Lang, for instance, is studied here through the lens of one of his most culturally suggestive films, while the work of Frank Capra (born in Palermo), for instance, is not. This study is not concerned to determine the nationalisms or national attitudes of particular people, then, but to examine the signifiers of culture or of cultural nationalisms as they are articulated within particular textual or cultural systems. (Partly in order to emphasize this point, I have included chapters on films by directors who, although their work is associated with European art-cinemas, were American-born.) In its analysis of Hollywood films by European directors, this study attempts to elaborate a theory of differential textuality in Hollywood cinema. When filmmakers enter with one set of stylistic or narrative codes an institutional system of representation characterized by a different set of codes, what kinds of representation result? How do these codes interact with, struggle against, redefine one another? The directors whose work is under analysis here migrated to, or were imported into, the Hollywood system with the preexistent "passport" of a style, a reputation, a pedigree, which, in its interaction with Hollywood's institutional edicts, reveals much about the particular codes of either institution.

At the same time, I have not proceeded by means of a systematic comparison of particular filmmakers' European work with their Hollywood films, but rather have tried to define the stylistic textures and ideological dispositions of the films such directors worked on in Hollywood in relation to the received practices and cultural assumptions of Hollywood or art-cinema representations at large. I do not assume that the directors' emigré status inevitably confers on these filmmakers a critical, privileged perspective in relation to the traditional codes of Hollywood representation (though that may sometimes be the case). However, I do take such an assumption to shape important aspects of the production, exhibition, and reception of the films they made in Hollywood. To be sure, my focus in relation to this topic is on the forms of representation the institution of Hollywood produces when it incorporates what it projects as differential or "foreign" elements—precisely, in this case, the *styles* of European filmmakers—and it is this aim that justifies the book's method of close analysis of individual films. The title of the introduction, then, should be taken to refer not to the directors as historical people, but to the films they made in the Hollywood system:[3] it is the films themselves that, residing within and produced by the institution of Hollywood, remain in complex ways "alien" to it.

A basic assumption of this study that should be articulated at the outset is that, despite the differences between them, both Hollywood and the various European cinemas function as cultural institutions with parallel aims and aspirations. Both are also, obviously, at the same time, constituted as social and economic institutions, and it is frequently the interaction between these related but differing forms of institutional imperative that determines the specific kinds of representation either produces. In defining Hollywood and European cinemas as cultural institutions, I mean to underline the various practices of regulation, mediation, and codification that characterize cinematic institutions more generally. Such institutions serve the social/cultural function of eliciting cinematic "pleasure," defined in its several ways, in consumers. This in turn guarantees the self-generation of the institution as an economic entity, setting into motion rounds of exchange, inducing audiences to buy tickets so the next round of films may be produced. In order to assure these functions, cinematic institutions produce regulatory mechanisms to render their products not only recognizable but desirable: codified practices of style or narration, marketing practices that disseminate knowledge and create curiosity about particular products.

The regulatory functions of cinematic institutions are not limited to the need of the institutions as economic entities in industrial society to accumulate capital; they must also, as cultural institutions, appeal to large-scale aesthetic desires, mass fantasies, widely accessible mythologies. Though I elaborate such positions at various localized phases of the book's argument, this study will make little theoretical sense if the reader cannot assume a certain basic correspondence, in the terms defined above, among modern industrial cinematic institutions. It will make just as little sense, however, if the reader does not accept crucial distinctions between the specific regulatory, mediatory practices of individual cinematic institutions, which is precisely what makes the migration of terms from one institutional system into another so culturally suggestive.

The European cinema as a cultural institution, indeed, has traditionally been understood by contrast with the Hollywood cinema in its narrative patterns and its stylistic effects. In this much-recited contrast, Hollywood has been seen as the holdover of the values of nineteenth-century classical realism, naturalizing, tempering, and disseminating these values on a scale without precedent even in the realist novel. Drawing upon traditional rhetorics of stability and ideologies of coherence, the Hollywood cinema fulfills its self-appointed function to mass-produce mass fantasies and, in doing so, gains worldwide dominance in international film culture as early as the 1910s. The European cinema, meanwhile, is in these narratives a united front—an all-but-undifferentiated "art-cinema," in the currently accepted designation in media studies—in its opposition to Hollywood's domination, valuing character over plot, expressive subjectivity over genre formulae, exploratory style over codified procedure, skeptical inquiry over populist faith, critique over affirmation.[4] Clearly, this schema is redolent of, indeed dependent on, the traditional oppositions between European and American national cultures. Even if one is inclined to resist the sharpest polarities at work in this schema, these films of European filmmakers in Hollywood remain illuminating examples of a particular strain of cultural hybridity, of the conjunction of cultural realms that has defined so much of cultural production in the twentieth century. Taken as a body of related works, however diffuse, these films play out complex issues involving cultural modernism and its relation to mass modernity, cultural hierarchy and the construction of value, and "national" culture and its place in an *inter*national context.

In its earliest days, before the coming of sound, film was often heralded as the great cross-bred, popular, international art. Rooted as it was in the ground of images, the medium was hailed for its potential to transcend national boundaries of language. To be sure, the rise of early cinema is marked by substantial and uninhibited borrowings across national lines, especially in the cinemas quickest to develop such as those of France, Britain, and the United States. The rise of the "chase" as a basic narrative pattern, the use of free-form compositions, and the staging of parallel action from shot to shot all resulted from a kind of cooperative cross-referencing among the work of such early directors as the Frenchman Louis Lumière, Britain's James Williamson, and the American Edwin S. Porter. The anarchic freedom, even the gleeful plagiarism, of such borrowings was enabled by an absence at the time of restrictions later to be imposed, such as limitations on national trade or the institution of international copyright laws. These transactions were also made possible by the adaptability and accessibility of the formal devices in question, which could theoretically be brought to bear on narratives of any national culture.

Even then, however, a certain assertion of national/cultural property rights dictated such transnational influence. One of Porter's early films, drawing on narrative structures and stylistic patterns previously developed in French and British one-reelers, such as Williamson's *Fire!* (1901), nonetheless attempted to stamp a national pedigree on the film in its very title, *Life of an American Fireman* (1903).[5] In this film, Porter draws upon the "chase" structure of these earlier one-reelers in order to dynamize an affirmative vision of institutions of rescue produced by the modern city. Obviously, nothing in the "chase" structure—a goal-oriented line of action, contiguous shot relations employing recurrent image patterns to provide spatial orientation—could be said to be endemic to the cultures "originating" it, but the boldness of Porter's appropriations made the devices and the genre itself retrospectively come to seem quintessentially "American." Moreover, Porter adapts in the film the in-camera editing of the Frenchman Georges Méliès's "trick" films. In order to represent a large number of horse-drawn fire-carriages careening through the streets using only two actual carriages, Porter employs invisible splices in order to create the illusion that a single shot extends continuously, concealing the in-camera edits contained within the shot. In other words, as is clearly visible in the text of the film itself, Porter turns off the camera after the carriages have gone by, then resumes shooting so that the same carriages can pass before the camera again, giving the impression of a plenitude of carriages where only two actually exist. The use of in-camera editing in Méliès's films is whimsically apparent, playfully making objects appear to vanish from the screen without attempting to conceal the mechanisms of the "trick." In incorporating the device, Porter renders it in the terms of an invisibility of style already becoming prevalent in American film, providing an early illustration of the contrast between European cinema's overt self-reflexivity and American film's emergent aesthetic of illusionism.

Thus from its earliest days, the medium was defined equally by the counterimpulse to categorize national cinemas according to distinctly *national* styles, even by branding seemingly neutral stylistic or formal devices with a nationalist stamp. Long before André Bazin's film criticism of the early 1950s, which finally consolidated many of the conceptions of national style in cinema that continue to determine the field of study, the cinemas of industrialized countries thrived on the production of myths of nationhood and attendant developments in style that would serve to distinguish their products from those of other countries. These myths most often harked back to pre-industrial images of celebratory nationhood, as in the case of a film like Abel Gance's *Napoleon* (1927); or to canonical classics of national culture, as in the case of a film like F. W. Murnau's *Faust* (1926). These cases indicate the connection between emergent European cinematic styles and narratives of national culture. In each case, the distinctive stylistic attributes the films incorporate or initiate, attributes that function to demarcate the explicitly *national* styles of an epic impressionism in Gance's case and a folk expressionism in Murnau's, are shown thereby to be assuredly compatible with received national ideologies. Thus, the dominant styles of early European national cinemas at once differentiate themselves from the styles of other national cinemas and ally themselves with ongoing "great traditions" of the particular national cultures from which they emanate.

Lacking traditions historically remote enough to be represented with impunity in a still unrespectable, "low" medium, Hollywood cinema in its first decades often eschewed providing popular images of its national heroes or massified versions of its national literatures. Instead, the Hollywood cinema targeted specific subgroups, by representing immigrant experience in America, for instance, or opted to develop genres that, ringing variations on key precedents in literature or other cultural venues, were markedly film-specific in their narrative patterns and stylistic ingredients, if not in their general iconographies. The western, for instance, as has often been noted, has its roots in the "high" mode of James Fenimore Cooper and in the vernacular mode of Owen Wister, but the one-reelers of the Hollywood western, such as *The Great Train Robbery* (Porter, 1904), inevitably diverge from their literary predecessors by condensing the narrative patterns, abstracting the characters, and distilling the styles of those antecedents in a manner dictated in large part by the limitations of the new form. The ballad-like breadth of the later Classical Hollywood western, in turn, has *its* antecedents as much in the broad strokes of the "primitive" one-reeler as in the pseudo-epic thrust of the nineteenth-century frontier novel. The very novelty of the medium was thus co-opted as a figure for the "newness" of American culture itself, at least in Hollywood's projections of it.

At the same time that early Hollywood reconstructed such "native" cultural traditions in the terms of the new medium, Hollywood film became for many of the same reasons a repository for similarly broadly styled projections of European mythologies invoked in place of supposedly absent American traditions. D. W. Griffith's early costume dramas of the 1910s, for instance, from *Willful Peggy* (1910) to the relevant sections of *Intolerance* (1916), conjure up European settings for their melodramatic narratives, while the Edison studio's versions from roughly the same period of European Gothic horror tales, precursors of the 1930s cycle of Hollywood horror films, reimagine those narratives of other national cultures for American mass audiences. In the case of the 1930s Universal horror films, the narratives nominally retain the aura of their national origins in their fancifully imagined "foreign" settings, routinely augmented by the stewardship of a European director such as James Whale or Karl Freund and the presence of European actors in the cast. At the same time, the stories are remade in the terms dictated by Hollywood as an institution of representation, employing the narrative patterns and stylistic practices that define the institution, thus providing imaginary versions of national *difference*, allowing American audiences to imagine themselves gaining access via such representations to another country's culture—habits of dress and styles of decor, mannerisms, customs, social structures—while retaining the security of national *sameness* guaranteed by the films' status as products of Hollywood. In such ways has the cinema functioned both as a medium for national self-expression and a vehicle for national dispersal, permitting audiences to imagine themselves as part of "globally" defined communities theoretically independent of immediate or inescapable national grounding.

A vital tradition persists in Hollywood cinema, to be sure, of personal visions of European or international subjects. Films of the Classical Hollywood era such as *Broken Blossoms* (Griffith, 1919), *City Lights* (Chaplin, 1931), *The Scarlet Empress* (von Sternberg, 1934), *The Shop around the Corner* (Lubitsch, 1939), or *Letter from an Unknown Woman* (Ophuls, 1948) all formulate within the terms of Hollywood's dominant styles a representation of European culture—and in most of these cases with a European director guiding the project. The lack of a parallel tradition in European cinemas of the representation of American culture signals at one important level, in its obvious nonmutuality, the hegemony of Hollywood in international film culture. To argue that film culture has always been shaped by patterns of intercultural exchange is in no way to deny the fact of that hegemony, which has been at least equally crucial in the formation of that culture and which has in many ways determined the processes of that exchange. To be sure, the presence of Hollywood as a symbolic force in the products of European cinemas is felt largely, in a sort of phantom form, at the level of influence: Griffith's influence on the Russians, Erich von Stroheim's on Jean Renoir, Buster Keaton's on Jacques Tati, Alfred Hitchcock's on Francois Truffaut, Douglas Sirk's on Rainer Werner Fassbinder, just to name a few examples. As the examples of von Stroheim, Hitchcock, and Sirk suggest, a European component was always decisively formative of the Hollywood tradition. But Hollywood as an institution of representation has routinely thrived on the absorption of the energies of cultural production of European cinemas in far more literal, material ways, appropriating narratives of European nationality in lavish "costume" epics, importing "talent" in periodic raids on European national cinemas, or incorporating the very national styles initially articulated to differentiate particular cinemas from Hollywood practices: to cite some of the better-known examples, the incorporation of German expressionism into the horror film or of expressionism and the prewar French noir film into Hollywood film noir, of Italian neorealism into the postwar pseudodocumentary Hollywood crime-film, of the French New Wave and other "new" European cinemas into the New Hollywood cinema.

The real effects of Hollywood hegemony in international film culture have produced the narrative that still largely shapes our understanding of the phenomenon of European filmmakers working in the Hollywood studio system. Incorporating an aesthetic of "exile" redolent of cultural modernism more generally (as in Joyce's "silence, exile and cunning"), that narrative presents a vision of the Hollywood exile as a figure of pathos stripped of originary means of expression, denied access to the native national styles that would speak his authentic identity. The image of the exile always points backward insofar as it calls up the image of a better past and lamented home, a time before the loss of national belonging that earns the figure its pathos. In individual cases, this narrative may well bear its share of truth, especially since emigration to Hollywood on the part of many directors was prompted by historical and political calamities. The rise of fascism in Europe prompted the first significant wave of emigration during World War II, bringing to Hollywood such European directors as Jean Renoir and Fritz Lang, as well as Robert Siodmak, Douglas Sirk, René Clair, Julien Duvivier, William Dieterle, Billy Wilder, Michael Curtiz, or, with differently shaded circumstances, G. W. Pabst or Alfred Hitchcock. The Soviet invasion of Eastern Europe and its resulting shock-waves gave rise to the second influx at the end of the 1960s, contributing to the emigration of the Polish Roman Polanski and the Czechs Milos Forman and Ivan Passer, as well as such figures as the cinematographers Miroslav Ondricek, Laszlo Kovacs, and Vilmos Zsigmond, among others.

This narrative retains, in any case, a faintly nineteenth-century ring in its image of the humiliated exile exploited by the commodification of Hollywood and tragically destined to produce degraded versions of his "native" work in the European mode. Privileging European cinema-as-art over Hollywood commercialism, this narrative typically appeals to an equation between nativity and authenticity even as it invests somewhat paradoxically in traditional models of authorship and self-expression. What is presumed to certify the artistic superiority of European cinema in such models is its valuation of personal expression over popular demand. Yet that structure of feeling—apparently transcending institutional regulation in the first instance, enabling direct transactions between the artist's glorified subjectivity and the artistic product—is finally seen to depend on the *medium* of nationality. After all, if it were required only for the artist's inner essence to overflow spontaneously, thus producing dependably Great Works, that inspiriting flow should theoretically be able to proceed unhampered—anywhere, at any time. The notion of the commodified exile is ahistorical, not because the Hollywood films of European emigrés are or are not superior or inferior to their European works. Short of an aggressive appeal to empirical models of evaluation, such inferiority or superiority must in specific cases remain a question of individual preference or personal taste, interesting to the extent that they remain under the sway of the particular institutional hierarchies of culture in place at a given point in time and thus tell us something about the mechanisms of those hierarchies. Rather, it is ahistorical because it denies the institutional mediation of cinematic representation as such, perceiving such mediation only in Hollywood's oppressive regimes when in fact it is characteristic of all cinemas.

Moreover, that notion is rooted in ideas about the nature of cultural production that have their origin in pre-industrial society. The romantic notion of a high European culture not subject to opportunistic vulgarity or puerile consumerism brings with it, especially by contrast to the debasements of culture that notion typically projects upon America, a set of assumptions that smack distinctly of a theory of radical endowment. Rather than to assume the contiguity of cultures as a set of shared or received values and images transmitted over many social or cultural strata and evolving according to historical circumstance, this notion posits culture as the bastion of high acts of transcendent imagination. From this idea comes, in turn, the image of a culture-bearing class granted the power to confer value, legislate distinction, regulate production, dictate norms, and exclude difference. Considering Hollywood's prominence on the international film market, the "superiority" of European cinemas in this context must remain a strictly symbolic one. To be sure, it has historically been the prerogative of Hollywood as an institution of representation to seize and retain those very powers of control. Indeed, the complex transactions between Hollywood and European cinemas have been governed, as rigidly as by other forms of cultural hierarchy and national boundary, by converse symbioses of Hollywood's actual, material dominance and what has often been seen as the greater artistic pedigree of European cinemas.

The competition between these institutions of representation thus pits Hollywood's economic domination on the "market" against European cinemas' superior cultural legitimacy that eschews any vulgar notions of markets. Because of such double-edged correlation, the products of the dialogue between these insitutions are typically schismatic, contradictory, even antinomial, whether represented by the Hollywood movie that projects a fantasy-Europe as the dream site of strange and fearsome exoticism (such as Griffith's *Oprhans of the Storm* [1921] or, in a different way, *The Scarlet Empress*) or the European art-film whose disgust with American cultural colonization of Europe is matched only by its fascination with things American (*Breathless* [Godard, 1959], say, or *The American Friend* [Wenders, 1978]). Those conflicted qualities, however, have larger implications for the ideologies of Hollywood than for those of European cinemas, especially when we measure Hollywood's ideologies of certitude against art-cinema's valuations of ambiguity. As an institution of representation, Hollywood achieved its dominance by wedding a kind of totalized American populism to a form of monopoly capitalism that, in a quintessential instance of ideological mystification, the former was engaged to conceal. (Consider the number of Hollywood movies that attack monopolies, from *A Corner in Wheat* [Griffith, 1908] to *Citizen Kane* [1941] and beyond, an especially striking recurrence given Hollywood's status at the time of the second film as a corporate monopoly.) Basic to the Classical Hollywood model of representation are such features as linear narrative and stable, normative patterns of identification. These strategies, in turn, aim to produce the effect of an ideology of coherence that theoretically excludes contradiction and thereby insures the continued generation of the institution that subtends them, matching the institution's economic functions at its cultural levels. The ideological structure of Hollywood as a system of representation excludes threatening contradiction by, whether in complex or simple ways, excluding *difference* itself. In so doing, it produces various illusions of unity—of a unified infrastructure, of a homogeneous audience—as well as, in the same instance and by virtue of the same strategies, such noteworthy features of Hollywood ideology as casual racism, entrenched misogyny, complex xenophobia, forthright homophobia, and complacent patricianism, even while exuding an oleaginous, warm bath of tendentious pan-humanism. The conflicted, schismatic aspects of the texts produced by the encounter of Hollywood and European cinemas, especially in the specific form of European directors' migrations to Hollywood, potentially endanger both the massive confidence (not to say complacency) and the circumscription (not to say insularity) that undergird the various rhetorical unities and homogeneities of this institutional system.

Why, if this is the case, should the emigration of European film-makers to Hollywood, and the influence of European cinematic styles upon Hollywood films more generally, be so decisive a factor in the evolution of Hollywood as an institution of representation? It might be expected that an institution of the type I have described, so powerful, so monolithic, so hermetic, and so protective of its own dominant position, might be readily able to effect the exclusions necessary to render competing institutions harmless in their ineffectual encroachments. It is the case, moreover, that at various points in Hollywood's history, the presence of European technicians behind the scenes in film production has been greeted with fairly uncomplicated displays of a xenophobia akin to that which so many Hollywood films themselves express. When William Randolph Hearst sought in a fit of outrage to forestall the release of *Citizen Kane*, that unwholesomely foreign-seeming document that Hearst believed to be based on his biography, one of his most potent threats was to expose to the American public the extent of "foreign" labor employed in Hollywood. In some literal ways as well as in many symbolic ones, the presence of Europeans in Hollywood illustrates the internalization of *difference*, of otherness, in a system ordinarily concerned precisely to exclude such difference. The cultural politics of the European-in-Hollywood manifests an instance of "difference" permissible within the terms of the institutional system, an instance that nonetheless, despite its permissibility, threatens the enclosure of that system. If it is true that the most basic practices of Hollywood representation are exclusionary ones, then, the fact of European emigration can usefully be examined to reveal the dynamics of such otherness within a system characterized by its titanic resistance to the experience and apprehension of difference, its commitment to a vision of securely homogenized sameness.

While it would not be strictly accurate to define the set of films directed in Hollywood by European filmmakers as a *genre*, the films remain related as a body of work in their inevitable textual hybridity. To the extent that these works illustrate the process of dialogue between competing, collateral, or opposed cultural institutions, they participate in complex dynamics of resistance and assimilation, canonization and re-accentuation, as terms from one institutional system are translated, transported, reinscribed within another. Some readers may recognize the terms "canonization" and "re-accentuation" as inherited from the work of an important twentieth-century theorist of the novel, Mikhail Bakhtin, who also reflected extensively on the concept of hybridity in cultural formations. For Bakhtin, the novel as a genre functioned as a cultural system in which the languages of official, literary culture engage in liberatory forms of dialogue with other language forms such as provincial or dialect speech, professional jargon or technical language. The latter forms exist outside the realms of official culture, according to Bakhtin, but they find expression in the hybrid genre of the novel, which welcomes and thrives on them, and the resultant dialogue among these levels of language undermines the unitary, univocal, "authoritative" discourses of official culture that continue to attempt to articulate themselves in the genre. The dialogic impulse definitive of the novel thus threatens the traditional cultural, social hierarchies official culture enforces. Yet, because of this threat, according to Bakhtin, official culture produces the novel as a cultural system that works to exclude the "heteroglossia" of these multiple voices through a process Bakhtin calls "canonization." However, because the nature of the novel as a genre is at odds with that process, the process is itself always in dialogue with a counterprocess of "re-accentuation" whereby the heteroglot elements of novelistic textuality reassert their hybrid, differential force:

> [O]ther aspects of heteroglossia . . . may, at the given moment, already have lost their flavor of "belonging to another language"; they may already have been canonized by literary language. . . . It is precisely in the most heteroglot eras, when the collision and interaction of languages is especially intense and powerful, when heteroglossia washes over literary language from all sides (that is, in precisely those eras that most conduce to the novel) that aspects of heteroglossia are canonized with great ease. . . . In this intense struggle, boundaries are drawn with new sharpness and simultaneously erased with new ease. (418)

Although Bakhtin often treated the novel as a distinctive genre completely insulated from other forms of cultural production, his work has been used to illuminate issues in a wide range of cultural texts, including films. Certainly his notion of the function and interrelation of differential systems in cultural production has shaped how I have understood the interaction of Hollywood and European cinemas as cultural institutions.

Yet, although the films of European directors in Hollywood strikingly lend themselves to discussion of hybridization, heteroglossia, canonization, and re-accentuation, the liberatory force of these terms in this context is nowhere near so clear as Bakhtin takes it to be in the context of the novel. This is in part because Bakhtin sees the novel as, generically speaking, essentially hostile to the controlling institutional forces of cultural production that attempt to govern it. The Hollywood film as a generic form, on the other hand, is given shape by a very direct connection between textual effects and institutional government. While the Hollywood film, like the novel, may well be fundamentally defined by a constitutive generic hybridity, it has traditionally been understood (to put it in Bakhtin's terms) as a distinctly univocal, monologic form, exclusionist and "authoritative" even in its postures of populism. The dialogue between Hollywood-as-institution and European art-cinemas constitutes a telling instance of "polyglossia" as Bakhtin defines it, as the migration of "language-codes" across "language systems":

> The new cultural and creative consciousness lives in an actively polyglot world. The world becomes polyglot, once and for all and irreversibly. The period of national languages, coexisting but closed and deaf to each other, comes to an end. Languages throw light on each other: one language can, after all, only see itself in the light of another language. (12)

But this dialogue remains bound to the counterprocesses of the monologic institution that determines it, shaped by the institution's effort to stamp its authority upon the languages of the individual texts it engenders.

Rather than thinking of them as a genre, it might be more accurate to think of this set of films as manifestations of a particular style of subculture within the larger institutional system. Indeed, anecdotal accounts of the "colonies" of Europeans in Hollywood during World War II, for instance, suggest that the social realities of these emigrés, marginalized and joined by shared codes and cultural affiliations, were much in line with those of the "subculture" as it has recently been defined in the field of cultural studies.[6] The importance of style in subculture proceeds from subcultures' subordinate relation to dominant culture; style itself, in these models, provides a potential refuge from dominant practices. As Dick Hebdige argues,

> the challenge to hegemony which subcultures represent is not issued directly by them. Rather, it is expressed obliquely, in style.

The objections are lodged, the contradictions displayed (and "magically resolved") at the profoundly superficial level of appearances: that is, at the level of signs. . . . Style in subculture is, then, pregnant with significance. (367)

With these ideas in mind, I have tried to discover in the dialogical manifestations of style in the films under analysis here especially significant illuminations of questions about cultural modernism, cultural hierarchy, and national culture.

Such aspects of dialogic style, to be sure, illuminate directly the cultural dialectics these films repeatedly enact, particularly in regard to those three key issues. In the case of each of these three issues, the films by European directors in Hollywood serve as unusually complex mediations between the binary terms of the particular dialectical structures that have traditionally given definition to the topics. In the case of modernism, those terms are mass modernity and the cultural modernism that sets itself up in opposition to the former. That binarism, meanwhile, both produces and depends on a related one, between the "high" culture of modernism and the "popular" forms of mass culture. Because the dialectic between these terms here takes the form of the dialogue between the European cinemas that have traditionally allied themselves with modernism and the Hollywood cinema that finds itself relegated to the side of mass culture, these issues are always assumed here to be bound up, in turn, with the issue of national culture. To be sure, the latter issue itself takes on a decidedly binary logic as European directors find themselves defined as "alien" in Hollywood culture and in turn produce representations often driven to define, against the grain of the Hollywood institution, American culture itself as "other."

The definitive, even the initiatory, history of the place of the medium of film in the field of cultural modernism has yet to be written. This book is not that history, but because of the fundamental (though not always dependable) alliance of European art-cinemas with the energies of modernism and of Hollywood with those of mass culture, the dialogue between these institutions is always in some way about the confrontation of these cultural levels. The exclusion of film from the domain of cultural modernism is an inevitable consequence of the theoretical bifurcation between modernism and mass culture as cultural forms. The protective wedge cultural modernism sought to drive between itself and social modernity impelled many of the most characteristic tenets of modernism: its claim to a formal autonomy apart from the degradations and contaminants of social modernity; its avowedly critical relation to the subjectivities produced by modernity; its construction of expatriation as a privileged standpoint *outside* the experience of modernity. Considering that film could only be seen as an exemplary product of modernity, it is hardly surprising that many modernists, from Wyndham Lewis to T. S. Eliot, in their efforts to defend against what they saw as the degradations of social modernity, routinely vented their contempt for film as a medium of representation or as a cultural force.

It is equally unsurprising, and evocative of the rich ideological variegation of modernism as one of the key cultural dispersions of our time, that just as many literary modernists—from Gertrude Stein to Blaise Cendrars, from Antonin Artaud to James Joyce to Viriginia Woolf— hailed the possibilities of the medium to link the progressive representation of modernism to the mass accessibility of modernity. In response, the not-so-hidden project of film theory in the early twentieth century became the reclamation of film by the impulses of modernism. To take an exemplary and well-known instance, Walter Benjamin's "The Work of Art in the Age of Mechanical Reproduction" (1936) stages this reclamation as an attack upon modernist autonomy: "When the age of mechanical reproduction separated art from its basis in cult, the semblance of its autonomy disappeared forever"(226). For Benjamin, the artificial division of cultural modernism from social modernity could lead only to evasion of the historical transformations in aesthetics brought about by modernity and inevitably reflected in modernism. Challenging modernism's securely oppositional relation to modernity, Benjamin sets modernism in an "obverse" relation to modernity, positioning film as something like an isthmus linking the two. The representational procedures of film and their effects upon viewers, Benjamin argues, "lead to a tremendous shattering of tradition which is the obverse of the contemporary crisis and renewal of mankind" (221).

Implied in Benjamin's schema are fundamental questions about the modernist project. If modernism envisions itself as a critique of traditional bourgeois subjectivity, how can it fail to align itself with the transformational developments of industrial social modernity, such as photography or film, which themselves reveal "entirely new structural formations of the subject" (236)? Given the mutable, changing nature of modern subjectivity as Benjamin constructs it, in other words, precisely what subjectivity is it that modernism proposes to critique? The "difficulties [film] caused traditional aesthetics" (227), according to Benjamin, were mirrored in transformations in spectators. In this passage, Benjamin attributes a capacity for modernist defamiliarization to aspects of film form itself:

By close-ups of the things around us, by focusing on hidden details of familiar objects, by exploring commonplace milieus under the ingenious guidance of the camera, the film, on the one hand, extends our comprehension of the necessities which rule our lives; on the other hand, it manages to assure us of an immense unexpected field of action. (236)

Here the ramifications of an implicitly modernist, self-conscious subjectivity ("extends our comprehension") are poised in an intricate dialectical relationship to affirmative commodity reification more characteristic of mass modernity ("manages to reassure us"). This dialectic, in turn, leads Benjamin to refuse traditional cultural hierarchies that oppose "progressive" cultural modernisms against the "reactionary" representations of the mass media of social modernity: "The reactionary attitude toward a Picasso painting changes into the progressive reaction to a Chaplin movie" (234), says Benjamin, reversing the usual relation of "high" culture to "mass" culture.

Benjamin's remarks challenge key assumptions of modernist aesthetics, all but reversing as well the claims of modernism that only an explicitly oppositional art can function to transform bourgeois subjectivity. For Benjamin, both that subjectivity and art itself together with the latter's institutions of representation, are continually *predetermined* by the fragmentary processes of history. Indeed, Benjamin's rejection of surrealist aesthetics—that exemplary branch of modernism—was motivated in part by his sense of the insulated, unitary quality he attributed to surrealism. In his own work, Benjamin sought to create a "dialectical image of modernity" (Frisby, 217) by studying "the confrontation of bourgeois and materialist conceptions of history" (Benjamin quoted in Frisby, 201) rather than yielding to the division of cultural modernism from social modernity. It is in the name of this "dialectical image of modernity" that Benjamin, unlike many less important theorists of modernity, refuses to insulate the "progressive" from the "reactionary," the oppositional from the already-commodified.

It is even more instructive to read another classic text of film theory, Eisenstein's "Dickens, Griffith and the Film Today" (1944), as a comment on the relation between cinema and modernism. This is especially the case because Eisenstein in that essay arrogates a nominal modernism to "our cinema" (203), Soviet film, by explicit contrast to Hollywood, as represented by the body of D. W. Griffith's work. Drawing on the very categories Benjamin problematizes, Eisenstein faults Griffith for regressing into nineteenth-century classical realism or naturalist melodrama instead of progressing into the modernist crit-ical-formalism his work nonetheless, for Eisenstein, heralds. The three prongs of Eisenstein's critique are familiar ones. First, Eisenstein derides Griffith for insufficient emphasis on montage as *formal* prac-tice, "without which [film] cannot expand beyond the *narrowly repre-sentational*" (243, emphasis in original). This defect gives rise, in turn, to ideological reactionism: "The structure that is reflected in the con-cept of Griffith montage is the structure of bourgeois society" (234). Synthesizing Griffith's naturalist bias and reproduction of bourgeois ideology in a conventionally modernist maneuver, Eisenstein posits a historical trajectory in which "the classic dualistic montage esthetic of Griffith" (254) is built on and superseded by a Soviet aesthetic where "montage became conscious of itself" (251). This triadic evolution toward modernist self-consciousness is thus, in Eisenstein's model, complete with the experiments of Soviet montage.

As representative documents in the truncated cultural history of cinematic modernism, the texts of Benjamin and Eisenstein are linked by their valuation of cultural critique and formal self-consciousness. There are, however, crucial differences in these writers' sense of the relation of these two terms. Eisenstein's gestures of canon-making, his effort to define the field by terms-of-exclusion and draw up lines of cultural/national demarcation, contrast with Benjamin's implication that all films are, by virtue of their participation in cinema's innovative representational technologies or of their status as products of mass modernity, at least potentially "modern."

In those gestures of canon-making, Eisenstein makes explicit a nationalist dimension in the debate on cinematic modernism. In Eisen-stein's essay, the persistence in cinematic representation of elements of a formerly dominant, now-discredited realism is the central problem. Eisenstein treats Griffith's work as the site of confrontation of nine-teenth-century realism with an ascendant modernism, both seen as the legacy of Dickens. Assuming incompatibility between American mass culture and an implicitly European modernism, the question Eisen-stein poses here is how it is possible that Griffith's Victorian represen-tations of "America the traditional, the patriarchal, the provincial" (198) can coexist with the "tempestuous tempi" (198) of his latent mod-ernism, as reflected in the formal experiments of his editing patterns? Indeed, Eisenstein solves the problem, in part, by adverting to simi-larly residual energies in the *literary* manifestations of modernism in American culture: "The successes of such keenly modern works as Erskine Caldwell's *Tobacco Road* and John Steinbeck's *The Grapes of Wrath* . . . contain ingredients common to [the nineteenth-century melodrama of] rural poesy dedicated to the American countryside" (227). Thus, Eisenstein appeals to categories of nationhood in order to claim ownership of modernism for Soviet film: Hollywood may incorporate elements from different national styles, and it may even in some way "originate" modernist cinematic form, via Griffith, but that form can only find *true* expression in a national territory whose prevailing ideologies are already compatible with it. Eisenstein ends by excluding a retrograde Hollywood, despite its potential emergent modernism, from the newly reinsulated category of progressive cinema. It thus becomes clear that the essay's project has been less to delineate interplay among competing possibilities of film style than to shore up a totalized, purified European modernism against the encroaching bourgeois realisms of American mass culture (*Film Form*, 202–3).

This brief survey of critical problems attendant on the definition of a cinematic modernism is intended neither as a clarion-call for clearer definitions nor as a summons to more stably or rigorously conceived film canons. It is a noteworthy paradox, after all, that the amorphous definitions extant of cinematic modernism have produced no dearth of duly reified canons. This paradox arises, perhaps, as an effort to deal with the schismatic relation between modernism and mass culture. In many conceptions of cinematic modernism, Hollywood-as-mass-culture emerges as both *dominant* and *other*, both that which threatens to stifle a developing modernism and that which must be seen as retrograde by contrast to a fully wrought modernism. But, as Peter Wollen points out with an air of commonsensical brittleness:

> Hollywood is by no means monolithically different; the American cinema is not utterly and irretrievably other. To begin with, all cinemas are commercial; producers and financiers act from the same motives everywhere. (13)

Once we acknowledge the parallels of Hollywood and art-cinemas as institutions of representation, the formative exclusion of Hollywood from the domain of cultural modernism must be reevaluated. The interpenetration of the energies of mass culture with those of modernism that has defined so much important cultural production in the twentieth century problematizes the construction of either category as thoroughly insular or impenetrably monolithic.

In this study of a series of films made in Hollywood by European (or quasi-European) directors, the transactions of filmmakers from European art-cinemas with the institution of Hollywood shed light on the place of film in cultural modernism, the crises in traditional hierarchies of "high" and "mass" culture that result from both that placement and those transactions, and the ways in which national culture—in many ways the "unconscious" of cinematic representation—mediates those issues. The book's first part treats three films in relation to the issues mentioned. These films derive from the classical era of Hollywood filmmaking, and so this section attempts as well to contextualize the "classical" paradigm as it has traditionally been constructed. The first chapter deals with a film, *Sunrise* (Murnau, 1927), chosen in part because of its representative, canonical status. Meant thereby to function as a compendium of the issues and approaches of the rest of the book, the chapter is divided into three sections, each of which examines one of the three key issues named above. First, I argue that the film celebrates modernity in its representation of the modern metropolis; then I show how, despite the film's many potential points of entry into the field of cultural modernism, it is significantly denied such canonical status. In order to show this, I trace the film's reception in the representative modernist film journal *CloseUp*. This exclusion takes place, I argue, precisely to foster the distinction between cultural modernism and social modernity and to reconstruct cultural hierarchies threatened by the breakdown of that distinction, a breakdown the film's cultural status heralds. Finally, I discuss the film's representations of national culture to illustrate how the latter mediates issues of modernism and cultural hierarchy, identity and difference. Such mediation, of course, might be expected to be particularly forceful in films made in Hollywood by "foreign" directors. In the two subsequent chapters of the book's first part, I isolate first the problem of national culture, treating Jean Renoir's *This Land Is Mine* (1943) as a particularly charged representation of nationality in wartime Hollywood; then the problem of cultural hierarchy, treating Fritz Lang's *Scarlet Street* (1945) as an allegory of the interpenetration of levels of culture that the cultural politics of the European director in Hollywood set into play.

By the end of the book's first part, it should be clear to readers how the issues of cultural modernism, cultural hierarchy, and national culture, in their complex interrelations, define the cultural politics of the figure of the European director in Hollywood. What may not yet be clear by that point is the extent to which the politics of identity and difference are always simultaneously in play as those issues work themselves out in that context. Thus, the book's second part sets out to define the "differential textuality" emergent in various forms in Hollywood filmmaking after World War II as the classical model evolves. Those chapters consider practices of commodity differentiation within the institutional system of Hollywood film. Especially in capitalist economies, the need for such differentiation combines an ideology of plenitude with the need of such economies to refute their own monopolistic bent. Diversity within the economic system guarantees not only the putatively "free" character of the market, but its self-projected ability to produce a plethora of commodities sufficient to meet all needs. Such diversity, however, threatens the self-contained character of the economic system. In Hollywood's symbolic economy, such threats are typically circumvented through the institution of a whole network of sign-systems that function to differentiate closely identical commodities. Genre structures work to provide the illusion of narrative variety among films while regulating them all through the same set of conventional edicts; the "star" system yields the effect of diverse personalities that are in fact marketed identically; patterns of exhibition rely upon different sites (the "movie palace" versus the "neighborhood" theater, for instance) in which the same spectatorial experience is made available. Thus, the symbolic economy of Hollywood depends on the strict regulation of elements in circulation, by means of which the identity of commodities, required to secure the closure of the system that will permit such regulation, subordinates their still-proclaimed difference. A converse relation of identity and difference in regulatory economies, however, also obtains. The process of differentiation that is a necessary part of the economy's structure potentially undermines the strictures of regulation by negating the economy's self-identity, necessarily referring outside itself, to other, differential elements that the system replaces, substitutes, incorporates.[7] Thus, the structure of symbolic economies reflects the structures of alterity, otherness, demonology.

Continuing to explore and extend in part two implications of the key issues articulated in part one, I attempt to widen considerably the field of theoretical interest not by shifting focus, but by showing how questions of identity and difference always underlie those issues. To be sure, as opposed cultural realms, modernity and modernism exist in a demonological relation of identity and differentiation, as revealed in Andreas Huyssen's well-known theory of mass culture as modernism's "other." From the vantage point of high culture, mass culture is projected as strange, alien, other—as indeed, is high culture from that of mass culture. What happens, then, when those vantage points are suddenly revealed to be the *same* one? Or what happens when a putatively "alien" position, that of the European director, is articulated within the "native" tradition of Hollywood? To be sure, boundaries of national identity are similarly shaped by symbolic constructions of selfhood and otherness, identity and difference. The series of films under consideration here, continually shifting vantage points, problematize by their very existence as cultural objects these social and cultural boundaries, thereby troubling as well ordinary constructions of identity and difference.

In the most literal terms, as I have suggested above, questions of identity and difference are raised inevitably by this project's very subject: How are received ideologies of Hollywood representation (signifiers of "sameness"?) tempered or otherwise modified as they are filtered in some way through the perspective of a filmmaker (signifier of "difference"?) brought into the Hollywood system from outside? As will be clear, however, it is rarely the most literal level that will interest me here. Rather, though I do not assume that a film directed in Hollywood by a European director will always be an inevitably "polyphonic" text, I do assume—if only because of the exclusionist cast of the institution's structure—that it will always bear a complex relation to fundamental aspects of conventional Hollywood representation. The questions I address here, then, are these: How does the ideology of Hollywood representation conceive of what it defines as "sameness"? How does it conceive of what it defines as "otherness"? How is the nature of Hollywood as a nominally closed institution challenged or affirmed by those definitions, by historical circumstances that threaten the autonomy of the "classical" model of Hollywood filmmaking, and by the continued presence of European directors within the institution, who might construct or project terms of identity and difference in ways not conducive to the institution's closure?

The two-part structure of the book implies a historical approach to the materials. At various points, the book makes good on that implication in treating key historical questions that the book's structural framework raises, about the relation of modernism and post-modernism to Classical Hollywood and "New Hollywood" filmmaking, about the relation of classical to postclassical Hollywood cinema, about the material circumstances determining the transactions of European directors in the Hollywood system. Indeed, each chapter of the book's second part raises an important issue in the historical evolution of Hollywood as a system of representation after its "classical" phase to suggest how the cultural politics of the European director in Hollywood, or the relation of European art-cinemas to Hollywood more generally, played a role in regard to that issue. These chapters contextualize the theme of identity and difference as it is introduced here, respectively, in relation to politics, form, myth, and spectatorship in postclassical Hollywood film. Chapter 4 examines the breakdown of ideological consensus in the postwar period of Hollywood filmmaking; chapter 5 takes up Hollywood's incorporation of the formal experiments of European "new waves" within the terms of "New Hollywood" film; chapter 6 looks at the relation of residual mythologies of Classical Hollywood representation to the growing rhetoric of demystification and self-consciousness in New Hollywood film; and the last chapter treats the fragmentation of the "mainstream" audience in contemporary Hollywood. Where locally useful in individual chapters, I have tried to provide as much historical context as possible. The first chapter charts a detailed reception-history, for instance, while the last traces a complicated marketing-history. Because of the decision to construct the book as a series of close readings, however, historical argument emerges here largely through particular observations about specific texts.

This particularist, text-based approach to the materials is motivated by two considerations. First, useful historical treatments of the transactions between European art-cinemas and Hollywood films already exist, and my own arguments have frequently built upon and incorporated the valuable research of such previous studies. Those studies, however, are less committed to detailed, particular analysis than to surveys of directors' works or to general historical observation.[8] In that sense, I believe this book usefully complements prior work in the field by emphasizing close analysis of representative films above historical overview. More simply, the approach reflects my own habits and tastes as a critic, observing psychocultural ramifications of texts by bringing to bear a kind of reconstructed synthesis of deconstruction, cultural critique, and psychoanalysis that should not be unfamiliar to even casual readers of contemporary criticism (and that, I should add, I have tried to apply accessibly). In turn, these habits reflect a belief in the idea that the domain of cultural representation is always implicated in psychological and ideological processes, which are always implicated in each other. Recent approaches in film study to issues relevant to this book have frequently implied that "empirical" research is the most valuable avenue to understanding, say, the formations of national culture.[9] The critical approach of this project registers my disagreement. Indeed, this book attempts to define ineffable, distinctive features of these films' *textuality*—their schismatic attitudes, their stylistic complexities, their ideological structures, their emotional textures—that empirical research cannot apprehend. Certainly, in their status as "resident aliens" in the Hollywood system, the group of films under discussion here can be differentiated in many ways from conventional norms of Hollywood textuality, even as they often imitate or inhabit those norms. Even more to the point, however, these films taken as a group are strikingly distinctive in the effects of their textual being—in the particular qualities of their curiously univocal hybridities, their mitigated heteroglossia, their muted polyphonies. In addition to its more concrete aims, it is that texture which this study sets out to describe.

Part One

Classical Hollywood Modernisms

1

Hollywood as Modernism's Other: The Case of *Sunrise*

The first of three films the German film-maker F. W. Murnau made in Holly-wood, *Sunrise* has taken its place among the important works of cinema history since its release in 1927. Amid the ebb-and-flow of shifting patterns of taste over many decades, *Sunrise* has retained a remarkably stable position, neither falling victim to devaluation or critical renunciation, like, say, *Birth of a Nation* (Griffith, 1914), nor in need of rediscovery, as was, say, Keaton's work in the 1960s. Even so, the film's meanings as a cultural object are anything but stable. A Hollywood melodrama directed by a "maverick" emigré, the film illustrates the dialogue of seemingly opposed cinematic styles at a crucial point in the formation of "Classical Hollywood" as an institution of representation. In doing so, it situates itself on the cusp of an emergent cinematic modernism and an already institutionalized mass culture, gesturing at once toward the "high" culture of modernism and the "popular" culture of modernity and thereby signaling the crises of cultural value that beset these hierarchies in the age of "high" modernism.

Clearly, *Sunrise* is a "canonical" film, if any film can be so certified. But in what canon is it to be located? When Dudley Andrew concisely surveyed the "determining forces" upon the film's production, he cataloged factors that have by extension shaped its reception: "William Fox's position in Hollywood, Hollywood's position in United States culture, Murnau's homosexuality, the decline of German Expressionism, the function of the pastoral within recently urbanized

29

societies, the problem of Christianity in a capitalist order" (360). Each of these terms has been treated with greater or lesser degrees of emphasis in critical response to the film over the years, but in cautioning against an exclusionary focus on any one of these factors, against "fetish[izing] one aspect of the work" (356), Andrew effaces what they have in common: an understanding of the film as occupying embattled intersections among cultural formations. It is this aspect of the text I will focus on here, arguing that the film's position as a Hollywood product by a German art-film director whose reputation linked him to a tradition of Euro-modernism inevitably troubles its status as a cultural object.

Two of the terms Andrew pointed to in his contextualization of the film explicitly posit conflicted or potentially incompatible ideologies at work in or behind the text: pastoral versus urban, Christian versus capitalist. The remaining terms do so implicitly. The reference to Fox conjures up the quest for European prestige within the American culture industry, and the reference to Hollywood as a cultural institution in America connotes the opposition of "popular" to "serious" cultural forms in early cinema. The invocation of Murnau's biographically known homosexuality, especially in reference to the avidly heterosexual representation *Sunrise* apparently yields, can only suggest a confrontation with the codes of censorship or displacement within the Classical Hollywood model that work to render such sexualities invisible; or, alternatively, to make them visible only in clearly regulated ways. Finally, the reference to "the decline of German Expressionism," grounded historically in the movement's depletion by American recruitment and German emigration, gives us a picture of the film as the signifier of a tradition in crisis, diluted by its wedding to the opposing and ultimately dominant tradition of Classical Hollywood.

Given this multilayered narrative, it is no wonder that this admirably "elastic" (356) work, to use Andrew's words, guaranteed canonical status by virtue of its very "resilience" (356), should yet be so difficult to *place*, to contextualize in any secure way. Neither unproblematically "realist" in the classical mode, nor fully "modernist" in a clear sense, the film exemplifies both the late phase of a passing (and moribund?) movement and the initial consolidation of a vital tradition, at once crucial to constructions of Hollywood as a machine designed for the representation and production of the bourgeois couple and of critical interest to the study of gay authorship in cinema.

In light of the heady overdetermination of the film's contexts, it is necessary to resist the competing impulses either to assign it to the transcendental domain of the "masterpiece," as Andrew seems inclined to do in his near-definitive reading, or to fix it squarely within a single one of the ever-shifting canons among which it oscillates, as he rightly warns against. More to the point would surely be to examine specifically what about the film has led to this quality of overdetermination in its cultural placement. It is indeed the very malleability of *Sunrise* as a cultural object that is important here, since this malleability brings into clearer focus the status of the cultural oppositions around which the film's textuality simultaneously defines itself and is defined. The structures of canon-formation routinely depend on the closure of delimited cultural fields, but the very existence of *Sunrise* as a cultural object—central to certain canons, marginal to others, produced in one cultural institution but drawing upon energies of another—illuminates the impracticability of such closure.

Sunrise is characteristic of Hollywood films by European directors in its complex negotiation of textual and cultural levels, conjoining differential codes of style and ordinarily opposed levels of culture. On its release, the film was promoted as the "first international" production, and its "international" status consolidates the very oppositions it negotiates—between Classical Hollywood and German expressionism, between modernism and mass culture, between high culture and popular culture. The film was received as strange and foreign-seeming by the mass audience of Hollywood movies, but, as we will see, it was construed as just another Hollywood potboiler by commentators who allied themselves with a modernist aesthetic. The film's "international" status serves as one of the clearest signifiers of its connection to modernism, but that status accounted at the same time for the difficulty of "placing" the film—as well as for the impulse to "place" it at all. As Astradur Eysteinsson suggests in his study of modernism,

> While everyone seems to agree that as a phenomenon modernism is radically "international" (although admittedly in the limited Western sense of that word), constantly cutting across national boundaries, this quality is certainly not reflected in the majority of critical studies of modernism. . . . The urge to "secure" works, writers, and canons within the boundaries of national literatures does not originate in the present century, but in the case of modernism it does come strikingly to the fore. (*Concept of Modernism*, 89)

In the case of *Sunrise*, the "international" style of the film negotiates Hollywood mass culture with the Euro-modernist dispositions of German expressionism. In doing so, the film confronts the illusionism and escapist fantasy associated with Hollywood's commodity culture with the self-reflexivity and cultural critique of modernist aesthetics. Because of the apparent rift between that culture and those aesthetics, the "international" position of *Sunrise* results simultaneously in its alienation in Hollywood and its demonization in modernism. Yet, like many of the most suggestive Hollywood films by European directors, especially during the classical period, its very existence as a cultural object threatens that insulating rift between mass culture and modernism, high culture and popular culture, Hollywood film and German expressionism—and, in turn, thereby threatens the stability of clear demarcations between identity and difference, sameness and otherness, nativity and foreignness, in Classical Hollywood film.

Modernity, Visuality, and Urban Space

If *Sunrise* was finally rejected as strange and remote-of-sensibility by the American audiences for Hollywood films at the time of its release, it was certainly not because the film does not expertly and seemingly wholeheartedly don the chameleonic protective-coloration of its disguise as an ordinary Hollywood movie. In the emotive charge of its melodrama and in the sensational edge of its plotting, the film bears very direct affinities to Hollywood hits of the time, such as *Seventh Heaven* (Borzage, 1927), with which it shares a star, Janet Gaynor. The film's story follows the tribulations of an innocent rural couple from the decline of their relationship to its regeneration. At the beginning of the film, the husband meets a "City Woman," a vamp, who persuades him to murder his wife in order to join her in the city. The husband prepares to do so, but when the wife learns of his plot and flees, he feels intense remorse. When he runs after her, the two of them end up in a nearby city. The remainder of the film shows the renewal of their relationship as they discover the culture of the city, and ends, after they have endured the natural disaster of a storm at sea, with their return to the country and their ultimate reconciliation.

In the extreme polarities of its moods and in its traditional, sentimental concern with heterosexual romance, the film reproduces fundamental conventions of the 1920s Hollywood melodrama. Despite the film's seemingly secure grounding in so typical a genre, however, it incorporates important textual elements that undermine that security. Stylistically, the film draws heavily, especially in its first half, upon techniques of optical subjectivity and devices of intrusive formal experimentation characteristic of the tradition of German expressionism in which Murnau made his reputation. To be sure, that Murnau was brought to Hollywood at all indicates that this style was not regarded in the institution as fundamentally incompatible with the traditional procedures of filmmaking in Classical Hollywood.[1] Yet the modernist patina of his work, certified in its subjectivity and experimentation, inevitably troubles any simple account of the film's distinctive texture.

If it makes sense to talk about the "modernist" elements of a Hollywood movie at all, and of this Hollywood movie in particular, such discussion must always take note of the complex currents and countercurrents that inevitably disturb the flow of the discourse. In *Sunrise*, the current of romantic melodrama is met by the countercurrent of expressionist "avant-gardism." But the film's avowals of its allegiances to mass culture, by way of its ardent adoption of Hollywood genres, counter those signifiers of modernist textuality the film simultaneously contains. A developing line of modernist cinema contemporary with *Sunrise*, from the canonical avant-gardism of *Un Chien Andalou* (Bunuel/Dali, 1929) to the modernist-expressionism of *Diary of a Lost Girl* (Pabst, 1927), follows the tradition of literary modernism in defining itself against the social, cultural realities of modernity itself. These films, typically, expose the oppression of the forms of social organization, the backwardness of the technologies of progress, and the vacancy of the novel subjectivities they impute to the forces of modernity. Although Hollywood films of the time also sometimes project specific elements of modernity as constrictive or destructive, they more traditionally celebrate modernity itself as progressive toward the demotic utopia so many Hollywood films, consciously or unconsciously, herald.

The representation of *Sunrise* avows its affinities with mass culture by celebrating modernity itself. An important gauge of the relation of *Sunrise* to modernist canons and to the theme of modernity is to be found in its representation of the modern metropolis, usually registered in such texts of the time as the emblematic image of modernity as such. In more traditional modernist cinema, such as the films named above, the image of the city typically functions as an image of modernity's malignance. The "vision of modernism as an unending permanent revolution against the totality of modern existence" (Berman, 30) often projected an image of the modern metropolis as the very index of the chaos, alienation, and fragmentation of modern experience against which modernism typically opposed itself. The adversarial spirit often installed as a determining force in the forma-

FIGURE 1. *Sunrise:* The image of the city celebrates modernity. Courtesy Museum of Modern Art, New York.

tion of modernist canons—where negation guaranteed admission to the canon, affirmation exclusion from it—demanded aggressive critique of the conditions and the very forms of the modern city as an emblem of modernity, even if it was the metropolis itself that produced the new forms of representation characteristic of modernism (Williams, "The Metropolis and the Emergence of Modernism," 13–16). In *Sunrise*, conversely, the city becomes the site of the reconciliation of the couple who are the film's main characters. This point is in itself noteworthy, especially considering the number of films contemporary with *Sunrise* in which the city is figured as an obstacle to human contact, whether in the European tradition, such as *Pandora's Box* (Pabst, 1927), or in the Hollywood tradition, such as *The Crowd* (Vidor, 1928). The city section of *Sunrise*, however, is closer to the celebratory exuberance of an alternative and distinctively European contemporary tradition in representing urban space, that of the city-symphony film, such as *Berlin* (Ruttman, 1926) or *Man with a Movie Camera* (Vertov, 1926). In Murnau's film, the landscape of the city functions not merely as the location of the couple's reconciliation but as its very agent. In spite of a conventional quality of alienation the film's imagery periodically attaches to its representation of the city, its narrative insistently positions the city as a source of fully legitimated renewal.

The movement toward reconciliation in the plot is worked out in a series of discrete and curiously repetitive episodes that correlate the couple's reconciliation with the juxtaposed rhythms of the city itself. For example, when the couple takes refuge from urban overstimulation in a convenient doorway, Murnau repeatedly cuts away from them to an anonymous vantage point of a passing wedding procession on a street whose spatial relation to the couple has not been made clear. Later, after they have wandered into the church where the wedding ceremony is taking place, Murnau again cuts away from the couple's fervent embrace as the husband begs his wife's forgiveness to repeated close-ups of peeling churchbells. In both cases, a quality of dissociation from narrative as such functions to introduce these images in figural terms. Although the shots of both the procession and the bells are finally placed securely into the narrative logic of the film's diegesis, the initial deferral of such placement abstracts the images as visual tropes, thus synchronizing the couple's gradual reconciliation with these explicitly urban metaphors of rebirth. Perhaps more to the point, these metaphors, through their identification with the rhythms of the city itself, differ in character from the expressly inward qualities of figuration at work earlier in the film.

Placed beside another roughly contemporary and passingly modernist canonical film about marital reconcilation, *L'Atalante* (Vigo, 1934), to be sure, Murnau's film is striking in its comparative lack of the rhetoric of introspection in relation to the melodramatic theme of reconciliation, positioning the Hollywood film more closely to the "objective" sensibility of mass modernity than to the "subjective" one of cultural modernism. In Vigo's more typical film, reconciliation is secured through a rejection of the values of the city. This rejection, in turn, is signalled visually through a return from objective imagery to a more interiorized, elemental imagery presented as analogous to a quality of restored inner tranquility. The movement toward reconciliation in the narrative of *L'Atalante* coincides with increased intensity of identification with the estranged characters as individual figures, as well as with a more rigorous focus of narrative energy in relation to the characters. In her perceptive monograph on *L'Atalante*, Marina Warner traces a progression she sees in that film from an initial representation of the city as "a private kingdom of desire" (52) to a greater "realism" as the city's obstruction of Jean and Juliette's romance becomes more pronounced. Warner goes on to oppose the image of the barge where the couple achieved union, industrial yet pastoral, to that of the city that separates them: "The barge, by contrast to the city, now takes on the character of a magical space of safety and dreaming" (55). According to Warner, then, *L'Atalante* participates in a conventional rhetoric of romance, aligning reconciliation with private experience, with a radical interiority, conceiving the city as a distinctly *public* space that threatens the private, pastoral, metaphoric, ineffable, and archetypal space, the world elsewhere, of romance itself.

Expressing some consciousness of such rhetoric, *Sunrise* challenges it decisively even as the film similarly seeks, like *L'Atalante*, to validate, even self-consciously to idealize, the domain of romance, in keeping with the conventions of the lyric melodrama of contemporary art-cinema. In *Sunrise*, by contrast with *L'Atlante*, not only does the narrative become increasingly diffuse as the film proceeds, but the very formal devices associated with identification or introspection, such as subjective compositions, intense close-ups, and point-of-view shots, used amply in the film's first third chronicling the couple's estrangement, are eliminated almost systematically during the narrative process of reconciliation. In *L'Atalante*, reconciliation can be achieved only by leaving the city behind, resuming a kind of pastoralized subjectivity, while in *Sunrise* the phases of reconciliation are correlated with the journey through the city itself. Both films deal with, to return to Andrew's phrase, the "function of the pastoral within recently urbanized societies," but Vigo's depends on a conventional opposition of country and city while Murnau's negotiates this opposition in a manner with, in turn, large implications for the other seeming oppositions around which the film takes shape.

The important difference of Murnau's film in its representation of the city as an emblem of nascent modernity may be seen clearly in a single sequence, as the couple cross a city street after their symbolic remarriage. In the sequence, the camera tracks behind the couple as they move forward, arm in arm, absorbed emotionally in each other and oblivious of the dense traffic encircling them. As they cross the street, the cityscape in front of them is dispelled in a supple dissolve by a matte-shot perspective of a pastoral landscape. A sudden series of cutaway shots to details of massed traffic—a sounding horn, a foot pressing against a brake—is followed by an equally abrupt long shot of the couple embracing amid a traffic jam, the cries of irate motorists bringing an end to their romantic revery. As an image of modernity, the sequence appears to be evoked uncannily in Walter Benjamin's later discussion of film and modernity: "Film corresponds to profound changes in the apperceptive apparatus—changes that are experienced on an individual scale by the man in the street in big-city traffic, on a historical scale by every present day citizen" ("The Work of Art in the Age of Mechanical Reproduction," 243). The sequence also suggestively condenses several prior moments in the film. It answers the earlier sequence of the husband's tryst with the vamp, in which a parallel matte-shot projects a stylized cityscape behind the two figures in place of the preternatural bog where their meeting takes place. It also echoes the earlier sequence of the couple's arrival in the city when they are buffeted by the dizzying rhythms of the city streets. The condensation of these earlier episodes illustrates by contrast a marked shift in the film's conception of urban space. Initially associated with longing and its rupture, as when the vamp taunts the husband with nocturnal urban images, the city is here coincident with fulfillment and mastery, as the couple's reunion magically and comically delivers them from the city's supposed threat. Both conceptions are clearly dependent on psychic projections worked out formally through the matte-shots. The first, the image of the city-in-the-country, is an image of fragmentation fraught with the surplus energies of its own displacement signified by orgiastic movement as well as by the use of unrestrained split-screens and superimpositions within the image. On the other hand, the image of the country-in-the-city is one of serenity and wholeness.[2] Both images, by contrast to more typical modernist assertions of their incompatibility, figure the congruency of city and country—and, by

implication, the public and the private, objectivity and subjectivity—
but the latter perhaps paradoxically finds compatibility as well in the
subject-positions potentiated by either milieu. If in *L'Atalante*, as
Warner argues, enchantment is only possible in refuge from the city,
in *Sunrise* it is shown to be available in the city itself, as this magical,
pastoral image indicates.

Although *Sunrise* reproduces many conventional conceptions of
the city familiar in cinema of the 1910s and 1920s, then, the film ends
not by rejecting the values of the city, as in *L'Atalante*, but by connecting the couple's reconciliation to their experience of urbanness. Here
again, the rhetoric of objectivity born with the couple's arrival in the
city is significant. The journey through the city is figured as a successive movement toward a kind of celebratory specularity, a pleasurable
acceptance of an explicitly *visual, objectified* urban culture. Indeed, this
explicit visuality may be clarified by noting that the disposition of the
couple after their symbolic remarriage strikingly resembles that of
Walter Benjamin's figure of the *flâneur*. In Anne Friedberg's account,
the *flâneur* is "the quintessential paradigm of the subject in modernity,
wandering through urban space in a state of distraction" (34–35). For
Benjamin, the figure of the *flâneur* serves as a crucial emblem of modern subjectivity because, a wandering observer attentive to the city's
contingency and ephemera, his gaze is (theoretically) both passive and
engaged: he neither actively resists the city's chaos and fragmentation
by mobilizing his own gaze against it, nor takes refuge in nostalgic
pastoral, longing for the sense of rootedness, psychic or actual, presumably lost with the very emergence of the city. Rather, for Benjamin,
the *flâneur* refines *a new kind of looking*, at once produced by the city and
uniquely responsive to it, receptive to urban fragmentation, taking
pleasure in the voluptuary chaos and sensory overstimulation the city
is often, in early reflection on modernity, said to introduce.

The narrative of *Sunrise* divests itself of the conventional rhetoric
of subjectivity in relation to the couple as they gradually assume their
positions in the visual culture of the city. As the film progresses, the
couple take their places as tranquil *objects* of a public gaze rather than
anxious *subjects* of an individualized look. Again, the projection of the
pastoral scene after their symbolic remarriage is a crucial turning point
here. The image can only be understood logically as a virtual or hallucinatory derivation from private consciousness, yet its lyric force
derives from its shared, projective character, strikingly evocative of the
nineteenth-century optical novelty of the panorama, a precursor of
cinema used predominantly to project rural images in urban spaces,
connected directly by Benjamin to the emergent forms of subjectivity

of the *flâneur*: "The city-dweller . . . attempts to introduce countryside into the city. In the panoramas the city dilates to become landscape, as it does in a subtler way for the *flâneur*" (quoted in Friedberg, 24). Thus the image conflates optical subjectivity with the mobilization of an outward-turning, projected, public gaze.[3]

At the most literal level, the couple's excursion in the city is a movement from a visually charged invisibility at the beginning of their sojourn—as Benjamin characterizes the longing of the *flâneur*, "to be in the midst of the world and yet to remain hidden from the world" (quoted in Friedberg, 29)—to an ultimate exhibitionism. On their arrival in the city, the couple remain unseen by oblivious city-dwellers who hurry past them and by the drivers of vehicles that swerve wildly around them. When they emerge from the church after their symbolic remarriage, the gathered celebrants look at them with ill-concealed disappointment at seeing ragged peasants rather than the resplendent bride-and-groom they expect. Yet the subsequent scenes in the street and in the barbershop figure an emergent, redemptive visuality around mirror-images. The couple first look at photographs that seem to mirror them, on display in a shop window, then at reflections of themselves in the window glass, and finally in an actual mirror in the barbershop in preparation for their visit to the photographer. In larger terms, the couple's activity in the course of their day in the city betokens systematic movement toward novel forms of visual experience. After they commission a photograph of themselves, imaging themselves through this process of commodification, the couple attend a carnival where they dance uninhibitedly before an enthusiastic audience of urban spectators. It is important to note here not only the trajectory from visual subjectivity in the film's first section, with its attendant rhetoric of psychological isolation, to distanced objectification in the city section, with its attendant rhetoric of social communion. Equally important, again, is the coincidence of the thematics of reconciliation, conventionally associated in romantic melodrama with privacy, introspection, subjectivity, with this narrative trajectory.[4]

The most important point here is that the film's supple negotiations of tropes of city/country, especially as they take shape around terms of modernity and visuality itself, provide a way of focusing its negotiations of the styles of German expressionism and Classical Hollywood. The point may be clarified through an analysis of the pivotal sequence in the barbershop, where the play of modes of visuality, thematics of modernity, and rhetorics of subjectivity effects an important shift in the film's tone. Indeed, the sequence is crucial in the coincident shift already noted in the narrative placement of the couple itself. The preceding third of the film relies heavily on the rhetoric of visual sub-jectivity associated with expressionism, using superimpositions to sig-nify mental processes, isolating individual characters in narrative space, and organizing sustained sequences around the point-of-view of single characters. The episode leading up to the boat ride, for exam-ple, employs such devices exclusively in relation to the character of the husband, while the episode of the boat ride itself makes similarly intense use of such devices exclusively in relation to the character of the wife. By contrast, the space of the barbershop is constructed around the newly interconnected viewpoints of multiple characters, including two—the barber and the "Obtrusive Gentleman" (as the credits identify him)—who do not figure prominently anywhere else in the narrative.

One useful way to understand the formal reorientation marked by the barbershop scene is in terms of a shift away from Murnau's "imagi-nary space" ("Secret Affinities," 37), as Thomas Elsaesser (following Eric Rohmer) characterizes it, to a construction of space more in keeping with—again in Elsaesser's words—"the clipped realism of the Ameri-cans, with its reliance on shot-countershot, the variations of angle and constant reframing for the sake of keeping up pace and momentum" ("Secret Affinities," 36). The sustained and exclusionary focus earlier in the film on the husband's point-of-view as he tortuously considers mur-dering his wife and the subsequent focus on the wife's point-of-view as her husband's plot dawns on her both provide clear illustrations of Mur-nau's characteristic procedures of "imaginary space." Viewed by Elsaesser and others as an essential aspect of Murnau's style, "imagi-nary space" defines spatial logic according to a rhetoric of subjectivity. According to Elsaesser, "Although almost always taking its cue from the 'real world,' [Murnau's "imaginary space"] finds its coherence in the urgency of a desire, an obsession, an anxiety or a wish" ("Secret Affini-ties," 37). An example Elsaesser gives is the scene in *Nosferatu* (1923) where Harker discovers the vampire's coffin. In that scene, Elsaesser argues, the coherence of narrative space is disrupted by an oneiric or primary-process logic signified by, for instance, "breaking the rules of continuity editing" so that the viewer is "unsure of what exactly Harker has seen" ("Secret Affinities," 37). Thus, though not explicitly Lacanian in Elsaesser's version of it, Murnau's "imaginary space," signifier of his expressionist style, has ties to Christian Metz's conception of the work of figuration in *The Imaginary Signifier* (1982): a moment of "perceptual block[age]" (Metz, 274) consciously or unconsciously working against secondary discourse through condensatory or metaphoric operations expressing psychic processes.

An example occurs in *Sunrise* when the husband awakens after fitful sleep and remembers his murder plot. The memory is worked out through a conventional shot/reverse-shot visual structure, a close-up of the husband suddenly stricken with terror, widening his eyes as he looks out-of-frame, followed by a shot of the bundled reeds he has gathered the night before to aid in his plot. The rhetoric of the shots implies through the shot/countershot structure—typical, as Elsaesser points out, of the "clipped realism of the Americans"—that the husband actually sees the reeds, that his glimpse of them is the source of his horror. But the narrative context has made clear that the reeds are concealed elsewhere, in a backyard shed, belying the implied literal contiguity of the shot/reverse-shot. Moreover, although we have seen the husband carefully cover the reeds in a previous shot, the close-up of the reeds in this shot, zooming in on them dynamically, contradictorily reveals them fully uncovered, signifying through both the image itself and the figural zoom the husband's anxiety of discovery. The conventional suggestion of spatial contiguity between the shot and the reverse-shot makes this a striking example of "imaginary space," rooting it in the secondary discourse of the classical shot/reverse-shot schema—"taking its cue from the real world," in Elsaesser's phrase—yet (in Metz's vocabulary) primarizing it through a process of formal figuration.

On the face of it, then, the barbershop sequence displaces the subjective visual rhetoric of "imaginary space" and expressionist style with more conventionally objective devices of the Classical Hollywood model, stably balanced frontal compositions and attentiveness to spatial continuity as well as a heavy reliance on *"plan americain"* composition.[5] The sequence begins with a precisely symmetrical composition with the camera placed outside the shop's entrance, a dual-paneled glass-and-steel doorway, immediately striking for its hypermodern sleekness of design and its largeness of scale. The door's transparency allows the viewer to see the busy shop in the depth of the composition, but it also allows the proprietor to see the street, so that when the couple tentatively enter the composition, the vigilant proprietor immediately opens the door with exaggerated cordiality to hurry them into the shop. If the connection of visual consciousness to urban experience previously in the film positions the couple as anxious subjects of the look who themselves remain unseen, from this sequence on they become objects of a generalized, public gaze. The architectural design of the barbershop itself establishes fully a connection between specularity, consumerism, and modernity that the preceding sequences have already implied.

The couple's reinvention as modern subjects is the implicit project of this section of the film, and this project requires their initial placement here as consumers. The see-through doors and the self-reflecting mirror are markers of a specifically modern, panoptical decor that functions to promote the visibility of the shopgoers, the consuming subjects, enabling them readily, the sequence suggests, both to be seen and to see themselves, but necessarily fragmenting the potentially connective, intersubjective, and consequently holistic character of the public look. In the most literal sense, the man and woman are immediately separated from each other when they enter the shop, and much of the rest of the sequence shows their frustrated efforts to see one another across the busy public space, craning their necks and peering awkwardly into mirrors.

One of the pivotal functions of the scene in the barbershop is to introduce an altered emotional texture, displacing the atmosphere of melodramatic anxiety of the film's beginning with one of light-hearted whimsy that will dominate the following third of the film. This displacement coincides with other apparently schematic and interrelated stylistic or formal shifts—from a rhetoric of subjectivity to a rhetoric of objectivity, from a kind of quasi-expressionism to the "American style," from a reliance on the construction of imaginary space to the increasingly complex but comparatively literalized spatial logic of Classical Hollywood. These shifts, in turn, depend on the alternate editing and conflation of eyeline matches and point-of-view shots that are crucially determinant upon classical narration in film.[6] In these terms, the sequence would mark the stabilization of a style previously characterized by disruptive excess. Symmetrical alternation between shots of the wife seated in the shop's lobby and shots of the husband entrapped in the barber's chair assures a quality of balance and visual coherence. Moreover, while this structural alternation continues to be motivated by characters' looks, these looks are freed of the fetishistic quality and the association with anxiety that attend them in the film's earlier segments, a freedom due in part to the slippage between point-of-view and eyeline matching that classical narration with its requirement of stabilized omniscience occasions. When the wife watches anxiously as a beautician offers the husband a manicure, for instance, the editing patterns alternate between close-ups of the nervous wife and shots of what she sees, so that the viewer may register the beautician's resemblance to the vamp. A more extreme close-up of the wife as her concern grows is intercut with alarmed reaction from the husband and impatient, mysteriously contemptuous reactions from the barber, before the husband finally refuses the manicure to the wife's relief. If

this sequence were to be executed according to the previously dominant logic in the text of imaginary space, its logic would circulate
around tropes of the wife's pervasive anxiety, making them central to
the scene's visual formation, as in the earlier scene of the attempted
murder, where the wife's point-of-view governs the visual presentation of the husband as a monstrous figure. In the event, however, the
wife's anxiety is entirely neutralized by the integration of multiple
viewpoints that has the effect, in keeping with the "American style,"
of objectifying the action. No character's response or viewpoint is privileged or presented as formative of a sequence's structure, though the
manicurist's viewpoint is actively excluded. Rather, all are subordinated to a newly privileged rhetoric of omniscience in keeping with
the tenets of classical narration.[7] The overt rhetoric of point-of-view
remains in place, but its introspective, disruptive force is contained
through a maneuver of displacement. In the shots described above, for
example, the close-up of the wife looking at the husband motivates a
subsequent shot of what she sees, but the latter shot, a frontal view of
the barber chair, is manifestly distinct from her vantage point from an
angle of forty-five degrees. Thus, the character's look remains structurally determinant upon the visual construction of the sequence, but
it now functions to articulate what will be presented as a coherent and
neutral narrative space, distinct from the subjective points-of-view of
the characters, that is merely one instrument in the arsenal of classical
narration.

This gradual movement in the film toward the Classical Hollywood style, as a model of representation produced in and by mass
modernity and participating in its cult of "objectivity," reflects the
film's celebration of mass modernity itself. Yet the quality of stabilization in the style of the middle third of *Sunrise* is interestingly complicated by the residual recurrence of potentially disruptive elements
within its framework. The integration of multiple viewpoints may
have the effect of objectifying the action or reorienting the spectator,
but it also introduces a new set of distinct formal problems of its own,
threatening classical stability. After all, it is possible to conceive of the
integration of viewpoints in the barbershop sequence not as the
orderly imposition of formal, hence ideological, coherence but on the
contrary as a destabilizing *multiplication* of viewpoints that, through a
kind of sensory overload, thwarts the very control it was presumably
called on to guarantee. Critics as different as Mary Ann Doane and
Robin Wood have stressed the film's compulsion toward control in
their interpretations of *Sunrise*, noting the film's effort to "enclose and
thus sustain its own represented world" (Doane, 71). This drive

toward control is frequently identified with the impulse of classical narration itself. According to Doane, "the manifest desire of the text" is "to control its own reading" (71). Such a claim, however, is dependent upon a conventional theory of classical textuality, as an enclosed, self-regulating system that functions to eliminate contradiction and to produce and regulate normative desire. As both representative text and cultural object, *Sunrise* challenges the closure and self-regulation of classical textuality.

At one level, the barbershop sequence functions to promote a certain narrative equilibrium with obvious ideological effects. The couple's reconciliation, completed in the previous sequence with all the trappings of classical closure that bring the film's first movement to an assured conclusion, is fully *re*assured in this sequence, all potential threats to the couple's renewed couplehood systematically rendered triumphantly nugatory, thus presumably bringing the circulation of desire under control, at least at the text's thematic or representational level. One by one, each new threat—the manicurist, the Obtrusive Gentleman, and the potentially alienating space of the shop itself—is eliminated or overcome, the manicurist rejected, the Obtrusive Gentleman vengefully brutalized by the husband, and the alienating space of the shop successfully negotiated when the separated couple are reunited at the end of the sequence.

In spite of the manifest concern here with a thematic of renewed normality, of restored balance, however, crucial elements of the sequence work to foreground the very dynamics of enclosure and control whose repression the classical model, at least in its available versions, would seem to demand. An important element of the sequence no critic has noted, for instance, is its emphasis on the barber's look during the action involving the manicurist. In a series of curiously insistent close-ups, the barber is shown watching the visual interaction of wife, husband, and manicurist with an expression by turns derisive, resigned, bemused, or aroused—an expression that is, finally, unreadable. The barber has already been introduced as a principle of control, firmly guiding the unwilling husband into a chair, holding him there despite his protests, and kneading with comic force the husband's recalcitrant face in preparation for thorough grooming. But the emphasis on the barber's look once the possibility of desire springs up with the appearance of the manicurist shows the barber's comic resignation to what he manifestly cannot control. In the extreme close-up, the barber looks from the manicurist to the husband, then rolls his eyes slowly upward and tilts his head back in an attitude of genteel disgust. The continuing unexpected attention to the barber's look makes even more apparent the sequence's complete repression of the manicurist's look. These shots thus punctuate, by contrast to the neutral shots of the manicurist that register her obliviousness of the couple's distressed attentions, the barber's exclusion from the networks of desire bounded by the integrated looks of the other characters.

Even as this exclusion is registered in the film, prominent signifiers associate the figure of the barber with explicit suggestions of eroticism. The close-up of his contemptuous face is stylized to evoke signs of orgasm as well as of disgust, and the continuing movement of the barber's off-screen hands against the husband's face causes the barber's head to palpitate suggestively, an effect heightened by the extremity of the close-up itself as well as by his suggestive positioning at the husband's back. The barber's reaction is linked through insistent *typage* with effeteness or prissiness, and his former assertions of firm control give way here to a posture of ineffectuality secured fully in the film's rhetoric when the husband, seeing his wife beset by the Obtrusive Gentleman, rises inexorably from the chair, erect and imperious, and pushes the barber aside in spite of the barber's formerly superior force. Thus, at the very moment the text's desire appears to be to assert control, specifically control over the desire represented *within* the text, its circuits become overloaded, as it were, strained by the very mechanisms intended to regulate them. In other words, if what finally destabilizes this sequence is its perplexing emphasis on the barber's troubled reaction to desire as the film represents it, that emphasis is not only made possible but, in some sense, *produced* by the presumably objectifying, neutralizing devices—in this case, integrated points-of-view—that are central to definitions of the classical model. The barber is the first of a series of representations in *Sunrise* of male figures emphatically defined as marginal to the regulated circulation of desire within the film who consequently disrupt or block its circulation. The investiture of an unmistakable though circuitous identification in these figures further troubles the conventional reading of the film as a simple reproduction of the conventions of Hollywood romance.

The point takes on even more resonance as the film's placement of the viewer in ever more distanced spectatorial relations to the couple in *Sunrise* becomes more pronounced. Once the barber's disruptive status is registered, the earlier shot of his hands against the husband's face assumes a retrospectively heightened resonance. The shot participates in the rhetoric of Chaplinesque comedy that comes to dominate the film's middle third, signified in the husband's dramatic expression of surprise, but seen in the light of the barber's pointed exclusion from the circulation of desire, the shot is striking also in its quality of tactile sensuality. The close-ups of the barber seem initially to present a disdainful attitude toward what the film would have us see as conventional desire because of the particular signifying chain in which the shots find themselves, bound by the triangulated looks of the husband and wife at the heedless manicurist.[8] But the second-order meaning of the close-ups presents the barber's own desire in figures of arousal and orgasm. The shots may thus be read as embedded in a quite different though superposed causal chain from which the logic of the sequence would appear to dissociate them, where the barber's physical contact with the husband's face *causes* the barber's arousal. The point is especially suggestive, given the film's drive in its second half to continue to yield a stock of images powerfully fraught with a rhetoric of sensuality that have, however, been drained of their explicitly erotic undercurrents, especially once the figures of the husband and wife have ceased to function as stabilized nodal points of viewer identification.

The action surrounding the Obtrusive Gentleman provides another example of how the film's strategies of containment give rise to the very possibility of disruption. After the threat posed by the appearance of the manicurist has been surmounted, a close-up of the wife registers the intense relief of her expression. The following shot is a neutral long-shot of the wife's position at the screen-right end of a long bench. Fully in keeping with procedures of classical textuality, the patterning of shots here works to emphasize emotional content of dramatic action without overtly stylized or expressionist articulation of such content. Moreover, the contruction of space around the bench the wife occupies is characterized throughout much of the sequence by conventional procedures that promote the illusion of spatial coherence. Though never shown in literal relation to the opposite space occupied by the husband, this space is defined clearly enough in its figural relation to the alternate space through the matching of shots according to characters' eyelines and the symmetry of shot-alternation itself. When the movement from shot to shot is not motivated by characters' looks, it is negotiated by matches-on-action or by the placement of significant objects as orienting pivots from shot to shot. For example, when the wife first takes her seat, a featureless metal globe occupies the space of the mise-en-scène beside her, and this globe subsequently becomes a pivotal object of continuity, always in view as the camera shifts positions over several shots. The narrative focus of the scene, as the wife strains to see her husband across the shop, is on the wife's separation-anxiety. However, the mysterious background object, unnoticed by the wife, draws the viewer's attention not only in the constancy of its placement across multiple reframings but by setting up a secondary enigma—What is it?—that is duly solved when a barber removes a warmed towel from it. Not only does the modernized towel-warmer serve as a stabilizing pivot-point within the mise-en-scène, then, but its presence occasions further linkage among shots when, for example, a reverse-angle follows the barber with the towel from the wife's space to the husband's, matching the shots on seemingly incidental action and thereby securing an even fuller effect of spatial coherence.

The shift to the long shot after the bit of business involving the manicurist is a moment of internal punctuation that announces both the conclusion of the previous episode and the initiation of the subsequent one involving the Obtrusive Gentleman. As a formal figure, it differentiates itself from previous camera set-ups that have been dictated by the various logics of matched shots. Here the reframing moves from a close-up of the wife to a long shot of the space she occupies without being, as it were, driven to do so either by the need to reveal the object of a look, as in the sight-links, or to resolve a visual enigma that has been posed just to negotiate alternating shots, as in the positioning of the towel-warmer. This is not to suggest that this long shot itself produces a rupture in the film's fabric, for it is as much in keeping with the habits of classical narration to articulate such overt syntagmatic punctuation as it is to disavow the drive to revelation that is fundamental to the classical text (both the drive itself and its disavowal, that is, are fundamental). What is striking here, rather, is the assurance with which the classical maneuvers of the sequence readily subsume the logic of imaginary space. In this episode, the Obtrusive Gentleman descends flirtatiously upon the outraged but helpless wife, pressing himself against her and divesting her of her flower, which he places into his own collar. The parallel and symmetrical quality of the sequence as a whole rhymes the barber's ineffectual disdain with the masher's boorish aggression, and these alternative masculinities are both promptly dispatched by the preferred masculinity of the husband, who rises from his chair with ripened virility, fully shaved and thus newly revealed as the matinee-idol he has really been all along, pushing aside the now-ineffectual barber and symbolically castrating the hapless flirter, cutting the flower from his lapel with a knife.

This symbolic castration itself illustrates the important point here most clearly. As the husband towers above the Obtrusive Gentleman, the film's rhetoric reimagines the husband in images of the monstrous much like those of the earlier scene in which he advances threateningly upon the wife during the attempted murder in the boat. The stylized, deliberate gestures as the husband reaches for his knife, the fragmentation of the action into highly charged close-ups, and the consequent protraction of the scene's tempo all point specifically back to the earlier sequence. The earlier sequence makes sense as an explicit representation of the wife's subjectivity, but the symbolic castration takes place, as I have argued, in a context of thorough objectification—so much so, indeed, that the symbolic dimension of the husband's violence, necessarily purged of any element of inwardness, is played for comic effect, treated as the hopelessly overdetermined, strictly superficial metaphor it must be in this completely exteriorized context. Moreover, the thematic logic of the sequence would have us see the husband's aggression not as an act of monstrous violence but as a valiant intervention on his wife's behalf, yet its nobility is comically undercut by the images of monstrosity the film proceeds nonetheless to attach to it. A residual effect of the logic of imaginary space that dictates the film's first movement, the scene decisively challenges the logic of classical textuality into which the film might have appeared to have moved. Thus, in spite of clear narratological demarcation between the film's first two movements, what they allegorize is not the stark opposition of incompatible styles but the self-reflexive interpenetration of mutually imbricated styles.

Critics of Murnau's films have routinely seen them as enacting tensions among mingled styles, as in Lotte Eisner's identification of Murnau's "oscillation between reality and unreality" (147). Such tensions, in turn, though often seen as engendering crises of representation *within* the text, have a way of clearly illuminating critical assumptions that construct the text. To illustrate the "oscillation" she perceives in Murnau's style, Eisner cites the epilogue of *The Last Laugh* (1924) as an example of realism because, she argues, its triumphal rhetoric deprives the figure of the porter in the film of tragic status. By implication, then, tragedy is opposed to realism in Eisner's reading, possibly because of what Eisner may see as tragedy's heightening, ennobling potential or its highly conventionalized nature. Other readings of *The Last Laugh*, however, precisely reverse Eisner's contention, finding realism in the bulk of the film with its intricately detailed social chronicle of humiliation and a betrayal of realism in the buoyant artifice and intrusive irony of the film's parodic "happy ending."[9] The point here is not to chastise such critics as misguided and hopelessly out-of-synch, but to suggest that such interpretive nonalignment necessarily reflects categorical negotiations worked out in the films themselves.

In their case study of the reception of *Sunrise*, Robert C. Allen and Douglas Gomery find that conflicting patterns of signification within the text met with changing audience response in the United States to the "German style" from which the film derives, accounting for the film's lukewarm reception. While the film's use of stars and particular narrative and generic patterns mark it as a product of Hollywood, claim Allen and Gomery, its distinctive and patently "experimental" styles—forced perspectives, probing cameras, expressionist acting, and self-conscious emphasis on off-screen space—"render the film unreadable as just another Hollywood film" (103). The authors track the process through which the latter styles, formerly welcomed as appealing exotica by American audiences, had gradually come to be associated with self-indulgence, extravagance, discomfiting strangeness, and pseudo-art. One key implication of their argument is revealed in their speculation that *Sunrise* might have been more favorably received as an import from Germany. What was understood as stylistic *difference* was viewed with pleasure by American audiences, then, only when securely insulated from what was perceived as stylistic *sameness*—the "American style." Intermingling the expressionist with the Classical Hollywood styles of filmmaking, *Sunrise* conflates modernist with mass-cultural dispositions—and in turn *difference* with *sameness*—in a manner that could only provoke something of a crisis in the received hierarchies of taste in film culture.

CloseUp on *Sunrise*: Cinema's Modernist Canons

Murnau's German films of the 1920s were important texts in the establishment of a modernist cinema in European film culture of the early twentieth century. With its sophisticated visual texture and its self-consciously elliptical, tonally unstable narrative patterns, *The Last Laugh* was particularly instrumental in the early articulations of a canon of cinematic modernism taking place at the time in such avowedly modernist European film journals as *CloseUp* or *Intercine*. As I have suggested, traditional modernist aesthetics excluded film as a medium altogether from the modernist canon because of the inextricable identification of the medium with the culture of mass modernity. The hybrid-modernism expressed in a journal such as *CloseUp*, however, even as it reproduced aspects of modernist culture's critique of traditional representation and of bourgeois subjectivity in general, negotiated the divide between modernism and mass culture in order to make a place for film within a thereby modified version of the modernist canon. Even so, *Sunrise* presented a challenge for the effort to forge a modernist canon in such venues, revealing a telling connection between conventional modernist antimodernity and the breakdown of traditional hierarchies of value in twentieth-century international culture. The celebration of modernity on view in *Sunrise* was much at odds with the traditional modernist critique of the sociocultural forms of modernity. The film's status as a product of mass culture further troubled its relation to the modernist canon, despite the signifier of Murnau's authorship as a gauge of the text's potential alliances with modernism. Rejected by popular audiences, *Sunrise* thus similarly became an object of sustained ridicule among avowed modernists who might have been expected to embrace it.

This response is represented in its most consolidated form in *CloseUp*, the international film journal so closely attuned to modernism that any effort to locate cinema within the framework of modernism must take it into account. The roster of the magazine's contributors alone—H.D., Gertrude Stein, Dorothy Richardson—certifies its ties to cultural modernism, and the journal's twofold goal was to broaden emergent definitions of modernism in order to include within their scope film as a medium; and to devise a distinctively modernist canon of specific cinematic works. The first of these goals culminated in the film *Borderline* (1931), a collaborative effort by the journal's contributors, directed by *CloseUp*'s editor Kenneth MacPherson. The film is an amalgamation of the journal's most highly valued cinematic styles, from compositions evocative of German expressionism, including some distinct echoes of Murnau's expressionist style, to editing in the Soviet tradition, with a lyric undercurrent derived from poetic imagism (further signified by the presence in the cast of H.D.)—all so highly wrought as if to yield in one fell swoop a full-fledged tradition of cinematic modernism. Although *Borderline* was repeatedly assigned at the time of its release to the category of the "avant-garde," the film stakes out a territory somewhere between a realist cinema that *CloseUp* vilified tirelessly and an avant-garde tradition of which the journal remained suspicious. The journal began publishing in 1927, contemporary with the early flowering of the avant-garde in international film culture, yet in spite of the journal's avowed support of "progressive" cinema, it tended to dismiss contemporary products of the avant-garde as shallow gimmicks. The journal's most severe dismissals, however, were reserved for "manufactured" products of "Fordist" cinematic industries, implicitly associated with a backward realism of which *Sunrise* ultimately became the unlikely representative. To trace the film's circuitous reception in the journal, therefore, is to see the crises of cultural value and cultural hierarchy resulting from the effort to elaborate a tradition of modernism in international film culture.

The donnish, Olympian house-style of *CloseUp* could not hide the fact that the journal was engaged in a hesitant, groping effort to forge an aesthetic of cinematic modernism in a cultural context where the exclusionary cast of modernism-at-large required that cinema be one of the first casualties in its formation. Contributors to the journal thus find themselves in the unhappy predicament of having to refuse many of the standard cultural hierarchies that would reject film altogether, consigning it to the excluded field of mass culture, while at the same time continuing to rehearse a conventional version of modernist aesthetics that would appear to rely upon those very hierarchies. Even though the texts elected for canonization derived from a tradition of European modernism, the journal repeatedly argued against a simple dichotomizing of American and European cinemas as emblematic of mass culture on the one hand and art-cinema on the other. As MacPherson himself puts it with characterist brio in an early editorial, "[P]lease deliver me from hearing any more the phrase *vile American-isms*. Otherwise I shall be forced to retaliate vile Europeanisms."[10] Appealing to unified visions of national/cultural identity, such defenses are always mitigated in *CloseUp* by the condescension of their undergirdings, as in MacPherson's characteristic follow up here: "American sentiment . . . is alright for America, for in this amazing land there is an essential naiveté of feeling" (1.4: 10). Another regular contributor, Winifred Bryher, appeals similarly to the category of "national psychology" (2.2: 45) to mount a "defence of Hollywood," but her more complex argument is that a veneer of falseness in American film grows from contradictions rooted in irreconcilable differences of sensibility she posits between America's "East" and "West": "The average Easterner approximates to Europe, talks a far better English than can usually be heard in London, and suffers to the point of sterility from overeducation. The Westerner is child-like, impressionable, superficial to an alarming degree, and vigorous" (48). Either internalizing or evading these "geographical" differences, according to Bryher, American movies are based on essential cultural contradiction rooted in them. In this East/West division, itself a displaced version of the Europe/America binarism, Bryher's argument not-very-subtly reintroduces by the back door the very opposition her "defence" seemed designed to break down—American sentiment, crassness, naiveté, the elements of *realism*, against European irony, sophistication, self-consciousness, the elements of modernism—and her concluding gambit furthers this opposition, transposing it to another level, when she recommends texts of *literary* modernism (by Elizabeth Roberts, H.D., and John Dos Passos) that she implies function to critique or expose the contradictions that "the mass of American movies" can only "reflect" (51).

In order to argue for a modernist aesthetic of cinema at all, *CloseUp* finds it necessary to revise modernism's wholesale exclusion of mass culture, the domain to which cinema has been assigned, as in MacPherson's reference equipped with carefully ironizing quotation marks intended to mock high-art contamination-anxiety, to the "'vulgar and tawdry' urbanities [of cinema]" (1.4: 8). Once such an aesthetic is presaged, however, the same contamination-anxiety creeps back in. This is seen not only in the journal's general treatment of European and American film but, more specifically, in the thinly veiled contempt of Bryher's reference to the "mass" of American movies—or, more fully, in a telling section of her alleged "Defence of Hollywood" in which a specifically *mass* psychology is attributed with a somewhat peevish tone to America itself: "[The space of the West] drives people together until the young Westerner is genuinely unhappy unless he is with a crowd. And cannot understand that Easterner or European may not share his feelings" (48). Particularly striking here is the conflation of Easterner or European, reintroducing the Europe/American division that had previously seemed to have been rejected.

Given both the ambivalently multivalent aesthetic of *CloseUp* and the mixed textual signals sent out vis-à-vis modernism by *Sunrise* itself, it is perhaps not surprising that the film became so crucial an index to *CloseUp*'s modernism-by-default. Even before the film was reviewed at length in the journal, it had already been installed as a touchstone, illustrating nothing less than a betrayal of cinematic modernism. Scattered references to the film even before its release treat its publicity materials with barely repressed derision. Reproducing publicity stills, for example, the journal captions them with archly patronizing descriptions that allude either to the pretensions or to the fetishization of technique that the journal imputes to the film (2.3). In a screed against the practice of publicity itself as "a parasite, a funny kind of growth" (2.3: 36–37)—though, oddly, distinguishing publicity from the evidently acceptable practices of business and advertising— the journal cites the studio's promotion of *Sunrise* as a foremost example of a process that "hides both the sign and the goods, till in time these are noticed chiefly in proportion to the amount of mistletoe that can be fostered over them" (37). Thus linked as a shoddy bag of "goods," a sow's ear remade as a silk purse, to the insidious mystifications of the culture industry, *Sunrise* is even dissociated by the journal from Murnau's authorship. Included grudgingly among *CloseUp*'s list of recommended films with works credited to their directors—

such as Ernst Lubitsch's *The Student Prince* (1926), Hans Keyser's *Luther* (1927), and even Cecil B. DeMille's *King of Kings* (1926)—*Sunrise* is idenitified as a "Fox film," with Murnau's name accorded only secondary status. Such maneuvers, by extension, dissociate the film from the expressionist tradition held in such high esteem by the journal, reconstructing *Sunrise* as a Hollywood product lacking the directorial pedigree even of a DeMille epic. Significantly, in one of the more neutral references to *Sunrise* in *CloseUp*, the film is named among "pictures appealable to the intelligentsia" (2.1: 36) in the run of Hollywood movies that "represent the taste of the proletariat" (36):

> Murnau has [combined proletarian showmanship with aristocratic art] in his first Hollywood picture, *Sunrise*. There is in it much beyond the appreciation of the crowd, but at the same time it contains elements of strictly popular appeal. Whether these elements are sufficiently strong to overcome the dubious effect on the general public of the picture's camera nuances and psychological subtleties, remains to be discovered. However, Fox, the producer of it, has put a cool million into it—and Fox is a wise showman. (37)

The scattershot intensity of these passing jibes served only as a dry run for the relentless vituperation of Robert Herring's lengthy review of the film, "Synthetic Dawn." The bulk of the review consists of Herring's snide plot-summary, ridiculing the film for anachronism, artificiality, and derivativeness. In the context of the *CloseUp* aesthetic, it is noteworthy that Herring locates *Sunrise* by implication in the very realm inhabited by the films on which the journal would ordinarily confer canonical status, between the classical realism of the Hollywood film and the formalist symbolism of the avant-garde. Herring first compares *Sunrise* unfavorably to the Hollywood melodramas it resembles, *Seventh Heaven* or *My Best Girl* (Taylor, 1927), then explicitly labels it a failed attempt at expressionism by contrast with *Nju* (Czinner, 1926): "So think for a moment of *Nju*, when Bergner returned from the dance, or stood by the fireplace, after she first saw Veidt. The light-waves there were thought-waves. Light was mind, and the figures were quivering accumulations of light. That is what *Sunrise* can't do, and wants to do" (2.3: 43). Viewed as neither conforming comfortably to the popular genres it mimics nor participating in the symbolist interiority it parallels, *Sunrise* finds itself positioned in the very divide between realism and the avant-garde where, at least in recent constructions of the concept, modernism resides. It is perhaps precisely the cultural overlap between

the space of *Sunrise* and that of the films favored by the *CloseUp* aesthetic—*Nju, Love of Jeanne Ney* (Pabst, 1926), *Mother* (Pudovkin, 1926),
or *The Joyless Street* (Pabst, 1927), for example—that accounts for the
defensive fervency of Herring's dismissal. Just as the popular rejection
of *Sunrise* turns precisely on the film's concerted merger with popular
forms, so the modernist demonization of the film stems from its dal-
liance with the rhetoric of modernism. In spite of *CloseUp*'s peace-mak-
ing efforts elsewhere with mass culture—as in the journal's half-
hearted "defences" of Hollywood—Herring's review ends with the
intemperate consignment of *Sunrise* to the field of mass culture in a
sneering phrase tellingly parallel to the title of a contemporary con-
demnation of movies-as-mass-culture by Siegfried Kracauer, "Little
Shopgirls Go to the Movies" (1927): "*Sunrise* tries very hard and succeeds in providing a Happy Hour for Housemaids" (44).

   CloseUp never explicitly invokes the concept of modernism as
such, even though the term was current during the years of the journal's run, as in Robert Graves and Laura Riding's *Survey of Modernist
Poetry*, published in 1927, the year *Sunrise* was released and *CloseUp*
first saw print. Its project of forging a modernist canon in film, however, is certified in definitively modernist assumptions that paradoxically determine the exclusion of *Sunrise* from that canon. One such
assumption is apparent in Herring's lordly proclamation, oratorically
echoing T. S. Eliot on *Ulysses* despite the differing value-judgment:
"The cinema should be the means of this age to express what this age
feels and there is nothing of this age in *Sunrise*. . . . Trying as it sets out
to do to be of no place and every place, of all time and no time, it succeeds quite elaborately in repeating the superficialities of every age
whilst giving expression to none of the complexities of this" (44–45).
Throughout the review, Herring ridicules the film's universalizing
rhetoric, equating its trading in archetype with a penchant for soggy
cliché: "Gaynor puts on the most peculiar hat, out of time—plaited
from Time's beard—and of no place" (40). When he claims that "we
get no feel of the city [in the film] because it has been given no life"
(41), he is similarly deploring what he takes to be a quite literal lack of
cultural specificity that unmoors the film from its "age."

   Like Eliot in his essay on *Ulysses*, Herring pursues an essentially
epochal line of argument, a millennial vision characteristic of high
modernism, positing a new age defined by unprecedented "complexities" that requires new methods, forms, even instruments, in order to
be properly represented. It would come as no surprise if, had Herring
taken the additional step of specifying the novel problems of modernity that *Sunrise* forsakes, they had turned out to be the standard ones

of cultural modernism that Eliot also recites—belatedness, fragmentation, alienation, formlessness. Where Eliot sees the *novel* as the privileged form of the modern age, however, "the expression of an age which had not sufficiently lost all form to feel the need of something stricter" (*Selected Prose*, 177), Herring assigns that position to cinema while striving to retain the underpinnings of an essentially Eliotic modernism.

A second important assumption underlying Herring's rejection of *Sunrise* depends upon modernism's critique of bourgeois subjectivity. A leitmotif of Herring's review is spurred by the film's subtitle, "A Song of Two Humans." The subtitle leads Herring to ask how the film defines the category of the "human." Discussing the film's action after the murder attempt, Herring writes as follows:

> [Gaynor] hops out [of the boat] (ah, you may say, in what contrast to her gay departure). And runs through a Californian wood. But the man catches her up. Forgive me. Once again, this is rather good, though Gaynor isn't herself nor anyone's self. She's Gaynor minus Gaynor. Weighed down by the wig. Perhaps she too wonders what a "human" is. (41)

For all its spritely bile, Herring's point here is based on a complex recognition of a growing dissociation—of sensibility?—perhaps implicit in the machinery of film itself, between self, star, and human-image. Each of these three models of subjectivity is posited as an empty category, but the emptiness is made manifest, in Herring's terms, by the continuing material interdependence of the three. In the triad, the human-image is the only constant quantity in the sense that, even when in Herring's terms Gaynor "isn't herself nor anyone's self," the photographed representation of her body remains present on the screen: "Gaynor minus Gaynor." If Herring believes the illusion of presentness itself vacates the categories in a kind of negative dialectic, he is not far from the critique of cinema mounted by certain philosophical modernists;[11] in that case, however, it is unclear how he can continue to uphold film as the hope of the modernist future.

What is clear, though, is that the categories have been vacated: "The 'humans' are in a restaurant. Now I have it, humans are robots. They do all they are meant to but they've no soul, no beings. They're just humans" (41–42). Again Herring aligns himself with currents of modernist thought, here more closely echoing Virginia Woolf in such a standard text of modernist aesthetics as "On Modern Fiction" (1920), for instance, than any of Eliot's precepts. One could interpret Herring's

critique here as simple dissatisfaction with the "materialist" approach
to character in *Sunrise* (the term is Woolf's, referring to realist fiction's
alleged denial of subjectivity) except that he seems as dissatisfied with
what the characters are as with what they are not. Throughout the
review, Herring subjects the signifiers of bourgeois domesticity to
relentless mockery: "Gaynor and O'Brien Realize What Marriage
Means . . . Good Wifehood, Little Lord Fauntleroy, Gladys Smith and
her Niece, and Arrested Development" (42). The ironic uppercase performs its deflationary function with caustic precision, making clear
that even if Murnau *had* succeeded in "put[ting] being into the
humans" (42), they might still have been found lacking in strictly thematic terms, for the "psychological insight" Herring misses here is of
an explicitly critical character. What he derides in *Sunrise*, clearly, is
the film's apparently affirmative standpoint, its seemingly uncritical
confirmation of the ideals of bourgeois union: "Men and Wives and
Other Women don't matter," Herring states flatly in his most explicit
gesture of privileging modernist representation over bourgeois experience, "except for the states of mind they cause" (43).

At one level, the *CloseUp* review denigrates *Sunrise* merely as
cheap sentiment and banal melodrama, but in so doing, Herring faults
the film for its refusal or its simple lack of engagement with these
modernist imperatives. The sustained attention the film drew from the
journal is accountable perhaps only in terms of the film's infringement
upon the territory of cinematic modernism that *CloseUp* was engaged
in defining. Such cultural trespassing presented a crisis to the *CloseUp*
aesthetic made manifest in the literally hysterical response of the journal to the film, but it was not a crisis that could be fended off by means
of such heightened vitriol alone, for it went to the heart of modernist
aesthetics itself. Above, I implied that a contradiction inhered in Herring's installation of film as modernist form par excellence even as he
promoted an Eliotic narrative of cultural breakdown and shamanistic
renewal through new and redemptive forms of representation. The latter implication becomes clearer if we return to Herring's conclusive
declaration with an emphasis on its definite article: "Cinema should be
the means of this age." To be sure, in the context of emergent narratives
of modernism at that time—say, Edmund Wilson's *Axel's Castle*
(1931)—the concept of a *cinematic* modernism could only be seen as
itself a contradiction, since modernism was by definition *a priori* that
which cinema was not. In the austere climate of Wilson's work, Wilson
could note cinematic qualitites of neosymbolism while dismissing film
itself altogether without appearing to broach any contradiction whatever, so hermetically had the categories already been sealed off from

each other, at least at the conceptual level (Wilson, 225–29). In order to define a canon of cinematic modernism in the first place, though, *CloseUp*'s contributors were necessarily obliged to conceive of the field of cultural production as contiguous, if not unified, so that film might fall somewhere within its purview; whereas modernism tended to conceive of that field as subject to the prior enclosure of preexistent hierarchies, those, broadly speaking, between bourgeois mass culture and the modernism that presumably opposed it. Often, this contiguity of the cultural field was admitted only grudgingly in the pages of *CloseUp*, or seen as an unavoidable by-product of a theoretically desirable class-consciousness. These tendencies are seen in this comment representative of the journal's refusal to dismiss mass culture out of hand: "[Most films] represent the taste of the proletariat. Wherefore, to criticize them or deplore them, is merely to take issue with the taste of the common people—and that is both futile and unphilosophical" (2.2: 36).

Only a conception of cultural production as a contiguous field, its products perhaps hierarchized but necessarily *inter*related, enabled the journal's placement of film at the center of "modern consciousness": "The cinema has become so much a habit of thought and word and deed as to make it impossible to visualize modern consciousness without it" (1.4: 8). If that conception markedly conflicted with the modernist bifurcations of the field of cultural production, particularly between its own productions and those of mass modernity, the *CloseUp* aesthetic sought to overcome such contradiction by, as it were, internalizing modernist demonology of mass culture. What is most striking about *CloseUp*'s treatment of *Sunrise* is not the film's ultimate consignment to mass culture but the threat perceived in the film's unconsciously acknowledged national/cultural hybridity. Herring can dismiss *Sunrise* entirely from the modernist canon only by disavowing its atavistic Expressionism, ridiculing its cult of the new (as evidenced by its self-proclaimed technical novelty), and denying the importance of its status as "the first international picture." Such of the film's clear signifiers of modernism must be effaced in Herring's discussion even as the seemingly inevitable consequence of their effacement, to force the film into the already reified mass-culture category, must be resisted. In fact, by the logic of the *CloseUp* aesthetic, the film's "failure" can be presented neither as a function of its position in mass culture, since that position has already been defined as somehow legitimate, nor as a consequence of its aspirations toward modernism, since to claim such aspirations for it would be paradoxically to plant it by implication squarely back in mass culture. Thus, as a cultural object,

Sunrise signals an impasse in the *CloseUp* aesthetic that must be seen as a reflection of larger conflicts within modernism itself that have problematized the position of cinema in the field of modernism since its inception.

Identity, Difference, and National Culture

A question implicit in the *CloseUp* responses to *Sunrise* is the question that any attempt to "place" a particular text always implies: Whose property is it? This question, in turn, is the same one upon which questions of national cinema ultimately devolve. If *Sunrise*, as a cultural object, threatens the dividing line between modernism and mass culture, it does so at least in part because it broaches the *national* division between Hollywood cinema and German expressionism. The narrative of Murnau's migration from Germany to Hollywood differs from the stories of later emigrés, who often sought refuge in Hollywood from political strife in their native countries, as in the cases of Jean Renoir and Fritz Lang. In Murnau's case, the director was lured to Hollywood, from a cinematic institution sustained by Hollywood capital, with the promise of access to money and advanced technologies.[12] In exchange for this, the institution hoped to gain international prestige by producing films directed by Murnau and to fend off international competition by incorporating the styles of German expressionism in some fashion into Hollywood's own representational arsenal. In the most literal terms, *Sunrise*, a product of Hollywood, is the property of Hollywood: in purchasing the signifier of Murnau's authorship, as it were, the institution of Hollywood bid to extend its ownership of cinematic commodities by assimilating foreign or differential terms into itself.

The institution could not do so, however, without either implying the prior incompletion of its own system or denying the essential "nativeness" of its own representations, thus potentially disrupting the certitude of that ownership. If Hollywood was in need of "foreign" talent, it might not be seen as having been initially *whole* (not to say stable, coherent, total); if such "foreign" talent could find a suitable home in Hollywood, the institution's representations might no longer be able to claim that quintessential "Americanness" they usually hoped to project. In order to function in the Hollywood system as a form of cultural capital, Murnau's authorship needed to be visibly articulated in the films he directed, and its signs needed to be taught to spectators so they could discover them in those films. Thus, the texts poduced of that authorship had to differentiate themselves from those of "native" filmmakers, the signs of whose authorship would be put to other uses by the system. Paradoxically, then, the effort of the institution to extend its ownership resulted not in the assured generalization of American national culture across national lines, but in the internalization and articulation of "foreignness" in Hollywood film that could only, in turn, upset the univocal coherence of representations of American national culture in that institution's products.

All of this is to say that *Sunrise*, in its reflections of national culture, occupies a liminal space complexly tied up with the film's borderline position between mass culture and modernism. Indeed, the liminal space to which the film finds itself consigned in the rhetoric of cinematic modernism resembles the liminal space the film defines for itself in its own textures. Setting oppositional, differential codes into dialogue—modernity/modernism, expressionism/Hollywood, high culture/mass culture—the film enacts a kind of textual liminality that defines its treatment of national culture as well. What happens in this textual dynamic, in effect, is that each term of these dyads migrates into the system of its opposed term, while retaining an intermediate status, literally *liminal*, refusing final integration into the system by negotiating differential terms. This dynamic results in a kind of suspended dialectic, an undecidability, that erodes the theoretical boundaries between each term and, residually, those between identity and difference themselves, the very epistemological categories that subtend such oppositions.

Though *Sunrise* is often interpreted in terms of its representation of national identity, the film avoids evocation of specific nationalities, at least at its surface level. To be sure, a quite literal problem confronts the film as it moves from country to city, that of how to retain in the second section the balladic rhetoric of the archetypal—of "timelessness" and "placelessness"—that has been so thoroughly established in the first. Signifiers of the rural, at least those the film happens to draw upon, situate themselves readily in a nominally "timeless" sphere. Critics at the time of the film's release noted the vaguely Eastern European climate of the film's rural setting, but the rustic habitations and quaint garments abounding colorfully in this section of the film could be equally at home in certain versions of rural America. Herring, for instance, designates the surrounding forest as distinctively "Californian." Signifiers of the urban, however, yield inevitable specificity, topographically or geographically—in styles of architecture, nationalities of language, habits of dress, makes and models of cars. The problem of the film's middle third, then, becomes that of representing an "international" city in this "first international film" while retaining the nominal "placelessness" that has defined its texture. The solution to the problem, in the event, is to empty these urban signifiers of their national, cultural specificity. Thus, while the film's celebration of urban culture may be seen to mark it as *anti*-modernist, its commitment to folk-tale archetype generates a conflict in its effort to represent modernity. At the same time, this concerted repression of the thematics of nationality reveals the extent to which issues of national style underlie and delimit the stylistic negotiations that characterize the film.

The irony of the film's having to efface signs of nationality in order to achieve "international" status is set into relief by its resort to a decidedly oneiric logic in the city section, perhaps meant to serve the function of transmitting the archetypal rhetoric of the country section onto the film's middle third. Such logic is evident, for instance, in the first shot that heralds the presence of the metropolis, the surprising appearance of a commuter train in the midst of a dense wood. The effect of dreamlike surprise here, of a certain spatial condensation, is heightened by the way Murnau frames the shot. It begins as a long shot of a sun-drenched wood, the wife fleeing in horror after the murder attempt with the already repentant husband in pursuit. As the camera pivots right to follow the wife—a tenuous camera movement at odds with the characteristic assurance of Murnau's mobile cameras—it startlingly reveals a train pulling into a station. Containing the juxtaposition of wood and train within a single shot, the shot's manipulation of off-screen space to create an effect of concealment and subsequent revelation emphasizes the unlikelihood in literal terms of the train's appearance in this rustic site. When the husband and wife board the train, the film yields its most flamboyant examples of forced perspective, causing the scenery outside the train's window, highlit in extreme contrast with the train's dim interior, to appear fluidly suspended in space, mercurially shifting and floating as if in a dream screen. Murnau's editing here begins the transition to the patterns of classical editing that will be complete by the time of the sequence in the barbershop; but what is striking here, as in the later sequence, is the interplay of this newly objectified texture with the oneiric logic of this sequence. The dreamlike representations of the scenery here are not linked to the points-of-view of the husband and wife, who in preparation for the growing narrative detachment from them during the rest of the film are pointedly shown to be oblivious of it. In this respect, the instance resembles the later effect of the projection of the rural scene after the couple's reconciliation in the city. Both examples rely on images of hallucinatory projection directed emphatically beyond the awareness of the characters, thus effecting in some literal way a gesture of self-reflexive irony.

The differing textual registers at work here result in a quality of undecidability, like that between differential codes of the film's negotiations of Hollywood and expressionist style. Those codes remain differential in some overdetermined way, gaining their meanings in the text as much by their relations to one another as by the spectators' experiences (or lack of it) with prior instances of Hollywood or expressionist style. Schematically dyadic, the relation between these two terms in the film's textual system nonetheless remains indeterminate because it does not appeal to a governing rhetoric of authenticity that would enable any one of the text's styles finally to be privileged as "dominant" in interpretation of the film. Indeed, it cannot do so, given the institutional requirement that the film find some ground between its status as a Hollywood product and its manifestations of Murnau's authorship. We cannot read the film's expressionist signatures as indicative of the "true" voice of the film, and thus of the triumph of Murnau's authorial persona, without denying the determining force of the institution's property rights upon the film's representation.

The question of authenticity is thus tied to the question of nationality. The ideology of nationhood is always an ideology of ownership, insofar as it implies one's belonging to a given nation-state and that state's belonging to its citizens. The condition of exile—loss of that belonging, of one's proper home, one's native tongue, one's fundamental birthright—points up, in negative terms, the traditional (and often unconscious) relation of authenticity to ownership, by revealing what happens when that relation is sundered. The rift between an individual and a native place, between the self and its "true" home, is frequently conceived in the condition of exile to entail a loss as well of "authentic" voice, to bring about the enforced necessity to speak in the language of another.

A quality of Bakhtinian "other-voicedness," to be sure, characterizes the texture of *Sunrise*, but if the film bridges the rift between national styles in its negotiations of Hollywood and expressionism, the result is to render either style, or even the dialogic style produced by their merger, potentially the film's "true" one, and thus to associate either at any given time in the text with constantly shifting positions of identity or difference. That quality of "other-voicedness," of an act of expression couched in language alien to the agent of expression, is evident in the film's narrative structure as well as in its visual style. The extremely digressive structure of the film as a whole, with its heavily marked shifts of style, tone, and narrative focus, has never been adequately dealt with in criticism of the film. Early reviewers who remarked on this aspect of the film simply saw it as a function of the film's dramatic failure in spite of its pictorial beauty, reading this aspect of the film in terms of a lack of the satisfying coherence already then seen as a staple of Classical Hollywood.[13] The general critical failure to confront the film's structural idiosyncracy can be seen in the assumption of many critics that the journey to the city somehow anchors the narrative, established clearly as a goal in the film's prologue that is then achieved in the middle third. In fact, in narrative terms, the couple's arrival in the city is strictly arbitrary. They do not set out for the city, and they end up there only because the wife happens to jump aboard the train that appears so fortuitously. The episodes in the city, too, are characterized by an effect of dreamlike randomness, a quality of contingency made more immediate by the unexpected shifts from naturalist melodrama to folk comedy, by the complete dissolution of narrative conflict, and by the consequent atomization of narrative anxiety—as if the now-irrelevant story of tragically triangulated romance has simply been put indefinitely on hold. Each episode is discrete and symmetrical, but no narrative logic dictates the sequence of the episodes themselves, and the couple, who repeatedly disappear and reappear surprisingly throughout this section to the end of the film, have ceased to function as a principle of narrative organization.

The shifts of narrative style in the film, like its negotiations of distinctive visual styles, challenge the possibility of a stable textual grounding against which to understand them. One way to account for the structural idioscyncrasy of the film, however, is to see it as a commentary on the terms, conventions, and conditions of Hollywood cinema of the 1920s. Each of the three sections of the film, with its distinctive tonal climate, emotional texture, and narrative focus, can be seen to imitate the style of an important Hollywood filmmaker—this despite the film's general reception as a distinctly Europeanized vision. The film moves from a mordant naturalism strikingly redolent of von Stroheim to the antic slapstick of a Chaplin, culminating with the storm and its aftermath in an approximation of the sentimental melodrama of a Griffith. The obsessional quality and the elemental imagery of the first section are very close to von Stroheim. The repetitious developmental structure of the gags and the carnivalesque settings in the second section, meanwhile, evoke Chaplin as tellingly as the conclusive search for the wife, with its direct allusion to the climax of *Way Down East* (1924), does Griffith. Moreover, the film's disjunctive structure, refusing the logic of standard coherence, accords readily to a logic of self-reflexive allusion that examines the three sides, as it were, of 1920s Hollywood. Interpreted in this light, *Sunrise* further undermines the concept of a "native" or "authentic" voice governing it. Instead, the film participates in a logic of pastiche, whereby given conventions and received codes come together in a single text, revealing the agency of their authorial arrangement only in the wake of their syntheses. Even if the elements of pastiche fuse smoothly, however, they remain indirectly "voiced"—signs, in Bakhtin's words, of "the image of another's language" (44):

> [They] in no way function here as the *primary means of representation* . . . rather, they themselves have here become the object of representation. . . . This novelistic image of another's style . . . must be taken in *intonational quotation marks* within the system of direct authorial speech. (Bakhtin, 44)

Though without the critical edge of parody, this adoption of received styles integral to the film's structure, its reproductions of "the image of another's language," disrupts the "directness" of authorial expression.

Sunrise has sometimes been read as an allegory of exile. Certainly, the film's concern with the construction and maintenance of "home" as a kind of valorized symbolic category is intense, perhaps giving the lie to the film's efforts to repress thematics of nationality in more literal terms. At the beginning of the film, the home is threatened by uncontained forces of sexuality. By the end of the film, with a rhetoric bordering on that of the romantic sublime, the couple has returned from their sojourn abroad, and home has been restored to its original condition of wholeness, stability, unity, and plenitude. This reading is dependent on a conception of "foreignness," however, which the film, bridging the divide between identity and difference, nativeness and foreignness, does not bear out. In fact, though the initial disruption of home is imputed to the diabolicalism of a "foreigner," the woman from the city, it is also shown to be a product of the husband's desire. Thus, the narrative suggests that such disruption originates in the home whose insulation and idealization itself produces the category of "foreignness." Moreover, the film's most intense affective investments shift porously and mercurially from identification with otherness to estrangement from identity, troubling the categories of "sameness" and "otherness" on which the ideologies of nationality itself are based.

To read *Sunrise*, at the level of its content, as an allegory expressing the exile's longing for national homeland accounts in part for the pervasive but unfocused, unanchored intensity of emotional affect that characterizes the film, but it does not account for the mercurial, schismatic quality even of that intensity. More sophisticated interpretations of *Sunrise* as an allegory have attempted to locate its allegorical dimensions at the level of its style, in particular textual codes. Janet Bergstrom's comparison of Murnau's German films to his Hollywood films relies upon a logic of displacement in arguing that Murnau's Hollywood films express alienation from his native style. Following Christian Metz's analysis of the "scopic regimes" of cinematic institutions, Bergstrom argues that the German and Hollywood cinemas of the 1920s were both rigidly codified and highly conventional in the terms of their representations, but that they remained nonetheless, despite these parallels, largely incompatible (187–88). Like theorists of 1920s Hollywood, Bergstrom defines the textual system according to its articulations of characters' looks. For Bergstrom, the system of the look in Weimar cinema is marked by a high degree of "abstraction" and "ambiguity." Such textual systems readily accommodated Murnau's thematic concerns, Bergstrom argues, which were determined by the imperatives of 1920s art-cinema. Echoing Elsaesser's conception of imaginary space, Bergstrom examines how specific codes of editing and composition in German cinema are "intended to elicit a contemplative look" (199) from the spectator. Articulated within the demands of the institution of German cinema, Murnau's films are expressive of such contemplation, "abstraction," and "ambiguity." Moreover, Murnau can use these devices in order to encode homosexual desire, so that these texts implicitly express Murnau's sexuality as well, even as they conform to the dictates of the institution. These effects of direct expression result nonetheless, Bergstrom observes, in forms of textual displacement that undermine traditional cinematic constructions of sexual difference:

> [F]emininity [in Murnau's films], insofar as it can be associated with eroticism or sexuality, has been displaced from the woman's body onto several kinds of substitutes. The woman's body is at a loss literally in that it has a reduced physical presence, lacking a sexual dimension; metaphorically, the symbolic function of the woman's body in establishing sexual difference is greatly diminished. (Bergstrom, 189)

In Murnau's Hollywood films, however, produced in a tradition that values narrative economy and visual concreteness, Murnau must *manipulate* the "conventions of narrative and visual action and economy of detail" (202), relying upon the "alternation in [spectators'] attention between narrative and non-narrative elements used to displace sexual identification" (202). To achieve similar effects in differing traditions, then—the supposed *displacement* of sexual identification— Murnau in the first instance works within established conventions, thus implicitly in his "native" voice, producing the ambiguous editing and abstract compositions of expressionism. In the second instance, however, he works *against* the established conventions of Hollywood, rooted in an objectivity presumably inhospitable to such effects, so that he can only express his authorship indirectly, in an estranged relation to the tradition in which he works.

Thus, Bergstrom sees displacement in operation in all of Murnau's films, but she perceives a kind of *double*-displacement in his Hollywood films. Literally displaced from his homeland, Murnau is denied access to the "abstraction" and "ambiguity" that make possible the "true" expressions of his German films and can achieve the representations he desires only through a kind of tragic indirection, working against the grain of the Hollywood tradition. Bergstrom's treatment of Murnau's homosexuality introduces the concept of displacement as a "successful" rendering of the director's desires:

> The displacement of desire from the woman's body to the man's, and, importantly, to other, more generalized substitutes, works because Murnau can call on a different sort of spectator convention [in his expressionist work] than is operative in most narrative films. (Bergstrom, 199)

Bergstrom's treatment of the representation of homosexual desire repeats the assumptions that underlie her claims about Murnau's immigration. The "displacement of desire" from the heterosexuality of the normative text to the homosexuality through which Bergstrom defines Murnau's own subjectivity "works," she claims, because despite institutional censoring mechanisms of German cinema that exclude overt representation of homosexuality, the abstract figuration of German film style allows its covert representation. The circuitry of such representation has already been defined as "displacement"—as if homosexuality itself were always only to be understood as an aberration from normative heterosexuality. A logic of displacement determines Bergstrom's treatment of the relation of differing textual systems, where elements from one system, once transmitted to another, will always be named as displaced, just as homosexuality will always be seen as the substitute for normative desire.

Bergstrom alternates between essentializing displacement as the nodal point of self-consciousness and demonizing it as the locus of unconsciousness in representation. On the one hand, she argues that "Murnau's displacement of sexual investment in the image" is therefore "lost to abstraction" (202), yet she claims that "Murnau's use of convention . . . can help us see new possibilities for the cinematic representation of sexual identity" (202). Here, Bergstrom may be following her chief influence, Metz, who alternately identifies displacement in cinematic representation with profound psychic evasion on the one hand, and with the very forces of meaning itself on the other: "Displacement keeps a good distance away from the truth of the unconscious, it proceeds via substitutes" (269), Metz claims at one point, while asserting at another, "Displacement and condensation are not 'qualities,' still less devices of meaning. They are meaning itself" (270). In Bergstrom's terms, however, the codes of differing textual systems retain an *essential* grounding in the system presumed to originate or to authenticate them, thereby certifying their "truth." Bergstrom grants the possibility of self-consciousness of expression in Hollywood representation, for instance, but that self-consciousness is always marked as itself *alien*—the displaced by-product of the European art-cinema in which it was initially articulated. In its projection of the circuitous psychic passage from one system to another, substituting a false term for a true one, the rhetoric of displacement must always privilege one over another.

The logic of displacement has traditionally held sway in discussion of the cultural politics of exile, and in particular in the case of European directors in the Hollywood studio system: the exile who loses his or her homeland is also deprived of her or his native voice, so that any further expression will be seen as "displaced" from its proper point of origin through the vehicle of its "artificial" or "borrowed" languages. It is worth noting, however, that for a theorist like Bakhtin, the concept of displacement was irrelevant to the polyglossia of textual systems because one is always speaking, in Bakhtin's terms, in "the voice of another." Thus, for Bakhtin, the concept of "alien" discourse does not necessarily imply estrangement because it is simply an intensified version of the paradigm for all human expression, which is always characterized by the incorporation of differential languages and by indirect, because borrowed, discourses. As Michael Holquist points out, defining the concept of "alien" speech in Bakhtin,

> *Cuzoj* [other] is the opposite of svoj [one's own] and implies otherness—of place, of point of view, possession or person. It does

not (as does "alien" in English) imply any necessary estrangement or exoticism; it is simply that which someone has made his
own, seen (or heard) from the point of view of an outsider. In
Bakhtin's system, we are all *cujoz* to one another by definition.
(*The Dialogic Imagination*, 423)

In its amalgamation of conventions borrowed from the languages of
Hollywood cinema and German expressionism, *Sunrise* as a text is
"alien" in this sense of the word. In suspending its own textual system
among many determining oppositions, the film opposes the logic of
displacement, which is bound up with traditional boundaries and
hierarchies, social, cultural, and national. In rendering identity and
difference themselves undecidable categories, it denies a stabilized
grounding for selfhood that in turn renders the category of "otherness" itself diffused.

The question of identity and difference in cinematic representation is predicated on the logic of identification that particular texts
work through: Who is the "self" of the text? Whom is the spectator
asked to identify with? Whom, on the contrary, is the spectator asked
to conceive as "other"? From this pair of questions, the relevance of
these categories to the issue of national identity should be clear: Who
is conceived as "native" in the text? Who is projected as "foreign"? If,
in examining operations of identity and difference in this film, I turn
now to questions of *sexual* identity and difference, it should not be
assumed that I am either abandoning the topic of national culture or
identifying sexuality with nationality. Rather, I am proceeding from
the assumption that conceptions of identity and difference governing
any textual system have complexly parallel implications for all the
forms of identity and difference—of class, race, ethnicity, national
identity, sexual identity, cultural affiliation—articulated within that
system. Moreover, the issues of sexual identity and national culture
are hardly unrelated except in the most rigidly categorical conceptual
schema. As Stephen Heath points out,

> Any political discussion of cinema and nationhood has to involve
> discussion of sexual difference, but that in no sense, or in a reac-
> tionary sense only, can be conceived of as the "addition" of some
> "further problem": the latter discussion is there in the very terms
> of the former as point of contradiction and struggle in represen-
> tation, in the institutions of representing, in the property of
> images and sounds in relations of men and women, their con-
> structions. (*Explorations in Film Theory*, 186)

Indeed, these issues are as integral to one another as modernity is to modernism, high culture to mass culture—and as, indeed, those oppositions are to structures of identity and difference, as specfic cultural manifestations of conceptions of selfhood and otherness, nativity and foreignness. In the "other-voiced" climate of *Sunrise*, identity and difference are constantly shifting ground and exchanging position, and the viewer is repeatedly asked to identify with what has been defined as "otherness," to assume a position of estrangement in relation to what has been defined as "sameness." Thus, the vertices of familiarity and strangeness themselves are redefined in the film's textual system.

The representation of women's points-of-view in *Sunrise* works out this suspension between identity and difference insofar as they are split between narrative and non-narrative dimensions of the text. An example is in the initial appearance of the milkwoman later shown to be the wife's confidante. Her first appearance in the film, because it is entirely unforegrounded, disrupts the film's narrative texture even while it is necessitated by required backstory information. After the initial melancholy dinner-scene that introduces the couple, where the husband yields to temptation and leaves the wife alone as he goes to meet the vamp, Murnau cuts to a sudden reverse-shot of the milkwoman, who describes to an interlocutor the couple's former happiness. This prompts the film's lone flashbacks, the first a single shot, comic in its sketchiness and abbreviation, depicting the couple's past carefree state. It is significant that, instead of simply introducing the flashback from an omniscient vantage-point, the narration insists on making the milkwoman its vehicle, even though to do so intrudes emphatically on the narrative rhythms that have been established. The languorous tempo of the dinner scene is achieved through use of long takes, stylized slowness of movement by figures within the frame, and painstakingly painterly compositions. Moreover, the scene contains only one previous reverse-shot, the husband's point-of-view of the wife, so the reverse-shot of the milkwoman is both temporally disruptive, an intrusion on the scene's measured, unvaried pace, and spatially disruptive, since the viewer has been unaware of the milkwoman's presence in the dramatic space of the room before the shot reveals her.

In fact, several prior visual cues suggest the solitude of the couple. For example, the sequence begins and ends with shots of first the husband and then the wife in identical postures, seated at the table in the narrow foreground of a deep-focus shot evoking the marriage of the painterly traditions of still-life and portraiture. Both figures are shown in attitudes of lonely contemplation. Because these shots negate the presence of a witness within the narrative, the sudden appearance

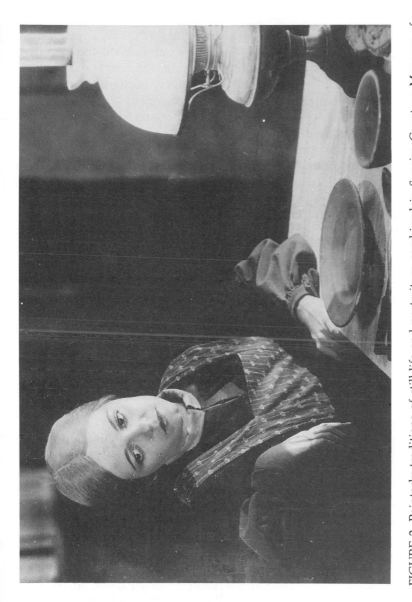

FIGURE 2. Painterly traditions of still-life and portraiture combined in *Sunrise*. Courtesy Museum of Modern Art, New York

of the milkwoman seems to issue from an abstracted space apart from the literal diegesis, an effect heightened by the character's association with the metacommentary of the flashback. Though the milkwoman's look is fundamentally constitutive of the scene as a whole, since she turns out to have been watching all along from the space occupied by the camera, its curiously undefined position outside the narrative proper as a source of narrative information or metanarrative commentary renders her look insubstantial, effectively bodiless. Thus identified with narrative processes as such, the figure is also registered as disruptive of the text's continuity, thus positioned as an intrusive, differential element within it.

A similar dynamic attends the figure of the vamp. A very literal figure of "foreignness," intruding from outside on the couple's happy home and disrupting its stability, the vamp also becomes a vehicle of narrative point-of-view at crucial points in the film. Initially associated with threateningly uncontained sexuality, the vamp is positioned in the film's final third in an abstracted narrative space, like that which defines the milkwoman, granted an uncanny access to narrative omniscience. The husband's return and the search for the wife, for instance, are both presented as seen by the vamp, herself unseen by the community, from a series of impossibly divergent viewpoints. Here, it is important to note that the vamp is positioned as an object of the narrative's irony. She mistakenly believes the husband has murdered the wife according to their plan, and so misinterprets all she sees as evidence of his crime and her triumph. Yet she remains the focalizer of the narrative events, thus a potential figure of identification. This double-focusing takes shape in the playing of the dominance of the vamp's point-of-view throughout this section of the film against visual figurations of her bodily absence that accompany it. Most striking is a long-held shot braketed by insistently lengthy point-of-view shots as the vamp witnesses the search. Foregrounding both the vamp's presumed exhibitionism and the viewer's visual inaccessibility to her body, the shot is held on the empty space of the vamp's room as, immediately off-screen-right, the vamp dresses to go out. The vamp's presence in relation to this empty space is marked by the garments she throws from off-screen into the range of the camera, as if performing a kind of invisible striptease. One of Murnau's stealthiest manipulations of off-screen space, the shot works to place the vacant space of the room in a cannily metonymic relation to the vamp's absent body. At the very moment when the vamp seems allied with the narrative itself, her point-of-view driving it, the film sardonically positions her teasingly outside the range of the viewer's gaze. In this case as well as in the case of the milkwoman, these figures are positioned as *subjects* of narrative discourse, their points-of-view determining the movement of the narrative. Yet they are also positioned as *objects* of disruptive desire within the narrative proper or abstracted metaphorically at meta-narrative positions. In the last scene, for instance, the milkwoman expresses her gratitude to the sailor who has rescued the couple at sea, and he responds avidly to her attentions, but another woman steps forth from the crowd and bluntly cuts off this increasingly erotic transaction. Traditionally, the hierarchy of the gaze in cinematic representation has been gendered to produce the male as subject of the gaze and the woman as its object. These representations in *Sunrise* may not finally challenge that hierarchy, but the shifting positions of these characters in relation to the hierarchy signals the shifing, chiasmic conception of identity and difference in the film.

The conventional hierarchies of the construction of the gendered gaze are troubled as well by the film's construction of the male look, illustrated most persuasively in the series of marginal male figures initiated with the barber and culminating with the rescuer whose attentions to the milkwoman are so bluntly circumvented. The structural relatedness of this cluster of male figures is clear in the analogous ways in which they are represented. While the vamp and the milkwoman are centered as subjects of desire thenceforth identified with the drive to narration, each of these male figures is shown, as in the case of the barber, to be positioned *outside* the networks of desire and peripheral to the narrative's development. As in the case of the barber's look, moreover, the emphasis on these characters' looks works to disperse audience identification, to negate the possibility of erotic mastery usually associated with the gendered hierarchy of the look in Hollywood cinema. The clearest instance of structural relation among this set of figures is seen by comparing the Obtrusive Gentleman of the barbershop sequence with the Obliging Gentleman, as he is named in the credits linking him obviously to the other figure, who appears later in the scene of the folk dance. As is the case with each of these figures, this figure is shown engaged in a frustrated interaction with another character that momentarily stalls narrative development. Whereas the Obtrusive Gentleman does so in an expression of aggressive desire, though, the Obliging Gentleman does so in an effort to protect female purity, to keep the female body covered.

The Obliging Gentleman figures in one of the Chaplinesque gags that characterize this section of the film—the model here appears to be *The Rink* (1916)—involving the shoulder-straps of the dress of the woman beside him, which keep falling down but which he obligingly replaces. At first, the woman expresses indifferent gratitude to him for his vigilance about her stubborn clothing, but when the man in frustration pulls down one of the shoulder-straps before it can fall again, she slaps him. The gag's sideline status is established by situating the two figures literally at the sidelines of the action, watching the couple dance. The cutaway shots that introduce the characters register a look of keen disapproval on the part of the man, an expression as enigmatic as the barber's in the earlier sequence. Despite the insistently peripheral status of these figures, they function as filters through which to witness the action of the couple, distancing the spectator from that action by mediating it repeatedly through these figures of comical displeasure. Presenting its main characters through the vantage points of these peripheral figures, the film filters identification through marginality, identity through difference.

The operation of dynamics of identification in *Sunrise* bridges the traditional divide between the distanciation associated with modernist textuality and the emotional engagement associated with mass culture's habitual forms of textuality. Although the film demands constant emotional investment in the figures of the husband and wife, the terms of that investment shift markedly in the course of the narrative. The rhetoric of subjectivity in the film's first section functions to secure traditional forms of identification between spectator and character, assuring direct and largely untroubled access to characters' interiority. With the city section of the film, however, such access is gradually blocked, replaced by various structures of mediation, such as viewing the couple no longer directly but as they are seen by other characters. Although such mediating structures herald growing distance between spectator and character, they are built around a continuing rhetoric of engaged sympathy characteristic of sentimental melodrama. The scene at the photographer's studio provides a representative example. At the end of the scene, the couple depart hastily from the studio, wrongly believing they have damaged the photographer's reproduction of the Venus de Milo. But the camera remains behind after their departure to register the photographer's amused reaction to their clumsy effort to hide the misperceived damage, thus positioning him as another of the male figures of sexual marginality through which the film repeatedly focuses identification. The narration here, no longer strictly guided by the protagonists' action, breaks its close connection with the couple by registering action that transpires in their absence, mediating the spectator's relation through the photographer's response, initiating the dominant pattern of the rest of the film. The film's narration distances itself from the couple's naiveté—their misrecognition of the statue—

yet guides the spectator's response through the figure of the photographer toward amused affection.

Far from positioning the couple as figures of the immediate identification on which sentimental melodrama thrives, such strategies work to render them as figures of foreignness in the film. Although the space of the city is in some literal way foreign terrain for the couple, Murnau repeatedly emphasizes not the strangeness of the city but the innocent misrecognitions of the couple. It is not the urban landscape itself that is alien in *Sunrise* but, rather, the couple's inability to deal with what the film presents as the familiar ground of modernity. Indeed, Murnau repeatedly draws attention to the city-dwellers' baffled looks at the couple, registering them as foreign to the realm of the city. Thus, the couple themselves are defamiliarized as characters, further distanced from the conventional structures of identification in Hollywood cinema.

Metz's distinction between primary and secondary identification in cinematic representation will clarify this point. For Metz, identification with character and narrative elements, though priviliged by the institutions of cinema, is subordinate to unconscious identification with the apparatus of film itself, its technologies of the visual, with the look of the camera that displaces, according to Metz, the spectator's primary identification with his or her own look. Although the spectator's relation to cinema is actually triadic in structure, for Metz, it is experienced in terms of an imaginary binarism—of an *immediate* relation of spectator to film, effacing the mediation of the psychically introjected apparatus. Although Metz sees all films as locked into this logic of the imaginary, he distinguishes between illusionist cinema that promotes secondary identification with character and plot and self-reflexive cinema that enforces recognition of primary identification with the cinematic apparatus itself. In spite of the fraught emotional climate of *Sunrise*, the film complicates conventional identification in its use of these mediating structures, as well as in its deconstruction of the gendered hierarchies of the look and in its orchestration of the triangulated gaze, exposing the triadic structure of cinematic identification. In doing so, it conflates something of the illusionist textuality traditionally ascribed to mass culture with the self-reflexive textuality attributed to modernism.

Conventional notions of identity and difference are intricately linked to the constructions of national cultures in associating the former with self, home, "native" place, the latter with otherness, wandering, "foreign" territory. A result of the play of these terms in *Sunrise* is to threaten the boundaries that define such oppositions. The final homecoming scene in the film illustrates the point. Culminating much that is distinctive in the film's texture, the scene combines a rhetoric of emotional sublimity with elements of emotional distanciation. The image of the couple's final, ardent embrace, the visual leitmotif of the final sequence, coheres with the extreme emotional amplitude—its sense of exceeding the ordinary scales of affect—of the sequence as a whole. Yet even here the film presents a reminder of the exclusionary structure of desire, in the comic encounter between the milkwoman and the rescuer that undermines some of the emotional momentum of the scene. This renders the couple's excessive engagement with one another potentially readable as narcissistic, and perhaps accounts for the curious double register of the film's end, suspended between ecstasy and loss, participating fervently in the fusion of the couple but expressing a sense of insuperable separateness from it. Moreover, despite the rhetoric of restoration and reconciliation that governs the scene, the couple's homecoming is associated not with a return to "authenticity," but with a final, overwhelming distillation of artifice. The most memorable image of the end of the film is the juxtaposition of the couple's embrace against an obviously synthetic sunrise. Surely this image, in the context of the film as a whole and the emotional grandiosity of this scene, cannot be said to ironize the couple's final embrace, but it does deny ultimately ontological affinities between "home" and "truth." The heavy reliance on artifice defamiliarizes the couple's home, so that the viewer may not even recognize it in the end. To be sure, the "home" at which we arrive at the end of *Sunrise* is not the same one we left at the beginning of the film. Thus, the last shots of the film cannot be said to chronicle a real homecoming, since it is the very idea of "home"—and all the concept implies about selfhood and otherness, strangeness and familiarity—that the film has investigated. The end of the film shows, rather, a *discovery*—the discovery of a "home" elsewhere.

2

Representation and Form: Representing Nationality in *This Land Is Mine*

n its very title, *This Land is Mine* (Renoir, 1943) registers both the historical crises the film seeks to represent and the representational crises this history engenders. Like the titles of other wartime Hollywood melodramas that deal with European fascism—*The Moon is Down* (Pichel, 1943) or *Hangmen Also Die* (Lang, 1943), for instance—that of Renoir's film produces by way of its earnest sententiousness, its pared-down declarative grammar, a forceful rhetorical gesture of reclamation. Yet the title's blunt assertion of ownership necessarily implies the interrogative challenge to which it responds: Whose land is it? In answer to this otherwise unasked question, in fact, the title may be understood as asserting either reclamation *or* usurpation, signifying either the triumphal liberation the film's rhetoric heralds or, alternatively, the fascist occupation of a small European town that its narrative chronicles. The title thus signals the conflicted nationalism of the film's representations, split between conventional Hollywood patriotism and a complex, *inter*nationalist vision of wartime national politics.

In spite of the title's first-person form and the sense of immediacy it implies, the sentence is spoken by no character in the film itself, but it appears as the patriotic slogan at the head of a leaflet distributed by underground resisters to the occupation. At a crucial moment in the narrative, the meekly apolitical schoolmaster Albert Lory (Charles Laughton) pockets the leaflet instead of discarding it, leading to his subsequent arrest. The Nazi officers who discover the leaflet on his person understand the slogan as a measure of Lory's guilt, but since the audience has witnessed Lory's repeated failures to resist the occupation, his arrest invests the title with a third potential level of significance, designating a third position possible in relation to the titular assertion of nationalist possessorship, that of ideological neutrality. One of the lessons of Renoir's essentially didactic film, however, is a familiar one in Hollywood's wartime narratives of European fascism. Such neutrality, the film tells us, though understandable in itself, will always be read in this historical context as *commitment*, as allegiance to *secret* resistance.[1] It is a lesson Lory has learned by the end of the film when, newly patriotic, he delivers himself of a protracted oration of nationalist pride, reclaiming the land as his, even though he knows doing so will mean facing the same fascist firing-squad he saw shoot down his mentor the previous night.

Still, the implied question—Whose land is it?—has not been answered with finality at film's end. This is in part because, released as the film was in 1943, the history it represents had yet to resolve that question. The near-universal criticism of the last third of Renoir's film is a function of the film's effort to achieve the semblance of ideological closure in the face of perceived historical indeterminacy.[2] In this sense, though the film has typically been singled out by critics for unusual abuse, it is fully representative of Hollywood's narratives of occupation, from the films named above to *Casablanca* (Curtiz, 1943). In each of these cases, the demand for narrative closure meets the threat of historical open-endedness, and in most cases, the threat is circumvented by transforming the conventions of a traditional "war" movie into those of a drama of personal conversion. Albert Lory's conversion, in *This Land Is Mine*, from apathy to patriotism, from cowardice to heroism, from pacifism to activism, can serve as a useful measure of the way wartime Hollywood modifies or reconsolidates its conventional edicts as it attempts to treat contemporary historical developments.

If critics find Lory's conversion less convincing than, say, Rick's/Bogart's admittedly different one in *Casablanca*, meanwhile, this is likely traceable to expectations of Renoir-as-auteur—famously celebrated, as for the bracingly open-ended conclusion of, say, *Grand Illusion* (1937), for his casual "off-handedness," his improvisatory spontaneity, his ideological agility and "openness."[3] These signifiers of Renoir's authorship contrast markedly with the imperatives of stylistic and narrative closure characteristic of Hollywood as an institution of representation. Thus, the apparent ideological overdeterminism of *This Land Is Mine* reveals much not only about Hollywood's confrontation with history but, at the same time, about Renoir's confrontation with Hollywood. Indeed, the nationalist debates the film narrates cannot help but take on greater resonance given the schism between the film's status as a Hollywood product and its function as a film "by" Renoir. Thus, the film delineates the relation between nationhood and property in a parallel question: Whose film is it?

Renoir's work in France of the 1930s frequently addressed prewar crises of European national culture in the terms of an explicitly Communist Popular Front politics, most famously in *Grand Illusion* or *The Rules of the Game* (1939). To that extent, Renoir's political affiliations would seem to be as potentially incompatible as his stylistic dispositions with the prevailing Hollywood ethos. It would be overhasty, however, to assume in line with traditional critical conclusions that Hollywood's dominant edicts flatly stifled Renoir's stylistic or political signatures, not at least in any simple way. Like that of other European directors of Hollywood wartime melodramas, such as Robert Florey, Douglas Sirk, or Michael Curtiz, Renoir's directorial influence upon *This Land Is Mine* was quite likely supposed to lend a rhetorical "authenticity" to the portrayal of European fascism, but it served perhaps inadvertently also to undermine the secure univocality of nationalism of the conventional Hollywood World War II film.

Even at its most secure, however, the representation of nationalism typical of Hollywood cinema of the time reflects larger categorical ncissions in modern conceptions of nationality as such. Debates surrounding nationality in the twentieth century have often taken up the issue of whether nationality is a specifically *modern* concept or whether it is coextensive—even identical—with *pre*-modern conceptions of political identity. According to the latter model, the concept of nationality has given shape to facets of human identity at least since the Middle Ages, even if it has in particular historical circumstances been subordinated to religious or dynastic forms of social governance. According to the former model, however, nationality is not a primordial source of identity, available wherever or whenever nations exist as political units, but an ideological and historically specific principle dependent on the social hegemony of post-Enlightenment rationalism, economic integration, and industrial media, each of these components functioning to produce large-scale effects of shared identity within national boundaries. To be sure, E. J. Hobsbawm and Ernest Gellner take nationality to be so historically specific that it can only be understood as a form of false consciousness. According to Gellner, this false consciousness derives precisely from nationalism's negotiation of premodern and modern conceptions of political identity: "[Nationalism's] myths invert reality: it claims to defend folk culture while in fact it is forging a high culture; it claims to protect an old folk society while in fact helping to build an anonymous mass society" (124). In Gellner's formulation, the cultural politics of nationality are thus revealed to be concomitant with questions of modernism and cultural hierarchy. It is in this context that Renoir's film takes on particular interest, dividing its energies between exposing the ideological bases of nationalism, by contrast to Hollywood's usual nationalist primordialism, and installing a "progressive" folk-culture-as-nation, by contrast to nationalism's (pace Gellner) inherent modernity.

Nationality as Ideology

Like most examples of Hollywood's wartime melodrama, Renoir's film is about crises of nationhood, but the overarching crises here are nothing but the logical outcome of the film's own already fairly explicit definitions of nationhood. The film's ideological burden is to wend its circuitous path to Lory's final speech in such a way as to legitimate ideologically a valediction that might otherwise appear to a bourgeois audience disturbingly revolutionary. In its critical class-consciousness and its open endorsement of sabotage, Lory's speech articulates a newly fervent nationalism that the film identifies as inspirational, by way of intense close-ups of Lory's fellow citizens as they listen. But the film's problem is just how to secure the effect of such inspiration, retaining its affirmative character while engaging in a vociferously didactic social critique at the same time. How, in other words, is it possible to articulate an explicitly *antifascist* ideology of nationalism in Hollywood's wartime melodrama, especially once fascism itself has been identified, as it is routinely in the genre, as a form of *hyper*nationalism?[4] To phrase the problem in more historically specific terms, how is it possible to mount a critique of European fascism without endorsing what was at the time the most clearly formulated alternative to European fascism, Communism?[5]

Lory's final speech makes the film's ideological program clear enough even as it throws this whole set of problems into unintentionally harsh relief. Advocating violent resistance and exposing capitalist complicity with the occupation, Lory calls for a form of *democratic* socialism to oppose the Nazis' "National Socialism." Lory's speech argues that the occupation, enabled by Nazi exploitation of a tacitly complicit capitalism, can be defeated only by collective action: "Naturally you wanted to survive—and the black market was the answer. You keep your business going by selling meat out the back door at ten times its price. Some to my mother, who was equally guilty, as I was in eating it. . . . I don't blame you for making money—You should blame yourself for making the Occupation possible—because you can't do these things without playing into the hands of the real rulers of the town, the Germans" (*This Land Is Mine*, 108). While covering its ideological flanks ("I don't blame you for making money"), the speech remains remarkable in its refusal to see the occupation as caused only by virulent Nazi aggression, conceiving it instead in terms of systemic social dynamics. In its clear assessment of collective guilt and ideological complicity, the speech culminates the film's refusal to conceive of national identity as a fixed, transcendent value.

It is just such refusal that plunges the film into the very ideological difficulties other Hollywood films of the time avoid precisely by presenting national identity as a redemptive social category powerfully reinforced by the threat of war. In spite of its obvious differences from Renoir's film, *Mrs. Miniver* (Wyler, 1942) is a key example of the more characteristic ideological single-mindedness of Hollywood's wartime melodrama. The thematic and narrative logics of the earlier film work systematically to *eliminate* the very kind of social critique with which *This Land Is Mine* provisionally concludes. In Wyler's film, such critique appears at the film's outset expressed by the Miniver son, Vin, who as the film opens has come down from Oxford with a headful of radical ideas critical of England's class structure. His relentless denunciations of the aristocracy, viewed by the Minivers in all their domestic wisdom as a harmless manifestation of youthful ardor, are considerably muted by his marriage later in the plot to an aristocrat, plucky granddaughter of a snobbish noblewoman. In the film's memorable final scene, the townfolk are gathered in a ruined church after the traumatic death of Vin's wife, who has been shot down during an air raid by German fire. The minister questions openly the comprehensibility of her death, but the potential bitterness of the film's climax is powerfully neutralized by sheer force of ideological will as the minister's rhetoric lurches suddenly toward uplift:

Why? Surely you must have asked yourselves this question. Why, in all conscience, should these be the ones to suffer? Children, old people, a young girl at the height of her loveliness— Why these? Are these our soldiers? Are these our fighters? Why should they be sacrificed? I shall tell you why! Because this is not only a war of soldiers in uniform. It is a war of the people—of all the people—and it must be fought not only on the battlefield but

> in the cities and in the villages, in the factories and on the farms, in the home and in the heart of every man, woman, and child who loves freedom! (*Mrs. Miniver* script, 831–832)

Thereafter, in a symbolic filial gesture, Vin takes his seat beside the formerly chastised noblewoman, his dead wife's grandmother. Sacrificing the figure of the wife on the altar of ideological necessity, the film thus insulates its version of nationalism by tying it inextricably to extended familial kinships and to related fantasies of class reconciliation, both of which in the film's paradoxical terms can be achieved only after Vin's explicit class consciousness has been repudiated or abandoned.

Although the minister's speech at the end of *Mrs. Miniver* is structurally and emotionally analogous to Lory's speech at the end of *This Land Is Mine*, the former works to exclude terms that would threaten the film's single-minded ideological coherence, its construction of a purely triumphal British nationalism. Lory's speech, on the other hand, cannot fail to introduce a certain ideological incoherence, however inadvertently, simply by pursuing the film's own thematic logic. The differing operations of ideology between the two texts define distinct positions in Hollywood's wartime melodrama. For a *Mrs. Miniver*, definitions of a stabilized nationhood along lines noted above are comparatively easy to secure through an appeal to specifically *British* cultural traditions—presented alternately as admirably entrenched or humorously quaint—and through projections of the Germans as faceless, anonymous enemies. The significant exception to the latter point occurs in a scene where a wounded German soldier takes Mrs. Miniver hostage in her kitchen. In its setting alone, the scene fully reveals the film's vision of war as a disruption of stable domesticity. The disturbing implications of the encounter—the threat of rape, the parallels between the soldier and Mrs. Miniver's own son—are kept insistently at bay by positioning the scene structurally to illustrate Mrs. Miniver's distinctively English pluck as she adeptly disarms the soldier and turns him over to the authorities with no maternal qualms whatever.

One of the few melodramas of occupation in Hollywood's stable, *This Land Is Mine* obviously cannot participate in the same strategies, simply *because* of its aspiration to depict life under occupation. Set in an unspecified country "somewhere in Europe," Renoir's film cannot exploit a presumed relation of cultural ancestry to its audience, as Wyler's seeks to do; nor, compelled as it is to represent the occupying forces as well as the citizens under their dominion, can it project the

Nazis as demonically *invisible* Others. Such literal obstacles to the film's participation in Hollywood's standard wartime ideologies of nationalism, however, cannot account for the film's ultimate ideological distance from a *Mrs. Miniver*. Where the latter film presents nationality as an invincible state-of-being, *This Land Is Mine* presents it as, precisely, an *ideology*, thereby subject to appropriation. In his often-cited discussion of the concept of "nation-ness," Benedict Anderson points to a formative slippage between the status of nationality as ideology and its parallel but overweening construction as a more essential or fundamental category of identity, a conflation to which Anderson recommends a kind of strategic assent: "[I]t would, I think, make things easier if one treated [nationality] as if it belonged with 'kinship' and 'religion'" (*Imagined Communities*, 15). If Wyler's film draws on familiar tactics in order at once to install and efface its ideology of nationhood, such as identifying family with nation, fantasizing classlessness, or demonizing enemies, Renoir's film all but reverses such tactics. (That the demonized Others of *Mrs. Miniver* are Nazis illustrates only that strategies of demonology sometimes find their proper objects.) Built as it is around speeches explicitly demonstrating characters' relationships to ideologies, *This Land Is Mine* is oddly scrupulous in its determination to grant the Nazis equal time. Moreover, the film's chief Nazi, von Keller, played by Walter Slezak, is invested with qualities of persuasiveness not evident in Slezak's other portrayals of Hollywood Nazis. As the scriptwriter Dudley Nichols portentously remarks of the film's conception, "There was no villain in the drama. We had ruled him out at the outset, for there are no villains in life but only human beings embodying elements of good and evil" ("The Writer and the Film," 8).

A glance at the volume *Renoir on Renoir* confirms that Nichols's sentiment echoes statements by the director himself. The avoidance of standard demonologies in *This Land Is Mine* may indeed be read in part as a signifier of Renoir's authorship, a function of the expansive humanity and generosity-of-spirit that, as standard critical surveys would have it, enable the Renoir of *Grand Illusion* to embrace warmly characters of all nations.[6] The vision of multinational fraternity of that earlier film grew out of a conception of war itself as shared tribulation. Although *This Land Is Mine* parallels *Grand Illusion* at important points, its exactingly "humanized" portraits of both Nazis and collaborationists, in spite of the film's avowed antifascism, derives from neither a perverse impulse toward fairness nor a recognizably characteristic breadth of spirit but, precisely, from the film's commitment to a vision of nationality-as-ideology. As Christopher Faulkner points out, "It is the tyranny of the *ideology* of Nazism for which Major von Keller is the articulate spokesman, and that ideology is shown to be effective—and attractive—because it masquerades as a superior humanism" (Faulkner, 133).

Tellingly, Renoir makes this point by paralleling von Keller's breezy fascism with the committed humanism of Lory's mentor, Professor Sorel. Aside from quite explicit localized cross-references between the characters' speeches, the parallels are made even more overt through attendant parallels of dramatic structure in two scenes that assert pointed similiarities between the characters. Both scenes present a paternalistic figure lecturing with fatherly wisdom a respectful subordinate, transmitting ideas welcomed or already shared by the underling, who, however, is yet unable to articulate those ideas clearly. The first is a scene between Lory and Sorel following an air raid in which Lory's terror, presented as a sign of his political cowardice, has been nakedly revealed to the entire school. Preaching a form of "moral" resistance to fascism, Sorel admonishes Lory gently: "Love of liberty isn't glamorous to children. Respect for the human being isn't exciting. But there's one weapon they can't take away from us—and that's our dignity." The remark is explicitly echoed by von Keller in a later speech about nationalist "dignity." The particular verities Sorel values—"love of liberty" and "respect for the human being"—are those of a democratic liberalism that von Keller rejects, but the appeal to verity itself is fundamental to the rhetoric of both leaders. Ordered to censor schoolbooks, Sorel expostulates, "Very well, we must burn [the books]. We can't resist physically. But morally, within us, we can resist. We contain those books, we contain truth, and they can't destroy truth without destroying each and every one of us." Similarly, von Keller, while investigating an act of sabotage in the parallel scene, instructs the rail foreman George Lambert about the state of pre-Nazi Germany: "A country without food, without arms, without honor. But the people were not bad, they were only waiting to be told the truth." Further, both figures conceive of nationhood in terms of endogenous political struggle. "It's going to be a fight—it *is* a fight, but if the children admire us they will follow us," proclaims Sorel, linking political power to pedagogical influence. Von Keller's later account of the rise of National Socialism echoes Sorel's rhetoric: "I fought in the streets for our Fuhrer. . . . For my class it was either kill or be killed. But we won, and now we are brothers." In spite of the differing ideologies voiced by these two figures, their conceptions of political order are shown to correspond fundamentally. Both celebrate the virtues of powerful leadership whose justice can be measured through an appeal to Truth, and both weigh the virtue of nations as a symbolic extension of familial kinships, as a kind of extended "brotherhood" or "family of man." Thus defining nationhood as ideology, the film inevitably introduces a potential threat to its own ideological agenda. Clearly favoring Sorel's democratic liberalism, the film nonetheless underlines here not the irreconcilability of that ideology with fascism, as might be expected, but rather the commonalities of these seemingly opposed ideologies.

The treatment of the character of George Lambert further illustrates the film's refusal of standard imperatives of Hollywood's wartime melodrama. Typical of its genre in its methodical placement of characters as representative of ideological positions, the film accordingly positions Lambert in the narrative as the representative of the collaborationist mind. Lambert's exposure of Paul, the saboteur-brother of Lory's secret love and Lambert's fiancée Louise, is the plot's pivotal moment. Most noteworthy about the film's treatment of the Lambert character is its brisk refusal to heap scorn upon him as the despised betrayer of the film's favored ideology. Indeed, the rhetoric surrounding the character makes plain that he has been conceived in some measure as a genuinely tragic figure rather than as a figure of contempt. In the context of the film's meticulous schematism, the emotional fervor it grants to the Lambert character in what is presented as his authentic torment over having turned Paul in is especially striking. Significantly, Lory's later conversion from apathy to commitment takes place, by contrast, entirely off-screen, even though we may assume it too, like Lambert's, follows a dark-night-of-the-soul after Lory has witnessed Sorel's assassination. In spite of his status as the narrative's central figure, Lory's moral dilemma and subsequent conversion are presented as given, without dramatization, even at the risk of rendering his final speech dramatically otiose. Even though Lambert is a peripheral character, however, his agitation is accorded full-scale dramatic treatment in intense close-ups of his solitary remorse, marking the film's only effort to render inner experience and its only indisputable moment of emotional correspondence with Renoir's earlier work. Indeed, the scene of Lambert's suicide suggests that of Bouldieu's death in *Grand Illusion* in its forthright deployment of symbolism and in its heightened emotional register. Preparing to kill himself, George releases a dove from his office window and drops the flower he has been wearing in his lapel on the floor. (Compare to the symbol of Rauffenstein's geranium in *Grand Illusion*.) Apparently attempting a kind of melodramatized understatement, Renoir tilts the camera downward, barely noting the gun Lambert retrieves from his drawer, refusing to punctuate it by focusing on the object. The camera remains trained on a delicately lit shot of the lorn flower as the off-screen gunshot sounds, causing the camera—in a final example of the scene's rhetoric of emotional immediacy—to tremble.

The presentation of the collaborationist as a figure of pathos complicates the film's ideological objectives, its critique of fascism, even in spite of a schematic structure that should by rights guarantee simplicity of ideological design. At the most basic conceptual level, to be sure, Lambert resembles a crucial type in the Hollywood wartime melodrama, the contemptible worm who cravenly betrays the cause in order to preserve himself, like Ugarte (Peter Lorre) in *Casablanca*. The casting of George Sanders in the role initially reinforces that conception. Usually cast as a sadistic villain, like the Nazi in *Man Hunt* (Lang, 1941), or an emotionless cad, like the critic in *All About Eve* (Mankiewicz, 1951), Sanders is enjoined here to play wildly against type, presenting Lambert's profascism not as a form of hateful complacency but as a product of human confusion, and emphasizing the poignancy of his final desperation. One of the plot's more improbable elements, Lambert's engagement to the openly antifascist Louise, serves to reinforce both Lambert's humanized status and, more importantly, the film's conception of nationhood as ideology. Though the film will end by figuring Lory and Louise as its idiosyncratically idealized couple, it does not seek, in order to achieve that idealization, to eliminate the Lambert figure by caricaturing him. Especially given the film's near-complete indifference to the thematics of romance, the romantic quasi-triangle of *This Land Is Mine* is unconventional in its refusal to specify a favored suitor.[7] Moreover, in its eagerness to present Lambert as a potentially legitimate object for the love of the film's heroine, the film finds it necessary to disregard the ideological unsuitedness of the collaborationist Lambert to the resister Louise. The scene in which Louise discovers the depth of Lambert's collaboration and breaks off their engagement thus becomes a crux of the film's ideological dispositions, since it combines the necessity to extend sympathetic understanding to collaborationism with an explicit amplification of the film's twin commitments to liberal democracy and to the resistance of fascism. Significantly, the scene follows soon upon that of von Keller's dialogue with Lambert and finds Lambert echoing von Keller while adapting the latter's ideas to Lambert's own rhetoric of pacifism. In the context of the film as a whole, especially after Lory's explicitly *anti*pacifist final speech, such rhetoric is ultimately found to be untenable, but in this scene it is granted a very real persuasiveness. Except for her initial resistance, the anticollaborationist Louise can articulate no response to Lambert's arguments, by contrast to the eloquent defenses of fascism supplied for von Keller: Instead, she dithers, "I haven't the right answer yet for the things you've said, but I feel—I *know* you're wrong."

If nationhood is to be defined as a function of ideology—rather than of, say, race, birthright, or some other form of political nativity—then the rhetoric of persuasion takes on the power to confer or alter the status of nationality. Certainly the didactic spirit of *This Land Is Mine* evinces clear recognition of this implication, but it is a mark of the film's unusual relationship to traditional Hollywood ideology that it not only parallels ideologies it could easily present as absolutely distinct but, until Lory's final speech, furnishes the mouthpieces of *opposing* ideologies with the most persuasively, fully wrought arguments. Indeed, though von Keller's dialogue with Lambert is presented at some length, a later, narratively crucial dialogue between Sorel and Lory enters the film only by Lory's fatuous and sketchy report: "Professor Sorel explained a lot of things to me I didn't understand. Now I know why our country fell: Some people were more afraid of our own workers than of the enemy." The scene between Louise and Lambert illustrates the film's fascination with ideologies it identifies as false while also exposing the vapidity of Lory's designation of the "enemy," a designation he himself implicitly rejects in his last speech, where he directs his criticism not at the forces of the occupation but at his fellow citizens. For if nationhood is to be understood as ideology, the threat of false consciousness and its real political ramifications can no longer be attributed to some reassuringly *foreign* enemy. As the parallel speeches of Sorel and von Keller both make clear in their different ways, acknowledgment of the ideological basis of nationality either produces or results from *endogenous* conflict, internalizing enmity and introducing the possibility of antagonism among countryfolk.

Nationhood and Family

However improbable it may be in story terms that the film's most overt antifascist would, in the movie's backstory, have betrothed to its outwardly most avid collaborationist, the engagement of Louise and Lambert extends this theme of internalized enmity into the very realm the wartime melodrama customarily called on to secure stabilized nationality, the unit of the family. Positioned between the exuberant, uncomplicated nationalism of a *Mrs. Miniver* and the I-Married-a-Nazi paranoia of a recognizable proto–Cold War wartime subgenre represented by, say, *The Man I Married* (Pichel, 1940), the scene of Louise's breakup with Lambert exemplifies a central theme of the film as a whole, the disruption of kinship structures by incompatible ideological identifications. In *Mrs. Miniver*, Vin's initial ideological radicalism never threatens the family because it is recognized as inauthentic from the outset, no contest for the normalizing force of the family structure. To a very real extent, however, *This Land Is Mine* is entirely structured around the dialogues of schematically paired kinpersons whose familial ties are troubled by ideological split between resistance and collaboration, and the film's didacticism is aimed almost as unbendingly at critique of the ideology of kinship structures as it is at that of fascism.

Three central pairs—Lory and his mother, Louise and her brother, Louise and Lambert—work out rigorously three distinct types of kinship structure, parental, fraternal, and sexual. Lory's relation to his mother provides the fullest formulation of the conflict the film posits between nationalist ideology and familial stability. The film goes to great lengths to show Mrs. Lory's machinations to detach her family from political life, only then to reveal both the insidiousness and the inevitable failure of such efforts. Indeed, Mrs. Lory's attempt to ward off the intrusion of politics into her family results, in the terms of the film, in the infantilization of her son. Emphasizing the repetitious sterility of the Lory household's daily routine, the film presents the son's relation to the mother through images of infantile orality. A key image of their first scene, for instance, connoted in a striking close-up as a suggestive emblem of maternal dependency, is the bottle of milk Mrs. Lory has procured on the black market. The regressive character of the relationship sketched here is depicted most clearly in the scene in the schoolhouse cellar during an air raid, while the students look on with derision as a terrified Lory cowers and huddles, with clear suggestions of fetal imagery, in his mother's arms. In contrast to the usual procedures of the wartime melodrama that consolidate national identity around idealized representations of the family, *This Land Is Mine* presents kinship structures it defines as profoundly *un*healthy in order to show how, in the film's terms, such structures *enable* the occupation. Lory's infantile dependency on his mother and Mrs. Lory's exploitation of the political situation to retain control over her son are circumstances Lory explicitly cites as giving sanction to the occupation in his final speech: "My mother got me extra food—and milk—by a subterfuge, and I accepted it without facing the fact that I was depriving children and people poorer than we were of their portion." Earlier, the relation of mother and son, constructed as primitive in some literalized Freudian sense, has already been threatened by political difference when Lory, in one of his pre-resistance gestures, rejects the official newspaper as lies, whereupon his mother, defining the resisters as "troublemakers," counters, "At least we have order [under the occupation]." In the terms of the film, then, Lory's proper course of action is to sever the regressive bond with the mother by joining the resistance, a suggestion the movie seals by making the mother complicit in Paul's assassination. After he has taken this course, significantly, the film can achieve its desired closure only by absenting Mrs. Lory entirely from the narrative. The film's vision of family as an obstacle to political virtue rather than an extension of national identity can broach no possibility of reconciliation between mother and son after Lory joins the resistance, so Mrs. Lory disappears jarringly at the film's climax.

The disturbance of kinship ties by political identifications is seen as well in the brother-sister relationship of Paul and Louise. Though a member of the resistance, Paul poses as a collaborationist even to the disapproving Louise. Early in the film, the audience is shown Paul's activities of resistance, including the act of sabotage on which the plot turns. The tension in the Paul-Louise relationship is shown to derive, in this film otherwise decidedly short on irony, from an ironic contrast between Paul's publicly avowed political identity, criticized by the antifascist Louise in spite of her own relationship with the collaborationist Lambert, and the actual one to which the audience is privy. A further irony is registered in the consequent fact that familial disaccord ensues between the characters in spite of their actual political alliance, whereas Lory's relationship with his mother is superficially marked by domestic harmony in spite of their growing political differences, unacknowledged by the characters even as they are made clear to the audience. When Louise discovers that Paul is the saboteur being sought by the Nazis, her response, according to the script, is "pride and joy."[8] Differences between the shooting script and the actual film in this scene point up the film's keen sense of disaccord between national identity and family bonds. In the script, Louise's discovery is remarked in stuttering emotion so overwhelming it does not even permit her to utter the detested word "collaboration":

> LOUISE: Oh Paul, I'm so happy. (*crying brokenly*) I thought—I thought—
>
> PAUL (*with great tenderness*): I know what you thought. Never mind. (54)

Where the script presents a dramatic reconciliation, however, the film registers more forcefully the troubling implications of Louise's former suspicion of her brother. As she embraces Paul in the film's version of the scene, Louise proclaims, "Now you are the brother I have always been so very proud of! Oh Paul, now I can believe in you again." The unusual syntax of Louise's speech, with its curiously slipped tenses, reveals the film's strain as it tries to gloss over Louise's previous disillusionment with her brother regarding his seeming collaboration. What the film has painstakingly chronicled until this scene is the crisis presented to ordinary modes of human kinship by nationalism-as-ideology, with its inevitable potential to divide families, so it is perhaps not surprising that this scene of reconciliation should seem both somewhat perfunctory and oddly overelaborated.

The example of the Louise-Lambert pairing, already discussed, illustrates that such political division, in the film's terms, betokens no distinction between consanguineity and collocation. If the imperatives of nation demand choice between collaboration and resistance, such choice is as likely to sunder "natural" kinships of blood as it is to disrupt established kinships of marriage. Further, the film's eagerness to make this point, evidenced in its apparent indifference to the narrative illogic of the Louise-Lambert relationship, demonstrates its concern with symbolic forms of kinship in spite of its refusal to conflate family with nation. Identifying such conflation as basic to the ideology of nationality, as in von Keller's appeals to universal brotherhood, the film goes on to portray social structures as fundamentally inflected by family structures, extending the features of the latter. Significantly, a noteworthy feature of the family structures represented in *This Land Is Mine* is the general absence of fathers. The overwhelming, regressively Oedipal character of the Lory household obtains even though the father is nowhere present, mentioned only in a passing neutral reference. Thus, what the film represents as Lory's irresolution of Oedipal conflicts, his failure to progress beyond infantile connection to the mother in order to assume the position of father, is not traced back to any literal paternal oppression. Instead, the film seems inclined to locate the problem in its representations of society at large, equating political inertia with arrested emotional development. The traumatized, fatherless world of the film's unspecified country thus becomes in miniature a battleground between symbolic fathers, Sorel and von Keller. At the same time, the film's characters, divided schematically between political identities as resisters or collaborators, are divided equally schematically in their relations to the Law of the Father. The male characters are defined as either poised on the brink of marriage, about to assume the Law of the Father, like Paul or Lambert, or beyond the pale, incapable of ascending to the Law of the Father, like Lory, too childlike to participate in the symbolic network of sexual kinship that confers paternalist status. The film entirely lacks any representation of the centralized, stable family of many a wartime melodrama, and both of the film's symbolic fathers, Sorel and von Keller, through their status as "bachelors" (Sorel's self-identification), are signficantly detached from *literal* family structures, explicitly defined in both cases as having chosen ideology over marriage.

Sorel's remarks to Lory, when he learns of Lory's ineffectual desire for Louise, clarify both the film's enforced distinction between its symbolic fathers and its (absent) literal ones, and its need to envision Lory as painfully split between the sociopsychic conditions of childhood and fatherhood. In one of his speeches, Sorel forges the link the film insists on between his commitment to liberal humanism and his status as symbolic father: "Oh, like all young men, I fell in love but . . . she died, and I found a great comfort in my work. *Our* work. My family became this school." Lory is here both identified with Sorel, as a fellow schoolmaster with a potentially equal commitment to the "life-work" of humanism, and contrasted with him, revealed as inadequate to such idealism. As schoolmaster, Lory's position of shared power in the social order makes his assumption to the Law of the Father possible, but Sorel's gentle condescension, treating Lory as a child, points to the failure of this possibility. Equally significant here is Lory's manifest inability to control his classroom, where the schoolboys taunt him openly. Similarly, Lory's relationship to a neighbor boy, Edmond, is at once enthusiastically brotherly and constrainedly fatherly, split between intense identification and an uncomfortable impulse to paternal vigilance. In the early scenes, his wish to walk the boy to school is linked to nothing more than guileless, childlike affection. Later, however, in one of the film's two brief references to Nazi anti-Semitism, he protects the boy from an anti-Semitic attack at school. When the boy's father is arrested with Sorel by the Nazis, Lory's instinctual resistance expresses itself openly for the first time. The film's tendency to work out tropes of political identity by aligning them with symbolic kinship structures is illustrated in the same scene when Louise, comforting Edmond after his father's arrest, delivers a motherly kiss to Edmond and a parallel one to Lory, calling him a "brave boy." Though a lingering close-up shows Lory to be excessively moved by the kiss, its asexual nature makes clear that, in the film's terms, Lory cannot become an object of Louise's desire until he has rid himself of infantile identifications and assumed the symbolic fatherhood the film is at pains to assert from the start as one of his available roles.

The film's notably overdetermined ending yields, in one sweeping rhetorical gesture, a triumphantly paternalized Lory, a newly love-struck Louise, and the reinforced possibility of a securely liberal national identity for the traumatized nation-state, bringing together literal and figural formations of kinship the film has manipulated throughout only to find they will not be so readily reconciled. That such reconciliation is the project of the film's conclusion is fully evident in its very overdetermination. Lory's new-found authority has been amply exhibited in the confident oratory of his final speech in the courtroom, so his circulation through his now-orderly classroom, reading with orotund paternalism from the "Rights of Man" as his spellbound students look on with misty-eyed admiration, serves only to reconfirm it. Both his liberal proclamations and the perfunctorily eroticized kiss he exchanges with the newly smitten Louise, in clear contrast to their earlier kiss, illustrate his welcome acceptance of Sorel's political legacy, as does his parallel destiny to Sorel's when the Nazis escort him away in the film's penultimate shot. In these terms, Mrs. Lory's significant absence from the final scenes, corollary to the absence of literal fathers throughout the film, suggests Lory's final victory over regression, correlating the repression of the mother with the emergence of the Law of the Father while equating nationalist heroism with triumphal marriage—even as the narrative makes clear the marriage of Lory and Louise will never take place. A widely circulated publicity still for the film emblematizes the film's need to collapse figural and literal kinship after seemingly having validated the former at the expense of the latter. In the still, Louise, Lory, and Edmond are positioned in a conventional family grouping, the male figures standing rigid while Louise enfolds Edmond in her arms with poised, maternal dignity. The position of her hands on the boy's chest reveals a wedding-band she wears nowhere in the film itself, and the arrangement of the figures suggests a literal familial kinship the film's plot belies, since Lory and Louise are never married and Edmond is the offspring of neither. So distant is the content of the still from the action of the film itself that its relation to the film can only seem eerily dissociated, as if it existed in some postnarrative limbo—an effect heightened by the backgroundless quality of the photo and the surreal postures of vacuous dignity of its figures. Especially given the film's refusal to invest its image of the family with a conventionally positive valence, the idealized, Miniver-like portrait of its publicity materials serves as a prominent sign of the film's hedged ideological bets. For if the film achieves its desired closure—the celebration of nationalist heroism and the consequent reestablishment of liberal nationalism—by collapsing figural and literal kinship, it cannot do so without high cost to its representations of nationality in more general terms.

In *Children of the Earth*, Marc Shell argues that the tension between literal and figural conceptions of kinship is basic to the ideology of nation, underlying the incest taboo that, for Shell, serves in turn to stabilize and regulate the structure of the nation-state:

> The literalist view, even as it belittles the figural as merely fictive, itself involves a key fiction, namely, that we can really know who are our consanguineous kin. . . . Likewise, that my lover may be my consanguineous kinperson is a logical reality, and this merges with the oneirological nightmare that my lover is my consanguineous kinperson. The particular family dissolves in the republic of dreams. The literal disappears in the figural. (4)

In *This Land Is Mine*, the social order imposed by the occupation, as noted by Mrs. Lory and registered visually in emphatically geometrical configurations of social collectives, is viewed as artificial and oppressive, but it is counterposed against a critical vision of the social *dis*order it controls, which is finally identified in Lory's final speech as having somehow allowed the occupation. Clearly, one of the unavoidable implications of the internalization of guilt in the film's representation of its imagined country's occupation is that a weakened patriarchy permits foreign takeover: the absent fathers of the film's destitute country permit the entry of the false figural fathers of Nazidom. Refusing to reject altogether the imperatives of patriarchy itself, with its need of symbolic father-figures, the film can only envision political strife as a confrontation of opposed figural fathers, where ideology functions to legitimate some fathers while invalidating others. Similarly, the unmarried status of all the film's principal characters serves both to undergird the film's critique of the family and, somewhat paradoxically, to underline its vision of social disorder. In the first instance, the film draws on the resister/collaborator . dichotomy to illustrate its conception of national identity as ideologically structured. Having shown how resistance is harmfully limited or threatened by the demands of family structures, however, the film then proceeds to attribute social disorder to what it perceives as weakened family structures.

As a gauge of the film's collapse of literal with figural kinship, this double-bind is well illustrated by the treatment of the Louise character, especially since she is the character most insistently shaped by

FIGURE 3. Publicity still from *This Land Is Mine*. Courtesy Museum of Modern Art, New York.

the film's ideological regime, without much regard for any external logics. As we have seen, Louise's attachment to Lambert coexists with her open resistance to fascism, and her subsequent disillusionment with both Lambert's collaboration and Lory's cowardice must give way with remarkable abruptness to her final unadulterated, idealized sexual love of Lory after his speech. Though the film absolutely requires this shift in order to secure its ultimate placement of Lory as a legitimate father-figure, the shift can be achieved only through repression of the figural kinships the two characters have previously enacted. Once a student at the school where she now teaches with Lory, Louise, as the film opens, is Lory's colleague but is betrothed to Lambert. Thus the Louise character potentiates a full range of the patterns of figural kinship. In relation to Lory, she may be linked as wife because of his desire for her, sibling because of her position as his fellow teacher, and daughter because of her status as former student. She herself alternates between treating Lory as a brother-figure, as in the dinner scene where her response to him parallels her responses to Paul, and as her child, as when she calls him a "brave boy." Lory's painfully fumbling efforts to express his desire cannot conceal an unconscious acknowledgment of these multiple possibilities with their implication of an incestuous undercurrent to his desire: "Louise, I know I'm not young—and you're so young in mind—I remember the day you graduated—I was already teaching then—and the day you came back to teach your first class. I was worried about you—and so happy when I saw how the children loved you." Yet even at the risk of making this undercurrent disturbingly explicit, the film does not shirk its obligation to eroticize the Louise/Lory relationship in the final scenes. Intense, softly focused close-ups of Louise during Lory's final speech express mingled pride and longing, not only through the framing of the shots and the expressions of the actor (Maureen O'Hara), but through the visual placement of Louise in the composition with her chin resting delicately on a balustrade as she listens raptly, eyes glimmering moistly. Their final kiss merely seals a representation rooted in the *contingencies* of kinship, through these multiple kinship possibilities, but blooming into the triumphal *idealization* of kinship.

In fact, this collapse of figural with literal conceptions of kinship is the defining function of a key problematic in the film that can be put quite simply. On the one hand, the film defines national identity as ideological structure, but on the other it idealizes constructions of *figural* kinship after having strategically detached questions of nationality from questions of *literal* kinship. A contradiction is thus presaged, especially if we make the conventional assumption that the workings of ideology comprise contingency, particularity, the sundry forces of the literal. Indeed, this problematic emerges clearly in a number of seemingly contradictory impulses basic to the film's structure. If, as I have argued, the film defines nationhood as ideology, then on what ground is one such ideology to be favored over others, especially after their affinities have been acknowledged? Given the conception of nationality-as-ideology, in any case, with its subtending rhetoric critical of a universalizing false consciousness, like von Keller's, that may be nullified through dialectical attentiveness to particularities of experience, how can the film take ultimate refuge in the idealization of figural kinship structures? Somewhat more concretely, given its critique of the ideology of nationhood, how is the film able to conclude with a triumphal rhetoric of nationalism that is fairly conventional in its marshaling of the concepts of heroism, courage, and pride, in spite of its overtly revolutionary edicts? The film ends with Lory being led to his death by the Nazis, but instead of expressing outrage at such literal perversion of justice, the film seeks to earn its nominal pathos by presenting the event as Lory's higher victory, outside ideology, in the realm of moral truth celebrated earlier in the film by Sorel, whose fate Lory, in an irony the film must neutralize, will now share.

Literal versus Figural, Particular versus Universal

With such questions, it may well appear that we end up precisely where we started, with the film's need to preserve a domain of universal truth against encroaching ideology, or, to put it in the terms of this chapter's introduction, against the onset of an unfinished history. Even if so, however, the dynamic still reveals much about the representation of national identity in this film and, by extension, in Hollywood's wartime melodrama in general. But such scission may be part of an even larger cultural current in which Hollywood representation participates. Especially in their twentieth-century versions, debates about nationality often presuppose a relation of paired dyads—literal and figural, particular and universal. In this context, nationality is seen to depend on complex interconnections among these terms. Insofar as it is manifestly a social construct, nationality is a figural form of identity, yet it achieves its resonant force by claiming to extend "literal" structures of kinship. Similarly, though the imposition of nationhood requires the particularization of a citizenry, distinguishing some countrypersons from others by virtue of conferred nationality, it also marshals a form of universalism that purports to elide individual difference *within* a given nationality. In *Children of the Earth*, Shell points up what he sees as the general impossibility of "the attempt to attain universalist kinship structure . . . within a world of nations" (193), arguing that "it is partly the free-floating conditionality of kinship terminology that allows for the nationalist and universalist ideology according to which any person stands, or stands potentially, in relation to any other person as a kinsperson" (4–5). In other words, the dissolution of literal into figural kinship structures that, for Shell, enables nation-building in the first place, especially once the nation has been defined as a social extension of "natural" kinships, gives rise to a troubled confrontation of particularist and universalist dispositions as nations attempt to sustain themselves as viable units: "[T]he veneration accorded to universalism is as disturbing in its political implications as the particularist nationalism that universalism pretends to eschew but actually merely defines by polar opposition" (193).

The problematic of nationhood in *This Land Is Mine* takes shape around a trio of opposed terms—exogenous versus endogenous national conflict, figural versus literal kinship structures, and particularist versus universalist nationalisms—that, as Shell's formulations suggest, are inextricably bound up together in the ideology of nationhood at large. In Renoir's film, as in many of Shell's examples, each pair troubles the others in their interaction. As a drama of occupation, *This Land Is Mine* finds itself positioned between narrative of intranational and international conflict. Neither fully endogenous, brother-against-brother, nor clearly exogenous, brother-against-other, the film's narrative conflict generates scenarios in which one's literal brother becomes unknowable, in which families are divided between opposed political options, in which enemies are unrecognizable by outward appearance (as in the subplot involving the frustrated search for the saboteur). Yet, having identified the danger of Nazism's universalizing rhetoric of brotherhood and having opted for a particularist ideology that recognizes such rhetoric as the mask of imperialism, the film counterposes its own fraternity, both explicitly nationalist and rhetorically universalized, where the Lorys, Louises, and Sorels of the world may mingle eternally in their bower of universal truth.

Such balance, if so it can be called, between particularist and universalizing tendencies is an ideological rarity in wartime Hollywood's representations of nationality, where, as in *Mrs. Miniver*, an overarching universalism is the rule. Paradoxically, however, the conventions for representing nationality in wartime Hollywood accommodate such balance readily, so that even if *This Land Is Mine* retains a certain distance from standard representations, it finds, in effecting its particular ideological operations, an unlikely ally in Hollywood's received conventions. If the film combines an un-Hollywood-like rhetoric of ideology-critique with a typically Hollywoodian vision of universalized virtue, that mixture is crudely readable as a structuring tension concomitant with the Renoir-in-Hollywood signifier. Even though contemporary reviewers of *This Land Is Mine* derided the dislocated quality of the film's fictive country, such coy allegorization or representational abstractedness is in fact quite characteristic of Hollywood's versions of Europe, even when the geographical referents are openly acknowledged to be unmistakable, like the representation of Germany in *The Great Dictator* (Chaplin, 1940).[9] Indeed, in many ways, *This Land Is Mine* typifies Hollywood's representations of wartime Europe, through complexly mingled strategies of displacement and projection, revealing how a tension between particularist and universalist tropes of nation inform such representations fundamentally. For instance, by virtue of its nonspecificity, the unidentified country located "somewhere in Europe" in which the film is set accommodates simultaneously signifiers of the particular and the universal. Such textual signifiers as characters' names and the conclusive invocation of the French "Declaration of the Rights of Man" combine with extratextual signifiers, like Renoir's own nationality and the historical fact of France's occupation by Germany, to invite a reading of these signifiers' "real" referent as "France." Such particularity, however, is undermined by the film's effort, as James Agee noted at the time, to "internationalize" (36) its setting. Thus, for instance, the Francophone potential of characters' names like Martin or Lambert is diminished through Anglicization in pronunciation.

In an essay of 1949, "National Types as Hollywood Presents Them," Siegfried Kracauer compares prewar, wartime, and postwar Hollywood conceptions of national typology. This study continues Kracauer's work on the concept of the "collective soul" in the context of national identity, begun in *From Caligari to Hitler* (1948), a book that greatly influenced the implicitly national dimensions of film history. From his study of a range of films Kracauer concludes that such typologies are shaped by the relations of national ideologies to one another and by the imperatives of contemporary political exigencies. For Kracauer, these factors determine the distance between particular representations as projections or as actualities:

> Our concepts of a foreigner necessarily reflect native habits of thought. Much as we try to curtail this subjective factor . . . we still view the other individual from a position which is once and for all ours. . . . Whether our image of a foreign people comes

close to true likeness or merely serves as a vehicle of self-expression—that is, whether it is more of a portrait or more of a projection—depends on the degree to which our urge for objectivity gets the better of naive subjectivity. (258)

Hollywood's images of England, according to Kracauer, are likely to be "objective" because of "common traditions" between British and United States culture, while its images of Russia incline toward "subjective" projection because of a historical lack of cultural interaction and because of basic ideological antagonisms. Yet, as Kracauer recognizes, because "a people is not so much a fixed entity as a living organism that develops along unforeseeable lines" (258), such images themselves undergo significant shifts, so that wartime Russia, for instance, is often represented favorably as an ally of the United States while postwar Britain is curiously marginalized in Hollywood's representations, perhaps, as Kracauer speculates, because of "the uneasiness with which Americans react to Labor rule in Britain" (263) after World War II. The latter point especially implies the determining role Kracauer sees of ideology, or at least of specific political trends, upon Hollywood's favor in its representation of foreignness, conferring what Kracauer calls "in-group" or "out-group" status on particular nations in particular political circumstances.

A synthesis of the particularist/universalist issue with Kracauer's categories is easy to achieve, for in practice Hollywood's representations of nationhood, especially in the politically volatile contexts of World War II, particularize its "out-groups" while universalizing its "in-groups." Tropes of nationality on view in *This Land Is Mine* illustrate the tendency in Hollywood's versions of Europe to draw upon strategies made available by received conventions in order to balance universalist identifications against politically exigent dissociations. By allegorizing the setting of *This Land Is Mine*, for instance, the film is able to exculpate its citizens under the banner of individualist democracy while demonizing forms of societal "weakness" that permit foreign occupation. The townspeople are projected as quasi-Americans in their courageous resistance and in their commitment to republican liberty, but as pan-European in their exploitation of black marketeering and their complicity with fascism. The double-binds of the film's ideological infrastructure thus enable a double focus on its thematics, where its strategies of de-specification permit the association of all virtues with a more-than-implicitly *American* ideal of democracy and the relegation of all vices to a position of clearly marked foreignness.

Without mentioning *This Land Is Mine* directly, Kracauer's essay suggests some literal reasons for the allegorization of French nationality in the film. Kracauer notes here both Hollywood's vanguardism and its rhetoric of indirection in dealing with prewar European crises:

> At the very moment when the European crisis reached its height, the American screen first took notice of the Axis powers and their creeds. *Blockade* [Dieterle, 1938], a Walter Wanger production, initiated this trend. It denounced the ruthless bombing of cities during the Spanish civil war, clearly sympathizing with the Loyalist cause—which, however, was left unmentioned, as was France, the villain of the piece. (263)

France's status as an "out-group," contends Kracauer, is made clear in *Blockade* without recourse to explicit representation of the country or its national types. Other wartime melodramas, such as *The Fallen Sparrow* (Wallace, 1943) or *Casablanca*, similarly level mitigated criticism at French collaboration—since, as Renoir's own somewhat defensive comments on the didactic purpose of *This Land Is Mine* imply, American individualism often projects such collaboration as a consequence of personal weakness: "I did this film, which was not intended to be shown in France but only in America, to suggest to Americans that daily life in an occupied country was not as easy as some people might have thought [because of 'propaganda attempting to represent all of France as collaborationist']" (*Renoir on Renoir*, 17). Given the well-certified "out-group" status of Vichy France in Hollywood, then, it is not surprising that the setting of *This Land Is Mine* should be allegorized into rhetorical indeterminacy.[10]

The specific manner in which the setting is visualized clarifies the film's dual relation to Hollywood's images of Europe, particularizing "out-groups" while universalizing "in-groups." The opening sequence crystallizes the film's detailed specifications of German nationality even as French nationality is methodically elided so that it may later be allegorically celebrated. Constructed around a precise, tightly organized shot/reverse-shot schema uncharacteristic of Renoir's usual procedures, the sequence works out visually the German occupation of the town by juxtaposing the literal icons of invading Nazism against general emblems of native national identity that have been emptied of their specificity. For instance, under the credits appears a somewhat generic statue commemorating victories in World War I, showing a soldier crouching for attack above a patriotic plaque. This image is followed by the camera's portentous tilt downward to reveal a discarded

FIGURE 4. Reverse-field editing reveals city center in *This Land Is Mine*. Courtesy Museum of Modern Art, New York.

leaflet at the base of the statue announcing Hitler's invasion. The juxtaposition of the statue as an internationalized marker of all-purpose patriotism against the specific reference to Hitler initiates a pattern that organizes the whole sequence, systematically contrasting inflammatory images of historical Nazism—goose-stepping soldiers, swastikas, the Nazi flag—with signifiers of a generalized nationalism, such as the vaguely European town square of the opening scene, with its cosily pre- or protomodern architecture. Indeed, the sequence's visual rhetoric depicts the inexorable eclipse of this generalized nationalism by a fully particularized Nazism by condensing the energies of the former within the symbol of the statue. In each of the sequence's successive reverse-shots, the statue recurs as a pivotal image from shot to shot as the invaders surround it, gradually occluding the camera's vision of the statue until it is no longer visible. A final reverse-shot, startlingly revealing an imposing municipal building formerly withheld from view, shows von Keller shaking hands with the town's mayor. This final shot seals the sequence's representation of Nazi penetration of the town's civic centers.

A contrast of the shooting-script with the finished film reveals here the reliance of the film's universalizing of nationhood upon not just a generalization but a certain anonymity of presentation. In the script's final scene, for instance, after Lory's speech, as Louise and Lory return to his classroom, the script includes a scene in which various citizens greet Lory with respect and new-found national pride on his triumphal march through the town (*This Land Is Mine* script, 110–11). Such a scene is inconceivable in the film itself, because of its overall tendency to render the citizens as a faceless, generalized mass. (When in Lory's final speech specific citizens are singled out for criticism, the individuating close-ups that accompany his comments are quite jarring because the characters have not been previously introduced.) Similarly, the script describes an opening sequence that depicts the town's day-to-day life before the occupation in shorthand scenes introducing a full range of characters. In the film itself, however, the opening sequence shows the Nazi invasion of the town square from a generalized point-of-view, depicting those townspeople who are singled out as strictly anonymous figures. In the first shot of the sequence, for example, the open, empty space, eerily depopulated in its tensed, pre-invasion state, is disturbed by the lone presence of a generic boy who runs into the street only to be snatched back inside his generic house by his generic mother.

These qualities of generalization and anonymity are both necessitated and made possible by the conventions of Hollywood studio-shooting.[11] As evidenced by other of his American films, *Swamp Water* (1941) and *The Southerner* (1945), Renoir's American period was marked by a pioneering insistence on location-shooting in the name of fidelity to regional milieus. In his comments on *This Land Is Mine*, however, Renoir links both the film's decidedly un-Renoiresque shot/reverse-shot editing and its obviously studio-shot ambience to the didactic purpose of the film:

> Nichols [the co-writer] didn't think about the stage setting. I was the one who made him think about it. . . . [I]t was a bit of a propaganda film. . . . So I thought we'd better be cautious so as to change the editing . . . the only method is a secure method, and that is why you have to have shots, reaction shots, master shots, medium shots. (*Renoir on Renoir*, 16–17)

That Renoir saw the project as an opportunity to exploit the conventions of studio-shooting for particular ideological ends is best illustrated in the film itself by a later sequence in the square when Lory discovers his mother's intervention in his arrest that has resulted in the killing of Louise's brother. The sequence is noteworthy for combining an open acknowledgment of the artifice of studio-shooting with an improvisatory rhetoric more in keeping with Renoir's characteristic styles. In the scene, Lory is faced with the revelation of his mother's betrayal of Paul to Lambert in order to secure Lory's release from prison. Rejecting his mother vehemently in the plot's key turning-point, Lory marches off with new-found resolve to confront Lambert. Lory's reaction to his mother's revelation is one of violent disorientation, and that reaction is figured visually through an unstably moving camera, in powerful contrast to the fixed camera positions of most of the film but much in keeping with the stylistic openness and spontaneity ordinarily attributed to Renoir. The camera swivels back and forth to follow Lory as he lunges in and out of its range, pursued by the grasping mother, and Renoir punctuates this passing permeability of the frame-space by way of the surprising entry into the composition's fray of various anonymous citizens who wordlessly join this public domestic struggle, ineffectually cuffing Lory or pulling at his mother. At the end of the sequence, such rhetoric of improvisatory openness is undercut abruptly by a sudden immobile high-angle shot that reveals unapologetically the stage-bound quality of the setting by punctuating the artificiality of the housefronts and the reedy, hollow character, heightened by the camera's distance, of the stage-sound.[12] Yet the suggestion of Renoir's free-form open-style persists in the unconventional angle of Lory's trancelike exit from the frame, an off-centered lurch that undermines the traditional comparison of the film-frame to the proscenium-stage. Manipulating conventions of studio-shooting, the scene encapsulates the film's use of those conventions to ally its conceptions of anonymously virtuous nationhood with the enforced artifice of the Hollywood studio.

Kracauer's measurement of the "objectivity" of Hollywood's representations of nationality relies upon quite literal units. For Kracauer, significantly, the "realism" of such representations resides largely in location-shooting. On this basis, not surprisingly, he declares postwar examples of neorealism the most "objective" cinematic versions of national typology, freest from projection by virtue of the very literal, photographic fidelity enforced by location-shooting. Discussing a group of studio-shot Hollywood films about wartime Britain (including by implication the most successful of these, *Mrs. Miniver*), Kracauer speculates, "Produced in response to powerful domestic urges, these films, I assume, would have misrepresented English reality even if they had been shot on location" (268). Thus, even if location shooting cannot guarantee the "objectivity" of a given representation, the implication that studio-shooting in such cases always entails projection is clear. With even more bracing literal-mindedness, Kracauer assumes that the necessity of casting American actors in such films inevitably clouds the films with an ideological bias that is apparently, for Kracauer, otherwise avoidable. For instance, Kracauer argues by examining strategies of casting that Hollywood's dramas of British imperialism "had a definite bearing on domestic [American] issues": "[T]he elder colonels in *The Lives of a Bengal Lancer* [Hathaway, 1934] and *Gunga Din* [Stevens, 1939] fell to the charge of English actors, while the young protagonists, heroes or cowards, were played by stars genuinely American" (268)—thus distancing the latter, by implication, from an otherwise glorified imperialism.

Similar dynamics are at work in Hollywood's wartime melodramas, where foreignness is typically represented as something of a constant quantity, effortlessly distinguished from patently American identities but undifferentiated in itself. Thus, for instance, foreign speech is marked stylistically in these films by vaguely European, usually British, accents that cast back fancifully to the projected or imagined "original." In the always exemplary *Casablanca*, for instance, the French Louis Renault is played by Claude Rains, with Rains's Britishness straddling a boundary between difference and sameness crucial in the construction of the character. Synthesizing the threat of cultural alienness with the security of cultural ancestry projected upon the

British, the film can initially vilify the character's collaborationism (albeit affectionately) but ultimately redeem him in friendship with the American character Rick. The projected nationality of *This Land Is Mine* is constructed through a Britishness that has been similarly encoded. Significantly, von Keller is enacted by an actual German, but the citizens are enacted by American or British actors, with the cast's spunkiest Americans (Maureen O'Hara and Kent Smith) in the roles of the most clearly ennobled resisters, Louise and Paul. The other characters are shaped according to a Britishness encoded at its first level, like Rains's in *Casablanca*, as *non*-British, a stand-in for the also-absent signifier of French nationality, so that characters' betrayals are accounted for by their foreignness while their triumphs coincide with their gradual Americanization.

A final effect of the film's specific evocations of German national identity as against the effacement of its other nationalities is that the film's ultimately favored ideology of nationhood can be identified, in an important sense, only negatively. In its fantasy of pan-European resistance, *This Land Is Mine* generates a fictive nationality defined only by its opposition to fascism, characterized chiefly by its status as *non*-German. Here again the film's fugitive attunement to ideology-critique complicates the issue. As an emblem of fantasized multinationalism, the statue in the opening sequence prepares for the film's implied comparison of fascism with other forms of nationalism. Although the statue serves as the displaced site for representations of the country's victimization, it is itself presented with a faint but distinct edge of parody. The soldier's pose in the statue—stealthy, aggressive, wild-eyed—signifies the violence underlying patriotism, and the generic properties of the statue lend it an otherworldly aspect, like that of Hollywood's representations of Europe more generally, that the film plays here for a kind of remote comedy. If such moments illustrate the film's sense of the ideology of nationhood as subject always to cooption, they finally give way to the film's vision of the collapsibility of nations into an ideal of republican liberalism. It is thus important to the film's project that its principals be fashioned as "schoolmasters," custodians of the archive of classical liberalism. Shoring up the artifacts of what Lionel Trilling in a similarly exuberant spirit of universalism would call the "liberal imagination," the film deploys references to Voltaire, Plato, Juvenal, and Tacitus as eternal signifiers of the liberal democracy that the film calls upon for its definition of virtuous nationhood. The clearest instance of how these signifiers operate in the text is, perhaps, the conclusive recitation of the French "Declaration of the Rights of Man and Citizen." At one level, obviously, this scene marks the reinstatement of the seemingly excluded national signifier—France—in its explicit appeal to this document of the French Revolution, an artifact of the decisive historical emergence of modern conceptions of nationalism. At another level, however, the recitation denies the document its historical particularity even as it is invoked. For instance, the declaration is read in Lory's lilt-ingly stentorian tones in a form both abridged and abutted, deleting the text's more notable exclusions, such as its denial of suffrage to women and to some men, while playing up its nascent political individualism.[13] With this characteristic maneuver, the film perhaps unconsciously broaches the conflation of the French declaration with the American Bill of Rights, culminating the film's tendency to project political weak-ness as *foreign* while establishing political strength as implicitly or potentially *American*.[14]

"Foreignness" in Laughton's Star Text

The presence of Charles Laughton in the role of Lory attests to both the complexity of this dynamic and its link to Renoir's particular uses of Hollywood conventions. As himself a European in Hollywood, Laughton emblematizes in his performance the dynamic of stylistic and cultural hybridity formative of the film's ideological structure. By the time of *This Land Is Mine*, Laughton's status as a prestige-object in Hollywood's value-system was thoroughly established, but the intri-cate relation of that status to Laughton's star text as it continued to evolve has not been noted.[15] In the thirties, Laughton's high-art pedi-gree consigned him to roles variously coded as demonically rapacious, as in *Mutiny on the Bounty* (Lloyd, 1935) or *Les Miserables* (Boleslawsi, 1935), or pathetically monstrous, as in *The Hunchback of Notre Dame* (Dieterle, 1939). Each of these cases projected a fantasy of Europe not only by adapting texts of European high culture (or what could be con-structed as such) but by positioning the figure of Laughton against a decisively *American* star—respectively, Clark Gable, Fredric March, and Maureen O'Hara—who, though perfunctorily encoded as Euro-pean in the particular terms of the stories, remained securely apart from the oppressiveness of the represented milieu by virtue of his or her literal and unconcealed Americanness.

Though a "star" in some sense of the word, Laughton was never presented as a focus of audience identification, unless rendered as a figure of the pity due to the grotesque, the mitigated sympathy extended to universalized otherness in Hollywood's economy, as in *Hunchback*. Laughton's star text worked out a very particular relation to the idea of foreignness specifically through Laughton's association with presumably unhealthy masculinities. Either a relentlessly avenging authority-figure or a milquetoast excluded from the networks of authority, Laughton in role after role stands in a troubled relation to the Law of the Father, alternately shown as investing it with insidiously exaggerated force, as in *Les Miserables*, where he plays the dogged inspector, or else pitifully failing to answer its imperatives, as in *The Suspect* (Siodmak, 1945), where he enacts the role of an effetely bourgeois murderer. This stark dialectic in Laughton's star text was again typically reinforced by the simultaneous presence of another star figure defined as explicitly American, virile, and upholding properly the very Law of the Father Laughton's characters transgress. Exceptions in Laughton's career to this bipolarized pattern only clarify the unfettered circulation of tropes of foreignness among Laughton's star codings, as in *The Tuttles of Tahiti* (Charles Vidor, 1942), in which Laughton plays a genial patriarch, where the free-floating foreignness of Laughton's star text enables the actor's quite unlikely Carribeanization, illustrating yet again the undifferentiated quality of Hollywood's projections of foreignness.

The codes of Laughton's foreignness may well have been set in play by his high-art position or his unassailable status as "serious actor," itself associated with a projected foreignness, but that position also guaranteed a certain moderation of those codes. In a related context, Janet Staiger argues that the codes of Erich von Stroheim's foreignness finally resulted in the exclusion of von Stroheim, as both "star" and auteur, from Hollywood as an institution; if Staiger is correct, it is worth asking why Laughton did not meet a similar fate (see *Interpreting Films*, 124–38). In part, the answer is to be found precisely in the bipolarized character of Laughton's star text, especially by contrast with von Stroheim's consistently identical characterizations in his performances in Hollywood films. The very extremity of these poles made it possible for audiences to view Laughton's characterizations as distinct from the actor's person, as yet another function of Laughton's Europeanized, high-art status as performative virtuoso. With a certain theoretical irony thus interposed between Laughton and his roles, the actor's relation to foreignness, though constant, was somewhat tempered.[16] Thus, in some of Laughton's most popular roles, he begins in a position of otherness but is successively assimilated into sameness, reassuringly revealed as "one of us" and deserving thereby of a certain provisional identification. In *The Ruggles of Red Gap* (McCarey, 1935), for instance, Laughton enacts a very British butler who undergoes a quite literal process of Americanization, while in *It Started with Eve*

(Koster, 1941), the audience is supposed to have no trouble envisioning Laughton as the father of the hyper-American Deanna Durbin.

Laughton's performance in *This Land is Mine* bears the burden of imparting an emotional coherence to the film's didactic trajectory. Both the performance's own shape and its embeddedness in the text as a whole draw upon a rigorous consciousness of Laughton's star text, relying upon and synthesizing recognized poles of Laughton's star text in order to ease the extreme transition from cowardice to heroism in the Lory character. Moreover, Laughton's performance is manipulated self-consciously by Renoir's direction in much the way we have seen Renoir manipulate the Hollywood conventions of studio-shooting, so that Laughton's performance becomes, in effect, a text on which signs of Renoir's authorship are inscribed.

Laughton's foreignness, already in operation in his star text as I have outlined it, is further elaborated in *This Land Is Mine* by way of a clear difference between Laughton's acting style and that of every other actor in the film. By contrast with the conventional Hollywood acting of the others, with their rigid postures, artificial gestures, and pre-programmed line-readings, Laughton's performance is remarkably supple and improvisatory. Even amid the heightened oratory of his final speech, Lory's aimless, unconscious hand-gestures—picking his nails, rubbing his knuckles along the banister as he speaks—attest to the gangly looseness of Laughton's performance. Just as Renoir works the artifice of studio-shooting into a free-form stylization that undergirds the film's representation of nationality, so he constructs from Laughton's performance a complex text on the surface of which a range of the film's animating tensions play: literal/figural, real/stylized, American/foreign. Laughton's proto-Method acting is made to embrace a range of expressive possibilities that end in the temperance of his encoded foreignness and permit his ascension to the quasi-Americanness the film requires.[17]

This point is best seen, perhaps, in the movement of the performance from quiet naturalism to extremely stylized expressive frontality, a movement coincident with the character's movement from collaboration-by-default to resistance. The early scenes of Laughton's performance are characterized by mumbled, inconclusively inflected line-readings and by insistently half-formed gestures designed to play up the character's lack of commitment. Renoir emphasizes these aspects of Laughton's performance by placing the actor in background or sideward positions in the composition. For instance, in the street scene where Nazis question Lory, Louise, and Paul about resistance leaflets, Laughton is positioned in a decentered, background position even though his cowering retreat is manifestly the focus of the shot. Here Laughton's detailed, discomfiting rendering of the character's cowardice is in especially marked contrast to the broad, sketchy performances of the other actors, in keeping with standard Hollywood performance styles. Similarly, Renoir stages Lory's profession of love for Louise with Laughton behind the mesh of a screen door, turning constantly away from the camera as he recites his lines in a fragmentary manner. This stylized naturalism gives way to a less-mediated oratorical style, more at home in a Hollywood movie. The transition is accompanied by a shift to visual frontality that aligns it not only with Lory's new-found resistance but with his ascension in the film's terms to an acceptable masculinity. In the court-scenes, Lory is initially contrasted visually with other figures, male representatives of justice, who are viewed in conventional frontal close-ups while shots of Lory seated in the witness-box are framed in ironically asymmetrical long-shot, Lory's head at the very bottom of the frame with an expanse of empty space above it. When he rises to speak, however, filling this empty space, he attains visual superiority over his fellow patriarchs, a superiority now emphasized by the clear modulation and full confidence of his speech. Drawing upon this shift from Laughton's Method-style to more conventional Hollywood oratory, Renoir uses the text of Laughton's performance in order further to modify Hollywood's conventions of representing foreignness.

3

Masscult Modernism, Modernist Masscult: Cultural Hierarchy in *Scarlet Street*

A scenario familiar to fans of film noir occurs at an important moment in *Scarlet Street* (Fritz Lang, 1945). The agents of officialdom have surrounded Johnny (played by Dan Duryea), a young tough presented alternately as hard-boiled and dandified, and they demand of him some information the audience knows he is able to provide. With a simpering smile and a cool, deliberate gesture, he deflects their attention from himself and, without compunction, indicates his devoted paramour, Kitty (played by Joan Bennett). Her initial disbelief gives way to dawning fear of the intransigence of his accusation, and she cowers and pleads, effectively convicting herself by protesting too much, crying ardently, "No, Johnny, no!" Eventually, though, she realizes her fervent denial is useless, realizes that she, like so many *femmes fatales* before her who despite the cognomen proved more fated than fatal, will have to take the fall.

The obvious conventionalism of the scene in formal terms, however, is belied by its content. In spite of the heightened rhetoric of the scene, both verbally and visually—reminiscent, say, of Sam Spade's unyielding accusation of Brigid O'Shaughnessy at the end of *The Maltese Falcon* (Huston, 1941)—it depicts not the culmination of the plot's mystery but the initiation of a plot-within-the-plot. The officials are agents not of the institutions of law but of the institutions of culture, a bohemian painter, the owner of a chic gallery, and a highbrow critic. Moreover, Kitty is being accused not of murder or robbery but—perhaps even more ignobly to judge from her response—of painting. At the same time, the accusation is complicit with a kind of robbery, since the paintings in question are in fact not Kitty's but the work of Christopher Cross (Edward G. Robinson), a mild-mannered cashier who has become smitten with Kitty. Interconnecting forms of culture and modes of appropriation, *Scarlet Street* reconceives the conditions of forties film noir, producing in place of the expected conventions a parable about shifting cultural hierarchies in wartime and postwar America.

Both this reconception itself and its range of applicability, whether inadvertent reflections of a contemporary Zeitgeist or functions of the self-consciousness many critics have been inclined to attribute to Fritz Lang, are best understood in the context of anxieties of the thirties and forties about the ascendancy of mass culture and consequent crises in the construction of cultural value and, more generally, cultural organization. In turn, as has often been remarked, such anxieties were themselves produced by the newly energized drive toward a *national* culture in the first half of the twentieth century. On the one hand, *Scarlet Street* opens itself to such exact cultural placement by way of, for example, the scrupulous specificity of its setting, New York and its environs in 1934, but on the other hand closes off such interpretation in a series of uncannily analogous refusals. Thus, for example, the film contains no signifiers, however oblique, of the "Great Depression" in spite of the clearly specified date of its setting; and thus it insists deceptively on its title as designating an actual location in the city, thereby evoking a nonreal, allegorized Greenwich-Village-of-the-mind much in keeping to be sure, with its stylized visual representations of the urban landscape. The tension here between cultural specificity and incipient allegory serves handily to link the film to traditional constructions of film noir. The genre has often been seen as reflecting the disillusionment of American culture during World War II in its images of alien cities, asocial private eyes, and threateningly uncontained female sexuality. At the same time, it has been seen as culturally anomalous, precisely *failing* to speak its society's concerns and instead turning inward upon itself to ever more exaggerated styles, morbidly isolated psychologies, and increasingly closed narratives.[1]

Juxtaposing reflexive realism against nascent modernism, this scission is of much the kind around which anxieties over the rise of mass culture took shape in critical writing of the United States of the thirties and forties. The potential confusion of art allied with widespread cultural assumptions, the "popular," and art as the product of fiercely individual sensibility, the "serious," prompted defensive spasms of cataloging, classifying, institutional organizing, designed to reassert these distinctions in the face of their perceived erosion. Yet such distinctions themselves derived from a powerful and often unremarked series of assumptions. Dependably linking modernism, hence high culture, with Europe and mass culture with America, the very intellectuals who resisted and derided mass culture during the thirties and early forties, as Andrew Ross demonstrates, found themselves recruited to "underwrite and legitimize the new rules of *consent*" (42) of the postwar settlement, a task "determined by the new exigencies of a *national* culture, defensively constructed against foreign threats and influences" (43). The very categories one cultural moment insistently separated, then—high and low, kitsch and avant-garde, European modernism and American mass culture—a corresponding moment found it useful to conflate.

Film noir is the key genre in this schismatic relation of European modernism and American mass culture in Hollywood. The noir films of the 1940s melded the hard-boiled detective stories of American popular fiction to the expressionistic styles of European art-cinema, and many of the formative films of the genre were directed by European emigrés such as Billy Wilder, Robert Siodmak, or Fritz Lang. Lang is an especially crucial figure in the evolution of the genre because all of his Hollywood films draw significantly on the patterns of film noir and because the atmosphere of his German films, such as *M* (1931) or the *Dr. Mabuse* series, fed into these patterns quite directly. Despite the range of his German work from popular serials to art-films, Lang came to Hollywood with the unqestioned pedigree of a "serious" filmmaker.[2] Embodied in that range is the abiding interest in the powers of mass culture and the formation of social and cultural hierarchies that continued to manifest itself perhaps even more forcefully in Lang's Hollywood films. Against this background, it is no wonder if Lang took the opportunity of remaking a European art-film, Jean Renoir's *La Chienne* (1932), in the form of a Hollywood noir movie as an occasion to meditate on the interrelation of cultural levels in modernist art, producing a perhaps inadvertently self-reflexive document reflecting the cultural politics of the European director in Hollywood. It is no less surprising that this document should be so concerned with the question of art as *property*, registering the connection between national culture and property rights. As a film made for popular consumption in a pseudomodernist genre by a European emigré associated with the quasi-avant-garde movement of expressionism, *Scarlet Street* is both a crucial index and a key example of this scission.

Modernist Masscult/Masscult Modernism

Before Kitty has unwittingly appropriated Chris's paintings, before she assumes the role of *producer* of culture, she looks at them, inhabits the role of *consumer* of culture. Not for the first time in the film, the spectator is asked to share this position. A slow dissolve from a previous shot to one of Chris's canvases is subsequently revealed, in the next shot, to be the vantage point of Kitty's perplexed gaze as she examines the paintings. The canvas shows an urban space in aggressively flattened perspective, a series of storefronts crowded together, flanked on both sides by lampposts throwing light in crisply outlined inverted-V-shapes, with the gridiron of an elevated railway arching over the whole scene. Over the lamppost at the right is coiled a serpent, tongue protruding, head extended, to the left, in the direction of a woman clothed in black standing beneath the other lamppost, facing front, seemingly indifferent to the threat of the serpent. In the film's composition, Kitty's posture before the painting humorously suggests the labor of failed comprehension. She cranes her neck and leans inward, and in the next instant when Johnny enters she gestures extravagantly for him to join in her interpretive travails. Even in collaboration, though, they remain professedly befuddled. Although Kitty fully shares Johnny's incomprehension, however, she also recognizes a certain coarseness in his expression of it. When he says, "I don't get it—snakes on the El!" she replies, with only half-mocking haughtiness, "You just don't know art." Clearly, the source of their confusion is a lack of recognition: even while they see the painting as a potential commodity, expressing surprise that anyone might pay for it, they dispute its value as a reproduction of reality. Yet later, when Johnny takes the painting to a pawnshop, the pawnbroker vents his contempt for the work as being *too* clearly representational. Casting a jaded eye on the canvas, the pawnbroker sneers, "That's my pawnshop, ain't it? . . . And that snake—strictly from the Bronx!"

Chris's work triggers a crisis of response, forcing a confrontation between the styles of modernism exemplified by the painting and the assumptions of mass culture represented by the comments of Kitty, Johnny, and the pawnbroker. For Kitty and Johnny, the painting is inaccessible in its meaning and, therefore, in their view, may or may not be of value. For the pawnbroker, who knows his commodities even if he doesn't "know art," the conventions of the painting are familiar enough, identical to those of what the "village longhairs" are "peddling" for the "price of the canvas." In either case, as an emblem of modernism at the hands of mass culture, the painting is an object

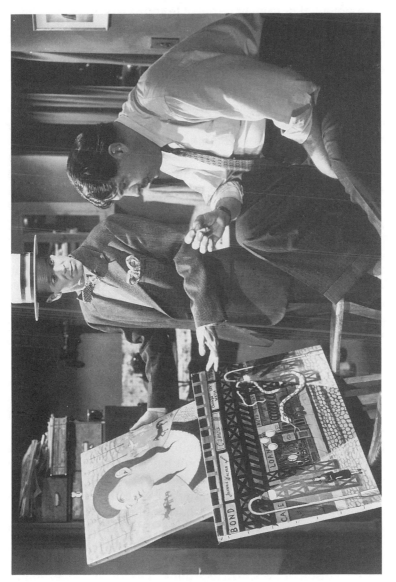

FIGURE 5. *Scarlet Street*: Modernist art on the mass-culture market. Courtesy Museum of Modern Art, New York.

demonized by those who would commodify it precisely because of its refusal, real or imaginary, to yield to immediate commodification. For Kitty and Johnny, finally, the *meaning* of the painting is irrelevant except as a potential detriment or possible spur to its exchange-value, and they don't expect to get it. When the work's cultural value is certified by the critic Janeway, they are unsurprised since, denizens of mass culture that they are, it would seem they have long since recognized the rigid lines that separate levels of culture and the particular place they themselves occupy along that strata.

At this level, the cultural narrative the film reproduces seems to be that of modernism's victimization by an encroaching mass culture that threatens it from below. Significantly, Kitty and Johnny are defined in the film less by the marks of their class than by the habits of their tastes. A "working girl" longing for upward mobility, Kitty has quit a menial job and has been pressed into prostitution with Johnny as her pimp, but the film eschews criticism, typical of the Hollywood social-problem film, of a class structure that sustains a market in which people themselves become commodities and, instead, displays tirelessly what it posits as the relentless vulgarity of the characters, mocking their unreflexive hostility toward high art, their strivings for cultural legitimation, and the barrenness of their cultural aspirations. Johnny's straw hat and Kitty's general attire function as signifiers of the characters' petit-bourgeois leanings, and the phonograph records Kitty compulsively plays define the level of their cultural grounding. The first time in the film we see Kitty and Johnny in their domestic habitat, Kitty languishes on a fake-posh sofa reading a popular magazine while a record skips on the phonograph, repeating bars of a Crosby-like crooner's rendition of "Melancholy Baby." Especially after Kitty's contemptuous reference earlier to Johnny's gift of a volume of Shakespeare's plays, the tableau serves to define her as a vulgarian who fails even to attend fully to the cultural detritus with which she insists on surrounding herself. So vacant has Kitty been rendered by the junk she consumes, presumably, that she does not even notice the skipping of the record. Even as she dismisses the Shakespeare book as a useless irritant, she does not notice what the film registers as the genuine irritant of the record's mechanically reproduced hiccough, which Johnny finally corrects with blunt impatience. In its criticism of Kitty, the scene mutedly echoes T. W. Adorno's less delicate critique of mass culture as the poison of the spirit. One thinks specifically, for example, of Adorno's remarks on "regressive listening" as a by-product of the institutionalization of the culture industry, especially as "tied to production by the machinery of distribution" (*Culture Industry*, 42): "Not only do the listening subjects lose, along with the freedom of choice and responsibility, the capacity for conscious perception of music . . . but they stubbornly reject the possibility of such perception" (*Culture Industry*, 41). The labor of perception gives way to a condition, like Kitty's, of distraction, detaching cultural preference from aesthetic perception. Clearly, the crooner's recording means no more to Kitty than do Chris's paintings; the difference is that she does not see the recording as demanding her comprehension. Even though—in the film's terms at least—the recording, too, defies comprehension with its arhythmic stutter and mechanically suspended meaning, Kitty is shown to be untroubled by this mechanically produced fissure in meaning, reserving her scorn for that effected in the paintings. As Adorno elsewhere refers to the uncannily "illegible" quality of the phonograph disc as mass-produced object ("Form of the Phonograph Record"), so Lang contrasts the inscrutability of the record, unnoticed by Kitty, with the inscrutability she and Johnny contemptuously attribute to Chris's work.

The point could not achieve any real resonance, though, if the film itself did not strategically contrast their responses to the paintings with another immanent response associated with the film's impacted irony. The film's critique of mass-cultural taste depends further on a marked contrast between the way Kitty and Johnny respond to Chris's painting and the ways the viewer is cued to read it. The first time this painting appears is after an exterior shot of Chris, having just haltingly expressed his love for Kitty, leaving her apartment. In the shot, Johnny crouches beside the staircase waiting for Chris to leave. The ostensible purpose of the shot is to present an image of the couple's duplicitous exploitation of Chris's naiveté. As Chris leaves, however, the shot gives way slowly to the subsequent close-up of the right half of Chris's canvas in Kitty's apartment, effectively superimposing in an extended dissolve the stealthily crouching figure of Johnny against that of the stealthily uncoiling snake. Matching the figures graphically, the painstaking transition presents the painting, in effect, as Chris's unconscious recognition of Johnny's serpentine character. Although Chris never recognizes Johnny as the man who attacks Kitty in the street in the film's first sequence, he is instinctively wary of Johnny, as he remarks to Kitty several times. The slow, deliberate pan across the canvas from the snake to the female figure reveals the threat to Kitty Chris unconsciously perceives Johnny to pose and, with its starkly controlled force, serves to legitimate Chris's allegorical rendering of their situation. The female figure in the painting is a direct precursor of the explicit portrait of Kitty Chris paints later in the film, and Kitty's failure to recognize what seems to the viewer an obvious representation of her first encounter with Chris becomes yet another instance of the limitations of sensibility for which the film will vilify her. The painting's allegory, made fully clear by the film's overdetermined rhetoric, nonetheless remains utterly opaque to its subjects.

Yet the firmly grounded irony of this narrative point is threatened by the subsequent identification of the first shot of Chris's painting with Kitty's gaze. The same pan that clarifies the painting's implicit allegory describes the stubborn arc of Kitty's misreading. The viewer's first glimpse of Chris's work earlier in the film has already posed the problem of precisely what attitude toward his painting the film expresses. In that scene, Chris is visited at home on Sunday afternoon by a co-worker to whom he reveals his artistic hobby, displaying his current work that his harridan wife, Adele, has relegated to the bathroom. The painting depicts the flower given Chris the night before by Kitty during their first meeting, but it represents the flower in a stylized manner reminiscent of Van Gogh's impressionism. Chris's co-worker registers his own incomprehension, contrasting the actual flower on the sink beside the easel with Chris's fanciful representation: "You see *this* when you look at *that*?" Here Lang reinforces the co-worker's incredulity with a quick, agile pan from object to representation, setting the radiant flower of Chris's imaginings against the limp, drooping one of reality. Both the breathless speed of the camera's motion and the sudden whimsy of the soundtrack music insist upon the absurdity of the contrast, even as Chris explains himself with a good-natured platitude about painting "feelings," not things. Thus aligning itself with the co-worker's bemusement, the film's rhetoric here expresses the same ambivalence toward Chris's work that emerges later in the shot that doubles as a clear display of the painting's meaning and a point-of-view—Kitty's—from which to register its opacity.

Chris's attitude to his own work, in turn, illuminates the film's ambivalence to it. At the beginning of the film, although he poses as a "professional" painter to Kitty, he clearly regards painting as little more than a hobby, a way to fill the free time his co-worker bemoans for its vacancy on his Sunday afternoon visit. Chris glorifies his hobby with a series of art-appreciation clichés, as in his rhapsodic monologue to Kitty early in the film: "I put a frame around something and then it grows. . . . Every painting, if it's any good, is a love affair." It is significant that Kitty's thinly veiled mockery of these notions at the time does not prevent her, later in the film, from appropriating them just as she appropriates the paintings themselves. When she and Johnny mar-

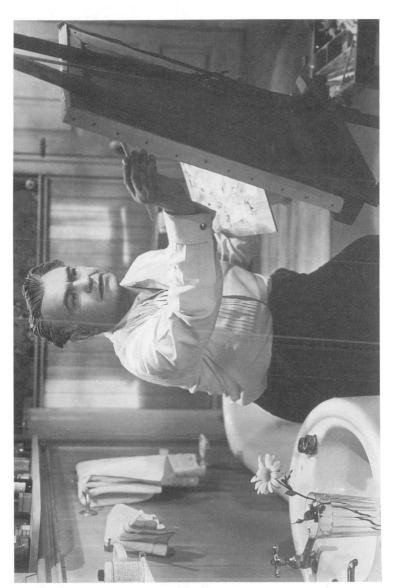

FIGURE 6. Christopher Cross's "Sunday painting" in *Scarlet Street*. Courtesy Museum of Modern Art, New York.

ket Chris's work, she parrots these sentiments with trancelike conviction as she tries to pass herself off as their painter to the critic Janeway. Kitty's easy co-opting of Chris's remarks reveals their ready-made character, points to their initial status as received ideas, perhaps "authentic" in Chris's expression of them, but clearly suspect even in their authenticity, superficial and amenable to appropriation as they are. Even though Chris would place himself within genealogies of "high art," the viewer is cued to understand his conception of such traditions as itself suspect. For example, when he justifies his hobby to the hostile Adele, he invokes Utrillo's copies of postcards as a model for his own work. Thus, in spite of Chris's cultish, ardent romanticism of art, the viewer is repeatedly asked to see its attendant frivolity and philistinism.

The status of art in the film is rooted in the contexts of mass experience. Chris is contrasted with his co-worker, whose leisure time is empty, by way of Chris's access through his painting to forms of "authentic" subjectivity shown to be unavailable to the other man. The contrast is solidified, in fact, in the film's opposition of work to leisure. If the opening sequence conflates the two, the film ends by showing the two domains to be so separate as to become incompatible when Chris loses his job because of his involvement with Kitty. In the opening sequence, an office party introduces Chris as a member of the labor force. His anonymity in this context is registered in the curious circuity of the film's opening. A car pulls up to a club, a woman of aristocratic bearing sends the driver inside, a woman of the working class watches the driver's entrance, the driver signals a waiter, the waiter enters the office party where a speech is underway, the figure standing at the head of the table addresses those seated around it, all identically dressed in formal attire. This complex, protracted relay defers the film's centering on its protagonist, and although Chris is seated at the table, he is not initially singled out. It is not until his employer, Hogarth, ceremoniously presents him with a watch to commemorate his anniversary with the company that Chris is finally individuated from the group. At that point, Lang cuts from a long shot of the table to a panning shot of the watch being passed from hand to hand along the table, ending with Chris. Significantly, though he will be the focus of the plot, Chris is singled out not by any prior narrative edict but as a result of Hogarth's expansive gestures, initiating another relay of deferral before Chris, previously with his back to the camera as just another member of the group, is seen in close-up. These formal dynamics present Chris, in effect, as an emblem of mass man in the workplace, anonymous, deindividuated, responding in untroubled synchrony with the other members of the group—laughing, for instance, at Hogarth's jokes. Even though the occasion is a social one, the hierarchies of the workplace remain in force, and even though Chris is ostensibly the guest of honor at the party, Hogarth's hurried presentation of the trinket—with the conspiratorially apologetic quip "Can't keep a woman waiting!"—renders Chris's gratitude excessive, an example of his submissiveness, naiveté, and manipulability.

Chris's "free time" stands in an oppositional relation to his labor by way of the hobby of his painting that presumably expresses a subjectivity his labor represses. Chris's co-worker, meanwhile, is a type of Adorno's vacuous subject of mass culture for whom "free time" can yield only boredom and docility, which, in turn, signify his blithe unawareness of his own radical *lack* of freedom. Adorno's comments on the ideology of "free time" in the social construction of labor are telling in this context: "[U]nfreedom is gradually annexing 'free time,' and the majority of unfree people are as unaware of this process as they are of the unfreedom itself" (*Culture Industry*, 163). Chris's painting may no more signify a full awareness of the dynamic Adorno describes and the film illustrates than it signifies conscious awareness of Johnny's threat, but it clearly sets Chris apart as a subject of mass culture from every other character in the film. Measured against the aimlessness of his co-worker, the duplicity of his boss (who is "stepping out" with his mistress), or the vacuity of Kitty and Adele (with their mindless records and radio programs), Chris's leisure time pursuits emerge as positively touched with inspiration, offering the possibility of his retaining a form of subjectivity in the face of mass culture's encroachment, and of his resistance to mass society's colonization of his time.

If this is the narrative the film offers, it contradicts Adorno's pessimistic viewpoint on the fate of "free time" especially in relation to the "hobby ideology" (*Culture Industry*, 165). From the possibility that the hobby might indeed serve as a genuine source of liberation or potential site of resistance to the work/free-time structure, clearly, Adorno dissents unequivocally. In the film itself, in fact, Adorno's remarks on this subject are echoed most explicitly by the character most indelicately caricatured among all the film's stylized gallery, Adele. Although she has clearly never heard of Utrillo, she yet pronounces Chris's work nothing more than a pale, amateurish, and even aberrant imitation of the master. Later in the film, seeing Chris's painting displayed in the gallery window under Kitty's name, Adele is quick to accept Kitty's authorship. Her subsequent accusation that Chris has stolen the work of "Katherine Marsh" implies an otherwise unacknowledged change of heart about the value of the paintings themselves. Marsh must be a genius, Adele reasons, since the same paintings she chastised as Chris's work now go for five hundred dollars each. On the one hand, Adele's initial pronouncements are validated by the satire the film directs at Chris's status in mass culture as a mere functionary. On the other hand, however, that validation is itself undermined by the more vehement satire directed at Adele herself, making the question of the paintings' value an important site of the narrative's own half-acknowledged crises.

Gender and Representation

It is significant that the reversals of cultural value the film represents—whether they dictate the logic of the narrative or are dictated by it—are constructed as insistently across lines of gender as across lines of taste or class. Indeed, the key moments of such reversal take shape around the parallel figures of Adele and Kitty. Like Kitty, Adele is positioned as a consummate consumer of the very mass culture Chris holds in contempt, when he pays it any attention at all. One of Adele's prize possessions is a portrait of her dead first husband, Homer Higgins, and the banality of its representational rhetoric is heightened by its central place in their living room. Chris explicitly identifies the portrait as kitsch: "That isn't painting, that's mud—done by a photographer," he declaims in a moment of uncharacteristic force, linking the painting's kitsch status to its naively realist aesthetic.[3] The accompanying shot of the picture adopts a low angle that emphasizes the comic bravado of the husband's pose, with his chest thrust forward and his head thrown back in a posture of paternalist swagger. Not only, then, does Adele value a painting the film is quick to mock, but she laps up radio soap-operas and, reportedly, goes to "the movies"—where, significantly, the phrase has been made to bear the imprint of a condensed range of cultural activity—every week. Moreover, what the film envisions as Adele's relentless oppression of Chris is linked to this very set of cultural attitudes. Adele herself contrasts the potent masculinity of her first husband with the ineffectuality she assigns to Chris, and the presence of Homer's portrait serves as a continued reminder of Homer's ripe, upright virility as against Chris's humble, hunched demeanor. Adele's longing for a radio Chris cannot afford to provide shows her, at once, as an ideal subject of administered culture and, consequently, an emasculating influence upon a male subjectivity that *resists* administered culture. Just as we may assume that Adele enthusiastically acquires such commodities as the "large economy size" of soap advertised on the ironically titled "Happy Household Hour," so in this instance she is shown to harbor a desire, manufactured by the culture industry though she herself does not recognize it as such, whose frustration is displaced upon acts of aggression toward her thenceforth "victimized" husband. In the film's clearest assertion of the link between Adele's status as feminine consumer and Chris's fate as emasculated male, Chris dons an apron to wash the dishes so that Adele can listen to "Hilda's Hope for Happiness" on the radio. Clearly, Chris himself recognizes this connection, on which the film insists, even if Adele cannot: when Adele chides him for his inability to give her a radio, he bitterly rejoins that he too feels trapped; and Adele lacks the insight to read his response as anything but a *non sequitur.* "Have you been drinking?" she demands.

The film's coolly anxious images of a destructively domesticated masculinity are undergirded by a construction of domestic space itself as a province of female power. The Cross home is presented as a stifling enclave of bourgeois domesticity. A habitation that is literally the property of Adele, who was Chris's landlady before their marriage, it is also the product of Adele's compulsive organization, as in the clearest instance of its symbolic order's according a central position to Homer's portrait and marginal positions to Chris's paintings. That the space doubles as a site of emergent, initially disavowed but finally internalized paranoia (a point to be taken up later) is seen in the striking dialectic of Adele's presence during the visit from Chris's coworker, when she is both figurally absent and strangely ubiquitous. The apartment's bourgeois adornments, from the kitschily ornamented screens around which the action is framed to the portrait of Homer, are signs of Adele's ubiquity that have become introjected in Chris's hyperactive superego, as when he pretends, for fear of arousing Adele's ire, not to have invited his friend, or refuses a cigarette for fear she might disapprove. Even more striking are moments during the scene when Adele's sudden appearance is presented as comically but violently intrusive even though a most un-Langian use of deep space, constantly framing Adele in background doorways, has repeatedly reminded the viewer of her presence. As Chris shows his friend the painting of the flower, for example, the bathroom door in the depth of the image swings open surprisingly to reveal Adele, who shrieks and withdraws slamming the door behind her. Even in his bathroom retreat, Chris is subject to Adele's intrusive, vigilant gaze, and the sequence ends, significantly, with an emphatic image of Adele's reassertion of her control over the domestic space. In the final shot of the sequence, we see Adele dispose of the flower Chris has been painting, dropping it into the off-screen toilet with a gesture of comically exaggerated distaste.

Kitty's position in the narrative is structurally analogous to Adele's since Kitty is seen as an alternative object of Chris's desire, but the analogy extends to the film's thematic level since Kitty's more covert emasculations of Chris are similarly presented as a function of her position as "the eternal consumer, the object of the culture industry" (*Culture Industry*, 142). Indeed, the film asks us to see Kitty as no real alternative at all, not only by foregrounding her obvious duplicity but by insisting on visual parallels between the Cross home and the apartment in which Kitty, at Johnny's behest, coaxes Chris into setting her up. Both spaces make clear the imaginary quality of Chris's access to patriarchal authority, and they do so in quite literal terms by disrupting the illusionary binarism of the couple—either bourgeois (Chris and Adele) or antibourgeois (Chris and Kitty)—through the introduction of a third term, Homer or Johnny. Homer's central position in the symbolic order of the Cross home has already been noted, and Lang further emphasizes it by making his portrait comically omnipresent, as when Chris is in the kitchen and the portrait of Homer in the adjacent room continues to loom large, centered perfectly in the kitchen doorway. Repeating this dynamic, Chris's traumatic discovery of the sexual nature of Kitty and Johnny's relationship is revealed in highly charged images that visually figure Johnny as central and Chris as marginal in relation to Kitty within the composition. Organized as a sort of parodically epiphanic revisitation of the primal scene, the moment of discovery parallels quite literally the street scene of Chris's initial encounter with Kitty and Johnny at the beginning of the film. As in that scene, so here Chris occupies a narrow space on the left of the composition, with Kitty and Johnny centered in a high-lit, internally framed background engaged in an ambiguously stylized *pas de deux*. In the later instance, the staging of the action behind decorative screens evokes similar visual patterns of sequences in the Cross home, again figuring Chris's relegation to the margins of phallic authority as a product of woman's desire objectified in the organization of domestic space.

Indeed, when Kitty first takes the apartment, the landlord hopes to impress her by displaying drawings on the wall by a previous tenant, the artist "Tony Rivera." Kitty's expression shows that she is markedly unimpressed, however, even when the landlord claims that "Some people pay a lot of money for those." That Kitty intends to efface these remaining traces of male subjectivity is shown at the end of the scene when she curtly remarks that she will replace the wallpaper with one of her own choosing. Again important is the manner in which these lingering traces are contextualized culturally in the film's rhetoric. Kitty's dismissive attitude toward the work of "Rivera" situates it within a hierarchy in which it is opposed to, and superseded by, a cultural level where taste is defined neither as autotelically oracular nor securely insulated but, rather, as part of everyday experience— defined, that is, by consumption instead of production, by buying wallpaper instead of by fashioning artworks.[4] At the same time, the imagined threat to high culture posed by a feminized mass culture points to the already problematic status of the former. Indeed, the figure of "Rivera" here may be seen as an absent analogue to the figure of Chris elsewhere in the narrative, questioning both the "high" position of a nascent modernism and its assured maintenance by an untroubled patriarchy. Just as the modernist disruptions presented by Chris's work are challenged by certain unreadable tonal inflections in the film, by the seemingly unconscious quality of its representations, and by the production of the work in the light of the "hobby ideology," so the seriousness of Rivera's work is similarly at issue here. Though Riviera's work is initially presented by the landlord with an ambivalent reverence, the artist is also said to be an "illustrator" of "magazine covers," showing him to be collusive with the culture industry the film has already chastised. Moreover, the function of his work, however Kitty may dislike it, is decorative, refusing the modernist imperative of an enforced distinction between a nonutilitarian art and the modes of everyday life. Even if the figure's name is intended to echo that of Diego Rivera, whose site-specific murals famously circumvented just such modernist imperatives, both the work itself and the wry substitution for the exotic "Diego" of the Euro-Americanized "Tony" conjure up the specter of a debased modernism. That its perceived debasement derives from projected anxieties about female power has been suggested; a final image from the film should solidify the connection between such anxieties and those concerning cultural hierarchy. When Kitty demands that Chris polish her toenails (in one of the film's most famous set-pieces), the circle of signification is neatly closed. Here Chris's desire for Kitty engenders self-debasement, since the demand to which he assents is an expression of open contempt on Kitty's part. At the same time, the energies of cultural production signified in Chris's wish to "paint" Kitty, to render her portrait, have been irrevocably displaced upon the commodities of fashion that will literally inscribe Kitty's body, a dynamic Kitty scornfully remarks as she brandishes the nail polish: "All right, Chris—paint me!"

Initially linking its fantasies of female power to its anxieties about cultural decline, then, the film proceeds to renounce those fantasies as it evades the very anxieties that gave rise to them. From the start, the authority of Adele or Kitty is viewed with a typically strangulated satire, as a form of aggression deriving from the delusory idealization of what the film would have us see as an unhealthy masculinity—that of Homer in Adele's case and that of Johnny in Kitty's. In the end, Adele and Kitty are duly "punished" by Chris—the one through Chris's unexpectedly cunning plot involving Homer and the other in a moment of instinctual, animal rage—and thereafter Chris is seen in a series of elegiac images as a type of the tragic, romantic wanderer, haunted not by the memory of his crime or the pain of his guilt but by a kind of masochistic half-awareness of his exile from his own desire.[5] In both cases, Chris's punishment of the women takes the form of a pseudotriumphant restoration of phallic authority, whether literally, by slyly reuniting Adele with the formerly beloved, now-horrifying figure of Homer or less literally, by seizing the ice pick to murder Kitty. Yet this final, brutal divestment of woman's authority merely reenacts a gesture that has already been completed in the film's own symbolic order, and it is significant once again that this anterior disavowal of female authority is ultimately worked out through the representation of Kitty's and Adele's relation to Chris's painting as emblematic of cultural production.

In both cases, that relation is one of initial distance and subsequent appropriation. Adele first derides Chris's work, then hastily accepts its value upon seeing it exhibited under another name; Kitty's initial response of indifferent incomprehension is followed by literal appropriation when she assumes authorship of the work. Having seen how this dynamic places Kitty and Adele within the film's conception of a threateningly ascendant mass culture, we will now find it useful to examine the relationship the film constructs between cultural authority, gender, and the gaze. In both cases, Adele and Kitty strike attitudes of cultural authority that only reveal them to be objects of various jokes circulating within the film. Thus particularly charged moments of female looking function to foreclose subjectivity and consequently undermine the very authority such moments might be thought to produce—as, for example, in Kitty's laborious and uncomprehending acts of looking at Chris's paintings. It is worth noting that after Kitty takes on the disguise of "Katherine Marsh," the intensity of her visual connection to the paintings is defused: at the most literal level, she is not seen looking at them again—is, in a key sequence, seen pointedly *not* looking at them—in spite of the appearance of narcissism her masquerade entails, converting as it does, taken on its own terms, Chris's wanly longing portraits of her into eroticized *self*-por-traits.

Likewise, Adele's relation to the paintings is defined by a curt dialectic of looking and refusal-to-look. Adele's overt marginalization of Chris's work early in the film is worked out, in part, in her refusal to look at it. Her encounter with Chris's painting of the flower, appro-priately set in the bathroom, illustrates this refusal. Glancing at the painting as at some particularly loathsome piece of offal, she promptly turns her back to it in another of the film's grandly overstated comic gestures, with an air of haughty dismissal, consigning its object, the flower, to the toilet as if to brand the work itself waste matter as explic-itly as Chris earlier does Homer's portrait when he labels it "mud." Late in the film, when she sees his paintings displayed in the gallery window, Adele is once again confronted by Chris's work in a moment of surprised revulsion in spite of her willful, purgative efforts to pre-empt it from her gaze. Although a particularly fraught moment of rev-elatory vision, the scene is marked by its clear sense of tonal distance. The literal distance of the camera from the action, with little editing to provide a conventional breakdown of the scene's components, renders Adele's theatrical gesture of surprise on seeing the paintings broader and more ludicrous than it would be if, say, a prior point-of-view shot had clarified the object of her surprise. Further, a long shot is held as Adele enters the gallery and, seen behind its plate-glass storefront, confers with its owner in animated gestures that are again exaggerated by the shot's distance, withholding the figures' conversation and thus presenting them rather like specimens being observed with detach-ment under glass. A seemingly triumphant discovery by Adele of Chris's deception, giving her the upper hand over Chris, the scene is really a joke on Adele, like the literal gag, further reducing the possi-bility of viewer identification with her, of her becoming entwined in a dog's leash just before seeing the paintings. The significance of the absent point-of-view shot in the scene becomes clearer when the scene is compared to that of Chris's discovering his portrait of Kitty in the same window at the end of the film, after her murder. Even though the ostensible point of the scene is to register Chris's *lack* of response to the painting, in contrast to the amplitude of Adele's response in the earlier scene with its call for rhetorical emphasis, the later sequence is exe-cuted with precisely the conventional forms of emphasis missing from the earlier one, thus constructing a dramatic space for Chris's gaze however distracted and affectless he is shown to be. In this context, the denial of Adele's point-of-view and its effect of ironic detachment become powerful indices of the film's severance of its constructions of female authority from its versions of cultural authority.

Kitty, too, thinking she has gained a measure of power in assuming the authorship of Chris's paintings, has succeeded only in positioning herself—or more properly in being positioned by Johnny—as the object of a larger joke on the part of the film. That she takes on this disguise at all further exemplifies the threat the film sees to a shifting cultural order of an insidious female authority. In the film the critic Janeway makes explicit the lines of cultural demarcation Kitty's charade crosses, even if he only implicitly remarks the affront that results from it: "I can usually tell if a painting is by a man or a woman," he says with more than a trace of effete pride, adding that her work is "not only original but it has a masculine force." What is perhaps of most interest about this moment of cultural transvestism is the extent to which it becomes, however briefly, central to the plot of *Scarlet Street* only to be rendered something of a red herring after Kitty's murder when Chris himself, apparently without regret, in his new-found canniness, ascribes authorship of the work to her. Replicating the film's strategy of asserting female subjectivity only to negate it, the subplot complicates the issue considerably. Surely in the terms of the film neither Adele nor Kitty can win at the film's own game: just as Adele's belief that she has Chris's number only sets her up to become the unwitting victim of Chris's plot involving Homer, so Kitty's appropriation of Chris's paintings, far from procuring for her a measure of cultural power beyond the sexual power indicative of the *femme fatale* she is styled as, only puts her more fully under Chris's sway. Indeed, instead of expressing anger on discovering Kitty's appropriation of his work, Chris observes happily, "I guess this gives me a little authority around here!" No matter what position Adele or Kitty stakes out in relation to Chris's work and, by extension, cultural authority at large, it is shown to be the *wrong* one, and it may indeed be to procure this very ideological effect that the film keeps its own response to the work ambiguous. Whether they hold the work in contempt, in any case, or reach a pseudo-epiphanic understanding of its value, whether they "get it" or not, the women dependably remain objects of a kind of wry, insulating, and curiously unmoored wit pervading the film

Such dynamics of gender construction reveal the film's stake in reinforcing standard polarities of gender while presaging the erosion of cultural levels that itself, given the much-noted mutual imbrication of gender and cultural hierarchy, should challenge those very polarities. In her work on masquerade and feminine film spectatorship, Mary Ann Doane notes the omnipresence in cultural representation of "a certain excessiveness, a difficulty associated with women who appropriate the gaze, who insist on looking" (27). The context of her discussion is that of the psychoanalytic construction of woman's relation to the body in tropes of "closeness," "merging perception and intellection" (23), as against male "distance" in which a *retrospective* relation to representation, knowledge, and understanding obtains. Following from this assertion of woman's necessarily extreme identification with the originary image of the mother's body is the claim that "modes of looking," constructed around the experience of sexual difference, are culturally assembled in a manner that "prevents the woman from assuming a position similar to the man's in relation to signifying systems" (23), leaving open for the female spectator only the possibilities of, on the one hand, masochistic pleasure in her objectification in the image, or, on the other, a kind of textual transvestism, a masquerade, that allows her by thus "appropriating" (20) or "reversing" (20) the male gaze to share in the joke of which she would otherwise only be the object. Doane traces the "narrativizing [of] the negation of the female gaze" (28) through several Hollywood films of the forties before presenting, as its "perfect encapsulation" (28), an analysis of Robert Doisneau's 1948 photograph "Un Regard Oblique." The photograph, she argues, elaborates a "sexual politics of looking" (30) that initially purports to center the female gaze, as does the "woman's film" of the forties, but ultimately negates it by, in this instance, first withholding its object, the picture outside the spectator's view, and then framing it within the triangulated arc of the male gaze.

The relevance of Doane's analysis to my argument should be clear enough in the largest sense, and indeed her systematic treatments of the representation of female subjectivity in classical Hollywood cinema have influenced my own comments on constructions and interactions in *Scarlet Street* of power, the gaze, a crabbed dialectic of "closeness" and "distance," and a potentially empowering crossgender masquerade that ultimately "itself remains locked within the same logic" (21) it might have been seen to challenge. What I want to draw attention to here, however, is a form of cultural specificity Doane herself does *not* in this case emphasize, apparently finding little to choose between the scopic regime of, on the one hand, Classical Hollywood with such of its productions as *Now Voyager* (Rapper, 1944) and *Leave Her to Heaven* (Stahl, 1945) and, on the other, the high-art museum-pieces of Doisneau and, specifically, this, "one of the most famous photographs of the twentieth-century" (Kozloff, 25). Undeniably readable as a parable, a "drama of seeing" (Doane, 29), Doisneau's photograph also enacts a drama of cultural hierarchy and authority specific to postwar representations. Roughly contemporary with *Scarlet Street*, Doisneau's photograph strikingly shares some of its ambience, imagery, sensibility. The texts have in common arch depictions of middle-class gallery-going and the clouded aura of postwar "street"-realism, signified in Doisneau by out-of-focus background figures, in *Scarlet Street* by the Greenwich Village street-scenes, almost Carné-like but for their Langian geometrical control. Beyond these generic connections, however, both texts derive from the media of mass culture at a vexed moment in its history, yet both articulate elements of wartime and postwar cultural critique of the conflation of cultural levels. Whether one locates such critique during the 1940s in a tradition of dialectical philosophy (Adorno/Horkheimer), modernist aesthetics (Irving Howe or Clement Greenberg), or "highbrow" punditry (Dwight Macdonald), its basic claim remains constant: in this narrative, modernity with its new technologies and representational media, as distinct from modernism, heralds a breakdown of previously distinct cultural levels that impoverishes human subjectivity.

The relevance of Doisneau's photograph to this critique may not be immediately clear. In the photograph, a woman and man, possibly wife and husband, stand outside a gallery window looking at a painting on display. The painting is blocked from the spectator's view by the camera's position in relation to it, behind the canvas, facing the couple. But a second painting of a nude woman's back—immediately recognizable to any partisan of high culture, or any reader of Clement Greenberg, as an egregious example of kitsch—is fully visible adjacent to the first painting. While the woman in the street gazes fixedly at the unseen painting, the man gazes furtively at the visible one. Indeed, the set-up not only allegorizes gendered spectator positions, albeit with a tone of what is doubtless intended as airy humor, but implicitly differentiates the two paintings as cultural emblems. In these terms, the unseen work elicits explication while the visible one elicits desire. The woman's arm is positioned in an explanatory gesture, her mouth frozen in a determined attitude suggestive of earnest discourse, her face turned slightly toward the man as if in an appeal for intellectual assent, though her gaze remains trained on the painting. The man, meanwhile, pretends to be attending to the object of the woman's civilized enthusiasm. To be sure, as the photo's title would have it, it is the very obliquity of his gaze that makes the woman the object of the picture's joke, rendering her earnestness itself laughable. Thus the scenario links repressed male desire to an implied cultural hierarchy that would have the man take pleasure in the higher realm of intellection, that inhabited by his companion, rather than indulging the baser appetites promoted by kitsch. Yet the "moral seriousness" with which a Greenberg, say, might mount such an argument is, in Doisneau, displaced by a rhetoric of whimsy, affably presenting the man's desire as harmless foible, thereby yielding either the simple effect of "conspiratorial charm" (Kozloff, 25) or the more complex but obviously related one of "a complicity between the man and the presumably male spectator, operating to exclude the woman" (Doane, 40). Although the photograph's materials draw upon a familiar distinction between modes of cultural pleasure, the very complicity it establishes with the viewer undermines the distinction, showing the man's gaffe—harmless and undiscovered, after all!—to be "all-too-human" and whimsically exculpable.

Like *Scarlet Street*, Doisneau's photograph illustrates the interconnection between the maintenance of cultural levels and the organization of social power around sexual difference. Both texts, in somewhat schematic terms, dramatize the lure of opposed cultural options—modernism and mass culture in *Scarlet Street*, serious art and kitsch in the photograph—and in both cases the crisis engendered by the clash of these domains is negotiated by a figure of repressed male desire while the domains themselves are identified with by turns oppressive or duplicitous yet tantalizing women. Without meaning to assert more than striking correspondences between the works, it is clear that the woman centered in Doisneau's photograph parallels Adele in Lang's film as suggestively as the nude figure in the painting does Kitty. So clearly contrasted are these figures within the photograph itself that the woman in her fancy dress seems the very opposite principle of the painted figure in all her lusty nudity. In fact, the clothed woman is seen as almost excessively clothed, down to hat and gloves, in a manner encoded not only as bourgeois but as puerile and prudish. Interestingly, the text accords her a position of cultural authority insofar as it is she who speaks for the painting hidden from our view, and it is here precisely, as in *Scarlet Street*, the threat of female authority that dictates the text's logic, in this case requiring that the ordinarily valued discourse of serious culture be subject to mockery.

In *Scarlet Street*, that discourse remains the province of men, though not, as we have seen, without attendant crises. The film's implicit gendering of cultural levels works along lines like those laid out by Andreas Huyssen, who pursues "the notion which gained ground during the nineteenth-century that mass culture is somehow associated with woman while real, authentic culture remains the prerogative of men" (Huyssen, 47). Yet, curiously, the subsequent logic of *Scarlet Street* does not fall easily in line with Huyssen's analysis, developing this thesis, of Lang's earlier *Metropolis* (1927). With the burning of the false Maria at the end of that more decisively modernist document, Huyssen argues, "the expressionist fear of technology and male perceptions of a threatening female sexuality had been both exorcised and reaffirmed" (81). If *Scarlet Street* enacts a comparable gesture of displacement, projecting half-conscious cultural anxieties onto the female consumer just as *Metropolis* projects expressionist technophobia onto the "machine-woman," the later film nonetheless never quite completes its gesture of disavowal. The last ten minutes of *Scarlet Street*, a virtual catalog of cinematic un-pleasure, show first a bourgeoisified woman purchasing the portrait of Kitty, suggesting both the triumph of a feminized vulgarism and the ultimate, albeit illegitimate, canonization of "Katherine Marsh"; and finally the desolate, suicidal Chris exiled permanently from mass society, suggesting an ultimate failure by the social order to bring sexuality back under its control. Such images of alienation bitterly culminate a structuring tension governing the entire film, that between its quasi-Adornean thematics and its historical status as an artifact of mass culture, between its heritage of Euro-modernist critique and its fate, however it may be resisted, as a product of "the dream world of capitalist realism promoted by Hollywood" (Huyssen, 34). We have seen how these thematics work themselves out at the film's culturally inflected diegetic level or, alternatively, are prevented by an attendant cultural logic from doing so. In a last section, I want to argue that in fact the film, engaged initially in defending its own modernism, can really only illustrate a mutual dependency of seemingly opposed cultural levels that was at last asserted explicitly as part of the ideology of the postwar settlement. That this dependency, given the historical moment, could only entail as well a mutual *demonology* will be seen in the film's complex relation to the categories of "primitivism," film noir, and modernism itself.

Paranoia and the Introjection of Difference: Film Noir, Primitivism, and Modernism

"Primitivism" as a modernist attitude and film noir as an emergent Hollywood genre of the 1940s are linked as sites of intersection and extrapolation among differing national or cultural contexts. Each is defined according to some marked and clearly articulated *difference* in relation to dominant representation. In the Armory Show of 1913 that was so important in the formation of a modernist canon in the visual arts, for example, "primitivism" emerged as a self-conscious affront to an entrenched heritage of Western representation in its own declarations of kinship with tribal or totemic forms. In wartime Hollywood, meanwhile, film noir brought together "stylization and realism, foreign influence and domestic genre" (*Classical Hollywood Cinema*, 74–75) in its transformative lamination of expressionist style upon the native conventions of the detective story. Both "primitivism" and film noir, then, take shape within prior traditions where they are assigned residence as terms while retaining, or having attributed to them, a certain alienation from the tradition. More to the point, though that quality of alienation is in the first place a matter of literal cultural or national difference, it is readily taken over in both cases by a symbolic rhetoric of the "unconscious" sustained by an impulse to assimilate those elements experienced as *Other*. Thus, according to Hal Foster, the institutional assertion of affinity between the modern and the primitive functions as "an erasure of difference" (Foster, 50), co-opting the primitive as the "unconscious," the dark underside of an otherwise apparently normative modernism. The authors of *The Classical Hollywood Cinema*, meanwhile, after tracing the "patterns of nonconformity" (75) through which noir has been said to expose from within key assumptions of Classical Hollywood, conclude that "formally and technically these noir films remain codified: a minority practice but a unified one" (77).

Positioned as they are as "foreign" undercurrents within dominant practices, both primitivism and film noir are theoretically redolent of the condition of exile. In a book on expressionism, discussing the fate of the movement in Hollywood, Paul Coates makes the connection explicit in relation to noir style: "The expressionist legacy left Germany along with the directors driven abroad by National Socialism. Their sense of internal exile, of a world out of joint, became real exile" (157). Yet, although Coates is serious enough about the connection to claim that "if the noir style was also adapted by native American directors, it was because they too felt themselves to be exiles in their own country" (171), he finds that what he claims must finally be seen as the "elective affinity" (157) of expressionism and noir necessarily compromises either strain: "[A] mainstream American film could never be thoroughgoing in its expressionism" (188). What is noteworthy in this familiar synthesis that Coates narrates anew is the extent to which it represses the categorical slippage it relies on, rather, I would argue, as do many of the noir films themselves, *Scarlet Street* among them. Dependent on a conventional understanding of the "great divide" of mid-century culture, with expressionism in its "pure" state standing in for modernism and "mainstream American film," Hollywood the Devourer, for mass culture, Coates's argument posits distinctly modernist dispositions already afoot in the inmost den of mass culture itself, where one might have supposed they could only *derive* from the "foreign" influence they compromise, in the form of those romanticized "native" directors with their high-modern alienation. Located at a seemingly indefinable cusp, then, facing longingly back toward an originary European modernism now closed off from access by history while being pressed resistingly forward into an American mass culture eager to absorb it, film noir at the same time welcomes its own absorption as potential renewal and denies its own origins as nostalgic weakness. What defines the genre in many of its versions is precisely its ability to retain a foothold simultaneously in the groves of modernism and in the bastions of mass culture. Film noir thus becomes among Hollywood genres not so much a site of *intersection* between modernism and mass culture but the point of their already completed fusion, like expressionist *doppelgängers* who are hence revealed, as we should have known all along, to inhabit the same body.

My contention that certain moments in or understandings of film noir represent not simply an interaction or interdependence but rather a newly articulated identification between modernism and mass culture is hardly invalidated by the notorious difficulty of defining the genre. If anything, that difficulty proceeds from the prior identification itself, as in Bordwell, Staiger, and Thompson's treatment of noir's coexisting transgressive and "classical" attributes. Nor, more to the point, does the difficulty of placing *Scarlet Street* in some ready-made anatomy of noir make it any more difficult to see how generic patterns in the film effect a certain corollary categorical slippage necessary to its ideology. Although the film dependably finds a place in even the most exclusionary catalogs of film noir, its materials exemplify the diffusion of noir's generic and stylistic elements that critics have claimed continues, after an initial consolidation of the genre during the war years, in the decades following. Comic in conception, *Scarlet Street* is noirish in execution. Awash in the compositional shadings of noir, the film is nonetheless closer in its narrative structure and even in much of its tonal texture to boulevard farce than to hard-boiled detective fiction. The Punch-and-Judy prologue of *La Chienne*, in which puppets bicker comically about whether the story to follow is comedy or drama, signals a coyly self-conscious schism in genre that Lang's remake of that film intensifies by way of its noir associations.

Film noir has routinely been understood to challenge normative conceptions of masculinity in Hollywood's representations, but the genre typically does so by way of images of exaggerated virility and obsessively uncontrollable male desire displaced onto female figures represented as enigmatic, phantasmatic, unknowable.[6] The treatment of the figure of Chris in *Scarlet Street* implies a mockery of this conventional design. When, late in the film, Chris's embezzling has been discovered, Hogarth questions him about his motives in conventionally noirish terms: "Was it a woman, Chris?" he asks with grim solicitousness. In the generic context of noir, the question should ring with a kind of cynical resonance, fraught with echoes of, say, Walter Neff's confession in *Double Indemnity* (Wilder, 1945) to killing for "money and a woman." Yet so automatic and volitionless have Chris's crimes seemed, so obviously futile his desire, so bitterly matter-of-fact and antimystical the film's images of its *femmes fatales*, the question takes on comic overtones. If, as we have seen, the film imagines a patriarchy diminished by correlative cultural decline, Chris himself emerges as both patriarchy's last hope and the clearest sign of its demise. In a series of articles on Lang, E. Ann Kaplan reads several of his American films as nostalgic meditations on a lost patriarchy, finding in particular that Chris's "lack of sufficient masculinity [in *Scarlet Street*] causes the 'trouble' in the narrative, and brings about his destruction" (43). Not only does Kaplan's analysis insufficiently emphasize the film's representation of male lack as female projection, however, but it entirely ignores the film's corrosively satiric depiction of the very patriarchal figures whose loss of authority the film purportedly bemoans. If, as Paul Coates suggests, the "political unconscious" of film noir generates images of masculinity-in-crisis only to dispel them with the resurrection of a previously powerless father figure, the return of Homer in *Scarlet Street* is an instructive gauge of the film's complex links to noir. If in, say, *The Big Sleep* (Hawks, 1946) the crippled father of the film's opening is replaced by the newly potent one of its conclusion (Marlowe himself), in *Scarlet Street* the beaming specter of lost phallic authority in the person of Homer's portrait is revealed to have been all along nothing but a pathetic fiction—originating, again, in the film's terms, in woman's imagination. So intent is the film on contrasting the actual Homer with the portrait that his identity is, in fact, not explicitly affirmed on his return in the film. After some prodding, Chris recognizes Homer, but the audience is not cued decisively to share the recognition until much later, when a shocked Adele screams his name. As against the idealized portrait, the real Homer is haggard and bewhiskered, sporting an eyepatch, and he has not died the noble death Adele recounts but, on the contrary, has fled implication in a crime. (The distinction is so literalized that the published credits for the film usually identify the character not as Homer but as "Patcheye.")

If the film's corrosive vision of patriarchy itself as ineffectual and endemically corrupt is at odds with the mainline Hollywood noir's restorative impulses, the superficial absence of paranoia in *Scarlet Street* further troubles the film's central placement in the noir canon. Chris lacks not only the eroticized intensity of the noir protagonist but the constitutive paranoia that feeds it. For Dana Polan, such representation of paranoia marks film noir significantly as "another side" (194) of Hollywood in the forties, a set of modernist disruptions that give rise to "the possibility of a mutation in the practice of 'classical' narrative" (194). But the narrative of *Scarlet Street* takes pains to reveal fully at each turn the deceptions that propel the story, distancing itself from standard noir turns in its refusal to yield a "mystery." Consequently, the spectator is likely to experience Chris, caught up helplessly in a plot to which the viewer is privy in all its machinations, as not being paranoid *enough*, as failing with monumental obtuseness to suspect his own obvious victimization. This *lack* of paranoia on the character's part is worked out formally in the early scenes of Chris's thievery, noteworthy for the striking absence of the conventional trappings of suspense. Lang stages similarly the two scenes of Chris's theft of Adele's bonds and his first attempt to steal from the vault at Hogarth's. Both are executed around limply unemphatic action, without the expected volatile soundtrack music to portend the possibility of Chris's being caught. The tight framing of both sequences also undermines potential suspense, so that even Adele's appearance while Chris is in the act is not presented as an imminent danger through such standard devices as, say, sustained cross-cutting to provoke anxiety. (Consider how differently Hitchcock, for instance, mounts such scenes, as in, say, the thefts in *Marnie*[1964].) The insinuating dramatic flatness that results from such strategies evinces a curt refusal to melodramatize the film's materials.

If such withdrawal, such periodic stylistic asceticism, is the means by which the film inhabits noir and stands apart from it, this genre that inhabits Hollywood and stands apart from *it*, it is also the point of infinite regress where a connection between the film's noir status and its narratives of cultural value emerges. Lang's film repeatedly bids for sensibilities akin to those of modernism through particular formal or thematic dynamics that oppose self-reflexive irony to cultural paranoia. Such of Lang's films as *Metropolis*, *Secret Beyond the Door* (1948), *The Big Heat* (1951), or *Beyond a Reasonable Doubt* (1956), for example, trace the progression of more or less naive characters through the gradual discovery of *literal* conspiracies hitherto unimagined. In each case, whether the context is that of dystopian fantasy, reconstructed gothic, or urban crime-thriller, the narrative derives its constitutive irony from placing a character's misplaced faith in social structures against an actuality so much *worse* than anyone could have supposed that, as in *Scarlet Street*, the belated revelation of conspiracy calls forth only numbed, helpless submission or mindless, automaton-like vengeance. In a topography of noir, rampant paranoia may be seen as initially morbid but it is also presented as ultimately cathartic or fructifying, rendering conspiracy nugatory, as in *The Maltese Falcon* (Huston, 1942); producing recovery from its ashes, as in *Woman on the Beach* (Renoir, 1948); or revealing its threat to have been delusory, as in Lang's own anomalously affable *Woman in the Window* (1944). In these films paranoia begins as psychic paralysis, the tortured recognition of a disturbed and hostile order, but ends as therapeutic action, agent of restoration. Noir's common denominator, such characteristic paranoia is usually, in critical versions of noir such as Schrader's or Neve's, seen as the product of a cultural Zeitgeist, and it is precisely by replacing, at the narrative level, paranoia with a kind of structural irony that Lang seeks to situate his films as, according to the modernist precept, "the expression of a purely individual consciousness rather than of a Zeitgeist or a collective state of mind" (Huyssen, 53). Unlike the free-floating paranoia of noir that reproduces cultural anxieties not to critique them but to exorcise them ritually, however, Lang's self-reflexive irony posits in place of noir's defeated or imagined conspiracies *genuine* conspiracies at work in the structures from which that irony was called upon to distance the whole work. Perhaps the clearest way to put this point is to suggest that *Scarlet Street*, in spite of its narrative disavowal of paranoia, *enacts* something of the paranoia commentators have attributed to the Frankfurt School, with its vision of a diabolically *administered* culture. The paranoia the film shows as lacking in the perceptions of its characters, in other words, returns with a vengeance in the film's vision of cultural order.

Jacqueline Rose has argued that paranoia is a basic effect of the film-system, especially in the shot/reverse-shot figure, with its visual fields constantly shifting so that the identificatory subject of the gaze is repeatedly faced with the potential of an unpleasurable reversal, confronted with the possibility of becoming *object* of an appropriated gaze ("Paranoia and the Film System," 144–45).[7] Although the disavowal of paranoia in *Scarlet Street* persists through the end of the film, its return in the form I have suggested takes something of the shape Rose describes. An example occurs in the scene of Chris's final theft when, by contrast to the earlier thefts, devices of suspense withheld in the previous sequences are employed in a particularly bombastic manner. An elliptical shot/reverse-shot scheme, moving between shots of Chris in the act of theft and shots of Hogarth approaching, shows only partial action that in its clipped ellipsis makes Hogarth's approach seem menacing and accusatory when in fact it turns out to be in his usual spirit of glazed bonhomie. Since Chris's demeanor is resigned and passive throughout, the rhetoric of the scene seems notably over-stated, made all the more so by the cloying repetition on the sound-track of "Melancholy Baby." Heard earlier in the first scene at Kitty's apartment within the film's diegesis, the tune's migration to the metadiegetic level has rendered it almost unrecognizable—sour, obsessive, sinister, and derisive. The mocking refrain underlines Chris's continued passive indifference to capture, but, marked by its bombastic deployment as a threatening element of kitsch, it simulta-neously transfers paranoia that has been repressed in the narrative onto the operations of the spectator. Through its repetition in different forms, "Melancholy Baby" takes its place within an intricate cultural sign-system in the film that the viewer must negotiate, just as the noir protagonist must unravel a paranoia-driven knot of densely intercon-nected signs. Indeed, the paintings themselves function in the same way, linking neo-noir paranoia, modernist aporia and the threat of cul-tural instability to the very processes of reading the film itself.[8]

Like film noir with its complex traversal of modernist alienation and genre formulae, primitivism too is defined in part by its tendency to straddle cultural levels, from avant-garde to kitsch, from self-reflex-ive modernism to "naive" folk art, without being ultimately assimil-able to any one of them. The current fascination with ideas of the prim-itive in cultural studies derives largely, as in representative work by James Clifford or Marianna Torgovnick, from an understanding of the phenomenon as an ideological construction enabling cultural exploita-tion or political domination. In *Gone Primitive*, for example, Torgov-nick proposes to examine the "way in which the West constructs and uses the Primitive for its own ends" (18). Thus, her focus is chiefly on institutional appropriations of the primitive; on the assumptions vis-à-vis primitivism of such canon-making figures as Roger Fry, Michel Leiris, or William Rubin; or on the systematic demonization of the primitive in Burroughs or Conrad. Like most such recent work, Tor-govnick's work sees modern conceptions of the primitive largely as a function of cultural *projection*, implicated deeply in exclusionist politi-cal operations. Even when Torgovnick confronts, say, the superficially receptive assimilation of the primitive in modern art, she views that dynamic as an objectifying process of misprision: "Modern artists typ-ically valued primitive statues' allusions to conception, gestation, and birth. But they often interpreted these allusions to the reproductive cycle as displays of stark sexuality, reading the generative as the pornographic" (102).

The construction of the primitive in *Scarlet Street* takes place through a kind of formal *introjection* rather than through strategies of cultural projection. In the film, Chris's work is clearly enough marked as "primitive" that several contemporary reviewers (at a time, to be sure, when the primitive was staging a comeback on the art market) noted the signs explicitly. The reviewer for *Commonweal*, for instance, found that "in the film's most interesting scenes, it turns out that this budding artist [Chris] is a primitive painter of real merit; and his pictures, which we actually see, prove to be the movie's greatest asset" (Hartung, 483). It is significant that the reviewer's surprise comes not only from the valuation of the primitive he sees here, but from the unusually sustained visual access granted the film's viewers to Chris's paintings. That we "actually see" the paintings is noteworthy indeed, especially considered in the context of numerous films of the time representing painting as a cultural index in which modernist strains in art are vilified, made monstrous, grotesque, or excessive, precisely through *denial* of the viewer's access to the works themselves. The plots of such representative films as *The Two Mrs. Carrolls* (Godfrey, 1947) or the movie version of *Dorian Gray* (Lewin, 1945) turn upon mysterious unseen paintings, for example, and the depiction of the pathological nature of an artist-figure in *Woman on the Beach* is secured through a systematic process of concealment of his modernist work. Such overt demonization of modernist styles, associating them with decadence or psychological imbalance, is made even sharper by contrast to films of the time in which realist paintings figure prominently in the narrative, serving as a source of reliability or stability. In *Laura* (Preminger, 1944), for instance, a detective falls in love with the painting of a murdered woman, and the central visual placement of the conventionally realist portrait, assuring directness of access for the detective to the object of desire, is laden with a rhetoric of *present*ness later repaid in the narrative when the woman turns out to be alive after all.[9]

In many films of the time, modernism is clearly linked to hysterical projections of the primitive by contrast with a reassuringly stable realism. Indeed, much postwar cinema explicitly contrasts modernist to realist art by presenting the former as distortional, sexually suggestive, ultimately *primitive*, and the latter as authentic, veritable, advanced beyond the primitive through its mature contact with reality. If this catalog of oppositions is familiar enough, the reviewer of *Scarlet Street* quoted above adds an additional, telling term when he implies that the primitive has ordinarily been associated with the *unseen*. In the context I have tried to establish here, the link of primitivism as a synecdoche for modernism itself in postwar Hollywood to invisibility, concealment, the unseen, should immediately suggest a corollary link of realism to accessibility, revelation, the overt. Interestingly, postwar attacks on modernism in the popular press tended similarly, though perhaps unconsciously, to be organized around tropes of the seen and the unseen. An especially vituperative and paranoid screed, much quoted at the time, characterizes modern art as "psychological communism" because, in its abstraction, it asks the viewer to *imagine* its conception rather than granting the viewer the power, like realism, to *see* its execution, just as commmunism "requires the observer to imagine the non-existent beauties" of a Utopian order (as against, by implication, the above-board requisites of capitalism).[10] Thus modernism finds itself here allied with proto–Cold War conceptions of *covert* infiltration, linked to the possibility of a threat from *within*, of a foreignness that has been so thoroughly internalized as to evade detection. In an article on representation of painting in forties cinema (in which, curiously, *Scarlet Street* is not discussed), Diane Waldman implies a connection between an explicitly xenophobic vilification of modern art, seen as literally alien, and recognition of modernism's interplay with mass culture. In the films Waldman sees as representative, the effort to relegate modernism to a position of sheer otherness by association with ugliness and regressive distortion, in spite of its basis in "the very real class nature of artistic taste" (64), becomes ever more difficult to sustain in light of the shared cultural ground of modernism and mass culture. For Waldman, the seemingly opposed aesthetic dispositions of modernist and realist painting comprise a mutual "reaction against the economic, social, and technological change which is represented *in and by both modernism and mass culture*" (64, emphasis mine).

In line with convention, *Scarlet Street* associates the impulses of modernism with a rhetoric of the primitive, but by reversing the conventional oppositions—by, for example, compusively *revealing* Chris's paintings instead of portentously concealing them—the film demystifies the association considerably. The signs of the primitive in Chris's work emerge either through remarks of characters in the film or by means of allusions directed *beyond* the characters to the audience. The differing orders of these signs suggest the function of primitivism in the film to signify multiple forms of *difference*—cultural, sexual, national. The already-noted quality of unreadability attached to Chris's work circulates around this rhetoric of the primitive. On the one hand, it is repeatedly suggested, even at one point resignedly by Chris himself, that the styles of the paintings illustrate a simple "problem of perspective"; yet what is in one instance perceived as a problem, the mark of *something wrong* in the work's materials, in another emerges as a guarantor of the work's sophistication in allusive connection to canonical modernist canvases. For example, Chris's portrait of Kitty, with its level perspective emphasized by the framing of the elongated figure tightly against a slatted background, alludes clearly in these very techniques to well-known portraits by Modigliani, while other of Chris's works refer equally explicitly to other well-known primitivist texts, such as "A Peaceable Kingdom." However, since the allusive quality of the work is never acknowledged in the text—is, indeed, *denied* in assertions of the work's originality—the intertextuality that defines it remains stolidly *meta*textual, taking its place as yet another of the film's brisk but stifled ironies. Thus, Chris's work is frozen between homage and parody, between the tributary simplicity of folk art and the knowing allusiveness of modernism.

Obviously, this slippage is directly related to the film's strategy of suspending questions of the value of the paintings and even of the film's attitude toward them. Here, though, the pay-off of this suspension is the important point. Drawing on tropes of primitivism that negotiate cultural levels rather than exclude rejected terms and thereby protectively consolidate established categories, *Scarlet Street* sets into play a kind of mutual demonology among cultural levels reliant on the art's status as an index of difference within a reassuringly homespun context. On the one hand, the primitive strain in Chris's work is a visual analogue to what the film presents as his psychological simplicity and the teeming, unacknowledged passions roiling beneath it; at this level, his work is understandable as simply naive, childlike, the product of native talent, deriving from the rawness of folk tradition. On the other hand, the painting's primitivism is a site of the film's self-consciousness, foregrounding sophisticated allusion and intertextual play. The best example of the lamination of these terms occurs in the scene of the exhibit late in the film. The complex tonal texture of the scene enables a remotely derisive attitude toward the paintings to coexist with a bitter critique of the process of their commodification as art objects. Perhaps the most characteristically Langian set-piece in the film, the sequence is constructed around a truncated perspective echoing that of the paintings themselves, the camera trained on an otherwise featureless wall with a series of crisp dissolves revealing the paintings in arch, languid succession while the camera reorients itself with mordant precision in relation to the pictures. The interaction of the few paintings we have seen earlier in the film with those we have not seen before, emphasizing the shifting responses progressively elicited by the work within the film's structure, simultaneously plays up the groundless quality of the unfamiliar paintings in narrative terms—presenting them as if they have sprung from nowhere. In a characteristic deployment of off-screen space that, far from seeming to fulfill a lost plenitude, only punctuates the scene's sense of the frame-as-limit, its eerily sketchy quality, Lang shows the dimly irradiated shadows of gallery-goers falling airily, cartoonlike, across the paintings, hoisting cocktail glasses and murmuring inaudibly what we can only assume to be bland platitudes.

The rhetoric of the primitive in *Scarlet Street* enables the conjunction of modernism and mass culture that is so crucial a part of the film's project while, at the same time, permitting the film to narrate its unconventional privileging of modernism. The appeal to "folk art" categories as potentially redeeming Chris's work is especially suggestive here, since critique of mass culture in the years before and after World War II carefully excluded folk art from its critical purview, arguing that folk art potentially retains an unspoiled quality, untouched by the otherwise general co-opting of cultural production in mass society. In most versions, to be sure, the contagion of mass culture with its popular forms and its easy accessibility is found to originate in the more authentic domain of folk art, only then to become bloated, corrupted, and hypertrophied through mass dissemination. In spite of the general recognition of this continuum, however, the vilification of mass culture in such narratives depended to a large extent on its insulation from an idealized folk art. Indeed, one of this narrative's key narrators, Dwight Macdonald, publishing an expanded version of his "A Theory of Popular Culture" (1944), changed the title to "A Theory of Mass Culture" (1953) precisely to foster a distinction between vital, individualized folk art and homogenized, monolithic mass culture. Yet, for Macdonald, the very primitivism of folk art's cherished vestiges, its lack of "cultural roots" and "intellectual toughness," was bound to make it difficult even for folk art to resist "the spreading ooze of mass culture" (17).

The introjection of difference at work in both film noir and primitivism by no means liberates *Scarlet Street* from a postwar context in which newly virulent demonologies are called on to secure cultural homogeneity. As Freud makes clear in his discussion of introjection in *The Ego and the Id*, introjection participates as fully as *projection* in the rhetoric of alterity, with the important difference that it masters perceived otherness by *internalizing* it whereas projection does so by distancing the other.[11] Such dynamics in *Scarlet Street* are evident in its treatment of specifically *national* difference, a thematic never far from the film's deepest concerns. Internalizing "foreignness" by problematizing the modernism/mass-culture relation and by drawing on embattled rhetorics of film noir and primitivism, *Scarlet Street* characteristically goes on to disavow questions of national difference at its most literal level. For instance, no character in the film remarks on the central incongruity of national styles on which the plot turns, the production by the naive, unself-conscious American of art that can only be seen in terms of an ironic, distinctively European cast. This is in spite of the fact that Chris is finally cut off from secure ownership of his work by the operation of nationally conceived market-forces. As Kitty remarks—albeit unaware of the dense irony of her comment—early in the film, encouraging Chris to market his work in Europe, "You're never appreciated in your own country!" According to Andrew Ross, a key feature of the move toward a *national* culture in the postwar settlement was "the continuing *real* historical presence of European prestige within the American value system" (64). This contradiction, whereby the solidity of American national culture is shored up *through* its assimilation of European "high culture," is worked out quite literally in the presence of European directors in the institution of Hollywood cinema. These directors may retain the prestige of their European heritage, which functions in turn to impart an aura of artistic prestige to their films, but the works remain decidedly *American* products by virtue of the economic demands and insitutional structures of the Hollywood system.

At the end of "A Theory of Mass Culture," Macdonald calls for a revival of the "cultural elite" associated implicitly with European traditions, even though the bulk of the essay has argued specifically for an integrated *national* culture by, for example, contrasting American democracy with Soviet totalitarianism (in a section of the essay, significantly, added on its republication in 1953). The exclusionist cast of the movement toward national culture in intellectual debate of the time coexists with the nearly compulsive invocation of European cultural models. In the *Partisan Review* symposium of 1952, "Our Country and Our Culture," for example, often cited as an important document in the effort to forge a unified national culture in the Cold War era, most respondents proceed by a systematic contrast of American culture with European, as if the logic of such a contrast in this context were somehow self-evident. In fact, it may be clear that the Europe/America opposition is always implicit in the modernism/mass culture debate, but both Macdonald's work and the *Partisan Review* symposium are marked by the simultaneous installation of "Europe" as a catch-all, a touchstone of unlimited signification, and the systematic driving-out of "Europe" as a martyr to the cause of greater cultural *unity*. Leslie Fiedler's contribution to the symposium begins by declaiming, "The end of the American artist's pilgrimage to Europe is the discovery of America" (88), and by the time his comments have concluded, though he posits a conventionally symbiotic relationship between Europe and America, he expansively portends a new-found cultural independence for the American artist who has shrugged off suffocating European precedents, emerging as "perhaps unprecedented in the history of Western culture" (91). Assuming in its very title a triumphal unity of nation and culture, positioning national identity as a stable core around which to conceive of cultural production, the symposium at the same time guarantees that rhetorical unity through, by turns, expelling the figure of "Europe" from the discourse and, at the same time, striving for a simulation of "foreign" prestige—that of the very foreignness, to be sure, that has been exiled.

Such rhetoric must be seen to have an unusual resonance for the cultural contexts of *Scarlet Street*, this film haunted—in its source, its styles, its genre, its director—by the specter of an outcast Europe. If Chris Cross's paintings function as a kind of free-floating gauge of cultural "difference," their contestation makes them resist easy placement as well within emergent conceptions of national culture. If postwar narratives such as Macdonald's express anxiety about an increasingly *homogenized* culture, that fear seems at odds with the simultaneous call for a replenishing cultural *unity*. Both the triumphal unity and the feared homogeneity—another pair of uncanny cultural doubles—derive from cultural fantasies that *Scarlet Street*, as both representation and document, may long to share but can only disrupt.

Part Two

Identity and Difference: Post-Classical Hollywood and European Art-Cinema

4

Un-American Activities in 1950s Hollywood: Hollywood Reading Europe/ Europe Reading Hollywood

The 1950s in Hollywood has traditionally been understood critically as a period of retrenchment, solidifying postwar consent in tranquilizing, sterilized images of an imaginary, idealized culture. Though not without a certain legitimacy, this version of the era is based on a reductive conception of the function of power in cultural formations and of ideology in the specific formation of the Hollywood cinema. According to that conception, dominant forms of social order and cultural practice manage to assert their hegemony without question, only later to be subject to critique and subsequent dismantling—with the advent, as such narratives would typically have it, of the 1960s counterculture that finally demystifies the complacent false-consciousness of 1950s ideology. More recently, however, 1950s Hollywood has come under reinvestigation according to less reductive conceptions that posit forms of power not in terms of a single monolithic force imposed from above on a given order, but as a set of practices dispersed throughout that order, often disguised by that dispersal even to their practitioners.[1]

This chapter contextualizes such tensions of 1950s Hollywood ideology in relation to the dialogue of Hollywood and European art-cinemas. In the context of this book as a whole, this chapter requires some justification. Despite their obvious significance to this study's theoretical concerns, the texts under consideration here, Joseph Losey's 1951 Hollywood remake of Fritz Lang's M (1931) and Jean-Luc

145

Godard's theoretical recasting of Hollywood in his film criticism of the 1950s, seem to be at best tangentially related to the book's broad subject, Hollywood films by European directors. Godard has never made a film in Hollywood, and although it has seemed in the past as if he might—he was one of the French "New Wave" directors mentioned as a possible director of *Bonnie and Clyde* (Penn, 1967)—it now appears as if he never will. Losey, meanwhile, became in effect a European director only after he fled Hollywood in the 1950s in the wake of McCarthyism, going on to produce such classics of European art-cinema as *The Servant* (1963), *Accident* (1967), *M. Klein* (1977), and *La Truite* (1982). Yet these texts illuminate the dialogue between Hollywood and the European art-cinema all the more strikingly because they do so at a time when McCarthyism had rendered such dialogue irrevocably suspect.

European directors such as Billy Wilder, Alfred Hitchcock, Douglas Sirk, and Michael Curtiz continued to produce films in Hollywood throughout the 1950s. The rise of McCarthyism, however, lent new force to anxieties about foreignness and all its attendant forms of difference within the institution of Hollywood. The blacklist that sent so many Hollywood filmmakers into one form or another of creative and actual exile functioned precisely to exclude foreignness from the system. This exclusion took place both literally, targeting actual "foreigners" who were suspect by virtue of their being *non*-American, such as Bertolt Brecht, and figuratively, targeting Americans whose alleged identification with the ideology of Communism, itself projected as foreign by the House Committee on Un-American Activities (HCUA), made them *un*-American, as was the case with most of the original "Hollywood Ten."

It is into this latter category that Joseph Losey fits, and his work has a place in this chapter not only because of the stylistic modes redolent of European art-cinemas that his work of this period self-consciously adopts, but because of the *figural* "foreignness" in relation to Hollywood as an institution that results. In most accounts of Losey's work, to be sure, his American films figure largely as the *pre*-European period of his career, important only insofar as they served as preparation for the director's ultimate apotheosis in the European art-cinema, much as the Hollywood sojourns in the careers of such emigrés as Murnau or Renoir are traditionally understood as their *post*-European periods, or as interruptions of their authentic "native" work. A parallel example is that of Jules Dassin, who after making several Hollywood studio films in the 1940s, emigrated to Europe in the wake of McCarthyism. (Dassin, however, is perhaps more important for his continuation of a "Hollywood" aesthetic in Europe during the latter phase of his career, as in his use of London as a film noir location in *Night and the City* [1951] and his use of the conventions of American gangster films in *Rififi* [1955].) Though Losey's remake of *M* is fully important in its own right, it is meant to function in this chapter as indicative of a kind of resident-alienation *avant la lettre*, on the assumption that such figural positioning might well illuminate the cultural politics of the European in Hollywood in the age of McCarthyism *more* tellingly than another analysis of the seeming political quietism and insinuating formal subversion of Hitchcock's films of the period, say, or of Sirk's 1950s melodramas.

Godard's work in criticism during the 1950s, like his films of the 1960s and 1970s, is almost obsessively concerned with the image of Hollywood as an institution of representation. The treatment of Godard's criticism in this chapter is intended to follow up the discussion of Losey's *M* as a figurative "alien" in the Hollywood system by showing how, at a time when the institutional regulation of Hollywood as evidenced by the blacklist was at its most virulent, Godard and his colleagues at the journal *Cahiers du Cinéma* were engaged in revising accepted notions of Hollywood ideology to discover a decidedly progressive tradition at work underground, or in the margins, in the Hollywood cinema of the McCarthy and post-McCarthy era. If this chapter widens the frames of reference of this study as a whole, then, it does so in order to show the forms in which the dialogue between Hollywood and the European art-cinemas persists despite powerful regulatory mechanisms designed to circumscribe it. Finally, this chapter is meant to reveal the crucial link between that dialogue and the complex, schismatic operations of ideology in postwar Hollywood texts by showing how the monolithic forms of power the institution of Hollywood projects produce counterreadings, countermovements, rather than a dependably secure, inevitable hegemony.

In their discovery of a dual register, a kind of double consciousness, in Hollywood cinema, the HCUA and *Cahiers du Cinéma* find themselves curiously allied in the effort to reconceive the forms of Hollywood representation after World War II. The Senate committee shares with the proponents of the *politique des auteurs* the inclination to read Hollywood according to an interpretive model that posits a surface-level of signification that conceals or otherwise deflects attention from a nonetheless privileged depth-level. According to the HCUA, a seemingly humanistic "social-problem" film—*Crossfire* (Dmytryk, 1947), say—may actually be a Communist treatise in disguise; according to the critics of *Cahiers du Cinéma*, a seemingly innocuous soap opera—say, *All That Heaven Allows* (Sirk, 1956)—may in fact be seen to subject to systematic, titanic critique the norms of a society that yet remains incapable of perceiving the film as anything more than an innocuous soap opera.[2] In such interpretations, the deep-structure of the text, occulted within the appearance of cultural normativity, relies for its meanings on a doubled relation to the surface-structure: in order to function at all, the text must disavow its allegedly "alien" status to operate at a covert level of ideological interpellation. Thus, the very existence of such double consciousness depends on a disavowal of depth-models of representation, prefiguring aspects of postmodernist aesthetics: the surface must remain in place even as the text's deep-structure works to undermine its validity. The institutional differences between the HCUA and *Cahiers* are clear enough: the former an organ of American politics, the latter of European culture; the former bent on uncovering, regulating, and repressing the "deeper" meanings of Hollywood movies, the latter on unearthing, multiplying, and liberating them. But these differences are less important, in the current context, than the parallel interpretive models that unexpectedly link these institutions. It is a link with significant implications for the forms of representation emergent in postwar Hollywood, where such double consciousness often bound together seemingly contradictory ideological impulses. If right-wing hymns to populism could be unveiled as gestures of left-wing subversion, then mass-culture box-office hits could equally surprisingly turn out to be high-modernist ruminations on cultural vacancy. This chapter initiates the second half of this study by examining questions of political identity and difference in 1950s Hollywood, then by connecting those questions to the modernist rereadings of Hollywood produced by French auteurist criticism at this time, by Godard in particular. If Losey reads Lang and Godard reads Hollywood against-the-grain, however, this should not be taken to herald the easy victory of a "progressive" counterlogic over the dominant logics of Hollywood. Rather, it illustrates the definitive double consciousness of postwar Hollywood ideology, as manifested in the textual hybridity of Losey's film, at once inside and outside the system, and revealed by the transnational perspective of Godard's writing.

Losey's Lang

Film historians have tended to see the significance of 1950s Hollywood in two ways. Some see in this period the institution's last-ditch efforts to retain the monolithic cultural authority of its "classical" period, others the point at which a genuine countercinema arises *within* the institution of Hollywood itself. No matter which of these scenarios particular critics adopt, most agree that the period signaled a crisis for Hollywood as a cultural institution. The terms of this crisis are well known. In 1947, the Supreme Court declared the major Hollywood studios illegally monopolistic and ordered their divestment of control over exhibition. In the same year, the HCUA mounted its investigation, which would proceed for five years, into Communist infiltration of the film industry. The years following saw the economic decline of the major studios, the rise of competition from television, and the flourishing of independent film production circumventing the studio system. If these crises signaled a decline in the power of Hollywood as an institution of representation, however, that power was not readily relinquished. To compete with television, Hollywood produced the "blockbuster" films often seen as definitive in cultural histories of this era. At the same time, Hollywood began to produce "smaller" films to compete with the "foreign" film market, particularly with the Italian neorealist films of the postwar era whose immediacy of style and urgency of social comment made so many Hollywood films look all the more artificial and remote from social reality by comparison.[3] The latter strategy of competition illustrated a typical effect of such strategies at the time, insofar as it threatened the institution's own reactionism to the onset of crisis. That is to say, Hollywood films could not respond to the challenges of neorealism without altering or tempering some of the fundamental ideological dispositions of their representations, unless by producing ever more insular "blockbusters." The double-edged quality of the operations of ideology in 1950s Hollywood results in part from the conflict between this reactionism of the institution and the nominally "progressive" solutions it generated to these perceived crisis-states, making way for the rise of a new kind of reluctant self-consciousness that in turn laid the groundwork for the "New Hollywood" of the 1960s.

A final strategy of the institution of Hollywood to deal with crises of the 1950s is manifested in the rise of the remake during the 1950s. As a form of reactionism, this strategy frequently had something of the same effect of generating "progressive" solutions in practice, producing films that in their relation to their "originals" give rise to forms of intertextual interplay that serve as something of a prelude to the forms of genre revisionism that mark "New Hollywood" formations. The emergence of the remake as an important form in 1950s Hollywood need not necessarily be seen as coincident with the growing self-consciousness some critics attribute to that decade in advance of the New Hollywood discourses that emerge in the following decade, however. To be sure, many of the remakes of the 1950s present themselves as nostalgic throwbacks to a more "innocent" era—and, implicitly, a more lucrative market. For instance, "screwball" comedies of the thirties such as *It Happened One Night* (Capra, 1934) and *My Man Godfrey* (LaCava, 1937) were remade in the 1950s as, respectively *You Can't Run Away from It* (Dick Powell, 1956) and *My Man Godfrey* (Koster, 1957) in a transparent effort to reinvigorate a stagnant market by association with an earlier expansive one. Yet the avowedly intertextual condition of the remake inevitably implies a degree of self-consciousness, reconceiving earlier texts of Classical Hollywood film according to the evolving terms of the classical model of filmmaking. Thus, for example, Frank Capra's 1950s remakes of his own thirties films *Broadway Bill* (1934, remade as *Riding High*[1950]) and *Lady for a Day* (1933) can in part be seen as a meditation, however inadvertently self-reflexive, on the evolution of Capra's own work and its place in the Hollywood ethos, as well as on the relation of the "old Hollywood" to the "New Hollywood"—as *meta*versions of the prior films. In this light, *Pocketful of Miracles* (1962) revisions *Lady for a Day* by counterpointing the old Hollywood mode in the person of Bette Davis with the New Hollywood mode exemplified by Method actors such as Peter Falk. The film thereby yields a stylized fantasia on Depression-era themes, its self-consciously simulatory status foregrounded, in place of the naturalized contemporaneity of the earlier film's treatment of its themes and settings.

An important line of 1950s remakes consists of a set of European "classics" remade in Hollywood, such as *Human Desire* (Lang, 1954), *The Man Who Knew Too Much* (Hitchcock, 1956), *Interlude* (Sirk, 1957), *The Blue Angel* (Dmytryk 1959), or *Cabinet of Dr. Caligari* (Kay, 1962). Hollywood remakes of European films were not uncommon from the beginning of the sound period of movies. Often these remakes served to make a "foreign" film available in an English-language version, employing cast members from the original production, as in the cases of *Algiers* (Cromwell, 1938) or *Intermezzo* (Ratoff, 1939). On occasion, Hollywood used sources in the European cinema in a quest for more "adult" material, as was the case with *Scarlet Street*.[4] Either way, the act of remaking the European original functioned as a gesture of appropriation, an effort to capitalize on a proven product or to assert the power of the institution to incorporate and thereby neutralize competition from without.

Joseph Losey's remake of *M* (1951) is unique among this group of films in many ways. While most of these films engage in what they posit as a normalization of the original, as in the remake-in-name-only of *Caligari*, or else use the remake as an occasion to project exoticized versions of Europe, as in *Interlude*, Losey's film both translates its European source into an explicitly American idiom and updates the concerns of Lang's late-Weimar melodrama to contemporary Los Angeles. Where other such remakes of the time draw upon various forms of nostalgia, casting back to an original text by reproducing and transforming it, Losey's remake proposes itself in a homologous or xenogamous relation to Lang's film. In this way, the act of remaking *M* at once translates or interprets the European original and asserts its continued relevance to the social and cultural contexts of 1950s America. In doing so, Losey produced a distinctive example of the genre of films made by directors who later became, as a result of their work, victims of the blacklist. In an excellent critical history of this period in Hollywood, Thom Andersen designates this genre as *film gris*. The designation obviously ties this group of films to 1940s film noir, as well as suggesting the "foreignness" of these films in the context of Hollywood (Andersen, 183–85). Incorporating postwar influence of neorealism with social and psychological detail, this group of films was sufficiently committed to social criticism to challenge the stability of traditional Hollywood ideologies. Although the HCUA never proved the existence of Communist ideology in Hollywood movies, these were the films that most forcefully expressed "alien" ideologies within the institution of Hollywood, drawing the committee's attention to the filmmakers because of the work they actually produced rather than because of known aspects of their personal beliefs, commitments, and allegiances.

Losey's remake invokes a conception of Lang's art-cinema classic as the decisively prefascist document that, as it ascended to fully canonical status throughout the 1950s, the film would generally come to be seen as. Two of the key critical treatments of Lang's *M* during the process of its canonization, bracketing the decade of the 1950s, both see the film as a pivotal text in the turn toward German fascism in the thirties. In *From Caligari to Hitler* (1947), Siegfried Kracauer reads essentially the whole of German cinema between the world wars as a prelude to Nazism, with *M* presented as a particularly prominent fixture in this cultural history. According to Kracauer, *M* "anticipate[s] what was to happen on a larger scale unless people could free themselves from the specter pursuing them" (Kracauer, 222)—the "specter" of authoritarianism. In Kracauer's thesis, Weimar cinema reflects what he sees as on the one hand an unwholesome attraction to anarchy and on the other a longing for a redemptive authoritarianism. Though influential analyses of *M* since Kracauer's book have tended to view it as a "progressive" text critical of the social and cultural forces that precede and give rise to German fascism, Kracauer himself denies the film such status, opposing what he sees as the film's "pessimistic outlook" (223) to Weimar films that "manifest outspoken leftist leanings" (223) and thereby testify to "the existence of antiauthoritarian dispositions" (223) in prefascist Germany.[5] Yet Parker Tyler's treatment of *M* in *Classics of the Foreign Film* (1962) draws on crucial material from Kracauer's discussion in order to present the film as an antifascist cautionary fable, warning against the dangers of authoritarianism. For instance, Tyler recounts Kracauer's anecdote, reportedly related to him personally by Lang, regarding the Nazi Party's misreading of the film's working title, "Murderer Among Us," as a reference to the rise of National Socialism instead of as a literal reference to the Dusseldorf serial killer. If Kracauer relates this anecdote to expose a political naiveté on Lang's part which Kracauer sees at work in the film itself, despite its superficial critical pessimism, Tyler reconstructs the tale as a mark of the hortatory foresight he assigns to the film. Kracauer asserts of the serial killer in *M* that he "is not so much a retrogressive rebel as a product of retrogression" (222). In doing so, Kracauer by implication assigns the film itself to the category of the "submissive" cinema of Weimar culture, as distinct from the "rebellious" cinema that resists political domination.

The film's ideological "wavering between anarchy and authority" (222), as Kracauer sees it, combined with its patina of left-leaning critique, makes *M* strikingly ripe for rediscovery in 1950s Hollywood. Exploiting the quasi-progressivist bent of his source in Lang, Losey reconceives Lang's text in the pulpy terms of the B-movie melodrama, multiplying levels of textual doubling already at work in Lang's film by positioning itself in a mirrored relation to the 1931 *M*. The act of remaking *M* implies congruity between an imagined decadent Europe of the past and America's 1950s present, thereby exposing the presumed false-consciousness of Hollywood's dominant effort to construct that present in idealized terms. Addressing a society explicitly perceived as, like Weimar Germany, *post*war and, implicitly, *pre*fascist, Losey's film depends on complex layers of intertextuality in order to construct a complex parallel between the cultural histories of prewar Europe and McCarthyite America.

This intertextual project is sounded in the opening sequence of Losey's remake. The first image in the film is a location-shot Los Angeles street scene, the camera mounted on the rear of a streetcar, showing the dramatically graded slope of the receding street as the car ascends a hill. Over this image, the title is superimposed, the letter "M" in jagged outline, explicitly imitating the appearance of the putative sign in Lang's text when it is branded in chalk on the serial killer's back. Further, the letter is bordered by an ornamented rhomboid that again evokes a quite specific and resonant image from Lang's film, the serial-killer Beckert's reflection in a store-window, identically bordered, as he stalks a victim. In spite of these clear allusions, however, the opening shots of Losey's remake announce their literal distance from Lang's film. In its visual texture, the sequence shares the ashen, hard-edged graininess of the neorealist-influenced, pseudodocumentary crime-thriller that gained currency in the late-forties Hollywood B-movie. Against the stylized and abstract cityscape of Lang's film, Losey presents the inescapable realism of location-shooting—even if its stylization, too, is rendered systematic in the course of the film. Against the late-expressionism of Lang's film, Losey's yields a Hollywood-tempered neorealism. Transposing the terms of the earlier film, Losey's remake simultaneously invokes not the content or even the spirit but, precisely, the *textuality* of Lang's film by way of the graphic allusions of the titles. Through such strategies of reference and differentiation, the remake conjures its source not as the guiding principle of its stylistic procedures or its narrative patterns, but as an artifact in cultural circulation that, by virtue of that status, confers levels of meaning on the current text that are specifically *relational*. In other words, Losey's remake is not the conventional effort in 1950s Hollywood to reproduce the elements of a prior text and thus either retrieve or supersede it; rather, Losey's film presents itself *in relation* to its canonical source, thereby illuminating the relation of a particular moment in one cultural history to that of another, parallel one, implying a complex relation between "Europe" and "America" as symbolic cultural spaces.

Though contemporary reviews of Losey's film rebuked Losey for daring to "improve" upon the original, reflecting the already entrenched canonical character of Lang's text, it is in this *relational* context that Losey's variations on Lang's themes must be seen.[6] If Kracauer is right to see Lang's film as symptomatizing or submitting to cultural anxieties of its time rather than self-consciously rebelling against them, the clearest index of this tendency may be the film's representation of the figure of the serial killer as a product of the modern metropolis, exploiting the structures of an emergent consumer culture in order to satisfy his rabid compulsions. Given this conception, however fugitively satiric its tone, the film can only be seen to legitimate much of the paranoia it presents as pervasive and debilitating. Thriving on the impersonality and the anonymity, the sheer massification, of the city, the serial killer of Lang's film manipulates the structures and institutions the film sees as failing profoundly to serve the social functions for which they have been designed. Expressionist cinema, from *Cabinet of Dr. Caligari* (Wiene, 1918) forward, modernizes the archetypal Gothic tale inherited from Hoffmann by relocating it to the asylum, often deepening its horror by punctuating the incapacity of the modern institution to contain the morbid energies of the archetypally deranged mind. A structuring absence in *M*, the asylum figures as just such a failed institution, so ineffectually bureaucratized that it allows Beckert to escape its confinements. Similarly, the modern office-building with its labyrinthine architecture and complex alarm-systems designed to fend off the imagined threats of urban culture, serves instead to provide a nearly impenetrable refuge for Beckert as he flees.

Lang's film represents the city as a geometrically enclosed nightscape, a representation Kracauer sees as reviving images of earlier German films such as *The Street* (Grune, 1923) or *Berlin* (Ruttman, 1927) in its oppressive sense of urban "chaos":

> Symbols of chaos that first emerged in the post-war films are here resumed [in later films] and supplemented by other pertinent symbols. . . . But no one any longer reacts vigorously against [the society's] condition. (Kracauer, 186)

In the case of *M*, such symbols of "chaos" noted by Kracauer as "the rotating spiral in an optician's shop" (222) function to link the film's vision of social disorder to what it sees as a dehumanizing fetishism of commodities. The tradition of street realism in 1920s German film out of which *M* partly derives often registers the rise of consumer culture by emphasizing the cycle of commodities' circulation, from consumption to waste. For Kracauer, such emphasis disturbingly parallels people with commodities: "People in *Berlin* assume the character of material not even polished. Used-up material is thrown away. To impress this sort of doom upon the audience, gutters and garbage cans appear in close-up" (186). The opening sequence of Lang's *M* synchronizes the tragedy of the child's murder with a similar emphasis on the circulation of commodities. As has often been noted, the images of the child's toys, a ball and a balloon, become powerfully synecdochic figures of her fate. In *The Imaginary Signifier*, for instance, Metz uses the sequence as a key example of "metonymy presented paradigmatically" (Metz, 190). What has not been noted is how such synecdoche extends to the deceptive avuncularity of the serial killer, who exploits an imaginary connection to the child made possible only by shared reference to these mediating objects. His method of luring his victim is thus defined as a function of commodity culture, which enables a stranger to feign familiarity to a child by expressing pleasure in the commonly admired commodity, as when he praises her ball, or by manipulating her own consumerist desires in order to effect an insidious appearance of pleasurable identification with her, as when he purchases the balloon for her. The closure of the sequence with the desolate, soundless understatement of the images of the wasted toys—the tattered balloon caught in a telephone wire, the abandoned ball rolling of its own accord in empty, sun-drenched space—thus establishes a theme that will recur in many of the film's most potent images, such as those of abundantly filled shop-windows or plentifully arrayed kitsch-objects. As Kracauer implies, however, it is the quality of human distraction or of inattentiveness to these very images that is the significant point here. Kracauer's example of the spiral in the shop-window illustrates how the film directs its commentary on commodification from a position outside the narrative as such by constructing the image as a detail of the composition unremarked by the characters inhabiting the frame. The hypnotic quality of the spiral is a wryly shrill symbol of consumerism's lure, yet it serves only as a backdrop to the narrative of Beckert's pursuit of his victim. If *Berlin* reflects a historical moment at which human being has become inextricably bound up with the activity of consumption, noting this circumstance explicitly through its finely tuned symphonic montage, *M* consigns such reflection to a background position at least insofar as the film's visual emphasis is on the internalizing logic of mise-en-scène, located as it is in a visual domain potentially distinct from and unremarked by that of the narrative. Thus, the film superficially dissociates its melodrama from its social criticism, its dime-novel tale of serial murder from its ideology-critique of consumer culture, even as it proposes a causal link between these two levels.

Separated from Lang's by twenty years and a world war, Losey's film depicts a consumer culture no longer ascendant, interposing itself as a response to perceived social decadence, but both fully institutionalized and itself in decline. Indeed, part of the function for which Losey's film seems to draw upon Lang's as its Ur-text is implicitly to define the social conditions it represents. The film's near-apocalyptic vision of a blighted Los Angeles derives its pervasive though oddly unarticulated anxiety from a conception of the cityscape as decimated, fraught with omnipresent signs of a past trauma and bristling with portents of a future calamity. The retrospective construction of Lang's *M* as both a *post*war and a *pre*fascist document interestingly mirrors the self-positioning of Losey's film in a pivotal space *between* unnamed historical calamities. Like many Hollywood crime-thrillers of the time, such as *Call Northside 777* (Hathaway, 1948) or *Boomerang* (Kazan, 1947), Losey's *M* relies upon a newly assimilated formal rhetoric of Italian neorealism, including the use of location-shooting and grainy black-and-white film stock, to yield a representation of the city in the terms of a gritty street-realism.

Losey's film goes beyond the conventional Hollywood assimilation of neorealist technique, however, to achieve a distinct affinity with neorealist imagery. Like the war-ravaged cities of postwar Italian film, Losey's Los Angeles is a ruined landscape of vacant lots, rubble-strewn streets, and decrepit buildings. At the same time, Losey synthesizes this nascent Hollywood neorealism with the atavistic expressionism signified by the film's source in Lang. A comparison of key sequences in the two films reveals important differences in the construction of space between Losey's and Lang's films that illuminate this telling synthesis. Although Lang's *M* is routinely seen as occupying historically a cusp between expressionism and an emergent aesthetic of social realism in Germany, many commentators have followed Kracauer in emphasizing the film's reliance on conventions of studio-shooting to achieve its geometrical stylizations of space, thus seeing the film as persistently *inner*-directed, morbidly subjective, in spite of its apparent concern with social reality. Similarly, Losey relies on extreme camera angles and distortional lenses to create a stylized sense of space. Yet the pro-filmic elements at work in either text give rise to crucial ontological differences between the films. The enclosed, abstracted, rigidly arithmetical urban space of Lang's film is a function of set-design, most obviously in such famous instances as the opening sequence, the office-building chase, and the mock-trial in the garret with which the film closes. Marked by a similar construction of space as eerily formalized, Losey achieves such effects by manipulating and subjectivizing *found* locations. For instance, as the mother searches for her daughter in Losey's first sequence, Losey distorts space through strategically baroque camera placement, setting the camera at a severe angle at the bottom of the concrete stairway as the mother ascends it, prolonging the dreamlike duration of the sequence by holding the shot as she climbs and creating a sense of spatial disorientation by problematizing the relation of camera level to spatial vanishing-point. Similarly, the closing sequence of the mocktrial is shot in a Los Angeles parking garage, where Losey's charge becomes once again to abstrac-

FIGURE 7. Stylized space in the trial scene of Losey's *M*. Courtesy Museum of Modern Art, New York.

tify existent space. In the latter instance, Losey does so by means of editing patterns executed with a sharply formalist precision around a rigorously enforced 180–degree axis, thus subordinating the sense of "real" space to formal pattern. The sequence unfolds according to a stylized shot/reverse-shot organization with the figure of the killer positioned in the foreground as a pivotal link from shot to shot, destructuring standard operations of "suture" by using this axis to play up figural *dis*sociation of the shots rather than to assure their relational unity.

Focusing on expressionist studio-shooting, Kracauer argues problematically that this procedure itself accounts for the morbidly *inward* quality he imputes to expressionist cinema.[7] His argument implies an immanent relation of filmic to profilmic elements, as if the materials to be filmed themselves determined the form of their representation; yet in this case, in the terms of my argument, the "profilmic" clearly differentiates the *types* of representation on offer in these films. In the earlier version of *M*, a literally insular expressionistic stylization is called on to reify a critical vision of the metropolis, at once registering the "chaos" Kracauer perceives there and, at least rhetorically, distancing itself from such social disorder by representing it through the optic of a heightened formalization. In the later version, a synthesis of previously incompatible styles complicates the problem of critical distance. If Lang's film is divided between "retrogressive" (pace Kracauer) and progressive impulses, mounting a reactionary attack on the modern metropolis yet proceeding in a Brechtian spirit of critical distance and ideology-critique, Losey's film can be said precisely to reverse these tactics, presenting an explicitly leftist account of the city-in-crisis while inevitably mitigating such an account by means of an attendant rhetoric of psychological and social "realism."

In the most literal terms, Losey's synthesis of expressionism and neorealism serves the film's vision of the city as located at a point of historical shift, deploying imagery of neorealism on the one hand to signify past trauma and the stylistics of expressionism on the other to portend uncannily a sense of imminent social catastrophe. Yet this portentous cultural anxiety circulates freely through the film in spite of quite explicit social commentary of a type completely absent from Lang's film, which by rights should function to neutralize or restrict such anxiety. Where Lang's film envisions the city as a wholly bureaucratized conglomeration of failed institutions, Losey's places a presumably explanatory emphasis on the social causes of their failure. If the failure of the asylum is presented in Lang's film simply as a given condition, its ineffectuality itself positioned as the cause of social ills and a spur to thenceforth legitimated paranoia, in Losey's film that failure is seen as the result of insufficient social resources. Lang's film characteristically signifies the asylum, as so many of the institutions it represents, through an indirect, extended rhetoric of cryptography, by means of a succession of shots documenting the overwhelming surfeit of graphic texts—forms, letters, lists—generated within the institution. In Losey, the institution is never invoked visually, but its structuring absence is signified by a fuller account of its inability to serve its implicitly validated social functions. "The hospital is so understaffed," explains a member of the police force, "they free dangerous men." Lang's police force is presented alternately as comically inefficient or brutally invasive, all but indistinguishable in Lang's uncharacteristically breakneck patterns of cross-cutting from the underworld figures who, in fact, are shown to mobilize more effectively than the police. Losey considerably de-emphasizes the role of the police, emphasizing instead the culpability in social breakdown of more deeply embedded social structures. Where Lang explicitly parallels the chief of police with the leader of the underworld, showing the active participation of both in the search for the killer, Losey counterpoints a broad caricature of the city's mayor (played in proto-Mr. Magoo fashion by Jim Backus) against a stock political-boss figure in order, by contrast, to show their *removal* from the social actions they decree and control, thus implying the dependency of such control on the invisibility of power sources.

The figure of the political boss is a key image in 1940s Hollywood, as illustrated by such examples as Gettes in *Citizen Kane* (Welles, 1941), Norton in *Meet John Doe* (Capra, 1941), or Willie Stark in *All the King's Men* (Rossen 1949). Typically, however, this figure is called upon to individualize corruption, personifying it in the form of a single character whose rejection or elimination thus permits a triumphal restoration of social order, as in Capra, or else to reinstate a threatened populism by purging it of its implicitly fascist elements, as in *All the King's Men*. At the time of Losey's remake, this stock figure had been given new life by the recently televised proceedings of the neo-HCUA Senate committee, led by Estes Kefauver, investigating organized crime. These proceedings, significantly, were intended to expose central "boss" figures but were characterized by a frustrated ability to reach such figures through the protective networks of their underlings.[8] Losey's representation of the political-boss figure is given a decisively leftist spin by analogizing criminal and social bureaucracy, revealing not the inefficacy of social institutions as such, as in Lang, but the insidious mimicry by the corrupt of the very structures precisely designed to fend off corruption.

It is significant that the film's most explicit commentary on social organization is granted, without apparent irony, to the political boss himself. The scenes in his chamber stand in clear contrast to parallel scenes in Lang. The latter are characterized by constant changes in camera set-ups and mercurial, edgy editing rhythms that render the figures spatially unstable, unidentifiable, and consequently interchangeable. The parallel scenes in Losey are rendered with a quality of visual stolidity, each shot carefully linked in time and space to the previous shot, rendering the boss's henchmen in their carefully posed positions as a group of veritable "organization men" (in William Whyte's coinage, roughly contemporary with Losey's film) in clear hierarchy.[9] Indeed, the revelation of the boss himself as the figurehead of this hierarchy is rigorously systematic, drawing on precise cutting around hard diagonals, positioning the figure in stylized symmetry at the head of a long table. To be sure, the boss's speech addresses this hierarchization specifically, symbolically illustrating it in an another image of linear order by stacking inverted glasses: "The average citizen doesn't care one way or another whether [the police] catch us or not, unless the press stirs them up for political reasons. . . . In one way or another we service the entire community, from the bottom up." In spite of its mockery of bureaucratization, Lang's *M* paradoxically laments the ascendancy of the institutional state and the loss of secure social hierarchies; asserting the connection between legitimated state bureaucracy and suspect social hierarchies, Losey's *M*, meanwhile, bemoans the co-option of valued institutions by corrupting influences.

The figure of the serial killer himself, in Losey's version, is psychologized amply in order to function more efficiently as a register of the potential value of these institutions. As Losey puts it, "My point of view was that society was responsible for [the killer] and he was sick. And he was not to be judged by anybody excepting qualified medical people and in due process of law" (Ciment, 110). The argument indifferently made by the defending attorney at the mock trial in Lang— "This man doesn't need to be punished, he needs a doctor"—is readable in the earlier film as a form of errant sophistry, but it becomes the fundamental plea of Losey's version in its quasi-social-problem-film mode. Again, in Lang, the serial killer's condition, like that of society at large, is treated as a given circumstance, with no interest expressed in its possible causes. Though Lang presents the serial killer as a tormented figure, the horror of his compulsions is hardly posited as even remotely exculpatory, and in spite of the film's rhetorical subjectivity of representation, Beckert's psychology remains stubbornly inapprehensible, impenetrable, his appearance often distinctly problematizing the rhetoric of expressionistic subjectivity at work in the film. To take one notable example, Beckert's pursuit of his victims is granted an interiorized intensity through a focus on Beckert's point-of-view, yet the point-of-view shifts disorientingly at crucial moments during these sequences, rendering Beckert's viewpoint literally inaccessible. One long take, for instance, ostensibly begins as Beckert's literal point-of-view; this effect is reinforced both by the long take's apparent function as a reverse-shot, following a shot of Beckert looking, tracking the object of his gaze, and by the sound of his off-screen whistle, seeming to signify through its auditory immediacy that the shot issues from his specific vantage-point. Yet subsequently, as the long take proceeds, Beckert himself is surprisingly discovered *within* the shot, undercutting its status as his point-of-view. To be sure, the film's expressionistic rhetoric of subjectivity serves repeatedly to yield exaggerated visual images of Beckert's emotional impenetrability. In a famous long take, Beckert enters a cafe while the camera lingers outside, dollying in smoothly to view him through the obstruction of a trellis of intertangled, overgrown vines. The shot functions as a visual correlative not only of Beckert's disordered mind but of the film's distanced portrayal of the character.

The parallel sequence in Losey's version departs markedly from Lang's rendering of the scene, contributing to Losey's detailed psychologizing of the serial-killer figure. Not only does the camera enter the cafe, but the scene underlines the killer's tortured subjectivity by serving as the site of a kind of intermediate primal scene as the serial killer helplessly watches the death throes of a struggling bird. The serial-killer's psychosis in Losey is linked to his experience as an abused child, with his identifications split traumatically between cathection to the figure of the suffering child and investiture in the father's sadism. In his final speech, the serial killer recounts a prior experience of watching the innocent suffering of a bird, implying that he kills in order to master the unassimilable image of such suffering. The representation of the serial killer's psychology in explicitly post-Freudian terms, as against Lang's indifference to questions of psychological causality, simultaneously serves to contextualize the character in the terms of an explicitly liberal social vision. Conferring a conventional domestic history on the character, a revealed past inhabited by the familiar figures of the overprotective, suffocating mother and the distant, violent father, the film constructs the killer as a recognizable social subject, thus a potential beneficiary of the very social institutions—redemptively therapeutic or humanely punitive—that would seem to have failed him.[10] Such a conception permits Losey's film a rhetoric of closure famously absent from Lang's, where Beckert's fate is unclear and the question of his guilt is displaced onto an incongruous and notably half-hearted theoretical plea against capital punishment. In Losey's film, significantly, the gesture of closure is effected by the serial killer himself, who accepts blame with the film's final lines, referring to the attorney who has been shot down by the political boss: "He was a good man. . . . He's been punished, now it's my turn." The psychologizing of the figure depends as well on an extension of sympathy to him, as for instance in the scene of the chase, in which the killer expresses remorse to his hostage, the girl who was his potential victim. In Lang, Beckert takes no hostage: Losey's turn of the plot at this point might be thought to render the killer even more culpable, yet he is seen as worthy of pity because the product of clearly specified personal causes.

Losey's film remakes Lang's as a leftist vision of McCarthyite America, but it is characteristic of 1950s Hollywood in reserving the option to efface its explicit ideological identifications. To be sure, although Losey's film reconfigures the narrative of *M* in distinctly liberal terms, it inherits from Lang a decidedly conservative edge of paranoia. Both films satirize paranoia at the narrative level but reproduce it at a thematic level, deriding the characters' paranoid responses to the murders while elaborating a conspiracy theory of social organization. Losey's film attempts to make the xenophobic edge of 1950s American paranoia clear in transposing Lang's bitterly comic setpieces. The scene in Lang where hysterical citizens suspect a man's innocent solicitude toward a little girl in the street, for instance, takes place in Losey's remake in a movie-theater screening *The Red Shoes* (Powell, 1948), satirically linking the man's projected perversion to a penchant for foreign art movies.

Moreover, the free-floating paranoia of Lang's townspeople is given in Losey the explicit correlative of McCarthyism; citizens accuse one another of Communism with comic irrelevance at the slightest infraction. Yet Losey's vision of a society administered from above by nominally legitimated institutions and from below by diabolical "organization men" does not thereby free itself of its distinctly conservative politics. In *The Paranoid Style in American Politics*, Richard Hofstadter implies a fundamentally conservative basis for social paranoia, especially in its conception of the role of free will in conservative politics: "The paranoid's interpretation of history is in this sense distinctly personal: decisive events are not taken as part of the stream of history, but as consequences of someone's will" (Hofstadter, 32). Thus, for Hofstadter, the paranoid disposition merely exaggerates conservative individualism, emerging as essentially an inverse form of populism wherein the enemy is projected as a demonic free agent. According to Hofstadter, paranoia crosses national boundaries and spans political spectra, but in so doing it unites elements across those spectra that would ordinarily be opposed. An essential trait of paranoid style is its inadvertent breakdown of the clear definition of the very distinct categories it would seem to require: "[The] enemy seems to be on many counts a projection of the self: both the ideal and the unacceptable aspects of the self are attributed to him. A fundamental paradox of the paranoid style is the imitation of the enemy" (32). At one level, the internalization of "foreignness" on which Hollywood's remakes of European films is predicated illustrates this paradox strikingly.

Influential accounts of Hollywood in the 1950s have similarly emphasized how, theoretically, growing polarities in American culture resulted paradoxically in the erosion of boundaries among hitherto distinct political positions. In an important essay on Cold War cinema, for instance, Michael Rogin argues that the heightening of political demonology in postwar America troublingly revealed previously repressed similarities between demonizer and demonized:

> Demonology begins as a rigid insistence on difference. That insistence has strategic propaganda purposes, but it also derives from fears of and forbidden desires for identity with the excluded object. In counter-subversive discourse, therefore, the opposition breaks down. Its cultural and political productions register the collapse of demonological polarization in a return of the politically and psychologically repressed. (*Ronald Reagan, the Movie*, 237)

Thus, for Rogin, the "countersubversive" imagination that shapes 1950s Hollywood defines itself by *driving out* "alien" figures "who serve as the repository for the disowned, negative American self. The alien preserves American identity against fears of boundary collapse and thereby allows the countersubversive, now split from the subversive, to mirror his foe" (284). In the dynamic Rogin identifies here, strategies of differentiation collapse into protective imitation. Its result, as Rogin's analysis of 1950s Hollywood makes clear, is a set of politically illegible films in which ideological positions become increasingly difficult to define. Similarly, Peter Biskind sees 1950s Hollywood, in contrast to traditional readings of the period as an age of quietism and conformity, as an "era of conflict and contradiction, an era in which a complex set of ideologies contended for public allegiance" (4). Just as Rogin sees growing identity of subversive and countersubversive impulses in this context, so Biskind points to the indistinguishability of "right" and "left" political positions in 1950s Hollywood representations, as in his representative analysis of *High Noon* (Zinneman, 1951): "We know *High Noon* is a left-wing film. . . . But aside from its disdain for business values, it would be difficult to tell *High Noon* apart from a right-wing film. Once stripped of its historical context, it becomes indistinguishable from, say, *Dirty Harry* ([Siegel], 1971), which also ends with a human throwing down his badge in disgust" (48).

    In failing to disavow the conservative paranoia of its source, Losey's leftist vision inadvertently places itself in the main lines of 1950s Hollywood, at the putative "end of ideology" Daniel Bell identifies as the key emergent formation of 1950s American culture. According to Bell, the appearance of new forms of power in 1950s American economy—a "countervailing power," rooted not in modes of production but in modes of consumption, regulated not by competition among producers but counterpower of buyers and sellers—unites liberals and conservatives in response against these emergent forms, rendering former differences between the positions of liberal and conservative increasingly nugatory (Bell, 80–83). In the fiercely demonological culture of 1950s America, as these versions of cultural history would have it, lines of demarcation between conservative and liberal, left and right, become not more insistent, as one might expect, but less clearly marked. Losey's film works out this cultural tendency in the context of the dialogue between Hollywood and European cinemas by narrating an explicitly liberal social vision rooted in an allegory of anti-McCarthyism while retaining the safety net of Lang's essentially conservative cultural politics. Losey's film exploits the politically ambivalent character of its source to situate itself as yet another of the politically illegible texts that define 1950s Hollywood.

Godard's Hollywood

While a particular vein of self-consciousness thus continued to develop in Hollywood's encounter with European cinemas in the 1950s, a group of French intellectuals was simultaneously engaged in an important encounter with Hollywood that would alter the terms of Hollywood discourses in essential ways. The group of critics associated with *Cahiers du Cinéma* espoused a *politique des auteurs*, a policy of authorship that rejected the staid, "literary" products of the European "tradition of quality" in favor of the vital, "cinematic" films of Hollywood cinema. The auteurist critics reconceived Hollywood in the terms of postwar modernism, and in doing so, they negated its ties to classical realism and reversed the traditional hierarchies through which European and Hollywood cinemas had routinely been connected. If previous criticism saw the products of European cinemas as "art," the auteurists were inclined to dismiss them as moribund throwbacks to outmoded aesthetics. If previous critics saw Hollywood as the mass-culture commodity par excellence, the auteurists found new manifestations of "personal expression" therein, as theorized in the *politique des auteurs*. Moreover, these animations of modernism and cultural hierarchy took place in the context of postwar national cultures. The French auteurist rereading of Hollywood in the 1950s has been accounted for by Dudley Andrew in national, historical terms, as a postwar phenomenon caused by deprivation and subsequent plenitude: American films that did not reach France during the war were imported in bulk afterward, so that several years of Hollywood movies appeared on the market all at once (*André Bazin*, 97). While this circumstance may account for the prominence of American cinema in the developing film culture of postwar France, reflecting the predominance of Hollywood movies on European screens, however, it cannot explain the specific contours of the auteurist analysis of Hollywood film.

The example of Jean-Luc Godard's 1950s film criticism, selected in the volume *Godard on Godard*, is too idiosyncratic, too headily perverse and willfully smart-alecky, to be taken as representative. Yet Godard's rereading of Hollywood does exemplify in general terms the specifically national dimension, as well as its relation to modernism and cultural hierarchy, of the treatment of Hollywood cinema in 1950s French film culture. Godard's criticism has often been read through hindsight as describing a systematic evolution toward his work as a filmmaker, in which the image of Hollywood as a signifying system continues to figure importantly. While this reading may impose a false teleology on Godard's work in criticism, it does nonetheless get at the gradually emerging definition of a specifically *modern* cinema that his criticism develops, which is then self-consciously realized in his films themselves.[11] This conception of modern cinema is elaborated most clearly not only in the context of Hollywood film, significantly, but in the context of the relation of Hollywood to European cinemas.

Like his more conventionally auteurist colleagues, Godard implicitly identified the practice of Hollywood cinema, particularly as illustrated in the work of specific auteurs, with the emergent "modern" cinema they discover in 1950s film culture. To be sure, Godard's conception of a modern cinema is based on both theoretical and historical arguments. Theoretically, Godard defines modern cinema in terms of a self-referentiality that he locates in a given film's degree of historical awareness, its sense of its own position in the continuum of film history; or, alternately, in its own internally deconstructive logic, its self-critique of or self-reflection on the forms of cinematic representation it adopts. This definition of cinematic modernism subsumes elements of Godard's historical argument that modern cinema—or, as he elsewhere calls it, "anti-cinema" (30)—is one among many available modes of filmmaking, competing for dominance but doomed to coexistence, in 1950s cinema. Though the theoretical assumptions from which Godard proceeds clearly overlap with the historical assumptions underlying his argument, it will be useful to treat the two sets of assumptions separately in order to arrive at a clearer understanding of his emergent conception of Hollywood as the harbinger of cinematic modernism in postwar film.

The style of Godard's critical writing, laying the groundwork for his cinematic practice with its gravidly oracular approach and its playfully lapidary tone, typically renders the truth-value of his claims questionable. In their gnomic, epigrammatical structure, Godard's reviews often resemble pastiches of conventional critical practice, subjecting the pieties of such writing to an intemperately skeptical, convulsively parodic interrogation. In these characteristics, Godard's criticism itself exemplifies the modern sensibility his writing sets out to define. His ambivalent response to that sensibility, moreover, is reflected in the repeatedly avowed commitment of his criticism to values of simplicity, naturalness, and sincerity, despite the complex irony and flamboyant artifice of his own writing. It is largely from this complex of values, this budget of paradoxes itself given shape by the imperatives of 1950s French film culture, that Godard's response to Hollywood cinema arises.

The dense-pack idiosyncrasy of Godard's criticism guarantees that if a theoretical agenda is to be discovered at all in Godard's writing, it is available only through a kind of negative extrapolation. Godard's review of No Sad Songs for Me (Maté, 1950), for instance, may be the fullest treatment in his work of the essential self-referentiality he finds in Hollywood film, but it is so in its implications rather than in its assertions. Supremely indifferent to the ordinary protocol of film reviewing, Godard circumvents plot-summary and standard forms of evaluation in order to apprehend a sort of metalevel at which to gain critical entry to this seemingly conventional soap opera:

FIGURE 8. Close-up from *No Sad Songs for Me*. Courtesy Museum of Modern Art, New York.

The beauty of this film lies in our certainty about Margaret Sulla-van's heart. . . . Thus the classically constructed script here acquires considerable psychological force. Although it neglects space, it enables one to remain very close to the actress and to share her inner emotions. Some close-ups of Margaret Sullavan illustrate this. The effect of nervousness they produce springs from the degree of bewilderment they convey. They make us anxious about things where the actress may be quite composed. One cannot question the truth of this effect more than by mock-ing the confusion, so to speak, of the illusions which happiness assumes. Thus the cinema plays with itself. (21)

Godard's treatment of the close-ups of Margaret Sullavan here has something in common with other famous meditations on the close-up in film theory, such as Bela Balasz's discussion of *The Passion of Joan of Arc* (Dreyer, 1929) or Roland Barthes's paean to Greta Garbo's face in *Mythologies*. In each of these cases, the close-up is seen as an *excessive* sign, or a sign of excess, troubling the chain of signification, removing itself by dint of its supernal plenitude from the plane of mere represen-tation onto another level altogether, a domain of transcendent self-ref-erentiality. In Godard's review, the "classical construction" of the script cannot harness the excess and decidedly *un*pleasurable energies—bewilderment, nervousness, anxiety—that the close-ups produce. Thus Godard here implicitly posits a literal, representational level of textual-ity and a figural, *meta*representational level that exceeds and finally takes priority over the former: "The cinema makes reality specific. . . . If destiny and death are the cinema's pet themes, then there must be a definition of the human condition within the carefully controlled pre-sentation of the *mise-en-scène*" (21). Though Godard recognizes that *No Sad Songs for Me* is "a very simple film," he does not allow this recog-nition to prevent him from using it to support a heavy weight of spec-ulation about the nature of cinema itself. A characteristic maneuver, this rhetorical strategy reflects a very basic assumption: Godard sees film, essentially, as the locus of a convergence of multiple energies, wedding the ordinary, the random, the ephemeral, and the banal with the grandiose, the rigorous, the permanent, and the transcendent—deriving the latter from the former in the very mechanisms of cinema's operation. (As Godard elsewhere claims of Hitchcock, he "knows that the cinema is an art of contrast" [25]). Godard's valuation of Hollywood cinema derives from his sense of Hollywood as textually overdeter-mined, therefore best capable of harboring these multiple energies, therefore most characteristic of the art of the cinema as such.

In a series of theoretical gestures that effectively form a bridge between Bazinian realism and Kracauerian phenomenology in film theory, Godard assigns a redemptive function to film itself while resisting the transcendental or metaphysical rhetoric that might follow logically from such an attribution. He believes, with Bazin, that filmic representation reveals formerly hidden properties of its objects in some essential way—"Not man's view of things, but the view of things themselves" (20). At the same time, he believes, with Kracauer, that such representation potentially "redeems" its objects: "The cinema makes reality specific"—heightens it by reproducing it. Yet he refuses to accept the implications both Bazin and Kracauer, in different ways, derive from their premises, that such redemption transcends reality as such in mystical or metaphysical ways: "It would be useless," claims Godard, "for [cinema] to try to make more of the instant than the instant itself contains" (21).

Although Godard intermittently implies that the cinema is itself, as a technology of representation, specifically "modern" in some undifferentiated sense, his most suggestive uses of the word "modern" position it precisely as a differential term, distinguishing one type of film from other types. In his review of *Hollywood or Bust* (Tashlin, 1956), Godard declaims, "[T]he cinema is . . . too resolutely modern for there to be any question of it following any path other than an open one, a perpetual aesthetic interrogation" (58). Despite his conferral here of a "modern" valence upon the cinema as such, Godard elsewhere opposes "modern" film as one possible stylistic mode against alternative and presumably concurrent cinematic practices. Such distinction is evident, for instance, in the rhetoric of his reference to *Man of the West* (Mann, 1958) as "a lesson in cinema—in modern cinema" (117). In his sustained meditation on "classical" style in film, Godard contrasts what he takes to be the "modesty" of such classical stylists as Mankiewicz, Preminger, and Mark Robson with "the religious tendency of the modern cinema" (29).[12] In his effort to establish the "modern" as a kind of ontological category in postwar film practice, Godard rejects its use as a term of simple periodization. He is careful to refer to the "classical" Mankiewicz as "the most intelligent man in all *contemporary* cinema" (82, emphasis mine), while he sees Nicholas Ray, who rejects classical form, as opening up "the world of *modern* cinema" (64, emphasis mine).

In spite of Godard's fairly systematic efforts to forge distinct categorical realms here, the stability and comparative insularity of the categories are challenged by Godard's identification of modern cinema with Hollywood filmmaking. If the modernism of a film like *No Sad*

Songs for Me resides not in its narrative structure, which is defined explicitly as "classical," but in its metatextual channeling of the epistemology of cinema itself, Godard's responses to Hollywood more generally are complicated by his conception of Hollywood as a differential system of competing terms in which "classical" and "modern" intersect—as a *closed* system in which, to take up the vocabulary of Godard's review of *Hollywood or Bust*, "open" forms remain nonetheless available.

The specifically national dimensions of Godard's rereadings of Hollywood cinema further illustrate this conception of Hollywood as a system of representation. Godard's valuation of Hollywood cinema has often been seen as problematic, especially where critics find it difficult to square Godard's hyperprogressive politics with Hollywood's evidently retrograde ideologies. On occasion, this problem has been solved by dismissing the French auteurist view of Hollywood as a simple *mis*reading, the result of exoticizing projections of American film on the part of European intellectuals that repress the actual rear-guard nature of Hollywood ideology in favor of an avant-garde recasting of it.[13] In an important article on *Breathless* as a film that "articulates the troubled relationship between the Hollywood cinema and the European film market" (51), however, Dennis Turner argues that

> [the] homage paid to Hollywood by recent Continental filmmakers evidences a more complicated attitude toward America and American cinema than most critics have allowed. In the first place, however much their work was admired, the Hollywood producers were seen as oppressors, cultural colonizers whose power in Europe stemmed from a cynical manipulation of the film distribution system. (Turner, 52)

The complexity of Godard's attitude toward Hollywood is worked out in his treatment of Hollywood as a cinema that transcends national categories even as it is fundamentally shaped by them.

This point cannot be understood without a clear sense of Godard's conception, following Bazin, of film history itself as basically nationalist in its structure. In discussing European cinema, Godard repeatedly invokes for explanatory purposes categories of national style, mostly inherited from Bazin, as in his association of neorealism with Italian national sensibilities. Moreover, Godard routinely appeals to the Zeitgeist of national sensibility to account for the ethos of specific films from Europe. The following reference to Bresson is characteristic in its trebled extrapolation of dominant styles from national pedigrees: "[Bresson] is the French cinema, as Dostoevski is the Russian novel and Mozart is German music" (47). Moreover, Godard is concerned in his treatment of European film to differentiate national styles, as when he contrasts the Swedish Bergman with the Italian Visconti (79). In his treatment of Hollywood directors, by contrast, Godard is strikingly inclined to compare specific filmmakers to European precedents, finding analogies between a given auteur and a pre-existent European model. In his first piece on Joseph Mankiewicz, for example, Godard mounts a sustained comparison between Mankiewicz and the Italian novelist Alberto Moravia—no random choice, we may assume, since Godard later adapted a novel by Moravia in a film, *Contempt* (1963), that is with its mordant melodramatics and its mannerist emphasis on self-consciously "literary" dialogue, as much an homage to Mankiewicz as it is a version of Moravia.[14] More to the point, however, Godard aligns Mankiewicz's work not only with specific aspects of theme and structure in Moravia, but more generally with a whole ethos of Italian style, of a "mediterranean" (13) sensibility associated with particular qualities of style and treatments of character. Similarly, Godard declares Hitchcock "the most German" (24) of Hollywood directors, while he sees Anthony Mann's career as bearing direct affinities to that of Jean Renoir. This sense of Hollywood as both defined by nationality and outside nationality is evidenced by Godard's labeling of Hollywood as the "transatlantic" cinema, a term he sometimes uses to refer to Hollywood's composite of national styles (p. 24), other times simply to position it in relation, both literally and symbolically, to European cinema (p. 26).

Godard's characterization of European cinema is everywhere stratified by national boundaries while his characterization of Hollywood is marked by a sense of the fusion of multiple national styles. A quite different conception of nationality, in fact, informs Godard's treatment of European cinema from that which underlies his treatment of Hollywood. Where European cinematic traditions are seen as fundamentally *determined* by nationality in the first instance, Hollywood bridges national boundaries seen as unbreachable in the European context. Thus, Godard reads European cinemas according to traditional notions of universalist nationalism, but he reads Hollywood according to a complex vision of national differentialism. In one sense, Godard's attraction to Hollywood is of interest as a series of stylized projections of European nationality, as in his correlation of favored auteurs with European national styles. It is here that Godard's rereading of Hollywood most closely resembles other important responses to Hollywood in 1950s French culture. The French valuation of film noir, for instance, as it is represented in the exemplary volume *Panorama du film noir Americain* (1955), derives from a perceived resemblance between Hollywood film noir of the 1940s and such films of a past "Golden Age" of French cinema as *Pépé le Moko* (Duvivier, 1936). In such analyses, the multinational character attributed to Hollywood film constitutes that tradition as a richly mythic repository of the lost values of a prior national moment.

In Godard's work, Hollywood is seen as the last refuge of passing cultural practices made visible at once in their final glory and their fated ephemerality. Here again the reading of *No Sad Songs for Me* is suggestive, acknowledging the illusory materiality of Margaret Sullavan's presence in the film while arguing that the film self-consciously heralds the final oblivion of the objects it represents.[15] The intensity of this quasi-metaphysical response perhaps reflects an unspoken identification on Godard's part, conscious or unconscious, with the director of the film, Rudolph Maté, a European in Hollywood, perhaps most famous for his work as camera-operator on *The Passion of Joan of Arc*, and the attention to the film's close-ups here may well reflect the knowledge on Godard's part of that art-cinema classic, famous for the affective intensity of its close-ups, as an Ur-text of Maté's Hollywood films. Writing only a few years later, Francois Truffaut archly acknowledged such identification in auteurist responses to Hollywood film:

> If you are irritated by the extravagant admiration of younger movie lovers for the American cinema, remember that some of the best Hollywood films have been made by the Englishman Hitchcock, the Greek Kazan, the Dane Sirk, the Hungarian Benedek, the Italian Capra, the Russian Milestone, and the Viennese directors Preminger, Ulmer, Zinneman, Wilder, Sternberg *and* Fritz Lang. (Truffaut, 64)

Yet the metaphysics of Godard's response remain intensely affective. If cinema on the one hand confidently proclaims its capacity to apprehend being in space, fixing objects in an imitation of permanence, its temporality on the other hand undermines the appearance of such permanence, signifying the inevitable disappearance of things, the impernanence of being:

> Look at these stretches of heath [in *Strangers on a Train* (Hitchcock, 1951)], these neglected homes, or the sombre poetry of modern cities, those boats on a fairground lake, those immense

avenues, and tell me if your heart does not tighten, if such sever-
ity does not frighten you. You are watching a spectacle completely subjected to the contingencies of the world; you are face
to face with death. (24)

This dialectic of presence and absence everywhere informs Godard's
conception of cinema as such. The dialectic is worked out most fully,
perhaps, in the relation of Hollywood and European cinemas that
Godard's work proposes. In these terms, Hollywood is proposed as a
cinema of self-proclaimed *presentness*—presumably victorious in its
postwar condition, nominally unspoiled by the destruction of warfare
visible in spite of that nominal victory, allegedly unified in its national
ideology—that yields nonetheless a powerful image of the existential
absence that is the very condition of being itself. The Hollywood films
Godard most favors, clearly, are those that have since been canonized
as critical visions of the sterility and false consciousness of dominant
representations of 1950s American culture, but clearly, as in his reading of *No Sad Songs for Me*, Godard finds those dominant representations themselves immanently poignant in their delusory pojections of
presentness. European cinemas, on the other hand, are for Godard
allied to a kind of epistemology of absence, thus acknowledging the
"real" conditions of experience—bearing the visible traces of warfare's
destruction and the less visible ones of the waning of centuries of cultural tradition, still animated by a mournful nostalgia thenceforth projected upon Hollywood.

The "naturalness," "sincerity" and "honesty" Godard attributes
repeatedly to Hollywood representations may well signify both
Godard's own naive faith in Hollywood's technical virtuosity and thematic self-confidence and his mythic conception of American nationality as it is represented in Hollywood film.[16] It also denotes, however,
his keen sense of the pathos of what he constructs as Hollywood's own
naiveté, of its commitment to an imaginary aesthetic of presentness
that remains threatened by the ubiquity of loss. This aesthetic of presentness, in Godard's analyses, collapses into the self-consciousness of
negativity just as surely as, in his vision of postwar Hollywood cinema, nationalities themselves collapse into a differential vision of still-
universalized nationhood. Hollywood thus becomes, in Godard's
work, a kind of "floating signifier" (in Jeffrey Mehlman's phrase),
whose aspiration is "to search for the plenitude of a real object when,
in fact, what is at stake is a purely formal circuit of symbols"
(Mehlman, 11). The modernist impulse Godard locates in Hollywood
film is defined by the relation of this delusory plenitude, rooted in uni-

versalist myth, to that "purely formal circuit," described by the arc of transient, reticulate national styles. It is a circuit that Godard whimsically traces in its circulation in Hollywood cinema. Inclined to read Hollywood through the optic of a European modernism that continues to shape French film culture in the 1950s, Godard finds in Hollywood, where others perceive the death knell of modernism itself, the final forms a postwar modernism is obliged to take in an increasingly trans- or multinational culture.

5

Reinventing Otherness: *Petulia*, Art-Cinema, and the New Hollywood

In its opening sequence, *Petulia* (Lester, 1968) coolly announces its own strangeness. With blunt precision, two settings are juxtaposed, the institutional-gray corridor of a hospital set against a stage on which a rock group performs. The unsettling quality of the sequence depends on a series of sharp contrasts; the smoothly tracking long shots and crisp shifts of focus of the corridor contrast with the quick, elided close-ups of the band, and the imbalance between the sustained takes of the corridor and the brief, mercurial shots of the stage produces a tempo freighted with anxiety. Contrasts of sound, color, movement proliferate: the grayish glaze of the corridor, with explosions of red in the attire of the wheelchair-bound patients being rolled into an elevator, clashes with the less garish tones of the stage space; the alternating metallic resonance and hushed silence of the corridor with the frantic rhythms of the rock music; the immobility of the patients with the spasmodic movements of the singers; the tightly controlled movement of the camera in the corridor with the clipped, chaotic movement of the camera on the stage.

In the space of a few shots, a rhetoric of strangeness is fully elaborated at the beginning of the film, a rhetoric that self-consciously underlines the film's difference from commercial American cinema and its pointed association with European art-cinema. Through this rhetoric, *Petulia* emerges as a peculiarly characteristic instance of the differential textuality that comes to characterize "New Hollywood" filmmaking in the 1960s. In fact, the insinuating wit of the opening of *Petulia* is in the service of a throwaway gag. The sequence is designed

175

to create an interpretive rift in the viewer's association of disparate settings, to undermine received ideas about continuity and cinematic rhetoric in general, but here the interpretive problem is quickly resolved, without fanfare. The band, it turns out, is performing at a hospital benefit—"Shake for Highway Safety"—at which the patients, victims of traffic accidents, are guests-of-honor. Beginning with close shots that derive their enigma from the absence of any framing context except what appears to be an arbitrary and whimsical juxtaposition, the film's director, Richard Lester, extends the field of view gradually so that the viewer is able to see the "real" relation between these locations. If this connection becomes clear *literally*, however, the rhetorical effect remains unresolved. Why go to such lengths, the viewer may ask, to create a mystery where none properly exists, to suggest the overwrought, near-metaphysical convergence-of-a-twain where nothing more than a small dramatic point is to be registered?

Suspense and resolution are elements of any narrative structure, but *Petulia* insists at the outset on problematizing the relation of these elements to each other as well as to narrative structure itself. In doing so, the film admittedly achieves a dead-pan comic effect, emphasizing through the earlier contrasts the inappropriateness of the dour, joyless patients amid the festive surroundings in which they find themselves. In the context of the film as a whole, however, two other effects supersede this one. The film's opening gambit is the first of the textual disruptions that will characterize the whole film—thus, in effect, the first of its lessons to the viewer in how it is to be read. At the same time, the opening shots, precisely by going beyond the evident requirements of the narrative, foreground the stylistic excess that will mark the film as "alien" even to the presumably progressive traditions of American film in the 1960s. Among the most important films in sixties American cinema to deploy techniques previously associated exclusively with the European art-film, *Petulia* cultivates its alien status by rethinking the uncanny in literal terms.

The emergence in the late 1960s of a full-fledged "New Hollywood," nascent since the end of World War II, coincided with the progressive destabilization of the European-art-cinema/Hollywood-mainstream opposition that had been important in international film culture at least since the 1940s. Initially defined as the bastion of purified expression heroically resisting the relentless domination of Hollywood commercialism, art-cinema began to lose something of this position of cultural privilege amid debate in the postmodern vanguard about cultural hierarchy throughout the 1960s. As Steve Neale argues in "Art Cinema as Institution,"

During the 1960s and early 1970s in particular, at a time when polemics surrounding "popular culture" and Hollywood were at their height, Art Cinema was often defined as the "enemy": as a bastion of "high art" ideologies, as the kind of cinema supported by *Sight and Sound* and the critical establishment, therefore, as the kind of cinema to be fought. (12)

Moreover, as Pamela Falkenberg points out, the "bipolar" relation of these sytems of representation began more and more to dissolve into a recognition of their shared cultural ground: "If the art cinema is outside the commercial (Hollywood) cinema, that outside is not one of radical exclusion: the art cinema is also a commercial cinema" (44). One line of interpretation of New Hollywood cinema, represented by Neale's earlier, influential article "New Hollywood Cinema," sees it precisely as a site of dialogue between Hollywood and European art-cinema producing a greater degree of formal self-consciousness within what nonetheless remains, for Neale as for most critics, a normative or standardized Hollywood textuality. Whether such dialogue is cause or effect of the emergence of New Hollywood discourses, it significantly recasts the relation between these cinematic institutions, as Falkenberg argues at length, from one of insulation and resistance to one of engagement, transformation, and reproduction. Comparing Godard's *Breathless* (1959) to its Hollywood remake (McBride, 1983), Falkenberg argues,

> In both cases, division within the same (within the French cinema or within Hollywood) depends on an identity posited from a distance. This identity, of course, is also a rewriting: reproduction from a distance represents another transformation. (44)

Yet the dialogue between European art-cinema and Hollywood that engenders a "New Hollywood" in the late 1960s has most often been perceived according to a rhetoric of assimilation, whereby Hollywood swallows up the hitherto oppositional practices of art-cinema, thus rendering them harmless, commodifying them thoroughly, divesting them of their capacities for subjective expression and cultural critique. In such narratives, Hollywood may reproduce art-cinema practices, assimilating formal devices that originate in the opposing system of representation, but such reproduction will always be seen as performative *imitation*, transforming these elements only by stripping them of the myriad, glorified "high-art" functions they can signify, apparently, only within their "native" domain.

Such an approach to New Hollywood filmmaking reproduces standard modernist presumptions about the relation of self-reflexive textuality to traditional realist representation. Modernist aesthetics privileged self-reflexivity as opening a more viable access both to the Real itself and to the domains of Art-as-such. Typically, this was an explicitly *formal* self-reflexiveness, on which was conferred a kind of automatic political valence: no matter how retrograde the content of a given modernist text, so long as its form achieved the requisite self-reflexivity, it could still be seen as "progressive" in its capacity to subvert traditional realism, critique bourgeois subjectivity, and ward off the encroachment of mass culture.[1] Emergent terms of New Hollywood filmmaking, however, render such presumptions increasingly difficult to sustain. Influential accounts of New Hollywood practice routinely see it through the lens of a persistent *sameness*: in spite of superficial differences from Classical Hollywood practice, these accounts would have it, the ideology of Hollywood remains fully untroubled. Even these accounts, however, assume the dispersal of energies of a formerly monolithic model. In *The Classical Hollywood Cinema*, the authors conclude with a brief coda on "the persistence of a mode of film practice." They argue that New Hollywood film practice indeed incorporates differential terms, but that these terms remain delimited by the conventions of "classical" textuality: "The New Hollywood can explore ambiguous narrational possibilities but those explorations remain within classical boundaries" (377). Yet their survey of New Hollywood practice proceeds by way of a sustained comparison of Hollywood texts with texts of European art cinema: *Tout va Bien* (Godard, 1972) and *The China Syndrome* (Bridges, 1979); *BlowUp* (Antonioni, 1966), and *The Conversation* (Coppola, 1974). Thus, the authors implicitly acknowledge the dynamic of textual *differentiation*, whereby Hollywood texts differentiate themselves through identification with non-Hollywood texts. For Thomas Schatz, this practice continues the capitalist practice of commodity-differentiation, in which commodities retain their sway by proclaiming their uniqueness. The effect of this, for Schatz, is a new kind of Hollywood textuality:

> [T]he vertical integration of classical Hollywood, which ensured a closed industrial system and coherent narrative, has given way to "horizontal integration" of the New Hollywood's tightly diversified media conglomerates, which favors texts strategically "open" to multiple readings and multimedia reiteration. ("The New Hollywood," 34)

Given this new "openness," it seems clear that any adequate theory of New Hollywood textuality must be a theory of difference—of how texts differentiate themselves and of how the Hollywood system conceives of the differential terms it announces itself to be incorporating—even if one concludes that Hollywood's ideological regimes remain securely in place.

Art-cinema at least since the French New Wave routinely imitated practices of Hollywood filmmaking, reproducing Hollywood genre conventions and formal patterns, even in some cases using actual Hollywood stars (*Breathless* is only one case in point), often for overtly critical or deconstructive purposes. Thus, art-cinema's reproduction of Hollywood styles transforms them into the terms of a modernist self-reflexivity. Before the New Hollywood, however, Hollywood filmmaking achieved its domination in the international film market through a clear differentiation of its products from those of art-cinema that relied upon the exclusion of the most basic practices of the art-cinema. Before the advent of the New Hollywood, in other words, art-cinema "imitated" Hollywood routinely in a mode of detached irony, but Hollywood's "imitations" of art-cinema functioned only to *delegitimate* Hollywood's access to such forms. This dynamic reflected larger cultural presumptions whereby mass culture's forms and traditions were widely available to modernist textuality, and deployed often for parodic purposes, but the forms of modernism itself were not—or, at least, not perceived as—reciprocally available to mass-cultural texts. The relation defined here, then, is in both cases one of non-mutuality and opposition. Art-cinema opposes Hollywood in this model, however, through maneuvers of explicit critique, reproducing the terms of Hollywood filmmaking in order to transform them by displacement, reflecting a complex attitude toward American cinema as a form of cultural colonization.[2] The relation between Hollywood and European art-cinema had typically been predicated on an implicitly chiasmic structure in which Hollywood's literal economic dominance in the international film market was offset by the presumed artistic superiority of art-cinema. The latter, in these terms, strove to speak nominally "authentic" forms of cultural identity and to retain its purified status apart from the networks of commodification. New Hollywood assimilation of previously excluded art-cinema practices extended its colonization into a territory formerly uncharted—that of "high art" with its presumed expressive idiosyncracy and its manifest contempt for the very commodification and standardization associated with Hollywood. It could not do so, however, without jeopardizing its own dominance, at least at the symbolic level, by measuring its own actual market domination against art-cinema's imagined aesthetic superiority. New Hollywood assimilation of art-cinema practices only rarely operated according to a logic of critique or of satirical undercutting; more often, it was understood as the very source of New Hollywood novelty—a new "frankness," "adultness," or "honesty"— admitting into its system terms that would, in fact, potentially, subject the system itself to a kind of autocritique. In "New Hollywood Cinema," Neale argues that emergent practices of late-1960s Hollywood filmmaking threaten the fabric of classical textuality, but he concludes that forces of stability endemic to the classic text—originating either in the text itself or in its reception—ultimately override this threat. Though Hollywood's dialogue with art-cinema may herald a breakdown of cultural levels whose alleged insulation had previously defined the relation of Hollywood and European art-cinemas, it does not in Neale's view challenge the foundations of classical textuality itself in Hollywood filmmaking. Specifically, Neale argues, the category of authorship remains in force as a stabilizing signifier, rendering the experience of apparently destabilizing New Hollywood textuality coherent through an appeal to conventional forms of human expressivity ("New Hollywood Cinema," 117–18).

Richard Lester, the director of *Petulia* and an important though often marginalized figure in the emergence of New Hollywood filmmaking, is an interesting test-case for ideas about authorship in New Hollywood discourse. Born in the United States, Lester made his name in England, beginning in the field of commercial television and advertising before making his first films, and this "transatlantic" quality of his biographical background readily translates into facets of his auteurist persona, with Lester's "original" national identity troubled by the permutations of his particular stylistic affiliations.[3] Thus, Lester emerges as something of a paradoxical figure, a native emigré, "foreign" to the culture yet produced by it, "alien" to the institution of Hollywood yet attuned to its commercial mystique. Associated early in his career with art-cinema-as-such, Lester even then was associated as well with a distinctively pop sensibility, as in the two films he made with the Beatles, *A Hard Day's Night* (1964) and *Help!* (1965). His film *The Knack, and How to Get It* (1964), though marked by a sustained rhetoric of spatiotemporal ellipsis subtending narrative experimentation characteristic of the most hermetic art-films, also reflected the cultural currents of "mod" London so effectively that Pierre Sorlin, in his book on the social ramifications of cinema in European culture, uses the film as a representative text in a discussion of the function of images from film in society at large (Sorlin, 7–20). Lester's work thus locates itself at a cusp between a progressive experimentation whose function had for-merly been precisely to guarantee the noncommodified status of the art-film, to differentiate the art-film from the commmercial cinema, and a welcome acceptance of the films' unavoidable place in com-modity culture.

If Lester's work thus challenges art-cinema's own prerogatives, these aspects of his work coincide with some of the most basic effects of New Hollywood cinema. Lester's negotiation of the terms of pop-culture and art-cinema—of the parallel spheres of commodification and that which defines itself precisely through its resistance to com-modification—results in a self-consciously "mod" style that is as definitive of late-1960s Hollywood as the later work of another nom-inally "foreign" refugee from advertising, Ridley Scott, is definitive of 1980s Hollywood. The comparison with Scott is not incidental, for both filmmakers elaborated distinctively postmodern visual styles, emphasizing qualities of surface-chic, imported quite directly from advertising but adaptable to a range of cinematic genres. Scott's visual style, with its immediately recognizable metallic luster, remains fully characteristic, for instance, in films as different as the Conradian historical epic *The Duellists* (1979) and the sleek neo-noir *Someone to Watch over Me* (1987). Lester similarly adapts the postmod-ern chic of his style to a range of films from the comic pastiche *How I Won the War* (1967) to the disaster-film *Juggernaut* (1974). The work of both directors in a variety of popular genres thus signals a decisive shift: If the classical *auteur* was typically identified with a specific genre—Hitchcock with the thriller, Ford with the Western, Mamou-lian with the musical, Capra with populist comedy, and Sturges with satirical comedy, and so on—the New Hollywood *auteur* ranges across multiple genres in a manner that potentially undermines the cult of "personal expression" underlying the concept of *auteurism* itself. (This identification of auteurs with genres in Classical Holly-wood may strike some readers as problematic, but my point here is to evoke the leveling, unifying function of *auteurist* analysis; consider the extent to which even auteurs known for work in multiple genres are often talked about as bridging or revealing deep correspondences between those genres—as in the case of Minnelli's negotiation of the musical and the melodrama, for example.) In the cases of Lester and Scott, to be sure, not only does the deployment of the rhetoric of commercial advertising bring with it connotations of a corporatized mystique, but the style itself, with its high-toned sheen and its nomi-nal rejection of depth-models in representing reality, is decidedly "impersonal" in its thrust.

Conflating foreignness and nativity, Europeanness and Americanness, high-modernist experimentation and precommodified style, Lester's auteurist persona reflects an important aspect of his work, employing distinctive modes of irony and satire but doing so *within* the frame of reference of the culture he represents. As a number of reviewers noted at the time of its release, *Petulia* is characterized in its distinctive visual texture by a delirious sleekness and a crisp-edged glossiness. This quality of visual texture is a central component of the film's concerted, time-capsule inventory of 1960s culture, chronicling the fads, fashions, and artifacts of 1960s culture in the very commercial style that is itself a quintessential product of the age. One contemporary reviewer remarked that there seemed little point in "deploring" this style, "since it is *the* style of the '60s" (Schickel, 12), while another complained that the film was stylistically both "modish" and "already dated" (Hatch, 29). In its implication that the film's style is itself nothing more than an ephemeral, passing "fashion," the latter point inadvertently highlights a crucial aspect of the film's hectic semiotics of 1960s culture. While the film represents the cultural detritus of its sharply delimited time and place—the "Summer of Love" in 1968 San Francisco, with its psychedelic ambience and its consumerized-countercultural milieu, its lovebeads and miniskirts and lava-lamps and roller derbies—the film's perspective is distanced, estranged, alienated.

Yet the film does not achieve these effects of estrangement by counterpointing its representation of 1960s America against stylistic patterns remote from the materials of representation, which through that remoteness serve to ironize those materials. To contrast *Petulia* with an approximately contemporary meditation on "mod" culture, *BlowUp* (Antonioni, 1966), is to see this point more clearly. Antonioni's landmark of European art-cinema (which may well owe something to Lester's Beatles films) scrutinizes its subjects from a steely distance gained by imposing a general stylistic asceticism upon its materials. Through starkly formalized compositions, severely wrought patterns of editing, and somberly drawn tonalities, Antonioni presents a vision of hipster culture that, although detailing it painstakingly, refuses even the suggestion of sensory responsiveness to or engagement with the terms or the pleasures of that culture. *Petulia*, rather, renders its vision of late-1960s counterculture in a style presumably "native" to that culture, thus achieving its distancing effects—presenting the culture itself as uncannily ephemeral—within the terms of the culture itself. This dynamic duplicates the relation of New Hollywood forms to art-cinema—a relation of simulation and transformation—that the film enacts.

Self-Conscious Narration in New Hollywood Film

Petulia bridges two distinctive approaches in 1960s "new wave" art-cinemas, the satirical cultural chronicles of new-British hipsterism and the narrative complexity of French New Wave cinema. The latter in particular proved a decisive influence on New Hollywood rhetorics. The New Wave influence on *Petulia* is best seen in the film's use of flashbacks specifically reminiscent in their temporal disjunction of the work of Alain Resnais. Like those of Resnais, Lester's flashbacks reject conventional cinematic cues such as the initiating close-up and subsequent dissolve leading into the flashback, as in such a quintessential example as the Paris flashback of *Casablanca* (Curtiz, 1943)—no random comparison, since Resnais's *Hiroshima, Mon Amour* (1959) alludes to that film (when its principal characters visit the "Casablanca" cafe) as both the seminal example of the classical model Resnais rejects and a signifier of the false consciousness, in this case of the cultural imperialism, which that classical model subtends. Lester's flashbacks, like Resnais's, are disjunctive within themselves, presenting fragments of action anterior to the film's story, disconnected segments whose relation to the plot is initially unclear. In the example of *Casablanca*, the flashback sequence is positioned strategically within the plot to resolve a newly elaborated narrative enigma. The crucial characters of the flashback (Rick, Ilsa, and Sam) have been clearly introduced, and the film's plot has raised a question about the relationship of Rick and Ilsa—What happened to them before the film proper has begun?—that must be answered before the plot can proceed. The classical flashback orients the spectator not only through its conventional cues, down to the establishing shot of the flashback itself with its imposing view of the Arc de Triomphe to provide immediate geographical orientation, but through its conception of the flashback as a coherent narrative, complete within itself, embedded within the plot. By contrast, the modernist ellipses of Resnais, especially *Hiroshima, Mon Amour* render the flashbacks inapprehensible in these terms except by accumulation.

In tracing Hollywood's deployment of New Wave techniques in *A Certain Tendency of the Hollywood Cinema*, Robert Ray focuses on the flashback as the most representative example: "As early as 1965, *The Pawnbroker* had assimilated *Hiroshima*'s unannounced, incomplete, out-of-sequence flashbacks that promptly became the staple of such commercial movies as *Two for the Road* ([Donen] 1967), *Point Blank* ([Boorman] 1968), and *Petulia* (1968)" (Ray, 288). For Ray, the fate of the device, like that of other devices originating in the art-cinema, is to be swallowed by Hollywood the Devourer, to be "assimilated" into the pitiless monolith of American film history as Ray constructs it. In this version, the device comes into being, it would seem, at some zero-degree of authentic expression only to become, through a process of imitation and reproduction, a "staple" of "commercial" filmmaking. Ray's argument thus repeats the standard narrative of origin, imitation, and commodification around which influential New Hollywood discourses have traditionally taken shape, not only lumping together a number of films that in fact employ the unannounced flashback in very different ways, but driving a wedge between the cultural formations of art-cinema and Hollywood and thus reinforcing the cultural hierarchies both traditions were, at their best, often engaged in dismantling.[4]

More recently, Maureen Turim distinguishes between the "modernist" flashback and the use of the flashback in Hollywood film, arguing that the latter typically "individualizes" and "subjectivizes" representation, positioning the flashback as a subjective function of character memory, while the "modernist" flashback, identified exclusively with European art-cinema, functions to challenge "the limits of the conventions of genre and spatio-temporal continuity" (Turim, 189). Though Turim admits that the flashback by definition troubles the continuity of linear narration, she finds that Hollywood flashbacks work against such disruption, tempering "the modernist potential of the flashback . . . by highly coded transitions and explanations that rendered the flashback as a conventional device" (Turim, 189).

The flashback of *Petulia* simulates the modernist flashback by designating multiple functions for the device in the film's narrative structure, avowing a degree of narrative self-consciousness crucial to the film's position in New Hollywood formations. One of the functions of the film's inserts is to announce the disparity of story and plot, *fabula* and *syujet*, events comprising the narrative and the arrangement of those events. Crucial information has been excluded from the story, clearly, and the inserts serve as disquieting, uncanny traces of that exclusion. One could put this, as well, in terms of the "return of the repressed": what has been excluded from the narrative makes its way back in through the eruptive inserts. Yet in spite of this rhetoric of "the unconscious," the inserts are not connected only to memory or, indeed, to the subjectivity of characters within the film. A look at the first occurrences of inserts in the film demonstrates the varied functions they serve, demonstrating that the use of the device serves more complex functions than a simple standardization or commodification of an initially "modernist" technique.

Because the film is not well known, and because its narrative is notoriously inaccessible (almost every printed summary extant gets the plot wrong), a brief plot summary is required before discussing the film's self-conscious narrative patterns. The film deals with a free-spirited young British woman, Petulia, married to David, the son of a wealthy family. Before the film proper begins, Petulia and David have encountered a young Mexican boy, Oliver, on a trip to Tijuana, and have been circuitously responsible for an accident that results in his injury. Stricken with guilt, Petulia takes mitigated responsibility for the boy, placing him with a Mexican family and sending money to support him. Meanwhile, she becomes drawn to the doctor who treats him, Archie, whose gentle humanity contrasts with the neuroses of her abusive husband. As she pursues a relationship with the recently divorced Archie, her domestic situation becomes more violent, but she continues to conceal the source of the abuse from Archie. The film ends on a bittersweet note with Archie and Petulia parting and Petulia, about to give birth to a child fathered by David, returning to her husband and, it is implied, the same patterns of abuse that have damaged her.

Through the uses of inserts, this already intricate plot is rendered more complex still. The first insert is perhaps the most conventional. It occurs in the first sequence after Petulia has followed Archie, leaving the benefit where they have met, archly negotiating the affair she assumes they will have, in spite of Archie's wry indifference to her. In the midst of their neo-screwball-comedy banter, a close-up of Petulia looking absently beyond Archie is followed by two point-of-view reverse-shots. What Petulia sees, through the glass doors behind Archie, is a car on a rotating platform to be raffled off at the benefit. The first of the point-of-view shots is a long shot of the car, the second a close-up of one of the tires as the car rotates toward the camera. The flashback follows, a series of quick shots with no sound, initiated by a graphic match between the tire of the car at the benefit and that of a car swerving in a street and running over the leg of a Hispanic boy. We then see the boy on an operating table, attended by Archie, and a zoom shot shows Petulia framed in a window, peering with concern into the operating room. From this temporal disruption, the narrative returns to the benefit with another close-up of the car's headlight followed by a close-up of Petulia, who resumes her conversation with Archie, apparently unperturbed.

Like Resnais's inserts in *Hiroshima Mon Amour*, Lester's retain some of the conventionalism of the classical flashback. The close-up of Petulia that initiates the insert, for example, links it clearly to Petulia's subjectivity. At the same time, also like Resnais, Lester replaces accepted conventions of the classical flashback with less recognizable ones. The shift from the time of the *fabula* to the time of the *syujet*, for instance, is signaled by the abrupt withholding of sound and by a shift in film-stock in the inserted shots, which are glazed with a monochromatic blue. In addition, the graphic match that parallels the rotating car at the benefit to the swerving one in the street further underlines the apparently subjective dimension of the insert. The viewer is meant to conclude, clearly, that Petulia is reminded of the accident by the similarity between the cars, thus triggering the flashback. The character of the memory is explosive yet ephemeral, leaving Petulia to go on with the prattling whimsy of her conversation in spite of the traumatic content of the flashback. The example, then, is directly comparable to the first of the flashbacks in *Hiroshima, Mon Amour*, in which the woman of Nevers remembers her German lover. The memory is triggered by a glimpse of her current Japanese lover lying in bed on his stomach, his arm stretched to his side, palm turned upward. Resnais introduces the flashback by graphically matching the Japanese lover's hand to that of the dead German lover, in a similar disposition. In both cases, then, the dirsruption of the *fabula* is shown to be a function of a specific character's memory, and in both cases that memory is represented as mercurial and involuntary, working to repress what it cannot acknowledge. Thus, the form of the flashback itself works to yield a vision of unmastered memory, of subjectivity-in-crisis, rather than the simple bourgeois subjectivity Turim finds in the standard Hollywood flashback.

The flashbacks in *Petulia* demand constantly shifting responses from the viewer because of the varied functions they serve in the film's narration. The flashbacks themselves not only draw attention to and help to resolve gaps in the plot, but also visually suggest relations among the characters in the narration's present tense as well as, in general, the troubled relation of the story's past to its present. The formal instability of the intercuts is further amplified by the expanding range of moods and tenses they encompass as the plot proceeds. Several of the intercuts, it soon becomes apparent, function as flash*forwards*, mercurial references to a *future* tense within the story, but because their presentation is rhetorically identical to that of the flashbacks these two types of intercut are initially indistinguishable from each other. During the scene in which his ex-wife Polo visits Archie in what she calls, with a kind of solicitous contempt, his "bachelor pad," brief intercuts depict a frenetic roller derby and a dark, orgiastic rock concert. Both shots recur later in the film in their normative place in the diegesis. The first recurs after Petulia has been beaten by her husband, David, when Archie, Polo, and their sons go to the roller derby, and the second during the two years of story time that the film compresses into a brief montage sequence. Because the flashforwards refer to events the plot eventually admits, the viewer is challenged upon recognizing the portended incidents in the present tense to rethink his or her intepretation of previous intercuts. In fact, the viewer can rarely be sure of the order—past or future tense—represented by any given example of the intercut as it occurs, but must attempt to situate each in the context of his or her indeterminate, continually altering interpretations.

Other examples of the flashforward serve to lend heavy emphasis to particular and often seemingly minute events. For instance, when Petulia has anonymously installed at Archie's an elaborate glass-and-steel greenhouse, he understands this as a gesture of gratitude and conciliation, and he exuberantly gathers a bouquet to take to her, but arriving at the Danner house he discovers that she and David have left together on a sailboat excursion. Standing bereft on the dock, Archie drops the bouquet into the water. In any case the shot showing this gesture would be fraught with desolation and frustration. With a precise cut on his gesture of dropping the bouquet, the shot abruptly counters the rhythms of the sequence in which it occurs, visually opposing Archie's resolute motion as he gathers the flowers to his impassive stillness as he stands on the dock. The shot's composition, too, centering Archie in a long shot, emphasizes his stolidity and solitude. These effects, however, are made more emphatic by the two earlier intercuts that have repeated this shot, though from different angles, so that its resonance when it recurs in the diegetic present-tense is enlarged, so that what might have seemed to be a small moment of pathos takes on a mysterious undercurrent of gravity. Thus, the shot at once achieves a powerful effect of truncation, underscoring the painfully unfulfilled reunion of Archie and Petulia, and a disturbing effect of resolution, culminating an enigmatic strain of imagery in the film.

In this sense, the flashforwards emerge as a key index to the extent of the film's narrative self-consciousness. In *Narration in the Fiction Film*, David Bordwell notes the theoretical or rhetorical similarity of flashbacks to flashforwards but goes on to differentiate them according to character subjectivity and authorial self-consciousness: according to Bordwell, flashbacks ordinarily represent character memory but flashforwards "cannot be attributed to character subjectivity; they constitute self-conscious narrational asides to the spectator" (79). Like Turim, Bordwell evaluates the effect of such devices according to the presentation of character, privileging modernist authorial intrusion over bourgeois subjectivity (as if the former were itself not fully amenable to bourgeois takeover). At times the flashforwards in *Petulia* can be understood as characters' speculations about the future. For example, when Polo describes her new lover to Archie, intercuts show her with Warren in attitudes of dignity undermined by the stylized sets and exaggerated colors around them. This intercut, like many of the flashbacks, is linked through close-up and diegetic context to a character, in this case Archie, who imagines sourly the comic postures of his ex-wife with her new lover. In fact, though, the intercuts in this sequence *do* recur in a literal diegetic context late in the film. Thus they finally emerge both as signs of Archie's jealous presentiments and as flashforwards to events in the story's future tense. If these flashforwards share the "teasing" character Bordwell attributes to flashforwards in general, allowing us to "glimpse the outcome before we have grasped all the causal chains that lead up to it" (79), they also reactivate the necessarily provisional status of the viewer's relationship to the text, forcing the viewer to recognize that relation as one to an intrusive and controlling narrator. Indeed, because flashforwards refer not to an anterior backstory already known to characters but to a yet-to-be-revealed forestory, they are by definition, according to Bordwell, "highly self-conscious and ambiguously communicative" (79), explaining "why classical narrative cinema has made no use of [the device] and why the art-cinema, with its emphasis on authorial intrusion, employs it so often" (79).

The self-conscious narration of *Petulia* relies on omniscient ranginess over the elements of the story and, at the same time, marked restrictions upon the accessibility of story information. In a way, the simultaneous availability of information, from events of the story to inner states of characters, is precisely what causes a kind of narrative blockage in the viewer's relation to the text. Insisting on the suspension of final inferences, the text also demands a kind of ultimate mastery. In the film's last sequence, Archie and Petulia meet in the hospital delivery-room years after their affair, and Archie, with a tone of careful consideration but in a manner of capricious whimsy, offers to take her away with him to another hospital: "I could call an ambulance. I've delivered plenty of babies. You have a fine pelvis. . . . We'd never be apart again." As he speaks, we see a soundless intercut of an ambulance, sirens flaring, moving through darkness. At the most obvious level, the intercut distances the viewer from the rueful seductiveness of Archie's speech, undermining both his earthy banter ("You have a fine pelvis") and his romantic platitude ("We'd never be apart again") by raising yet again questions of narrative sequence. Is this ambulance the same one that appears in the film's opening shot, an

ominous, ubiquitous *deus ex machina* ironically come to whisk the
lovers away to final happiness—à la the famous ending of that other
example of the contemporary brief-encounter/reconstructed screw-
ball-comedy, *The Graduate* (Nichols, 1967)? Instead of a flashforward
heralding the couple's final escape, though, the intercut turns out to be
something of a red herring. Lifting the phone receiver to summon the
ambulance, Archie reconsiders and the two bid each other farewell.
The shot of the ambulance must finally be understood, then—to adopt
the slightly grandiose rhetoric the final sequence calls for—as the
marker of a union that was not meant to be. Thus the film's stylistic
dependency on bathos and various forms of sleight-of-hand frustrates
the viewer's effort to master the intricacies of the text, even as its mar-
shalling of modernist techniques requires new forms of mastery on the
part of the spectator.

In their varied functions, the intercuts of *Petulia* simultaneously
signify lack and excess. If the inserts do at times serve the conventional
purpose of providing needed narrative information, they more often
draw the viewer's attention precisely to the fact that such information
has been withheld. Indeed, the inserts of *Petulia* densely laminate narrative lack upon stylistic excess, at once exposing the gaps upon which
the narrative act is predicated and enunciating an enigmatic narrative
complex. Consider, for instance, the examples in the sequence in
which Petulia arrives at Archie's apartment bearing a tuba. The
sequence contains two brief intercuts. The first shows Petulia hurling
a rock through a pawnshop window to steal the tuba; the second, in
languorous slow-motion, shows her falling to the ground, pushed by
a man standing erect beside her whose face is not visible. Though the
two intercuts are similar in execution—in their brevity and in their
placement within the diegesis, triggered by specific references or parallel gestures—each derives, as it were, from a separate narrative
order. The first could be called synchronic, since it springs from veri-
fiable action of the sequence: hoisting the tuba, Petulia refers off-handedly to "all that broken glass" at the pawnshop, and we cut to the shot
of the rock shattering the glass. The second, however, could more
properly be called diachronic, since it depends on the temporal order
of the narrative. The insert is connected clearly enough to the action of
the seqence: Petulia feigns her fall in front of Archie, and we cut to the
intercut showing the fall of the previous night in which she has actually been injured by David. Unlike the first, though, the second cannot
be understood strictly by an appeal to its relation to the sequence in
which it occurs, even if only because David's identity in the intercut is
concealed. Rather, this intercut makes sense only cumulatively, link-

ing itself not only to the diegetic moment that seemingly prompts it, but to a series of successive intercuts whose meanings are enlarged by their complex interrelation.

In a literal sense, then, the first insert exceeds the evident narrative needs of the sequence. Precisely because it is disconnected from any larger syntagmatic context, it is literally inexplicable. It may clarify Petulia's antic vandalism, permitting a glimpse of what we may now see as the destructive undercurrent of her playfulness, but it does so by obscuring her motive and raising new narrative questions. Is the viewer to understand her act of vandalism as random whimsy or as the harbinger of yet unacknowledged desperation? Why does Archie respond with such equanimity to her explanation of how she acquired the tuba, which—especially since he is not privy to the explanatory intercut—must surely seem to him mystifying? Such questions would not present themselves with much force if it were not for the intrusions of the intercuts, which thus complicate what might otherwise have functioned as a simple plot-device, yet another instance of Petulia's "kookiness," of the "I-Love-Lucy jazz" Archie sees as characteristic of her.

In this instance, the stylistic excess of the inserts derives from what may be seen as their gratuitous character. In the film as a whole, to be sure, the inserts participate in an overarching rhetoric of the uncanny. The inserts use repetition to set plot events in a relation of familiarity and strangeness that draws upon that rhetoric in a very literal way. Yet that rhetoric appears for much of the film to lack any real narrative grounding. The inserts seem initially accountable as signifiers of the trauma of Oliver, the boy whose accident is represented in the first several inserts. Yet the quality of portentous inevitability, of ominous foreboding, about the film's flashback structure implies a large, unmasterable trauma belied by the handling of the Oliver subplot. Clearly, in the terms of the narrative, Oliver is shown to have been badly abused, and his accident is indeed caused by the negligence of those who exploit him, but because he is shown in the story's present tense to have recovered from the past accident, and because the film's rhetoric makes much of his spunky resilience, his fate hardly seems to call for the inexorable fatalism, the intensely affective aspect of the film's structure. In fact, the structure of the film works out self-consciously a complex dynamic of repression and displacement dependent on an elision of Oliver's fate and Petulia's plight as an abused wife. Only halfway through the film does it become clear that the movie is a narrative of domestic abuse, locating such abuse in the context of more general abuses of commodity culture by paralleling the figures of Petulia and Oliver as subjects of that culture. Indeed, the film is structured, through its use of inserts, to lead the viewer to mis-readings of the Petulia character as Archie misreads her, as an irre-sponsibly free-spirited "kook," only then to draw attention to the nature of this misreading, to the misrecognition of signs of abuse in a culture in which abuse itself occurs in function of commodification. The film's denial of conventional mastery to the viewer through its self-conscious narrative patterns serves the effect of underlining the film's real but formally displaced subject, the repression of suffering in consumer culture. In the film's last sequence, a pregnant Petulia, splayed on an operating table, accosts a nurse in a tentatively bitter, frightened tone: "I thought you said I wasn't going to suffer!" The nurse responds matter-of-factly, "You're not suffering." Positioned before the emotional intensity of the final encounter between Archie and Petulia, this exchange seems to be merely a throwaway dialogue, but in the context of the film as a whole, it should be seen to have a forceful thematic resonance. It crystallizes what the densely ironic, self-conscious rhetoric of the whole film has taken shape around—the denial of Petulia's suffering.

Genre and Class in the Neo-Screwball

In these terms, in spite of the figure's association with an aggressively "mod" hipsterism, Petulia nonetheless emerges as a figure out of 1940s Hollywood melodrama, the long-suffering female victim represented through a rhetoric of pathos. The last shot of the film bears out such a reading of the character, fraught as it is with a quality of desolation and loss that has the potential effect—in its close-up image of Petulia's face as she calls Archie's name and is muzzled by an oxygen mask—of fetishizing the character's suffering. In spite of the film's postmodern surface, to be sure, it is characterized as well by a heightened emotional climate, a psychologically nuanced affective structure that might seem in direct contrast to the film's seemingly dominant tone of corrosive, misanthropic, broadly sketched satire. In fact, though, the film is dis-tinctly representative of New Hollywood rhetorics of formal self-con-sciousness in occupying a position that might be justifiably called *post-generic*, assembling the shards of various seemingly incompatible genres and relying for affective force on the conjunction of these multi-ple conventions themselves. Marketed alternately as a sophisticated comedy or a wry drama, *Petulia* fits comfortably into none of the avail-able generic niches of Hollywood discourse. Advertisements for the film tended to present this generic instability as the film's selling point by playing up the film's purported "sophistication"—redolent of that of art-cinema per se—but at the same time they were at pains to offer some generic identifiers, however intermixed, through an appeal to the recognizable category of the bittersweet "comedy-drama." The marginalization of *Petulia* from the emergent narrative of New Hollywood filmmaking is curious since the film answers both the crucial imperatives that determine that narrative. The narrative, like that of New Hollywood's assimilation of such formal devices as the New Wave flashback, is contingent upon an understanding of forms, in this case generic forms, as evolving from a zero-degree of sincere expression, through manifestations of various crises, to a point of achieved self-consciousness. The narrative thus depends on a contrast between "naive" genre pieces that reproduce received conventions and ideologies, those identified with the classical model, and self-reflexive genre films that manipulate and thereby subvert already discredited conventions and ideologies, those identifed with the art-cinema. With its mercurially shifting tones and flamboyantly "arty" style, *Petulia* clearly participates in the self-consciousness this paradigm demands.

Hierarchies of taste that produce such narratives, however, tend to marginalize the very genres in which *Petulia* has its roots, the "screwball" comedy of the 1930s and the "woman's melodrama" of the 1940s.[5] Largely absent from respectable film histories of the 1960s and 1970s, the thirties screwball comedy and the forties romantic melodrama were spectacularly rediscovered in the 1980s. Thomas Schatz's influential *Hollywood Genres* (1981) devoted a detailed chapter to the screwball comedy, putting it on the generic map just as Stanley Cavell's *Pursuits of Happiness* exhaustively demonstrated the genre's roots not only in folk myth and high comedy but, less expectedly, in Western philosophy. In spite of the reach of such underpinnings, both studies acknowledged the troubled place of screwball comedy within standard taxonomies of genre. Schatz accounts for this marginality by arguing that the genre lacks the "easily identifiable elements of setting and iconography" (151) of, say, the western or the gangster film. Moreover, if theorists from Robert Warshow to Christian Metz could readily trace the permutations of the western from its gung-ho roustabouting to its melancholy self-consciousness, how could a genre that thrives on forms of sentiment give way to the corrosion of postclassical cynicism? Can one imagine, in other words, an *anti*screwball comedy as readily as one can imagine, in Warshow's phrase, an antiwestern?

More to the point, what specific iconography the genre does offer is decidedly affirmative, further troubling the postclassical valuation

FIGURE 9. Screwball vs. Melodrama: Petulia's final entrapment. Courtesy Museum of Modern Art, New York.

of critique. In Schatz's account, the genre is demarcated by "a style of behavior (reflected in certain camerawork and editing techniques)" (151) that valorizes spirit, play, romance. Even if the genre animates tensions of class and gender in its frolicsome tales of heiresses meeting reporters, photographers, or absent-minded professors, it dependably resolves these tensions within the framework of the classical model. Indeed, Cavell sees the genre as essentially one of recovery or of rediscovery. In Schatz's view, such films "reassured Depression audiences that the filthy rich were, after all, just folks like you and me" (150). If the demystifying thrust seen in much New Hollywood discourse eventually to overtake the classical western could be seen as somehow latent even in the genre's earliest forms, it is clear that to coax a similar critique of ideology from the screwball comedy would on the contrary violate the deepest impulses of the genre.

Petulia attempts to achieve its critical vision within the terms of the screwball comedy, manipulating the conventions of the genre. The film's first shot, under the credits, is of the blue crescent of a half-moon from which a keening ambulance emerges, undermining from the start conventionally romantic iconography through such mordant juxtaposition. In the first sequence, Petulia and Archie may very well "meet cute," as per the requirements of the genre, but the elements of the uncanny already at work in the structure of the sequence disturb whatever reassuring generic familiarity might be the result. The plot of the film clearly reverses the formula of the screwball comedy. Like many crucial examples of the genre, it hinges on marital crisis and a reaffirmation of marriage, but in the event the nature of the crisis is diffused and the reaffirmation presented as only one more phase in the repetitious, destructive cycle the film's plot traces. *Why* does Petulia pursue an affair with Archie? Why does she return to David at the end of the film? At one level, the film's cool suspension of such questions, readable initially in the context of what the film wants to present as the enigma of Petulia's identity, finally serves as a decisive marker of its "adult" "sophistication." Sixties-style hipsters, after all, do not need the clear motivations for their actions classical cinema formerly required, and if the viewer is tempted to invoke decidedly antiscrewball concepts—such as those of pathology or sadomasochism, for instance—to name characters' motivations, this serves less to sever the connection of *Petulia* to tradition than to cast, in the standard fashion of New Hollywood discourse, a retrospective pall over the tradition itself. The genre of the screwball comedy has ordinarily been demarcated according to problems of motivation: what makes its characters "screwball" in the first place is precisely the free-style, improvisatory, and spontaneously associational quality of their behavior, and what troubles the relation of screwball comedy itself to the classical Hollywood tradition that produces it is the resulting narratological slipknots. *Petulia* reveals the unpredictable action of the screwball comedy to be not, as Cavell claims, the basis of a sort of idealist, liberating acknowledgment of self by other—where in *Bringing Up Baby* (Hawks, 1937), for instance, Susan instantly perceives David's Cavellian "essence" by sheer dint of instinct, just as Petulia does Archie's—but, rather, rooted in severe psychological lack or limitation.

The film's handling of thematics of class, inherited from the high screwball, similarly answers postclassical paradigms. Class antagonisms in the high screwball tend to be presented fairly schematically, either opposing images of wealth through starkly contrasting figures of the "good" rich and the "bad" rich, as in *It Happened One Night* (Capra, 1934), or alternatively, dissolving initially sharp class differences altogether into an affectional union designed precisely to negotiate these differences, as in *You Can't Take It with You* (Capra, 1937). In either case, however, this schematism dependably functions to reassure audiences that the filthy rich were after all just folks, allowing the films to revel in the (presumably) visually pleasurable spectacle of conspicuous consumption while falling back on the twin safety nets of satire and populism. Echoing Cavell, Robert Ray states baldly that "in its purest form, screwball comedy ignored class divisions to develop almost allegorical schemas of reconciliation" (87).

In keeping with convention, *Petulia* formulates class divisions around emblematic families, here the Danners and the Mendozas, the Hispanic family to whom Petulia entrusts Oliver after his accident. The Danners signify the sterile rich clearly enough, and indeed the rage David directs at Petulia seems to result from fear of his own literal sterility, his inability (until the end of the film) to produce an heir to the Danner line—itself a class-based issue in the terms of the film. The Mendozas, however, lack the compensatory earthiness the classical screwball comedy ordinarily confers on its images of the poor. Clearly, the Danners are exploitive and the Mendozas exploited, but, in the terms of the film, the Mendozas are not directly exploited by the Danners. Whatever motivates Petulia's choice of the Mendozas as Oliver's custodian, she appears to have made the choice with Oliver's interests in mind, without intending to exploit the family. Refusing to link the two representative families in a direct social relation of exploitation—an individual wealthy family taking advantage of an individual impoverished one—the film shows them both embedded in the same social structure of domination.

The houses of either family are visually constructed as identical domestic spaces, loveless and eerily vacated. In their visual textures, both homes are presented in images of dead space—depthless white walls and featureless backgrounds, drained of color or life. The first shot of the Danner home is especially telling, and directly evokes visually the parallel scene of Petulia's visit to the Mendozas. The first shot, a disorienting low-angle pivoting to follow characters' movement, shows David in the foreground, carelessly holding the phone on which he has just called Archie, whose voice is heard through the receiver. A distracted Petulia enters and circles David, who speaks to her with forced cheer, a kind of characteristic, gleeful sadism, as he blithely hangs up the phone. The white glare suffusing the shot is brightened further by the costuming of both characters in white and by the use of a lens filter that imparts a grey-white haze to the scene. The sequence at the Mendozas, similar in visual design, is similar too in its manipulations of that design to suggest repressed or unspoken content in the scene's dramatic materials. As Petulia puts groceries in the cupboards, Mr. Mendoza reaches past her for a glass of water, leaning closer toward Petulia and gazing at her with carnal deliberation. She turns away and the camera pivots to follow her, stopping abruptly on Mrs. Mendoza and Oliver framed in the doorway. At this point the shot ends with a cut to Archie's apartment and the scene of Polo's visit. Ending the shot on confrontation, with Oliver and Mrs. Mendoza casting accusatory gazes at Petulia, Lester reasserts narrative questions about Petulia's relation to Oliver, mysteriously implicating her in the accident.

Both of these domestic spaces are presented as otherworldly, curiously detached from their environs. When Archie goes to the Mendozas to deliver Petulia's message, he must navigate directionless passages to reach their house. In spite of the crowded conditions of the housing development where the Mendozas live, row houses snaking across a squat hill under an explosively artificial sky, the scene emphasizes the depopulated quality of the neighborhood and the isolation of the house. Where the Mendozas' is austere and barren, the Danners' house is lavish and imposing, embowered in metallic verdancy, yet it too is accessible only by empty though overgrown labyrinths, as well as by a mechanical lift serving as a kind of portage back to the world at large. Here too, emphasizing the parallels, Lester includes a scene showing Archie's frustration to traverse the space between the house and its surroundings.

This mitigated class-consciousness devolves upon the film's more general conception of contemporary consumer culture. The parallels the

FIGURE 10. Postmodern geographies in *Petulia*. Courtesy Museum of Modern Art, New York.

film proposes of the Danners and the Mendozas, as opposed to the conventional contrasts among classes in the screwball comedy, are rooted in the film's conception of emergent possibilities of social interpellation that, at least superficially, exceed the edicts of class as such. In the film's terms, class divisions break down in the wake of new possibilities of relation to culture itself. In "Periodizing the '60s," Fredric Jameson similarly argues that the decade produced a historical shift from conceptions of identity in specifically class-based terms to conceptions of identity rooted in cultural affiliations and declared allegiances:

> The '60s was . . . the period in which all these "natives" became human beings, and this internally as well as externally: those inner colonized of the first world—"minorities," marginals, and women—fully as much as its external subjects and official "natives." . . . It is, however, important to situate the emergence of these new collective "identities" or "subjects of history" in the historical situation which made that emergence possible, and in particular to relate the emergence of these new social and political categories (the colonized, race, marginality, gender and the like) to something like a crisis in the more universal category that had hitherto seemed to subsume all the varieties of social resistance, namely the classical conception of social class. (181)

For Jameson, the countercultural production of new subjectivities in the '60s developed from a historical shift in the politics of world domination. The '60s subject, now defined by race, gender, or some other form of cultural/political—as opposed to economic—identity, is the subject triumphantly "liberated" from past colonial domination. This liberationist bent of conventional '60s cultural rhetoric is one of the most prominent objects of satire in *Petulia*. To be sure, the film conceives of '60s culture as promising forms of social, countercultural liberation—"women's lib" or the new freedom of the Third World—only as a guise for more localized, renewed, and pervasive forms of domination that claim their power precisely by seeking refuge under the rubric of culture as such.

The character of Oliver is important to examine in this regard. Associated circuitously with a kind of glorified Third-World-ism, the Mexican Oliver attaches himself to David and Petulia when they are on a tourist's jaunt to Tijuana. On the trip home, David's fury is stirred when he interprets Oliver's presence as a consequence of Petulia's contemptuous assertion of David's inability to produce a child ("He's not mine!" screams David. "That's why you brought him here, isn't it?"). While treating Oliver with oleaginous declarations of affection, giving him the gift of a watch, David terrorizes Petulia with the threat of violence, positioning the boy as a counter between them in their sadomasochistic relationship. As Petulia tries to put the boy on a train to send him home, he runs off and is struck by a car. Petulia's guilt over the incident furnishes its melodramatic edge, but in much larger terms, the incident figures characteristically the power dynamics the film sees as pervasive in '60s culture, dynamics the film links not directly to issues of class but to forms of individual desire, of individual identity, seen as *culturally* determined in new ways. Oliver's presence at the Tijuana tourist-trap, where Petulia calls him a "little hustler," bespeaks what the film sees as his determining status as a *product* of the society-of-the-spectacle, exploiting the tourist-trap even as its very existence fundamentally determines his own inevitable exploitation; and his exaggerated valuation of the watch David gives him, a kitschy American trinket that clearly signifies for him some access to cultural authority, positions him as an avid *subject* of commodity culture. Though he can be seen as at fault in the accident that hospitalizes him—he attaches himself to Petulia, after all, just as she attaches herself to Archie—the film would have us see, rather, how his exploitation is made possible by his own desire, how Petulia and David achieve a form of domination over him by manipulating the desires predetermined by the society-of-the-spectacle. In other words, though Oliver is one of the newly legitimated subjects of '60s culture, and though the film makes much of his own sense of his autonomy, his function in the narrative is to illustrate the role of culture itself in new social relations of domination. Jameson argues that the '60s may well historically have written an end to colonialism as such, but this only, in his view, precipitated a possibly more insidious neocolonialism: "the end of one kind of domination but evidently also the invention and construction of a new kind—symbolically, something like the replacement of the British Empire by the International Monetary Fund" (Jameson, 184). In its vision of a society determined at every level by specfically *cultural* forms of domination, *Petulia* too recognizes the migration of domination from its former harbor in immediate, physical acts of political violence or in material class structures to its final refuge in symbolic structures of violence and dematerialized forms of cultural power.

Hyperreality and the Logic of the Simulacra

The flashback structure of *Petulia* replaces the coherent subjectivity of the classical text with the alienated, estranged subjectivities produced in and by postmodern American culture. It is important to note here not only the way in which the film's structure insists upon determining connections of cultural forms upon human subjectivity, but the manner in which this conception infuses the film's vision of '60s American culture as ascendant hyperreality. Even more to the point, that culture is defined in explicitly *national* terms, defamiliarized as specifically *American* by being presented systematically through the points-of-view of the text's parallel "foreigners," the Euro-Brit Petulia and the nominal Third-Worlder Oliver. Attracted to and fascinated by the alien culture of hyperreal America, Petulia and Oliver are distinct from the other characters in the film in their perception of that culture from a position of estrangement, a position with which the film affiliates itself in order to achieve its effects of defamiliarization. Projected as Other by virtue of their status as "foreigners," Petulia and Oliver are nonetheless figures of intense identification in the film's emotional economy. They are thus constructed, as characters, according to a complex conflation of an imagined alterity, by which they are set apart from the otherwise general sway of hyperreal America, and a presumed identification, by which they are positioned as focalizers of many of the text's responses to the images of American culture it generates. This dynamic of identification with what has already been defined as *difference*, while retaining a foothold in the realm of *sameness* that is the only position from which that difference can be projected, defines the text's semiotics of hyperreal '60s American culture.

The film is constructed around a number of set-pieces that represent '60s America as a virtual Disneyland of the mind, a Baudrillard-like festival of simulated realities. The hotel where Petulia and Archie tryst, the park in which they meet again, the paralleled tourist-traps of Tijuana and Alcatraz, the penguin exhibit where they have a final reunion, even the hospital where Archie works, one of the film's main settings, are all presented through a lens of flamboyant estrangement, of uncanny defamiliarization, as hypertrophied spaces of displaced realities. In a sequence in Golden Gate park, a guard hawks "Our Nipponkai souvenir pagoda where every item is the Real McCoy." The hotel, like the hospital, is shot through wide-angle lenses in monochromatic color, emphasizing brilliance of surface, and both spaces are characterized by a surfeit of technology that replaces even the most insignificant human activity and alienates humans from even the appearance of any immediate relation to one another. In the hotel, for example, the desk clerk appears only on a television monitor, giving instructions from some removed, virtual space. Typically, Petulia delights in the hotel's hypermodern design and hypertechnologized devices—stepping gleefully in and out of the bathroom, for example, to test the auto-matic light—while Archie remains indifferent to and even unaware of them. Throughout the film, to be sure, Petulia and Oliver take note of the very attributes of this cultural space—its surplus, its excess, its fas-cinating weirdness—to which the film most avidly directs the viewer's attention but of which all other characters remain more or less oblivi-ous. Thus, the film presents American culture as an alien landscape of hyperreality by avowing its own identification with the characters who, putatively, are themselves alien to that landscape.

Petulia and Oliver are objects of the text's most intense affective investments not only in this dynamic of identification, but in their par-allel status in the narrative as "victims" of commodity culture who become themselves objects (rather than the subjects they aspire to be) of the society-of-the-spectacle that so fascinates them. The oppressive conversion of experience into spectacle is felt in virtually every scene of *Petulia*, but nowhere more forcefully than in the sequences of the discovery of Petulia's brutalization and the aftermath of Oliver's acci-dent, paralleled by their placement in the narrative and by similar edit-ing patterns in either scene. In both cases, the emphasis in the sequence is on the failures of response of a gathered crowd of insen-sate, gawking onlookers, revealing the suffering of the characters as material for yet another enactment of the process of spectacularization. The key theorist of the society-of-the-spectacle (before Baudrillard, that is, and with a quite different set of assumptions), Guy Debord, emphasizes the simultaneous plenitude and alienation that define spectacle as a social form. The procession of spectacles that organizes *Petulia*, a veritable pageant of postmodern spectacle, is characterized by its surface richness and amplitude, its often overwhelming visual force, and the characters of Petulia and Oliver are at once most respon-sive to that quality of plenitude and most damaged by those effects of alienation. It is significant, indeed, that Debord describes spectacle according to a fairly explicit logic of the uncanny, linked to metaphors of *home*: "The externality of the spectacle in relation to the active man appears in the fact that his own gestures are no longer his but those of another who represents them to him. This is why the spectator feels at home nowhere, because the spectacle is everywhere."[6] In Lester's med-itation on the society-of-the-spectacle, the "foreigners" are most attracted to spectacle because its delusory qualities, its status as pro-jected reality that displaces reality as such, generalize their own feel-ings of foreignness from the culture that spectacle produces.

For Debord, spectacle is a latter-day, post-Marxist form of all-embracing false-consciousness:

> The spectacle is ideology par excellence, because it exposes and manifests in its fullness the essence of all ideological systems: the impoverishment, servitude and negation of real life. The spectacle is materially "the expression of the separation and estrangement between man and man." (Debord, note 215)

The critical vision of '60s culture on offer in *Petulia*, too, clearly posits the society-of-the-spectacle in terms of a generalized cultural expansion that serves to conceal a loss of unity and a growing estrangement—that is, indeed, the final form of domination itself. In the terms of the film, domination, far from being linked directly to class conflict, is thoroughly localized in "private" forms of relation, in the phenomenon of "domestic abuse," where violence is sanctioned precisely by being made private; and, at the same time, it is thoroughly generalized in the "domination of society itself . . . which reaches its absolute fulfillment in the spectacle" (Debord, note 36). The extreme poles at work in the structure of domination that the film finds in '60s American culture are themselves causes of the ascendant hyperreality the film sees, embracing such extremity, as having overtaken that culture.

The treatment of specific images of '60s counterculture in the film reveals both the film's conception of spectacle as false consciousness and its dual relation to structures of identity/difference. Far from being heralded as an authentically liberationist alternative to oppressive establishmentarianism, the countercultural currents the film represents are most virulently demonized as poisonous, threatening, and alienating. If the film imagines the populace of San Francisco as a horde of complacent bourgeois on the one hand, it envisions its countercultural counterpart as a mob of drugged hippies on the other. Grotesque close-ups of rock stars leering into the camera and offhanded glimpses of spiritless fads, as in the shot of Archie tattooing a young woman splayed on a hospital bed, represent the counterculture as such in images of carnivalesque monstrosity. Allying itself with the rhetoric of a countercinema that defines New Hollywood discourse, *Petulia* nonetheless demonizes the very counterculture that might be seen as that cinema's natural ally in the more general sphere of culture at large. Identifying with the putatively "alien" figures in the narrative in order to achieve its critique of dominant culture, the film at the same time vilifies the countercultural milieu in which such critique might have been seen to originate.

In spite of the film's sustained critique of the society-of-the-spectacle, its representation of '60s America is finally less in tune with the work of Debord than with that of another contemporary the-

orist, the ecstatically dyspeptic laureate of the hyperreal, Jean Baudrillard, and this attunement is importantly bound up with ideas
about simulation, origination, and the relation of these two terms.
For Baudrillard, simulation differs from imitation in that the latter
implies the reproduction of an original that both respects the
integrity and attempts to represent the essential attributes of that
original, whereas simulation reproduces its object in a manner that
denies that object's "origin" elsewhere, or its possession of any prior,
essential being. Where Debord's conception of the society-of-the-
spectacle retains the underpinnings of Marxist materialism, Baudrillard's ideas about hyperreality and the precession of the simulacra proceed from a wholesale critique of Marxist thought as itself
idealist in its bases. For Debord, spectacle is nothing but an expanded
form of commodity fetishism, still redolent, as in the quotation above
(note 215 in Debord), of the *material* relations among people. For Baudrillard, spectacle transforms commodity into pure representation,
replacing the materiality of commodities with the simulation of
material reality. Indeed, Baudrillard's notions of the hyperreal and
the simulacrum derive from a rejection of the Marxist distinction
between use-value and exchange-value. In classical Marxism, this
distinction underwrites ideas about social justice, where a society
based on "real" use-value, answering the actual needs of its citizens,
is found just, while the capitalist imperative of exchange-value,
transforming use-value and displacing such human needs in favor of
the shifting needs of an artificial market, compromises possibilities
for social justice. In Baudrillard's thought, this appeal to a "real"
basis of social relation is itself seen to be founded in mystification,
since "actual" use-value will always be subordinate to and consequent of ideological constructions of value as such. In mass society,
according to Baudrillard, the "original" as a gauge of the "real" and
the "actual" is obsolete—and happily so, since its dominion only
allowed the ascension to power of those who were able to gain access
to it—and the Marxist distinction between use-value and exchange-
value, assuming an illusory access to the real in order to instate the
authority of its own ideology, participated as fully as any representation in the logic of simulation—in the logic, to be sure, of "repres-
sive simulation" (*Selected Writings*, 114). On this basis, Baudrillard
rejects Marxist ideology-critique (like Debord's) as well as either any
nostalgia for some superior state before the ascension of hyperreality
or any utopia after hyperreality's exposure as false consciousness:
"The concept of critique emerged in the West at the same time as
political economy and, as the quintessence of Enlightenment ratio-

nality, is perhaps only the subtle, long-term expression of the system's expanded reproduction" (*Selected Writings*, 116), Baudrillard comments on the former point; while, on the latter, he argues:

> When the real is no longer what it used to be, nostalgia assumes its full meaning. There is a proliferation of myths of origin and signs of reality; of second-hand truth, objectivity and authenticity. There is an escalation of the true, of lived experience. . . . And there is a panic-stricken production of the real and the referential, above and parallel to the panic of material production. This is how simulation appears in the phase that concerns us: a strategy of the real, neo-real, and hyperreal, whose universal double is a strategy of deterrence. (*Selected Writings*, 171)

The logic of the simulacra alone, in Baudrillard's terms, circumvents what can thus no longer be called the "false consciousness" of the Real. The simulacrum overtakes the position of the real even as it obliterates the power of the real, refusing reference to a definable origin, yet its uncanny power comes from a structure that is itself as simulatory as the content of its images: though no longer determined as representation by the relation of an image to its original, the simulacrum continues to produce ecstasy by mimicking even that relation, consolidating its own hallucinatory power by asserting the resemblance of the real to itself.[7] It is no wonder, given the inescapability of hyperreality in postmodern culture as Baudrillard defines it, that he recommends an ecstatic surrender to its lure, for whatever pleasures such surrender may yield.

The attunement to Baudrillard's thinking that may be seen in *Petulia*'s representation of hyperreal America resides in the film's gravid and delirious participation in the styles of the hyperreal. The film's kaleidoscopic, wildly lumino-kinetic visual style, with its distinctively postmodern self-consciousness, signifies on one level the surrender to the force of the hyperreal that Baudrillard opts for. Clearly, the film delights in the visual pleasures of hyperreal space-and-time just as Petulia and Oliver take pleasure in the simulated commodities of the society-of-the-spectacle (Oliver's fetishization of the watch, Petulia's association with high fashion[8]). The film ends by defining these two characters' pleasurable reveling in hyperreality as a form of masochism: it results in Oliver's accident, while Petulia becomes not only the victim of her abusive husband, but is made to internalize guilt over his violence against her as a function of her position in the society-of-the-spectacle. Her desire for David is presented as another example of her attraction to the beauty of American hyper-real artifice: "You were the most beautiful thing I'd ever seen," she tells him. "When I first saw you, I thought, 'He can't be real, he must be one of those beautiful plastic gadgets the Americans make so well.'" Yet, though the effect of this may be to articulate a kind of Debordian critique of spectacular hyperreality, such critique coexists with a decidedly non-nostalgic, Baudrillardic sense of the lure of the simulacra. The film may well see '60s America as a decadent culture whose fleeting ephemera nonetheless retains the beauty of its passing weirdness, but it does not present American mass culture as, say, a degraded version of British high-culture—a strategy it might well have fallen into given Lester's association (albeit troubled) with British art-cinema, especially since the film to some extent works out these national/cultural interconnections thematically through the character of Petulia. Yet though Petulia looks on the spectacle of American cul-ture with the Nabokovian estrangement of the detached "foreigner" (and the relation between this film's vision of American culture and that of Nabokov's novel *Lolita* [1955] seems more than passing), she longs to participate in that culture, not to hold it at bay through her "alien" status as a Britisher.

It is at the level of visual style that the film's deepest affinities with the ethos of hyperreality remain clearest. Its intensely affective gestures of identification with the figure of Petulia notwithstanding, the overarching rhetoric of the film's postmodern style aligns it deci-sively with the properties of spectacle and simulacra that it nonethe-less presents as deciding her unhappy fate. In this sense, the film's own identifications are split between the fetishized main character and the very milieu that, in the terms of the film, oppresses her in spite of, or because of, her wish to be part of it. The ecstatic, hyperreal design of the film's style may simply amplify the emotional circuitry figured around the Petulia character, then, expressing a pleasurable engage-ment with hyperreal culture that mirrors Petulia's own. At the same time, however, it complicates the film's relation to the issue of cultural difference as such: Petulia is the demonized national other with whom the film asserts identification, yet, in its wholesale adoption of the styles of American hyperreality—presented as strange, uncanny, and gorgeous all at once—it deeply invests as well in the very formation that demonizes her.

This dynamic, in turn, duplicates the film's relation to art-cinema practices and to the rhetoric of the New Hollywood itself. Internaliz-ing these practices, the film yet continues to exploit them in order to differentiate itself from standard Hollywood fare; incorporated as constitutive elements into the textual system, they yet remain signifiers of otherness. Simulating otherness, the film distances itself from the Hollywood cinema by which it remains defined. It allies itself with these "foreign" practices, then, precisely to distance itself from the institutional practices to which it remains bound in a relation of sameness. Though the film internalizes critique of Hollywood commodification by taking commodity-culture as its subject, it nonetheless accepts its position within that culture by continuing to simulate its most distinctive forms of representation. In juxtaposing the latter with the practices of art-cinema which the text also internalizes, the film thus simultaneously denies the "origin" of these practices in art-cinema as such. In these ways, *Petulia* illustrates perhaps as clearly as any Hollywood film of the time how the logic of hyperreal simulation underlies the emergence of New Hollywood forms.

Mythic Self-Consciousness and Homosexual Panic in the New Hollywood: *One Flew over the Cuckoo's Nest* and *Deliverance*

I n film criticism, the formation of the New Hollywood tends to be understood structurally in two basic ways. One way of understanding it is in terms of the opening-up of the previously closed institutional system, admitting *formal* practices that had hitherto been excluded. The other way is in terms of an evolving revisionism at work in the system's own logics of internal coherence, such that the set of myths that had previously sustained the Classical Hollywood model gradually undergo a kind of systematic self-critique. The previous chapter examined the first of these assumptions through an analysis of *Petulia* as a representative text. This chapter engages the other assumption. In the terms of this assumption, Classical Hollywood is predominantly mythic, while the New Hollywood is defined precisely by its exposure, critique, and presumed eradication of formerly powerful myths. This truism conforms closely enough to the historical evolution of Hollywood filmmaking that some version of it underlies most accounts of the Hollywood tradition. Moreover, such accounts of New Hollywood filmmaking traditionally associate a kind of "native" myth with American film traditions and the encroaching, "foreign" self-consciousness that would challenge such myth with European art-cinemas.

It must immediately be pointed out that such assumptions are, like so many modern definitional imperatives, themselves bound up with at least one clearly recognizable myth, that of the dark age brought to triumphant enlightenment by regimes of knowledge steadily evolving toward superior, ideal forms. To recognize a myth's content, of course, is not to liberate oneself from the grasp of its form—especially since one way mythologies retain their power is by declaring themselves *outside* form, by setting themselves up as naturalized, eternalized, collectively shared stories that remain in a general and inapprehensible circulation that exceeds any of the particular forms they may assume. A version of a myth may be easy enough to identify in its specific contours, but as Mircea Eliade has argued, myth itself remains, at least in its own self-projections, timeless and outside history (Eliade, 36–37; see also, in general, Barthes, *Mythologies*). The enlightenment critique of mythology proceeds by claiming to humiliate this self-definition, to violate myth's sanctuary in archetype, to reveal its origins in time, and thus to restore myth to the history it could only pretend to escape and to expose such pretense as itself the mark of mythic false-consciousness.

Yet history itself, as Lévi-Strauss was not the first to point out, participates in a structure that mimics that of myth in its counterposing of the universal and the local: "History, which claims to be universal is still only a juxtaposition of a few local histories within which (and between which) very much more is left out than is put in" (*Savage Mind*, 258). Like myth—history's double, its shadow-form—history seizes its explanatory power by allying itself with universality and thus concealing the gaps in its narratives. Merely to expose the exclusionist nature of history, to reveal its gaps, is not effectively to humiliate history itself, which always retains that power because of this strategic alliance with "timelessness." The affinity of myth and history leads Lévi-Strauss, like Adorno and Horkheimer in a different tradition, to reject the simple binarism of naive myth and enlightened self-consciousness, opting instead for a conception of ritual experience imbued simultaneously by sacraments of myth and edicts of history, a dialectical conception in which the presumptions of enlightenment continue to be formed by the very myths enlightenment claims to oust.[1]

In high modernism, structures of myth were called upon repeatedly—in the work of Joyce, Pound, Eliot, and others—in order to reveal by contrast the quotidian, random, or degraded qualities of modern experience. Uses of myth especially in the work of Eliot or Pound signify the neoclassical bent of modernist aesthetics, alluding to traditions of antiquity in order to preserve learned heritage from the soiled textures of contemporary life. Yet the very juxtaposition of classical mythology with contemporary representation, necessary to shore up the former, threatens this aspiration. Imposed from above with austere or aggressive irony, such structures of myth frequently functioned in modernist texts as *formal* correlatives of the texts' content, often rendering that content opaque. "Myth" thus emerges in such texts, from Joyce's buoyantly remote echoes of Homer to Eliot's flinty reconstructions of Frazer, as the lingering aura of a "high" tradition feared lost. In that sense, it is to be distinguished from the unconscious myth-making imputed to the forces of mass culture, which in fact in its protective relegation to the level of form and in its critical functions, it guards against. To be sure, a key theme of *Ulysses*, for instance, lies in that novel's contrast of pop-culture myth-making with high-culture mythology, the former manifested in the novel's *content* as shared gossip, circulated rumor, public speculation, or mass-media legend-mongering, the latter manifested in its *form* as densely woven allusion. If *Ulysses* can be taken as exemplary, it illustrates the modernist critique of myth-making as mass naiveté and the modernist valorization of formal self-consciousness as a reaction against and corrective to popular myth-making. It also illustrates, however, the intricate connections between these textual levels, producing a kind of "mythic self-consciousness" at work in modernism.

The dialectical concept of mythic self-consciousness, in its refusal to separate or simply oppose these terms, is useful in understanding the break between Classical Hollywood and New Hollywood forms. Such a concept can serve as a counterbalance to histories that have, on the one hand, overstated that break by too readily accepting the purely mythic character of Classical Hollywood and the fully self-conscious nature of New Hollywood film; or, on the other, understated it by claiming myth as a determining condition of Hollywood ideology as such, and thereby asserting an untroubled continuity between Classical Hollywood and New Hollywood film.[2] The former approach errs in denying the operations of rhetorics of self-consciousness in Classical Hollywood and of persistent rhetorics of mythology in New Hollywood film; the latter errs in denying historical change in the evolution of Hollywood as a cultural institution. To be sure, the concept of mythic self-consciousness lends itself especially well to discussion of New Hollywood if one assumes that New Hollywood cinema is decisively characterized by a gradual opening-up at some levels, admitting terms previously excluded from its system, together with an effort to retain monologic closure at other levels. With its suggestion of competing, even potentially contradictory systems in dialogue—that of myth and that of a presumably demystifying self-reflexive textuality—mythic self-consciousness duplicates the structure of New Hollywood textuality itself. We can, moreover, begin with the schematic alignment of Hollywood with mass-cultural myth-making and European art-cinema with modernist self-consciousness, but if we shift the emphasis from the *content* of myth as such to the structure of the dialectic between myth and self-consciousness, we will see that neither term of the binarism can be securely insulated from the other.

The choice of texts in this chapter represents films drawing quite self-consciously upon traditional American mythologies but directed by filmmakers from European art-cinemas. Milos Forman, the director of *One Flew over the Cuckoo's Nest* (1975), emigrated to Hollywood from Czechoslovakia in the wake of the Prague Spring of 1968. A central figure in the "Czech Renaissance" of the 1960s, Forman earned a reputation in such films as *Fireman's Ball* (1963) and *Loves of a Blonde* (1967) for keen observation of self-contained communities in the style of a mordantly earthy naturalism. The director of *Deliverance* (1972), John Boorman began his career in England with a free-spirited, post–New Wave pastiche with the rock group the Dave Clark Five in a riff on Richard Lester's Beatles films, *Catch Us If You Can* (1965). In their Hollywood films, both Forman and Boorman have evinced continued interest in the structures of traditional American mythologies. In Forman's work, this interest has manifested itself in his being drawn to material about myths of American self-identity, more specifically myths of American counterculture, in such films as *Taking Off* (1971), *Hair* (1978), *Ragtime* (1981), and *The People vs. Larry Flynt* (1996). For Boorman, this interest appears in his systematic deconstructions—congruent with his status as a New Hollywood maverick—of traditional Hollywood genres, from the neo-noir *Point Blank* (1967) to the postwar war-movie *Hell in the Pacific* (1968) or the posthorror horror film, *Exorcist II/The Heretic* (1977). Significantly, both filmmakers integrate this fascination with American mythologies in their careers with periodic returns to more traditional art-cinema products, such as *Amadeus* (1983) or *Valmont* (1992) by Forman or *The Emerald Forest* (1983) and *Hope and Glory* (1987) by Boorman.

The particular subjects of *One Flew over the Cuckoo's Nest* and *Deliverance* introduce a final important term in this chapter, the thematics of homosexual panic. It is no coincidence that, as a rhetoric of mythic self-consciousness comes more and more to shape Hollywood discourses throughout the 1970s, the theme of homosexual panic returns obsessively in definitive New Hollywood texts. Indeed, a list of important films of the time reads like a virtual catalogue of the theme: *Midnight Cowboy* (Schlesinger, 1969), *Butch Cassidy and the Sundance Kid* (Hill, 1969) or *The Sting* (Hill, 1973), *MASH* (Altman, 1970) or *McCabe and Mrs. Miller* (Altman, 1971), *Little Fauss and Big Halsey* (Furie, 1970) or *The Last Picture Show* (Bogdanovich, 1972), the "Godfather" films of Coppola, *Mean Streets* (Scorsese, 1973), *Scarecrow* (Schatzberg, 1972), and so on. This thematic pattern derives from psychocultural tensions at the core of American ideology as such, but its obsessive recurrence in New Hollywood films of the late sixties and early seventies suggests as well a quite specific series of institutional resonances. If the New Hollywood heralds the breakdown of the closed, regulatory system of Classical Hollywood as an institution, it is not surprising that the invasion of the system by differential, previously excluded "foreign" terms should produce narratives of variously repressed forms of anxiety. Even when these terms were welcomed as the very forces that would reinvigorate the institution, they remained signifiers of *difference* in the system in relation to the signifiers of *sameness*, holdovers from the classical model, with which they interacted. Hollywood ideology had traditionally been able to recover difference *as* sameness, especially in its representations of class and race—the initially demonized rich who reveal themselves to be "just folks" after all, the black man deemed "acceptable" only after he is reconstructed as just like his white brethren. It remained to be seen, however, how the ideology of Hollywood would contend with the implication of the newly differential logics of the New Hollywood that sameness could also function as a form of difference—that the seemingly coherent genres of Classical Hollywood had really always been sites of confusion, contestation, and ideological tension, or that prevailing myths of American identity, far from providing any stable grounding for such identity, had been deeply discomfiting sources of cultural anxiety all along. It is just such fears as these that find expression in the many narratives of homosexual panic in New Hollywood cinema. Moreover, in its rhetoric of the relation of identity and difference, otherness and sameness, the logic of homosexual panic is parallel at deeply embedded levels to the structure of mythic self-consciousness. In the characteristic films of American mythologies recast by European directors treated in this chapter, that symbolic parallel reveals much about how the institution of Hollywood itself negotiates identity and difference during this period of change.

Cuckoo's Nest and the Logic of Closed Systems

With its narrative emphasis on institutional politics, *One Flew over the Cuckoo's Nest* reflects interestingly on the institutional structure of New Hollywood cinema itself. Therefore, the film is a particularly significant example of the problem of mythic self-consciousness in Hollywood cinema of the 1970s. Associated with myth through its rhetoric of allegory, the film also announces its ties, evident in its source in Ken Kesey's novel, to a countercultural tradition aspiring to ideological demystification. Critically manipulating charged images deriving from well-known repositories of American myth, the film simultaneously blunts its own criticism by appealing to received mythic discourses such as those of individualism and exceptionalism, as well as the pervasive "frontier" mythology routinely located at the core of American mythologies.[3] So potent is the story's relation to such quintessentially American mythologies that Leslie Fiedler revised that *locus classicus* of archetypal cultural criticism, *Love and Death in the American Novel* (1960), to include references to Kesey's novel after its initial publication. Another critic connects *Cuckoo's Nest* to received traditions of American myth by connecting it to archetypal, Fiedleresque scenarios of communion across racial lines:

> The real love affair in *Cuckoo's Nest* is that of McMurphy and Chief Bromden. . . . [This relationship] recalls that of Ishmael and Queequeg, or Huck and Nigger Jim; it revives a familiar American fantasy. (Farber, 97)

In this fantasy of the white man's union with the dark "other," the narrative thus recasts a traditional fantasy of difference in American culture. Still another critic attempts to define potential ideological conflict at work in the film, generated precisely by its presumed conflation of patterns of myth and levels of self-consciousness, by counterposing its allegorical narrative structure against its naturalistic style:

> It is precisely [Forman's alleged quest for realism] that encouraged some critics to view the film as being literally about problems of mental health. The film simultaneously pursues the objectives of coherence (through the use of classical narrative) and ambiguity (in its use of actors). It is a strategy that allows the film to work on a number of levels. . . . It is the film's uncertainties and ambiguities that allow it to work on an audience, avoiding an easy response to standard polemics. (*Five Filmmakers*, 73)

Robert Ray approaches the film from an opposite direction in his neo-Fiedleresque study of Hollywood film, meanwhile, proclaiming precisely its polemical failure, but the important point is that he proceeds nonetheless from similar assumptions. Citing the film as an exemplary instance of mythic self-consciousness, Ray argues that the film betrays the self-conscious myth-making of Kesey's novel "with its naturalistic style" by "largely ignor[ing] these references" (319) to pop iconography that self-deconstruct the novel's mythic levels. For Ray, the self-referential level of Kesey's novel renders its self-consciousness triumphantly predominant over its impulse toward myth-making, while Forman's film, eschewing such reference, reverses the hierarchy. Despite differing conclusions, both these critics imply a crucial relation of mythic content to formal style. This suggests, in turn, that the issue of mythic self-consciousness turns upon a confrontation of textual levels, with a narrative or representational level colliding with a formal or stylistic one to produce the paradox of mythic self-consciousness. It is worth noting here that such an approach implicitly revises applications of myth study to Classical Hollywood cinema. Earlier texts of "cine-structuralism," such as *Signs and Meaning in the Cinema* (1969, revised 1972), conceive of style as such as mere "noise," to be circumvented in order to gain access to the mythic level of texts, which exists independently of style (Wollen, 104–5).[4] In New Hollywood discourses, however, style is frequently conceived as the chief demystifying force in a given text, especially if the film's style has been visibly inflected by the practices of European art-cinema.

In spite of this shift of emphasis, analysis of the mythic elements of any text must remain, as Lévi-Strauss maintained, combinatory and diachronic, studying not only differential groupings of terms within a given textual system but its intertextual relation to larger systems of textuality, to other versions of the myths it narrates. At least in psychocultural terms, the immensely popular film version of *Mister Roberts* (Ford/Leroy, 1955) is an important intertext of *One Flew over the Cuckoo's Nest*. A comparison of that earlier product of Hollywood's postwar efforts to reconstitute the classical model with this later document of New Hollywood practices should usefully illuminate the relation of myth to self-consciousness in New Hollywood film. On first reflection, the earlier film, with its gung-ho comedy and its makeshift patriotism, might seem a far cry indeed from Forman's, with its gritty fatalism and its fickle radicalism. Yet both texts represent enclosed, hierarchized, all-male communities regulated by localized forms of institutional power—the navy in *Mister Roberts*, the asylum in *Cuckoo's Nest*. Moreover, both texts thematize questions of authority by positioning these communities allegorically as microcosmic versions of macrostructures, and the resulting narratives of authority, especially as it exists in the context of institutional power, are strikingly parallel. Indeed, in both cases, opposing figures of authority are played against one another in order at once to delegitimize nominally perverse forms of institutional authority and to relegitimate the institutions themselves.

In his remarkable work *Symbolic Economies*, Jean-Joseph Goux explores the generalization of economic practices across political, legal, sexual, religious, and cultural systems of representation: "The specificity of these practices and representations cannot keep us from discovering their profound community with regard to modes of symbolizing" (88). Without wishing to argue for the priority of any particular system, Goux attempts to establish how the construction and circulation of symbols in a given system is governed by an "economy" of regulation. Such systems of representation, for Goux, are predicated on an "economy" insofar as they depend upon a relation of matter to idea. Economies of money depend on this relation by substituting symbols of exchange for material referents, banknotes for gold. But there exist as well, according to Goux, economies of the body, of the psyche, of the social order, each reliant on the relation of a material base (the surface of the body itself, say, or the brain as an aspect of that body, or the material stratifications of class structure) to an ideational superstructure (sexualities, neuroses, demonologies). It is not important, for Goux, whether psychic, social or libidinal economies precede or determine the more "literal" economy of money, or whether the latter itself becomes metaphorized in the spheres of the psychic, social, or libidinal. Rather, Goux hopes by attending to the differential relations of circulation and exchange that control terms within given systems to arrive at a "a sociohistorical science of consciousness and the unconscious" (87). The effort to understand how symbolic processes work in social or psychic life has traditionally erred, Goux argues, in assuming that apprehension of the contents or referents of symbols yields their meanings. The latter assumption, however, mistakenly detaches thought, source of symbol, from the institutional contexts in which thought is made possible:

> [O]n this process of symbolization will depend, among other things, the *dominant mode of representation itself*—the dominant and dominated form of social consciousness. To show how the very form of social consciousness in a given mode of production and exchange is determined by the signifying, intersubjective,

"affective" mode of exchange, as a function of the dominant form of exchange—how it is determined by the *mode of symbolizing*, conditioned by the economic process—is to become able to consider consciousness (social or individual) no longer as a simple mirror, an unvarying agency of reflection, but rather as *constituted* in its very form, in its *mode of reflection*, by and in the process of social exchange. The "content" is what reflects, to varying degrees, real social existence, whereas the mode of reflection is completely and effectively determined . . . by the stage of the logic of symbolization in which the exchanges are located. (86)

Goux's ideas differ from those of traditional structuralism in emphasizing the regulation of symbols according to the logic of particular institutional economies. Such emphasis enables an attention to the formal or relational aspects of symbol-making to coexist with attunement to specific social or historical controls enacted upon the production of symbols. Moreover, it reveals how symbolization itself both reflects the operations of institutional economy and itself *is* the very process of exchange that produces such economies. In its negotiation of the levels of symbolic representation and institutional imperative, defining a space between the "real" and the "symbolic" that is the very province of myth, Goux's modifications of classical structuralism are useful for the study of myth in New Hollywood cinema.

Given the deeply embedded structural parallels between the two film texts under consideration here, it is not surprising that they share a number of more particular surface affinities.[5] Perhaps the most striking of these is the analogous gesture of rebellion, identification, and solidarity with which either text explosively concludes. At the end of *Mister Roberts*, the spirited but cowardly Ensign Pulver learns of the death in combat of the title character, who has demanded transfer to the battlefront from the inactive cargo-ship where the film is set; in response to the news of Roberts's death, Pulver, salutarily repeating an earlier gesture by Roberts himself, uproots and throws overboard the palm tree belonging to the ship's captain, who had been Roberts's nemesis. *Cuckoo's Nest* ends similarly with Chief Bromden discovering the lobotomization of his fellow inmate McMurphy, murdering him as an act of mercy, then uprooting a marble fount McMurphy had earlier struggled unsuccessfully to lift and hurling it through a window, making way for his own escape. In both cases, an ultimate symbolic gesture both underlines and implicitly redeems the martyred status of the text's protagonist, pointing at once to the tragic failure of the protagonist's individual rebellion against "the system" and, at the same time,

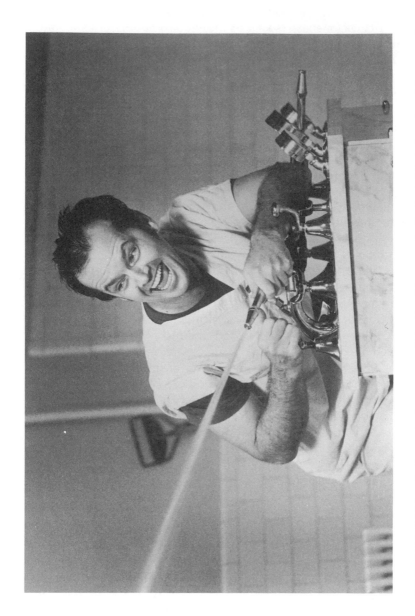

FIGURE 11. McMurphy's carnivalesque assault in *One Flew over the Cuckoo's Next*. Courtesy Museum of Modern Art, New York.

to the posthumous persistence of a spirit of "rebellion" fostered by the protagonist's nominally inspiring individualism.

The allegorical force of either gesture resides in its function as an effect of communitarian bonding. The uprooting of the fount in *Cuckoo's Nest* follows a passionate embrace between Bromden and McMurphy, with Bromden's murder of McMurphy, itself proposed as a salutary gesture in honor of McMurphy's lost individualism, markedly eroticized. The homosocial character of the bond between Bromden and McMurphy is further worked out through the image of the fount as a phallic emblem. Earlier in the film, McMurphy employs the fount's hose to spray his fellow inmates in a symbolic gesture of contempt intended to eliminate those very contemptible elements from the community's group-psychology. In that instance, the fount functions purgatively, as an extension of McMurphy's sense of his own phallic power, but in an immediately following sequence, the fount is transformed into an obstructive force, a marker of ineffectuality, as McMurphy tries unsuccessfully to lift it. In fairly literalized terms, the image of the fount is baldly overdetermined, standing in for McMurphy's possession of it in its limp condition and his final dispossession from phallic power in all its erect recalcitrance.[6] Thus, Bromden's later uprooting of the fount is a gesture of completion by means of which the phallus as signifier of social power is positioned clearly as the mediating emblem of the Bromden/McMurphy relation. Their relation is defined, therefore, as a quite explicitly *homosocial* relation, one of symbolically shared access to phallic power that must, as a condition of its being, disavow suggestions of literal genital contact. At the same time, the image of the fount functions in still larger terms to mediate the text's thematics of authority. Although McMurphy has in the end been exiled from phallic authority in some ultimate way, castrated-by-lobotomy, the film's vision of institutional authority demands that its narrative conclude with the image of Bromden's seizure of the phallus, a fantasy of liberatory fulfillment intended to compensate for acknowledgment of the radical lack that generates it.

In *Mister Roberts*, the image of the palm tree functions as a signifier of phallic authority in even more literalized terms, since it is the cherished posession of the ship's captain, a clear symbol of his authority, an object he is repeatedly seen tending lovingly in images charged with comically masturbatory connotations. Yet in the earlier film, too, as in *Cuckoo's Nest*, the aggressive usurpation of that symbol—Pulver's uprooting of the plant and throwing it overboard—does not herald a fully successful entry into an already constituted symbolic order but, rather, registers the impossibility of such access. In other words, as in

FIGURE 12. *Mister Roberts*: The Captain tends his palm tree. Courtesy Museum of Modern Art, New York.

Cuckoo's Nest, the phallus-as-such is initially given as the pivot-point between an imaginary subject and a symbolic order, between individualized desire and the institutional economy that produces and regulates such desire, potentiating exchange between these two levels, but secondarily posited as a mediating sign of a male-male bond sealed, *through* the mediation of the sign, in a common *rejection* of that order's edicts.

What characterizes these strikingly parallel symbols, then, is the overdetermined and paradoxically literalized status they achieve by virtue of their regulatory functions within closely analogous visions of institutional economies. By means of the microcosmic and allegorical structure they share, both *Mister Roberts* and *Cuckoo's Nest* envision the dynamics of institutional power in terms of closed systems, alternately seen as regulated and self-regulating, governed by principles of exchange and circulation of elements *within* the system.[7] In *Mister Roberts*, the floating microcosm of the cargo-ship is isolated from the larger structure of the military as such, largely separated from interaction with other ships, and the ship itself is clearly defined as an instrument of just such exchange-and-circulation, marginal to the activity of warfare, as Roberts perceives, but essential to its subtending economy, functioning to circulate needed commodities, as the captain proudly declares. To be sure, these differing positions between Roberts and the captain on the value of the ship's mission mark out the opposing positions the two figures occupy within the self-enclosed economy of the microcosm. The captain enforces principles of regulation, removing disruptive elements from this closed, microcosmic system, controlling their circulation, or mediating stabilized exchange of differential elements in order to neutralize threatening difference. Also a figure invested with institutional authority as the ship's second-in-command, Roberts professes an abiding confidence in the system's capacities for *self*-regulation, in the tendency of terms within the system to stabilize themselves, to siphon off or make productive use of excess energies or potentially disruptive terms freely permitted to enter into circulation, on the assumption that they will take care of themselves, or that the dependable workings of the institutional economy will take care of them. The two figures thus delineate opposed versions of institutional power, the former critically defined as eliminative and regulatory, the latter idealized as provocative and generative. To be sure, where the captain's deepest impulse, presented as aberrantly obsessive, is forcibly to take terms *out* of the institutional economy, Roberts's wholesomely genial instinct is to provoke their exchange and generate their production. In a memorable scene, for instance, the captain is enraged by the spectacle of shirtless men on deck, and demands that they cover themselves in spite of the sweltering heat, thus effectively removing the naked male body from the very free circulation that Roberts had previously promoted in permitting the men to strip. To be sure, the captain's regulatory impulse extends to the control of Roberts's generative instinct, as when the captain repeatedly censors the requests for transfer Roberts repeatedly produces—a very literal production of textual excess on Roberts's part which the captain compulsively strives to forestall. In the terms of the narrative, the captain's attraction to the character of Pulver is linked to Pulver's office as laundry supervisor, a role dependent on the purgative cleansing and recirculation of the very terms within the system—clothes—that had earlier come to emblematize the captain's oppression.

Although the narrative of *Cuckoo's Nest* is set within a very different kind of institution, its structural similarities to *Mister Roberts* produce a closely analogous vision of the dynamics of institutional power itself. In the terms of this comparison, the figure of Nurse Ratched occupies a position analogous to that of the captain in *Mister Roberts* while McMurphy, despite the obvious fundamental differences between the characters, occupies a position analogous to that of Roberts, claiming a share of institutional authority in his recognition, superior to that of his fellow inmates, of the institution's power. The institutional economy of the asylum, like that of the ship, is elaborated visually in detailed, rigorously measured sequences emphasizing routine, order, deadening rounds of regulatory procedure predicated on patterns of controlled circulation and exchange. Indeed, the symmetrical structure of the later film, beginning and ending with scenes depicting the spiritless daily rituals of the asylum, registers ironically the dependency of the institution's order on the exclusion of disruptive elements. In both the opening and closing scenes, Nurse Ratched is positioned in a panoptical cage at the center of the social space, regulating the anesthetizing music piped into the room, distributing patients' vaguely resisted medication, and otherwise insuring the regular operation of the institution's daily round with a kind of rigid tranquility.

The visual scheme of the film works out its narrative structure as a conflict between Ratched and McMurphy for control of the institution's economy. The principle of an excess superficially far more subversive than Roberts's, McMurphy nonetheless, like Roberts, enacts subversion by deploying the terms already in circulation within the institutional economy rather than striving to subvert that economy entirely. The wild party McMurphy orchestrates at the climax of the film, for instance, culminates in the literal subversion of the very instruments of Ratched's control—the record-player, the cage itself, the microphone—with the inmates invading the space associated with Ratched's power in order to turn these devices to newly liberatory, carnivalesque uses.

The differing relations of Ratched and McMurphy to the structures of the institutional economy they inhabit may be illustrated by comparing their manipulation within the diegesis of differing tropes of circulation and exchange—voting and betting. A central conflict between the characters is staged around McMurphy's raucous lobbying to watch the World Series baseball game on television and Ratched's primly brutal denial of this seemingly banal and harmless pleasure. In a significantly anal image, McMurphy bets the other men that he will "put a bug up [Ratched's] ass" so that she will relent, but Ratched cannily puts the matter to a vote in order to quell the issue. McMurphy's characteristic appeal to the bet and Ratched's deployment of the vote represent seemingly analogous but ultimately opposed forms of relation within the institutional economy. Both voting and betting function as *symbolic* forms of exchange, displacing exchange from literally, materially circulated terms or commodities onto figural substitutes for the latter. The two forms of exchange differ significantly, though, in the degree of this displacement. McMurphy's arrival at the asylum signals an immediate alteration of the institution's economy registered in the form of the bet itself: before McMurphy's arrival, we see the inmates play cards without stakes; afterward, we see them play the same games, now betting with cigarettes at McMurphy's instigation, a change that, as the film makes clear, transforms the terms of relation within the card games and registers more general changes McMurphy's presence brings about in the dynamics of the community at large. The bet functions symbolically to substitute a traded commodity for an assertion of power, both literalizing the possession of power by way of these visibly accumulated commodities and neutralizing its threatening force through the substitution itself, nominating it as a species of play or an effect of luck. Even so, the bet can only circulate within an already reified structure, invested in the question of power insofar as its signifiers by definition mark instances of win or loss.

Voting, too, implies a prior installation of power structures that either demand or claim merely to sanction it, thus bound up similarly in a competitive dynamic of winning and losing, of access to power or denial of such access. Yet whereas the bet necessarily foregrounds the conflict that generates it, a constituent symbolic element of a more literal contest, the vote makes such conflict itself an element in its structure of displacement. The ideology of voting typically locates voting within a utopian vision of *shared* power, with final consensus symbolically obviating prior conflict. Put in these terms, it is easy to see why voting is so routinely associated in Hollywood representations with a covert fascism while betting is linked to a glorified populism. Examples from two texts crucially representative of Classical Hollywood's ideology of populism clarify the point. In *Mr. Smith Goes to Washington* (Capra, 1939), for instance, voting is seen not as a central principle of democracy but as a shell-game that lends itself to fascist subversion, while in *Young Mr. Lincoln* (Ford, 1939), betting functions to restore populist order during a scene at a fair where Lincoln playfully cheats at betting-games in order to assure a "proper" outcome. According to the ideology of Hollywood populism, votes can be bought, and while bets can also be fixed, their status as a more *immediate* form of exchange, based on a presumably direct agreement between principals, touches them with the potentially redemptive individualism that underlies Hollywood's most basic mythologies.

In *Cuckoo's Nest*, McMurphy's bets are shown to disrupt or subvert oppressive power-structures while Ratched's votes are shown to reinforce and even to derive from those structures. Though her aversion to voting about the World Series yields an impression of collectivism, ostensibly legitimating the inmates socially by allowing them to voice their own interests, this impression is revealed as specious in the terms of the film. It is clear from the start that Ratched permits the vote only because she knows that the inmates have already been rendered docile by the institutional structures that serve as the predetermining condition of the vote. When McMurphy begins to draw in marginalized inmates to vote in his favor, Ratched hurriedly calls the meeting to a close, resulting in McMurphy's most damning accusation against her in the film, voiced to her superiors and rife with signs of the film's vexed neopopulism: "She ain't honest!"

In the case of both *Mister Roberts* and *Cuckoo's Nest*, the regulatory function of the institutions is contingent upon the institutional structure's enforced definition of itself as a closed system. This definition, in turn, is dependent on a rabidly exclusionist politics of gender. The putative self-consciousness of *Cuckoo's Nest* resides not only in the ironically foregrounded hermeticism and non-normativity of the institution that serves as its setting but in the replacement of emblems of *male* authority with the figure of Nurse Ratched in its retelling of its narrative of institutional power. Part of what guarantees the required insulation of the institution in *Mister Roberts* is precisely the exclusion of women, the removal not of desire itself but of what continues to be designated nonetheless as desire's proper object. Indeed, *Mister Roberts* begins with a scene of presumably whimsical voyeurism, in which men on the boat gaze through binoculars at women on shore, certifying the continued circulation of heterosexual desire despite the presumed exclusion of sexual difference but registering the relegation of that desire to the sphere of illicit fantasy. To be sure, the authenticity or humanity the film associates with Roberts's authority is shown to derive from his own curiously estranged identification with such desire, which the captain wishes simply to purge or repress. In these terms, it is significant that neither Roberts nor the captain is presented as a *subject* of heterosexual desire, but Roberts's erstwhile identification with the desire of his men motivates a central line of the plot, Roberts's effort to secure on-shore liberty for the men so they may satisfy what the film would have us see as their healthy lusts. Yet, just as the ascension to authority seemingly requires the disavowal of desire in Roberts and the captain, so the regulatory structure of the institution demands the exclusion of its normative objects. This dynamic, indeed, importantly determines the film's categories of authority, with the "humane" version of authority designated as that which acknowledges normative desire, the oppressive version as that which simultaneously demands such normativity while obstructing or negating its only possible expression.

It is not necessary to appeal to the many intellectual or cultural traditions that posit the recognition of sexual difference as the very origin of self-consciousness in the individual psyche in order to argue that *Cuckoo's Nest*, by centralizing its conflict around a particularly fraught experience of sexual difference, invests its retelling of myths of authority with a charged self-consciousness.[8] If the institutional economy represented in *Mister Roberts* secures its presumed mythic stability through a disavowal of sexual difference, that represented in *Cuckoo's Nest* announces its self-conscious relation to such myth by reorienting its versions of institutional authority around questions of gender. Even more to the point, the film's handling of gender politics devolves upon a canny analysis of gender's role in shaping cultural constructions of power. A comparison of the figure of the nurse in Kesey's novel with that in Forman's film, for instance, reveals that the latter considerably divests Kesey's representation of its archetypal resonance.[9] The larger-than-life, deindividuated bitch-goddess of the novel is replaced in Forman with a humanizingly detailed characterization emphasizing Ratched's position as *agent* of institutional power rather than as its foremost exponent. In a crucial scene late in the film, for example, the asylum's authorities debate whether to return the disruptive McMurphy to work camp, but Ratched argues for allowing him to remain in the institution because, as she argues, "I think we can help him." Not only does the scene undermine the identification of Ratched's power with the pervasive power of the institution itself by revealing her as an underling of male authorities, but it emphasizes her own marginalized position within the institution's hierarchies through editing patterns that conceal her presence until very late in the scene among the men who run the asylum. Moreover, the film leaves open the possibility that Ratched's declaration here of a humanely therapeutic motive is genuine. Further, although the film is structured dramatically around the conflict between McMurphy and Ratched, it takes shape at the same time around complex visual and thematic *parallels* between the figures. For instance, the arrival of the nurse at the beginning of the film sets up visual comparisons and contrasts to the arrival of McMurphy later in the film. Both are heralded by the abrupt, disruptive slamming of the gate around which both sequences are aurally framed, but the nurse's appearance is associated with institutional order, in particular by use of a telephoto lens that, emphasizing stylized shallowness of space, makes the figure's motion look regimented and automatonlike. By contrast, McMurphy's appearance is immediately associated with an excessive, unrestrained energy—kissing the cop who leads him in, greeting the character of the Chief with a stereotypical "How!"—heightened by the dynamic movement of the backward-tracking shot that captures it.

In spite of these clear differences, however, the film continues to emphasize analogous characteristics of the positions McMurphy and Ratched occupy in relation to the institution itself. For instance, the scene of McMurphy's electroshock therapy is paralleled strikingly in visual terms to the scene in which McMurphy, after Ratched's sexual humiliation of Billy Bibbitt, attempts to strangle the nurse. Both scenes employ severe high-angle shots, the camera placed in both cases directly above the supine object of its gaze, with hand-held cameras signifying the trauma of the experience and a final slow dissolve portending its dire meaning. Such visual rhetoric presents both McMurphy and Ratched as victims, not ultimately of one another but of the institutional economy they had strived to control but of which they must finally be seen only as elements, like the elements for whose circulation and exchange they had bartered. This structural parallelism is emphasized by scenes framed by the weighted exchange of gazes between McMurphy and Ratched, such as the group-therapy scenes that repeatedly begin and end with shots/reverse-shots as the two figures look at each other, matching the figures visually and underlining the identification that defines their conflict.

Although the narrative of *Cuckoo's Nest*, like the narrative of *Mister Roberts*, asserts the possibility of individualistic resistance to an otherwise pervasive institutional economy, it simultaneously counters such assertion with a clear sense of the embracing force of the institution's all-consuming power. *Mister Roberts* narrates its vision of institutional power in mythic terms by setting its narrative within an idealized and implicitly legitimated institution and by positing resistance to the institution's fully acknowledged oppression as a constituent part of its systemic economy: the figure of Roberts, in these terms, is both an arm of the institution itself, fundamentally committed to its functions, and a humane reformist who recognizes its localized failures. The suffocating oppression of human potential that the film registers fully is seen as a function of individual whim, not of institutional structure; the men suffer not because of the social organization of the military hierarchy itself, in the film's terms, but because of the captain's extreme neuroses. *Cuckoo's Nest* claims its erstwhile self-consciousness, meanwhile, by relocating its narrative to a less revered institutional setting, one that already thematizes a presupposed deviance from supposed normalities. Even if the later film retains a residual mythic individualism not far removed from that of its classical counterpart, then, it illustrates the ubiquity of institutions' assimilationist energies and tendency to eliminate disruptive forces, to remake resistance in the terms of the institution's needs.

The parallel appearances of Ratched and McMurphy, significantly, establish both figures, at least in the allegorical terms that shape so much of the film, as additive elements to the institution's otherwise closed economy. Initial slow tracking-shots through the asylum, before the arrival of the antagonists, signify both its claustrophobic hermeticism and, by way of the stifling quiescence of the film's opening, its stabilized constitution. Thus, especially since no other characters are seen leaving or arriving in the course of the film until the Chief breaks out at the end, the entries of Ratched and McMurphy position them both as subjects who come into the institution from outside, who enter it as alien or foreign elements, immediately destabilizing the system by making apparent in their confrontation previously latent power relations.

The issue of sexual difference becomes especially relevant here, for in spite of Ratched's regulatory function within the institution, her presence alone is seen to undermine the stability of this all-male system as, at once, a threatening image of phallic womanhood and, in more conventional terms of the constructions of sexual difference in psychoanalytic discourse, a disturbing signifier of lack, a presumed reminder to the institutionalized men of their own potential or already-effected castration. Because the film is attuned in its sidewise manner to the politics of gender in social organization, presenting as it does Ratched's position within the institutional system as itself a function of the institution's demands, it is possible to read the demonology of Ratched's femininity as an example of the text's self-consciousness. Though Ratched's collusive role as an agent of oppression is unequivocally linked in the film to questions of gender identity—it is impossible to imagine a *male* Ratched—the emphasis on her status as an element *within* the institutional system rather than as a controlling force *behind* it may be understood to reveal that identification of Ratched's femininity with insitutional oppression as the protective, illusory projection of male homosociality.

To compare *Cuckoo's Nest* with a contemporary art-cinema narrative of phallic womanhood such as *Seven Beauties* (Wertmuller, 1974) is to see a basic contrast in the films' treatments of sexual difference. The figure of the female commandant in Wertmuller's film is a monstrous projection of grotesque femininity, wielding an explicitly phallic riding-crop that becomes a signifier of her *non*arousal when the male protagonist attempts to conquer her domination by seducing her. The structural similarity of the two films resides in their staging of this struggle for domination of the disciplinary space, made self-consciously *primal* by being self-consciously *gendered*: in spite of the historical illegitimacy (as alleged by Bruno Bettelheim in his famous commentary on the film) of the figure of the commandant, it is no more possible to imagine a male commandant in the film than to imagine a male Ratched in *Cuckoo's Nest*. The scenario of *Seven Beauties*, however, is easier to assimilate to the psychoanalytic narrative in which the (projected) threat of female "lack" to the male ego gives way to (projected) fear of female plenitude, in turn giving rise to the male drive to master both anxieties by reintroducing the plenitude of the phallus— through heterosexual union, seduction, or rape. With its sardonic, Rabelaisian sensibility, the seduction scene of *Seven Beauties* can hardly be called a fantasy of male mastery, yet its grim parody of such fantasies implicitly validates simply by drawing on them the conceptions of sexual difference in which such fantasies germinate. In *Cuckoo's Nest*, Ratched's placement as a signifier of sexual difference does not generate among the inmates fantasies of sexual conquest, significantly, but instead provokes recognition of the dynamic of their own homosocial relations. A representative example of this point occurs when

McMurphy boasts to the other men that he can escape from the asylum whenever he wants to, whereupon one of the men comments, "Maybe he'll just show Nurse Ratched his big thing and she will open the gate." The important point here is that Ratched's entry as a signifier into the previously closed system brings with it not the need to incorporate or to assimilate the "alien" terms that accompany it—say, fantasized images of female genitalia. Rather, the intrusion of sexual difference here serves only to generate fantasy scenarios of sexual *sameness*, of what in these terms was *already* present in the system— *male* genitalia. Although it responds to femininity as a cause, as a signifier of difference before the appearance of which difference was presumably nugatory, the inmate's remark simultaneously registers an effect—the recognition of sameness *as* difference. In other words, what seems most significant about this eminently characteristic moment in the film is its illustration that Ratched's gender-*otherness*, as the film constructs it, gives rise to fantasized evocations not of femininity that may be seen to define that heterology, but of one man's penis as imagined by another man.

Thus associated with (perhaps unconscious) forms of displacement, Nurse Ratched's presence in the institutional system as a signifier of sexual difference conjures up not energies of heterosexual desire, as might be expected, but anxieties about homosexual panic. Though Ratched is linked throughout the film to images of symbolic castration, as when she denies Cheswick his cigarettes, her most literalized, palpable, and *bodily* threat in relation to the men is that of *anal penetration*. When McMurphy refuses to take his medication orally, she icily refers to "another way" of administering it—adding ominously, "But I don't think you'd like it." The reference to anal penetration here is associated with humiliation and characterized by a portentous indirection that effectively absents it. Immediately afterward, significantly, McMurphy turns to another inmate—whom he has nicknamed "Hardon"—and says, *"You'd* enjoy it, wouldn't you?"—symbolically rerouting the phallic to the anal.

In almost every way, the scene yields a classic scenario of almost-successfully-disavowed homosexual panic. Ratched's threat points up the penetrability of McMurphy's body and his subjection to an institutional desire—not, presumably, Ratched's own—that might render him doubly passive. Although she does not imply that he might take pleasure in this passivity, locating the humiliation in the penetration itself, both the terms of her threat and McMurphy's own reinscription of the joke when he reroutes it to "Hardon" make clear that such pleasure is at least viable. The logic of homosexual panic typically conflates sadism with masochism by, at once, fantasizing anal penetration as an act of violent aggression that debases its passive object with the mere potential of "pleasure," with the recipient's being perceived as having "liked it" or "wanted it"; and, at the same time, as an unnatural violation that paradoxically feminizes the aggressor whose desire it allegedly enacts or reflects. The logic of this dynamic, in turn, participates in a tripartite structure. A first phase in this logic is the recognition by the male subject of his previously denied penetrability, his vulnerability to imagined homosexual aggression; a second phase is his fantasy of another man's desire for such aggression. The third and determining condition of homosexual panic merges the introjection of the first phase with the projection of the second in the unresolvable anxieties that chart out the terrain of homosexual panic, compelling its subject before the fact (since the fact itself remains psychic fantasy) to imagine his own possible pleasure in anality, his own potential for such desire.

In her ground-breaking discussions of homosexual panic, Eve Sedgwick emphasizes the institutional deployment of such symbolic irresolution, which at once imposes an all-but-monolithic sexual normativity and refuses the possibility of complete disavowal of homosexuality: "Not only must homosexual men be unable to ascertain whether they are to be the objects of 'random' homophobic violence, but no man must be able to ascertain that he is not (that his bonds are not) homosexual" (*Between Men*, 88–89). In Sedgwick's early work, the structure of homosexual panic is analyzed principally in feminist terms as an impetus to the exchange of women among rivalrous men within distinctively homosocial settings. Such exchange, for Sedgwick, comes to operate as both a form of disavowal of homosexuality, with the woman functioning as "camouflage," and a form of participation in homosociality, with the woman signifying the intensity of the men's connection to *each other*. The threat of homosexual panic, then, is the threat that such exchange will fail to serve its purpose of camouflaging the intensity of the male-male bond, even as it is precisely these forms of exchange that precipitate that intensity. Initially dependent on the differential logics of gender, homosexual panic both denies and reinforces them: On the one hand it devolves upon a relation of sameness, "between men," rhetorically abrogating sexual difference; on the other, it projects a form of difference *within* that relation, casting the unwanted desire of the other as the signifier of difference between similarly positioned subjects in the relation—one defined by an anxious desire and the other, its object, by an absence of desire that, coupled with recognition of the desire of the other, gives rise to the anxious condition of "panic." Assuming a prior, stable moment of male-male relation *before* the intrusion or eruption of desire, homosexual panic itself participates in the logic of closed systems through which, in a narrative like *Cuckoo's Nest*, it achieves articulation. The subsequent moment of that intrusion of nominally differential elements, in these terms, brings about the loss of the integrity, even of a putative "innocence," of the male-male relation as a closed, nondifferential system of relation—as if the potential for desire were not always already present in any human relation.

Thus, the structure of homosexual panic repeats that of mythic self-consciousness. Both posit an initial state of systemic unity—the state of "wholesome" or "healthy" homosocial bonding on the one hand, or the state of pure and innocent myth on the other—subsequently disrupted by the intrusion of a term that, in fact, in either case, was already present in that initial state, or at least potential in it, potentially given rise by it—the homosexual desire *produced by* homosocial bonding, or the self-consciousness that comes out of compulsively reiterated myth. The original condition of purity and untroubled identity given as the determining state of either concept is itself illusory and implicitly mythic, for the homosocial is always bound up with the homo*sexual* (and vice versa) just as surely as myth is always bound up with self-consciousness—or, indeed, any term in a differential pairing with its projected opposite. Narratives of New Hollywood are similarly driven by such animating myths of initial, coherent identity troubled by the subsequent onslaught of difference—with the image of a classical model gradually challenged by differential, foreign terms originating outside its system which it can no longer comfortably dispel through assimilation. It is not surprising, therefore, that these parallel structures of homosexual panic and mythic self-consciousness should figure so prominently in the formation of these narratives.

Mythic Self-Consciousness in *Deliverance*

Like *Cuckoo's Nest*, *Deliverance* (Boorman, 1972) is a characteristic product of 1970s New Hollywood filmmaking in the way it situates itself in relation to traditional Hollywood mythologies. Also like *Cuckoo's Nest*, *Deliverance* represents a typical New Hollywood conjunction of archetypal narrative patterns from Fiedler-style "classic" American literature, particularly through its source in James Dickey's novel, and self-conscious stylistic patterns derived from European art-cinema, substantiated here again by the presence of a European director. The latter fact alone, in both *Cuckoo's Nest* and *Deliverance*, signifies the unapologetically (though not unmitigatedly) distanced, ironized relation of the film to standard Hollywood mythologies, as if despite their often stridently, archetypally *American* postures these texts required for their projects of demystification not the "native" touch of an American director but the alienated detachment of a "foreigner." Like *Cuckoo's Nest*, *Deliverance* draws upon and manipulates a rich stock of archetypes in order to deconstruct traditional mythologies of the frontier while reinforcing mythologies of the self that undergird them. Most importantly, *Deliverance* narrates a Gothic tale of homosexual panic, a literalized allegory on the order of that in operation in *Cuckoo's Nest*, that illustrates yet again, perhaps even more explicitly, the mutual imbrication of the thematics of homosexual panic and the dynamics of mythic self-consciousness in New Hollywood filmmaking.

Perhaps the most superficial, and therefore the clearest, gauge of mythic self-consciousness at work in *Deliverance* occurs at an obvious thematic level. The film's narrative of four city men attempting a leisure-time conquest of a soon-to-be-dammed-up river both ridicules the complacent frivolity of the men's mock-epic quest, revealing it as unconsciously collusive with corporate domination and class oppression, and at the same time participates in the multiple demonologies on which such a Darwinian ethic of survival must be constructed. An important part of the film's satire of the four weekend adventurers lies in their condescendingly superior and contemptuous attitude toward the rural folk who inhabit the space they seek to conquer, who *live* the "adventure" that the suburbanites can only experience vicariously, yet the film goes on to show the country-dwellers to be every bit as grotesque and monstrous as the city people believe them to be. As Carol Clover argues in an important analysis of *Deliverance* that sees the film as the crucial forerunner of the rape-revenge narrative in the 1970s and 1980s Hollywood horror film, the city/country duality at the heart of the film serves to clarify projections of class-based demonology that structure the film's narrative. A key paradox Clover points to in the film is related to my point here. These narratives of "urbanoia" in which city people in the country are beset by blood-thirsty or rape-bent country people, a line of representation that *Deliverance* initiates or at least refocuses, tend at once to justify urban guilt about the destruction of the countryside, while at the same time establishing the "exterminability" (Clover, 136) of the "rednecks" engaged in defending that countryside against urban invasion. This paradox may be seen as the legacy of the mythic Hollywood western, where attacks by "redskins" on frontierspeople were routinely presented as irrationally violent, motiveless onslaughts rather than as defensive maneuvers to protect a land under seige. In the wake of the post-mythic, New Hollywood western, which typically proposes to deconstruct the genre's myths by precisely reversing their terms, showing the frontierspeople as aggressive imperialists and the Native Americans as beset or victimized populations, the no-longer-tenable demonologies of race simply migrate to a congruent genre and transform themselves into demonologies of class. Yet the basic contradiction remains. If such narratives claim to deconstruct myth by criticizing the culpability for social oppression of a hitherto supposedly dominant class, how can they, or why do they, continue to demonize the very class whose oppression has been decried? In spite of the evident invasion by self-consciousness of Hollywood's systems of representation, then, these narratives cling to their decidedly mythic, populist Us-versus-Them bases, where it is still clear enough who the "Us" is meant to be and who the "Them" is meant to be. What becomes less clear with the advent of whatever forms of self-consciousness the institutions of Hollywood find they can no longer profitably fend off is what, precisely, is the relation *between* these terms.

Such problems are nowhere more in evidence than in *Deliverance*, perhaps the film that initially articulates them in their most consolidated form. The film's critique of the suburban sensibility is mounted fully in the opening sequence of the film, a structural montage that plays images of unspoiled landscape against images of industrial invasion, while the voices of the four main characters are heard blandly discussing their pilgrimage in voice-over dialogue. The abstract quality of the set-piece lends it an apocalyptic edge reminiscent of the climax of another vision of American culture by a European art-director, *Zabriskie Point* (Antonioni, 1969), a film to which the sequence alludes specifically in its final shot, echoing the last sequence of Antonioni's film, a long-held image of a pastoral scene decimated by an explosion. The portentous tone established here is continued in subsequent shots showing the arrival of the men in the haunted wood, such as an eerily canted angle on a dark horizon and an enmisted sky with the men's canoe-bearing cars gliding along the bottom edge of the composition. Such shots present the land itself in images of otherness, both neo-romantically exoticized and charged with Gothic uncanniness. At the same time, through these very associations, they register a satiric contrast of primitive space to urbanoid comfort. The specific shot in question, for instance, plays the archetypally Coleridgean landscape against the men's big, safe cars and expensive canoes for comic effect.

Significantly, the men are introduced here only through their voices, with only the character of Lewis clearly individuated from the group through his pseudo-Thoreauvian rantings, including a bitter indictment of the "rape" of the land. The other three figures in this dialogue-montage seem somewhat interchangeable, especially at the end of the sequence when in tandem they reject Lewis's views as "extremist." To be sure, Lewis's comments are satirized for their extremity even while they echo verbally the visual montage that accompanies them, depicting the "rape" of the land in very explicit visual metaphors that would seem to legitimate Lewis's claims.

If the film begins by deindividuating its principal characters, the process of the narrative will be the process of systematically differentiating them according to the terms of a predetermining self-conscious archetype.[10] The second sequence of the film, the men's first mutedly hostile encounter with the country people, uses compositions in long shot and wide-screen as a way of introducing the four characters without yet individuating them fully and without emphasizing any one character over the others. Though the film will eventually turn into Ed's story, there is little in the first half of the film to suggest Ed's narrative prominence over Lewis, Bobby, and Drew, and the wide-angled, wide-screen compositions are effective not only in depicting the men from the start as stranded within the very spaces they comically propose to conquer, but in further effecting this initial quality of interchangeability. At the same time, these compositions function to construct visually the relations of the suburbanites to the country-dwellers, which the film posits here in the terms of a *mutual* demonology—the condescension and suspicion of the suburbanites met with the skepticism and contempt of the country people. For instance, as Bobby procures fuel for the car, he compliments an attendant—"I love the way you wear that hat"—who responds shortly: "You don't know nothing." The composition is laid out with Bobby and the attendant occupying opposite ends of the frame, separated in the image by an imposing gas pump, the fragmentation of the screen space visually emphasizing the disconnection between the men's identities. Later in the same sequence, as Drew plays his banjo in a duet with a mentally retarded boy, another long shot contrasts the instinctually graceful dance of one of the rurals, expressing a presumably natural affinity with the music, with Bobby's awkward, arrhythmic clap. Though the scene can hardly be said to celebrate rural folkways, it does presage a certain idealization of what it presents as rural primitivism as preferable to civilized hypocrisy. Perhaps the best illustration of this point is in Bobby's off-handedly cruel reference to the boy:

"Talk about your genetic deficiencies. . . . That's pathetic." Yet, despite
the edgy hostility of this sequence, perhaps its most important function is to register a connection between Drew and the boy in the exhil-
aration of their banjo playing. It is crucial that this moment of seemingly authentic connection occurs at the very beginning of the film in
a general atmosphere of mutual suspicion among the characters, for it
proposes at some level the *bridgeability* of the gap between country and
city. If the film's initial assertion of complicity of the suburbanites in
economic exploitation participates in a rhetoric of self-conscious
demystification, the fantasy of an emotional affinity among classes
that might transcend class boundaries, even if it does not entirely
undermine the former assertion, certainly recontextualizes it in the
terms of a reconstructed mythos.

In an important way, paradoxically, the banjo-playing scene prepares the ideological way for the rape scene at the core of the film.
Bobby's reference to the boy is presented as cruelly ignorant, yet the
boy himself *is* irrevocably presented through an optic of "genetic defi-
ciency," not just as an autistic idiot-savant but as a threateningly
uncanny troll right out of Gothic fiction, complete with unreadably
featureless face and blank, assaultive gaze. Drew's pure pleasure in
the duet, then—"I could play all day with that guy!"—suggests that
the demonological relation of country and city, underclass and privileged class, can be neutralized by a kind of sophisticated and significantly class-based identification *downward*, just another version of the
condescension the film has already taken pains to criticize. Although
the boy too is shown to take in the duet a pleasure the film's rhetoric
seconds heartily, after all, immediately after the duet he reverts to an
unresponsive autism that gives the lie to the prior fantasy of communion. Thereafter, to be sure, Drew's pleasurable identification with the
boy is shown to be an outgrowth of the character's naiveté. As the men
enter the river, for instance, they again glimpse the boy on a bridge.
Drew greets him happily, but the boy does not respond, and the film's
technique here, an anxiously subjective tracking-shot under the
bridge, presents both the boy's unresponsiveness and his almost surreal ubiquity as a bad omen. Thus, the film itself participates in the
very demonization of the country-dwellers it represents as reprehen-
sible in the suburbanites.

The rape scene furnishes the most overt example of the latter
point, clearly, but before that scene and its implications can be treated
in some detail, it is necessary to consider what leads up to it in a larger
context in an effort to address how the film's focus shifts from critique
of the city people as metaphorical rapists of the land to positioning

them as victims of a literal rape. Though it may be too schematic to align the initial critique with an impulse to self-consciousness and the subsequent shift with a reversion to myth, such thematic reversal does clearly reveal the mythic overdeterminism that characterizes the whole text. The treatment of the character of Drew illustrates this point. Drew's initial identification with the mountain folk gives way, after the rape, to his somewhat hysterical insistence on reporting the murder of the rapist to the authorities, which in turn leads to his death on the river, the result either of an accident revealing his essential unfitness, his inequality to the demands of nature, or an act of revenge by the surviving mountain man, ironically giving the lie to Drew's ineffectual adversion to civilized law. Either way, the character's death is both an ideological necessity in the terms of the plot and the inevitable outcome of the film's gradually evolving logics. In a very real sense, the figure of Drew is necessarily sacrificed to the survivalist ethic the film provisionally adumbrates in its latter half. Moreover, in the terms of the film, this character is the only logical sacrifice insofar as his capacity for identification with otherness, seen as admirable at the outset of the film, must ultimately be rejected as a function of destructive innocence, weakness, and vulnerability. The first two of Drew's crucial functions in the plot are presented as fully congruent, as if an identification with otherness and a faith in social structures of legality were two sides of the same psychic coin. Thus, his third function—to die—becomes, if not the causal effect, both the logical end and the determining condition of those prior functions, revealing these attributes as inadequate responses to the physical, mental, and social realities on which the film proposes to meditate.

The larger point here is that each of the four characters serves a clearly defined function in an increasingly ruthless but ever more abstract narrative/thematic logic in the film. The point may be clarified by the terms of a series of interrelated questions regarding the narrative's trajectory: Why must Bobby be the character who is raped? Why must Lewis be the murderer of the rapist? Why, after having accorded nearly equal time to all four figures before the rape, must the film shift almost exclusively to Ed's point-of-view afterward? The answer already sketched above to another such question—Why must Drew die?—provides at least structural guidelines with which the remaining questions may be approached. Like Drew's, Bobby's placement in relation to the pivotal event of the rape itself emerges as a function of his general response to the country people. Where Drew responds to them with what the film ultimately sees as a naively imaginary identification, Ed with timidly complete withdrawal, and Lewis with open contempt, it is Bobby who responds to them most explicitly in the terms of a markedly *urban* condescension recognizable as such to the rurals themselves. The gas-station attendant's response to Bobby's patronizing politeness is a case in point, illustrating such recognition. A contrast of Lewis's and Bobby's contemptuous treatment of the rurals reveals that Lewis's contempt mirrors that of the country people for the suburbanites. To be sure, though Lewis is a city-dweller, he is most closely identified with the rurals in habit, demeanor, and sensibility through his dress, his accent, and his status as guide to his urban compatriots, certifying his greater connection to the land. When he barters with a rural to transport their cars, his contempt—"Fifty dollars my ass!" is his rejoinder to the man's offer—is taken as an acceptable element in the process of bargaining even as the other man calls him a "city boy." Though Bobby's expressions of contempt for the country people are veiled, the rurals respond to him from the start with far greater virulence, shown to perceive him as *more* contemptible because of the explicitly urban patina of his condescension.

In the opening sections of the film, crucially, Bobby functions, as well, as the principle of a sexuality repressed but uncontained by the dynamics of the group. After their first day of rafting, an exhilarated Bobby refers to the experience as "the best—no, the *second* best sensation I ever felt!" His conception of the trip in implicitly sexualized terms is further illustrated when he asks Lewis whether rafting is "how you get your rocks off," and boasts, when they are retiring to their tents for the night, that "I had my first wet dream in a sleeping bag." Though the other men respond with vague amusement to the obsessively adolescent bawdry assigned to the Bobby character, they do not participate in it, and it is even implied that they are made uneasy by it.

The latter point is especially significant in the context of the generic lineage *Deliverance* initiates, which routinely concerns itself with the production of an aggressive, collective sexuality by the very workings of male group dynamics. In films contemporary with *Deliverance* in New Hollywood film such as *Straw Dogs* (Peckinpah, 1971), the bonding of the male group relies on forms of allied competition and identification that lead logically, in the terms of the films, to acts of gang rape. Typically, in such representations, these acts result from the activation of sexual energies *within* the group that must then be directed outward so that they are not perceived as directed *at* the group. Thus, gang rapes of women in such films are an extension of an initially male-male erotic discourse, where the men's intimately violent partnership in rape becomes yet another way of engaging with and examining *one another's* sexuality; they also serve as an ultimate disavowal of homoeroticism, where the woman is usurped as an object in order for the men to prove that their desire is *not* for one another. That Bobby's "first wet dream" took place in the context of *male* bonding potentiates implications in *Deliverance*—no matter what the *content* of the dream (and it is significant that the dream's content is not made an issue here)—that are acknowledged only at an allegorical or structural level. Unlike many of the films that follow it, which tend to show how the generation of sexual energies in all-male groups gives rise to heterosexual rape *by* the group of an often randomly chosen woman, *Deliverance* concerns itself with a homosexual rape *of* the group that *remains* linked, specifically through the positioning of Bobby as its object, to unconscious sexual energies *within* the group. When, in response to Bobby's remark about his "wet dreams," Ed asks "How was it?" he concludes a characteristic round of earthy banter that includes revelation by one man of his state of sexual stimulation among the others, and the subsequent expression of interest by one man in another's sexual responses.

In *Deliverance*, to be sure, it is the very objectlessness of these responses that causes the crisis of subjectivity the film ends by registering, the unmoored quality of sexual response within the group that the rape paradoxically functions to underline. On the one hand, an open erotic discourse in an all-male group can itself be taken to signify assurance and certitude, demonstrating the men's ability to engage freely in such discourse because they know it does *not* implicate one another as its potential objects. Yet, in *Deliverance*, such certitude is challenged by the very free circulation of such discourse, so that the river itself, for instance, becomes an object of sexual reverie. In this context, the most "innocent" exchanges among the men can be seen to take on an erotic edge, as when Lewis asks Ed, "Why do you come on these trips with me?" and the latter replies, "I've wondered about that myself." Similarly, Bobby's physical exhibitionism preceding the rape, an offshoot of his near-obsessive erotic discourse, functions initially as a marker of the presumedly secure heterosexuality of the all-male group but challenges that security by the very terms in which it must be asserted. In a striking moment, Bobby jubilantly reveals his naked body as he covers it with insect-repellant while the other men, confronted with this insistent spectacle of male nudity, look discreetly away. Bobby's revelation of his body, like his constant stream of sexual innuendo, derives from an assumed freedom from inhibition based on the presumption of secure heterosexuality. He can reveal his thenceforth de-eroticized body knowing, because of this presumption, that it will *not* stir desire in those who see it. Yet such knowledge depends in some measure upon the revelation itself, since it cannot precede its own proof. To reveal the nude body within the all-male group thus at once asserts the presumed unassailability of the group's heterosexuality and inevitably simulates the forms of homosexual desire.

The rape scene itself functions as a textbook return-of-the-repressed scenario that links the film's thematics of class antagonism to those of homosexual panic. In the terms of the film's thematics of class, the scene allegorizes class negotiations in its mythic reversal of those terms, with the otherwise inexplicable impulse to rape by the mountain men functioning as an allegorical form of revenge, in response to their own class-consciousness. At the same time, however, it functions as an irrevocable literalization of the dynamic of homosexual panic. Bobby's rape humiliates all four of the men, the film would have us see, by making manifest an always palpable but previously denied relation of domination and submission among them, forcefully literalizing that relation in an otherwise unaccountable image of horrific anal penetration.

The rape scene powerfully emphasizes what the film sees as the shared character of this debasement, perhaps most strikingly in its marked *de*-emphasis on Bobby's postrape trauma. In one of a series of anxious stylizations in the sequence, the immobile frame is repeatedly broached by the disorienting, complexly orchestrated entrances and exits of the characters, weaving in and out of the screen space in the aftermath of the murder as they discuss a course of action. Throughout this part of the scene, Bobby's presence is almost comically peripheral as he wanders aimlessly in the composition's background, outside the intersubjective network being woven visually in its foreground through the abstracted interactions of the other characters. Alternating with this abstractifying of the frame-space in the scene is a portentous mobility of the frame itself, the camera slowly tracking and panning back and forth on the outskirts of the clearing. The latter technique, interposing trees, rocks, gnarled vines between the moving camera and the static scene, newly emphasizes the engulfment of the men by the space of the forest, in contrast to earlier scenes that have emphasized the men's separation from nature, shooting them through car windows, for example, in which the woods appear only as a reflection in the glass. At the same time, the camera's mobility continues to emphasize the *collective* trauma of the group over the *private* trauma of the rape victim, who continues to be glimpsed only in

FIGURE 13. Man engulfed by nature: *Deliverance*. Courtesy Museum of Modern Art, New York.

passing and who, for the rest of the film, is rendered very much as an absented figure.

Such emphasis reflects, in part, the seemingly contradictory functions of the scene—both starkly allegorical and grimly literalized, thus a clear test-case for the notion of mythic self-consciousness within the film as a whole if we align allegory with myth and literalization with self-consciousness. It is worth noting in this context that, given the framework into which the rape scene must be fit according to the film's own ideological precepts, it must be represented not through the viewpoint of the victim—the already scapegoated Bobby—but through that of an onlooker. Not the least of the ways in which the scene marks a turning-point in the film is in its function to shift the narrative point-of-view to that of the Ed character, which clearly dominates the remainder of the film. Since the film's point-of-view has been equally balanced among the characters prior to the rape, theoretically, the rape itself could certainly have been presented powerfully through Bobby's perspective, particularly since he is its victim. In the terms of this film, however, what most disturbingly thematizes male subjectivity is not simply for one man to be raped by another man; as we have seen, it is clearly not the trauma of the raped man the film wishes most forcefully to register. Rather, the most pressing trauma the film can envision is that brought on by being forced to *witness* the rape of a man with whom one identifies by a man with whom one cannot identify—a rape defined by gender *identity*, male-on-male, which yet emerges as a violation of perceived sameness, that of the all-male group, by invasive and virulent otherness, that of the demonized mountain-men. Prior to raping Bobby, the mountain men threaten Ed with castration as they tie him to a tree. The rape itself is presented not through the lens of Bobby's violation but through that of Ed's symbolic castration, forced to watch but powerless to intervene.

A comparison of the scene to an analogous one in one of the film's important intertexts, *Rashomon* (Kurosawa, 1950), reveals the later film's stake in displacing the horror of rape onto the trauma of witnessing. In the earlier film, the rape of the wife by the bandit is perceived by the bound husband as a transgression *by* the wife. In each of the versions of the rape scenario retold in the course of the film, however, this perception is registered only after the rape itself has been focalized through the perspectives of the rapist and the victim. In *Deliverance*, similarly, a triangulated scenario of rapist, victim, and witness raises the specter of the victim's implication in the rape—often a specter, to be sure, behind male-male rape, on the assumption that one man should be able to fend off another's aggression unless he really wants it. If Bobby's explicit eroticization of the homosocial space earlier in the film leads in the film's logic to his rape, Ed's veiled contempt for Bobby during the rest of the film after the rape is the function of a soured identification, one which must continue—in Ed's nightmares—*after* it has been poisoned. Ed's disgust as he watches the rape signifies an identification both self-directed, since he fears he will next be raped, and projected, since Bobby's subsequent stigmatization as victim differentiates him from the other men at the same time that it provokes a collective recognition of their own shared vulnerability.

In its fantasy of the violation by outsiders of an intersubjective community, a group of men initially bonded by identification with one another, *Deliverance* participates in myth-based demonologies the like of which the most retrograde Hollywood movie would have ample reason to be proud. Yet the film shows, just as clearly, the origin of such fantasies in the systemic structure of community itself, in projections of an illusory sameness, self-consciously undoing the myth that continues to determine the film's logics. Binding myth and self-consciousness in a scenario of homosexual panic, the film illustrates the mutual implication of identity and difference in New Hollywood cinema. If the New Hollywood projects itself as a previously coherent system disrupted by the invasion of differential elements, such as the self-consciousness of European art-cinema, it also projects, in films such as these, an unprecedented awareness of the mythic dimensions of that scenario itself in its new-found engagement with such rhetorical self-consciousness. *Incorporating* forms of representation formerly associated with European art-cinema with an abiding investment in Hollywood traditions, New Hollywood representation reconceives relations of difference and sameness in Hollywood film. Demystifying Hollywood myth while mythifying art-cinema's rhetorics of self-consciousness, New Hollywood film introjects the "difference" of art-cinema while projecting—and provisionally *rejecting*—the "sameness" of Classical Hollywood representation.

7

Cutter's Way and New Hollywood Spectatorship

The problem of cinema spectatorship is one of the most complex and elusive ones in media study. In order best to understand the many processes of film watching, should we study the habits of actual viewers, extrapolate intentions from the patterns of address in given films, or somehow combine these or other alternatives in a study of mediation of the viewing experience through extratextual forces? Should our study of spectatorship, in other words, be viewer-based, text-based, or context-based? Each possibility raises problems of its own. The investigator can never expect to gather conclusively a representative set of actual viewer responses, especially of responses to films of the past, and while the text itself may well signal in some ways the types of audiences it imagines for itself, to apprehend that textual level does not necessarily (even assuming it is so readily apprehensible) account for possible variability of responses or active counterinterpretations of a film's perceived intentions. I cannot hope to deal with all of these issues here, but it would be remiss to end this study without some commentary on how spectatorship in New Hollywood film has been influenced by the dialogue between Hollywood and European art-cinemas.

As Miriam Hansen has shown, pre-Hollywood American cinema assumed a high degree of differentiation in its audiences, particularly in regard to ethnic and class identities. By depending on viewers' familiarity with particular ethnic customs or habitual assumptions of class, for instance, many films from 1905 to 1916 afforded the pleasures of self-recognition to specific and varied, though usually working-class, audiences (Hansen, 68–76). Though such representations necessarily excluded audiences not directly identified with those identities, they often simultaneously provided those seemingly excluded viewers with the pleasures of exoticized spectacle, frequently tempered through a universalizing appeal to widely accessible conventions of popular entertainment, like burlesque pratfalls and visual tricks. The Classical Hollywood model beginning in the late 1910s, however, began to project a unified audience of white middle-class heterosexual spectators who were further projected, moreover, as distinctly "American." In fact, this model arose as a homeostatic and self-perpetuating system of representation to defend against a perceived onset of differences in the actual audiences. By generalizing *difference* into a form of *identity*, by presuming that variable audiences would find it possible to "identify" with the homogeneous subjects of Hollywood movies, the institution fused the pleasures of familiarity and strangeness by standardizing the commodity of pleasure itself. Even if that commodity was so divisible as to be atomic—subdividing itself, at least, into the pleasures of voyeurism, narcissism, discovery, illusions of plenitude, curiously intersubjective feelings of private experience before a public spectacle—it could still be held forth as the fundamental principle of cinema itself. Even if particular audiences happened not to "like" particular films, the driving force of cinematic pleasure-as-such retained its power.

Audiences educated in the films of European art-cinema of the 1960s and 1970s, and disillusioned by the social trauma of the Vietnam War, grew increasingly disaffected with the escapist products of Hollywood. Thus, with the New Hollywood, that set of rhetorics and practices that constitute the institution's effort to confront such perceived dissatisfactions, two things happened. The institution was beset by a registration of difference, of newly articulated identities demanding representation, unmatched since before the establishment of the classical model, and the terms of cinematic pleasure began to change substantially. Those previously excluded identities, for instance, were no longer so inclined to take pleasure in their own exclusion (even assuming they had ever done so), yet this demographic gain was often framed in terms of a kind of *loss*—of certain formerly unchallenged pleasures, or of a certain representational innocence, as illustrated in the oft-voiced exclamation of cinematic nostalgia, "They don't make 'em like that any more!" These two events, then, are clearly related, and the second half of this book has been concerned to trace aspects of differential textuality emerging from them in postclassical Hollywood film. This chapter attempts to define the relation between these events by showing how shifting patterns of distribution reflect changing assumptions about audiences' desires and pleasures. The most powerful challenges to the traditional Hollywood definition of cinematic pleasure came from the European art-cinema, which often asked viewers to set aside the quest for escapism in order to derive pleasure from putatively more "truthful" representations of reality. Entrenched practices of distribution and exhibition had long worked to separate these two types of cinematic pleasure in film culture by, for instance, insuring the existence of distinct "art-houses" apart from "mainstream" cinemas to which patrons could repair to nourish their longing for that *other* kind of pleasure, thus preserving the traditional definitions. This chapter examines the result when that distinction begins to break down.

Hollywood's Shifting Mainstream after Vietnam

In the development of New Hollywood cinema, Vietnam as a cultural signifier functioned largely as an absent principle, but in critical constructions of the New Hollywood it has been all but ubiquitous. In a representative essay that surveys overlap between the cultural discourses of Hollywood and Vietnam, Michael Anderegg notes that "the film industry had little interest in the Vietnam war as such" while arguing that, "as if to compensate for the absence of movies about Vietnam, movies themselves quickly became a central motif in the Vietnam mythology" (Anderegg, 16). As Anderegg's assertion implies, the exclusion of "Vietnam" from the terms of the New Hollywood may be seen as a result of an effort to sustain increasingly inviable structures of myth, to deny the trauma of history. The war itself, to be sure, has repeatedly been represented as an apocalyptic turning point, the "end of history," a historical trauma that differs from previous sociocultural traumas in American culture in having been generally recognized as somehow unmasterable.[1] If previous wars, in spite of their evident devastation, could be recuperated under the banners of *victory* and *justice*, the "loss" of the war in Vietnam made manifest a range of social corruptions and civic failures thenceforth seen to subtend it.

Many of the most influential narratives of the war see its pivotal importance in its having relocated a process of demystification associated with the war from the realm of ideology to that of history itself. In the best-selling *Backfire*, for instance, Loren Baritz argues that the historical phenomenon of Vietnam itself challenges basic American mythologies, but these challenges continue to be resisted by ideology, yet to be fully absorbed by the culture's representations. Arguing that myths of American nationalism led inevitably to the war, Baritz concludes that "[o]ur power, complacency, rigidity and ignorance have kept us from incorporating our Vietnam experience into the way we think about ourselves and the world" (Baritz, 349). If what is "new" in New Hollywood filmmaking is taken to be a critique of mythology, an effort to engage more immediately the historical real, it should theoretically be a simple matter to distinguish "new" from "old," the progressive text of New Hollywood cinema, allied with ideology-critique, genre revisionism, and confrontation with historical trauma, from its retrogressive opposite. In practice, however, such distinctions are complicated by the subjection to reconstituted forms of mythmaking of Vietnam-as-signifier in spite of its association with an ever more pressing, undeniable reality, itself now taken to demystify or humiliate those representations that would deny its force. Even more to the point, the very interplay of ubiquity and absence that defines Vietnam-as-signifier in the New Hollywood renders difficult the differentiation of New Hollywood texts from Classical Hollywood throwbacks—if, indeed, this is the important distinction—because, as Anderegg notes, even the "progressive" text of the New Hollywood tended to evade specific evocation of Vietnam, if not as cultural signifier than at least as historical reality. In narratives such as Anderegg's, then, Vietnam is the deep cause of change in American filmmaking, yet its status as an *absent* cause makes such shift difficult to mark.

Even given these more general caveats, the relation of a representative film such as *Cutter's Way* (Passer, 1981) to the issue of New Hollywood differential textuality in more local terms is curiously difficult to define. Emergent narratives of the New Hollywood were often predicated on a schematic division between studio-produced and independently made films, the former implicitly associated with traditional representation and the latter with a break from traditional form predicated on the assimilation of practices from the European art-cinema. In *New Cinema in the USA*, for instance, Roger Manvell neatly divides New Hollywood representation into "traditional" and "experimental" camps, the first occupied by Classical Hollywood auteurs like Cukor, Ford, and Hitchcock, the second encompassing avant-garde practices as well as independent filmmaking by directors like Frank Perry, such as *David and Lisa* (1962) (Manvell, 31–48, 122–26).

A history of the shifting patterns of production, distribution, and reception that characterize post-Vietnam Hollywood could be written with *Cutter's Way* occupying one end of a spectrum bracketed at the opposite end by, say, *Heaven's Gate*. Exemplary of the "small" film rescued from oblivion by new strategies of distribution, *Cutter's Way* would likely in such a hypothetical history find itself opposed to Michael Cimino's failed "blockbuster," with the latter conceived as an amorphously bloated enterprise that lays bare the desperate anachronism of big-studio marketing in contemporary film. If Cimino's movie, as legend has it, bankrupts the studio that produces it while *Cutter's Way* circulates through new channels of distribution circumventing studio control, both films, in any case, are set up simply by virtue of their positions within this dynamic in a troubled relation to "mainstream" filmmaking.[2] For whatever reason, clearly, the conventional practices of distribution can no longer accommodate such films, signalling either the outmoded status of the practices or the problematic nature of the films. Thus guaranteed a kind of extratextual "outsider" status, the films become readable in themselves as distinct from mainstream practice through properties of excess or delimitation: they are "problem" texts because they are alternately *too much* or *too little* like the Hollywood norm. In these terms, *Heaven's Gate* emerges as the hypertrophied myth-making epic resoundingly rejected by a postmythic age, while *Cutter's Way* is the self-reflexive film-of-quality that slips through the cracks in a newly but multiply ruptured audience-base.

Because Hollywood typically defines its own alleged crises in terms of narratives of altered proportion or contested scale, the David-and-Goliath scenario of confrontation between studio-blockbuster and small independent is by now a familiar gauge of Hollywood's crisis-points. Coordinating various crises through the years, the history of Hollywood since World War II yields other such suggestive pairings as *Imitation of Life* (Sirk, 1959) and *Shadows* (Cassavetes, 1958); *Dr. Dolittle* (Fleischer, 1967), and *Easy Rider* (Hopper, 1969); or—inflecting the point somewhat differently—*ET* (Spielberg, 1981) and *Blade Runner* (Scott, 1981).[3] What invests *Cutter's Way* with particular interest, however, is the changing profile of differential textuality, of the "outsider" film, it signifies. By virtue of its troubled history of distribution, the film is something of a cult-movie-by-default, yet its narrational strategies and patterns of audience address are significantly more conventional than those of such bona-fide and roughly contemporary cult movies as, say, *Liquid Sky* (Tsukerman, 1979) or *Repo Man* (Cox, 1984). By virtue of its novel channels of circulation, the film clearly qualifies for art-cinema status, yet its comparatively secure genre-orientation and its nominal deployment of "star" figures would seem to position it more closely to the Hollywood norm. To be sure, the film began as a full-fledged studio product, becoming only by something of a fluke an important test-case for post-Vietnam Hollywood.[4] What the film marks is the appearance of a new level of differential textuality in New Hollywood cinema, demanding rethinking of the blockbuster/indie paradigm.

A survey of the marketing history of *Cutter's Way* illustrates not only the curious process of the film's ascension to "cult" status but its suggestively problematic position within the blockbuster/indie paradigm. Originally released in New York with the title *Cutter and Bone* in March 1981, the film was pulled from distribution before the end of its first week's run after a damning review from the *New York Times* characterizing the film as hermetic, clumsy, and depressing—as, essentially, a failed mystery-thriller. This initial pan, however, was followed by several appreciative reviews in weekly papers, such as J. Hoberman's in the *Village Voice*, praising the film's "odd rhythms," "comic detail," and "grim lyricism": "[*Cutter's Way*] is the only Hollywood movie I've seen since *Raging Bull* [Scorsese, 1981] to suggest that the rewards of a second viewing could be even greater than those of a first" (Hoberman, 40). Both the terms of such praise, aligning the film with surreal, gritty B-grade film noirs like *Detour* (Ulmer, 1945), and the venues of its appearance perhaps suggested to United Artists that the studio had failed to apprehend the proper nature of its product. Such a possibility itself points to a shifting profile of cinematic textuality within the studio system. In any case, the turning point in the marketing history of *Cutter's Way* occurred when the film was turned over to the new "specialized" branch of United Artists' distribution operations, United Artists Classics. The film's title was changed, it was screened at several film festivals, and it was subsequently rereleased in limited distribution in June 1981 to more satisfactory box-office returns.

Such wholesale reinvention of a commercial failure as an art-house triumph was made possible, in effect, by the recognition of new *kinds* of "specialty" films, new categories less reliant on the standard oppositions of studio-versus-independent filmmaking, dominant cinema versus countercinemas, Hollywood versus art-cinema practices. The operations of United Artists Classics in the late seventies and early eighties clarifies something of the breakdown of these oppositions. Initially charged with the distribution of mainstream art-cinema items like *The Last Metro* (Truffaut, 1978) or curiosities like *Just a Gigolo* (Hemmings, 1981), United Artists Classics was largely associated with "foreign" films with commercial potential or cult-films-in-the-making such as *Gigolo*, whose cult status was certified by the bankable presence of David Bowie in the cast and by a delectably weird cameo-turn by Marlene Dietrich. While the association of United Artists Classics with the newly conglomerated United Artists suggested its continued ties to a mainstream aesthetic, the very appearance of this new branch of distribution made clear both the studio's acknowledgment of a reconfigured mainstream and its sense of the unprecedented marketing needs of new forms of cinematic commodity. On the one hand, surely, the workings of United Artists Classics can be said to illustrate the mainstreaming of the art-cinema in the late seventies and early eighties, mining the crossover potential from limited venues or arthouse circuits into wider distribution of such relatively unchallenging "art" films as *Last Metro* or *Second Chance* (Handford, 1980). Yet they must also be seen to illustrate the disturbance of a hitherto stabilized mainstream market no longer conceived as unassailably reliable in its reception of commodities. The category of the "specialized" film itself, all but unprecedented in Hollywood's marketing histories, broaches new ways of conceiving of the audience, opening up the possibility that an unsuccessful film is simply one that has failed to reach its proper target audience.

The example of another "problem" film rereleased through United Artists Classics, *New York, New York* (Scorsese, 1977), further illustrates the point. In spite of the resounding failure of the film on its first run, Martin Scorsese's musical pastiche was subsequently redistributed as a lost classic with previously edited footage restored, accorded the respectful treatment of a director's cut and thereby remade as an unjustly abused auteurist masterpiece at last properly targeted to the very art-house audience that might have initially been able to appreciate it. (This occurred, it should be noted, after the box-office success of *Raging Bull*.) Two points are relevant here. First, such marketing strategies of United Artists Classics derive from shifting conceptions of possibilities of spectatorship in the New Hollywood, emphasizing new efforts to target audience rather than to alter product. Second, a novel relation of Hollywood to art-cinema practices emerges in such marketing histories: the branch of distribution formerly reserved to showcase "foreign" product with mainstream potential is finally called on to handle the home-grown film that fails to adhere to the logic of the very mainstream perceived as eroding.

Positioned initially within that mainstream as a conventional example of the thriller genre, *Cutter and Bone* is called to account for its lack of action and its murky plot; reinvented as an art-house "legend" (as the ads proclaimed on its rerelease), *Cutter's Way* takes its place among the studio-produced or studio-affiliated films of the late 1970s and early 1980s that strive to synthesize sensibilities, formerly presumed to be distinct, of Hollywood and art-cinema. Such films include work by directors from the United States, such as Paul Schrader (*American Gigolo* [1981]), Terrence Malick (*Days of Heaven* [1979]), or James Toback (*Fingers* [1978]), as well as directors from Europe, such as Louis Malle (*Atlantic City* [1981]), or Jean-Claude Tramont (*All Night Long* [1983]). In that context, the film is celebrated for its rich ambiguity and for the cachet of its European director. Ivan Passer came to Hollywood from the same "Czech Renaissance" that produced Milos Forman, but his films of the 1970s did not gain the high profile Forman's did during that decade. Indeed, Passer at the time of *Cutter's Way* was already known for three "problem" films that he had directed in the United States, *Born to Win* (1971), *Law and Disorder* (1974), and *Silver Bears* (1978). Each boasted elements of "quality," such as George Segal's bravura acting in the first of these films, but none gelled into a mix that might satisfy audiences of more traditional Hollywood movies. Thus equipped with something of the mantle of the uncompromising maverick, Passer's seeming resistance to assimilate fully to Hollywood's institutional demands—a mark of "failure" in regard to his previous American films—in this event contributed to his function as a signifier of prestige-value behind the film.

Genre Hybridity in New Hollywood Film

Even if as a standard genre movie *Cutter's Way* is initially judged a "failure," the film's relation to genre interestingly illuminates its relation more generally to the shifting mainstream of New Hollywood filmmaking. With its narrative of a Vietnam veteran drawing his wife and friend into the investigation of a crime, it is possible to situate *Cutter's Way* within at least three intersecting generic lines. First, the film occupies a place at a pivotal moment in the development of Hollywood's representations of Vietnam-as-cultural-signifier, between the two "waves" of the emergent genre of the Vietnam film, from the apocalyptic representations of the war experience in the late seventies, such as *The Deer Hunter* (Cimino, 1977) and *Apocalypse Now* (Coppola, 1979), to the recuperative images of the mid-eighties, frequently depicting postwar experience, such as *Gardens of Stone* (Coppola, 1987).[5] At the same time, the film is organized around generic patterns that consolidated themselves throughout the seventies as the "buddy" movie. Finally, *Cutter's Way* continues the neo-noir resurgence initiated by such films of the seventies as *The Long Goodbye* (Altman, 1973), *The Conversation* (Coppola, 1974), *The Parallax View* (Pakula, 1974), and *Night Moves* (Penn, 1976).

Such admixture of generic signifiers is itself noteworthy in relation to the question of differential textuality. Narratives of the New Hollywood typically invoked the mixture of genres as an index of the new films' deviations from classical norms, where unity of genre subtended a range of desired unities. According to this narrative, a film such as *Bonnie and Clyde* (Penn, 1967) breaks with the classical model by mingling the western genre with the gangster film, exposing the mythic bases of both genres and violating unities of tone and style with this brash synthesis.[6] If *Cutter's Way* can be understood in these terms, moreover, the particular genres in which the film deals occupy an already anomalous position in relation to normative textuality, even before they are brought into dialogue with one another. In spite of certain critical assertions to the contrary, film noir continues to be viewed as an adversarial practice in relation to Hollywood cinema, and its seventies manifestations, according to Dennis Turner, even "'out-noir' the classic film noir" by "presenting their protagonists with 'unreadable' mysteries which defy solution" (Turner, 4). Similarly, the Vietnam film by definition breaks with the classic war film, replacing the latter's triumphal rhetorics of courage and heroism with images of chaos and disillusionment. The buddy movie, meanwhile, even though it has been called the quintessential genre of the seventies, lacks the distinctive iconography of the classic genre and remains therefore relegated to the margins in spite of its crucial importance in the formation of New Hollywood categories. Indeed, the genre is paradoxically both pervasive in contemporary American film and curiously indefinable, amorphous, ephemeral, essentially a *non*-genre, as even the trivializing designation by which it is named, as well as its frequent assimilation as a minor comic genre, attests.[7] Not only does *Cutter's Way* draw upon a generic fund already rife with markers of New Hollywood differential textuality, then, but it overlays these multiple generic patterns in defiance of lingering classical edicts about generic unity.

Yet the mixture of genres in *Cutter's Way* is not likely to be felt by the spectator as a severe violation of textual stability, if indeed it is registered at all. This may be accounted for in part by the relative compatibility of the genres the film juxtaposes. The buddy film itself has been seen as an outgrowth of Vietnam-as-cultural-crisis, enacting or recuperating relations between men fostered or threatened by the war and its representations (Jeffords, 54–86). A certain temperamental congruence between the genres emerges more clearly if one considers that one of the formative buddy movies of the seventies, *Thunderbolt and Lightfoot* (Cimino, 1974) shares a director—as well as basic concerns, images, and sensibilities—with one of the founding narratives in Hollywood's representations of Vietnam, *The Deer Hunter*. Similarly, accounts of the evolution of noir have routinely seen the Vietnam film as the former genre's ultimate haven, finding general connections of tone and style between the modes as well as more localized shared practices, such as the sustained use of voice-over narration (Hellman, 188–202).

Although the buddy movie, with its customary ethos of exuberant camaraderie, would seem to be at odds with the attitudes of noir, where typically relations between men are portrayed as overtly hostile, it is worth noting that this generic gap had been vigorously negotiated in Classical Hollywood by a director such as Howard Hawks. In Peter Wollen's survey of Hawks's career, for instance, the apparent distance between such Ur-buddy movies as *Air Force* (Hawks, 1945) and *Only Angels Have Wings* (Hawks, 1939), on the one hand, and such central noir texts as *Scarface* (Hawks, 1932) on the other, disappears in Wollen's influential account into the work's thematic unity: "For Hawks the highest human emotion is the camaraderie of the exclusive, self-sufficient, all-male group" (82). Indeed, a defining feature that closely links these three genres is their common concern with constructions of masculine identity, whether such constructions are seen as registering crises of male subjectivity or celebrating a protectively mythologized masculinity.

Although the question of generic hybridity continues to figure prominently in discourses about the New Hollywood, it had taken on a resonance of quaintness by the early 1980s, when *Cutter's Way* was released. Already by that point, talk of generic dialogue destabilizing classical unity seemed both to overstate the case for generic unity in the classical mode—as if genres had not been routinely combined throughout the history of Classical Hollywood cinema—and to miss the fundamentally diffused character of representative New Hollywood texts. The question of generic models in New Hollywood discourse often takes shape around the issue of genre revisionism or reconstruction. Such discourse necessarily implies a simply reflective notion of cinematic representation, in which localized shifts of generic patterning are accounted for by fundamental shifts in historical condition. Although such approaches routinely engage in a rhetoric of demystification, arguing that the historical real works successively to expose the false consciousness of the generically mythic, they often construct genre itself as essentially immutable, its basic premises unaltered despite superficial shifts of focus. Thus, as I argued in the previous chapter, although what in such narratives is said to define the New Hollywood is precisely its critique of generic mythologies, the narratives themselves remain predicated on the mythic resonance of genre.

In an effort to move beyond such models, Timothy Corrigan in *A Cinema without Walls* presents the very category of genre as itself fundamentally altered by contemporary historical conditions, even as he denies the ready accessibility of the historical real as an immediate, determining agent upon cultural representation. As suggested in Corrigan's subtitle—"Movies and Culture after Vietnam"—he locates Vietnam-as-signifier as the turning point in contemporary history. However, he sees its determination upon cultural production in complex and often circuitous ways. Corrigan argues that shifting and interconnected patterns of production, distribution, and audience address or response work to alter the very terms of film genre, yielding not simply the "corrected" genre models of so much New Hollywood discourse but the already palpable spectacle of "the debris of generic history" (160):

> [T]he very idea of genre seems to reflect the excess history that it cannot accommodate, since there never could be a film that represents the pure or classical genre that genre criticism and theory seems to need in order to sustain itself. But, especially with the generic pastiches of contemporary movies (the blending of sci-fi, romance and the western as one film, for instance) and the current critical positions that relentlessly try to use it (thematically more popular than ever in journals and at conferences), genre seems invariably to overdetermine, mimic, repeat, and shuffle its structures so excessively that what is mostly designated is a contemporary history that insists that it cannot be ritualized according to a single transhistorical pattern. The image of genre seems to taunt contemporary reception with its utopian possibilities only to turn those audiences back before its historical impossibilities. (138)

From this premise, Corrigan goes on to adumbrate what he calls the "generic hysteria" produced by the attempt to contain cultural histories within established genre patterns once the former have been acknowledged to exceed the representational capacities of genre. Thus, Corrigan's model reconceives a standard opposition in New

Hollywood discourse between critique and nostalgia, genre revisionism and genre reconstruction, classical throwbacks and progressivist modernism, positing a category both *post*-generic and nonetheless still bound by the mythologies that produced the genres that have presumably been superseded.

Contemporary film culture confronts the problem of how to retain a measure of cultural authority (read: continued box office) in a society defined by cultural projection or historical circumstance as increasingly heterogeneous, diffused, multiplicitous. The dispersal of generic energies occurs in film culture in tandem with other, analogous dispersals—of authorship, of narration—in a context where diverse representational practices now are theoretically available, in place of a former monolithic and stabilizing classicism, and where audience identity is congruently perceived as ever more fragmented. Thus, even in cases where "generic hysteria" may be read as self-reflexive, as in, say, *Paris, Texas* (Wenders, 1984), it continues to signify uncertainty, the loss (or abdication?) of authority, the "illegibility" of contemporary film. In the simplest terms, genre hybridity is the effect of a newly perceived need to address audiences seen as newly diverse, who will therefore require greater diversity of spectacle/attraction. In more complex terms, multiplicity of genre reflects the decentered subjectivity that is both cause and effect of the ascendant "cinema without walls" of contemporary film.

Coherence and Narrative Stability

Even on the most superficial level, the textual disruptions of *Cutter's Way* that might serve to connect it to forms of "alternative" film practice are not radically foregrounded. By comparison with the neo-noir films of the seventies mentioned above, for instance, *Cutter's Way* represents a marked retrenchment. Unlike *The Conversation*, with its ultimate disturbances of conventional narrative objectivity, *Cutter's Way* retains the signifiers of such objectivity in its negotiation of multiple character viewpoints and in its relatively stable grounding in a representation of external reality against which those viewpoints may be verified. As against the loose narrative structure of *The Long Goodbye*, with its contingent ordering of story events and its consequently rangy, disorienting narrative rhythms, *Cutter's Way* seems closer in construction to the tradition of the well-made play, a tightly constructed naturalist drama ordered around a causally focused narrative logic. Although *Cutter's Way* articulates explicit intertextual relationships with both of these prior neo-noir texts, then, its connection to "mainstream" Hollywood is more secure than that of either of the previous films. Taking up an explicitly post-Vietnam fascination with corporate culpability from *The Conversation* and a neo-Chandleresque class-consciousness from *The Long Goodbye*, drawing key images directly from both films, *Cutter's Way* employs ellipsis, irony, and narrative subjectivity only in modulated ways, thus potentially neutralizing such tactics as mere devices within—and assimilated by—an otherwise conventional mode of representation.

To be sure, signifiers of textual instability in the film are typically recuperated by an overarching narrative stability in which they function as constituent elements. For example, though the character of Bone is positioned to provide a certain narrative anchorage, his point-of-view is repeatedly elided at crucial and strategic narrative points. In the opening sequence of the film, the viewer is pointedly refused access to Bone's witnessing of the narrative's initiating event, in which a man—possibly the magnate J. J. Cord—dumps a woman's corpse in a back alley. The scene is organized around a close-up of Bone squinting into bright light, without a point-of-view reverse-angle to show what Bone sees. The reverse-angles that are supplied are distinguished from Bone's viewpoint, although the shots remain infused with a rhetoric of the subjective—of spatiotemporal fragmentation—that implies the viewer's alliance with Bone's vantage point. Congruent with the spectator's fragmented view of the event, Bone's own view is presented as incomplete. Indeed, a later cut back to the alley after Bone has left reveals what he has *not* seen, the woman's corpse—disturbingly condensed in the synechdochic image of her high-heeled feet protruding from a trash-bin. But in fact, in spite of this seeming congruency, the film emphasizes the enforced distinction between Bone's viewpoint and the audience's even more fragmentary one, so that the viewer is uncertain not only about what was really there, but about what Bone saw. Conventions of point-of-view editing in Hollywood cinema tend to imply, even in the absence of literally subjective shots, a correspondence between characters' viewpoints and narrative events, implying continued narrative omniscience in spite of heightened character subjectivity (*Classical Hollywood Cinema*, 31–32). Here, even if the viewer assumes initially that the fragmentary representation of the event is motivated by the need to register the obstruction of Bone's viewpoint, that assumption is overruled later in the plot when Bone's description of the killer far exceeds what the audience has been permitted to see. Bone's invasion of the Cord Oil office, ostensibly to deliver Cutter's blackmail note, is presented similarly through ellipsis.

As Bone tentatively enters the lobby, a cut returns the audience outside, so that the delivery is registered only by Bone's report, which turns out later to be false. It is significant that, although Bone repeatedly voices a reality-principle the narrative intermittently endorses, as when he labels Cutter's obsession with Cord a product of fantasy or paranoid delusion, he is the character most often linked in the film to the possibility of narrative unreliability. In each case, however, the momentary narrative gap is soon nominally closed by a logic of narrative causation.

Still, the film can be said to leave open two of the central enigmas around which its narrative takes shape: Is Cord the murderer? Was the death of Cutter's wife, Mo, an accident, a suicide, or Cord's second murder, with Bone as the intended victim? The interrelation of these questions clarifies the large implications they consolidate for the film's narrative procedures and their relation to questions of spectatorship. Contemporary film theory posits two basic drives behind the processes of spectatorship, the drive toward sadistic mastery on the one hand and toward masochistic psychodynamics on the other. Typically, the classical model of narration has been identified with an implied sadism, with its linear narratives, active protagonists, punctual climaxes, and satisfying resolutions yielding the pleasurable effect of final mastery for the implied spectator. That final mastery, however, depends on the intermediate potential of masochistic spectatorship, for classical narration itself usually incorporates elements such as suspense, reversal, or frustrated desire, components of masochism, on the route to conclusive viewer satisfaction. Even when the individual viewer does not experience ultimate satisfaction, then, as in the case of the female spectator who registers the objectification of women or the exclusion of female identification in the standard Oedipal narrative of Classical Hollywood, masochistic response is always potential in narrative construction. The viewer, that is to say, *desires* frustration in narrative in order that the effect of ultimate mastery be therefore produced all the more powerfully. A "cult" film is one that divides its audiences in terms of the kinds of pleasures it affords them. Refusing to produce the usual cinematic pleasure of mastery, the "cult" film typically excludes viewers whose responses are limited to that pleasure, "punishing" those viewers for such limitation by reveling in its own vulgarity or badness (as in the case of *Liquid Sky* or John Waters's films), or by systematically refusing the imperatives of classical narration, denying narrative climaxes (as in a Warhol film) or heightening them to such a frantic degree that they cease to function as climaxes (as in a "head" movie, such as *Performance* [Cammell/Roeg, 1970]) or closing with an anti–"happy ending" (as in, say, *Sid and Nancy* [Cox, 1986]). The target viewer of the "cult" film is one who delights in such punishment, surrenders the typical cinematic pleasures in favor of a kind of ecstatic, knowing *un*pleasure, discovers the novel pleasures occulted in the film, or identifies with the film's sadistic relation to the mass audience.

If the spectator's desire for the frustration of pleasure is an intermediate stage in the drive toward final, pleasurable mastery, the question of narrative closure becomes important in the positioning of the spectator between masochism and mastery. We might conclude that a film that achieves traditional, "satisfying" closure dispels intermediate frustration to position the viewer in a state of final mastery (as in a "feel-good" movie), while a film that negates such closure displaces mastery by asking the viewer to take a certain pleasure in that negation. In a suggestive analysis of *Cutter's Way*, John Caughie and Gillian Skirrow argue that despite the film's clear "cult" leanings, its narrative movement is toward the conventional closure achieved in what they see as the "redemption" of the Cutter and Bone figures in a final Oedipal confrontation with Cord. In their reading, Mo "dies to allow the boys to be redeemed as men" (58), while the question of Cord's culpability dissolves into the necessity of his construction as an archetypally demonic father-figure. In these terms, the textual disturbances of the film cannot be said to result from the irresolution of the questions above since such an appeal to an overarchingly symbolic Oedipal structure effectively resolves them. Admitting the "ultimately unsatisfying" nature of "this kind of Oedipal reading" (56), Caughie and Skirrow view the Oedipal dyad as determinant of the film's drive toward coherence, which they see, significantly, as ultimately unfulfilled: "The Oedipal, or its appropriation as a given structure, arrives as the resolution rather than as the problem, offering to contain the disturbance of the film within an acceptable structure of sexuality, ordering the deformities, trying to forget the bits that don't fit. But not quite succeeding" (60).

Even in more local terms, the issues of Cord's guilt and Mo's fate, however apparently unresolved, can be said to operate within a stable narrative scheme. In a film such as *The Conversation*, the open-endedness of the diegetic situation is predicated not on withheld or suspended resolutions but on a complete narrative macrostructure. In keeping with the conventions of noir mystery narrative, both *The Conversation* and *Cutter's Way* are inititiated by specific engimas that become objects of investigation that shape the plot. In *The Conversation*, however, that initial enigma is itself indeterminate. The elements of

the opening scene in the Coppola film are subject to multiple reinter-
pretations as the plot proceeds, and as in that film's key intertexts *Rear
Window* (Hitchcock, 1954) and *BlowUp* (Antonioni, 1966), it is not clear
what event, or even what kind of event, precipitates the narrative's
outset. By contrast to such constitutive undecidability, *Cutter's Way*
stabilizes its enigmas by articulating a range of possible resolutions
within the diegesis, in the terms of a fully enforced narrative logic.
Whether or not Cord is guilty, it is clear that a woman has been murdered; whether or not Cord murdered Mo, it is clear that she is dead.
Moreover, characters in the film are systematically aligned with potential viewer responses that further delimit—if not close off entirely—
narrative possibilities. For instance, the police label Mo's death an accident, Bone believes it is a suicide, and Cutter is convinced it is Cord's
second murder. Thus, signifiers of narrative indeterminacy, even as
they are allowed continued circulation in the text, are simultaneously
grounded in the film's status as "character study," replacing narrative
closure with a depth-model of psychological ambiguity that continues
to anchor narrative possibilities.

Though modified here, this model of psychological ambiguity
finds its precedent as much in traditions of European art-cinema as in
those of film noir. Despite the comparative narrative determinacy of
Cutter's Way, significantly, its narrative is grounded in a vision of traumatized subjectivity redolent of both noir and art-cinema representations, and correlative of the film's post-Vietnam politics. It is this conception of character—and, indeed, the film's very status as "character
study"—that most clearly focuses the relation of the film's "mainstream" status to its own avowals of differential textuality. At the same
time, the film's conception of a traumatized subjectivity is its strongest
link to the more obviously "radical" neo-noirs of the seventies. This
link may account for the distinct echoes of Caughie and Skirrow on
Cutter's Way in Dennis Turner's treatment of spectatorship and seventies neo-noir in general, with relation to *The Conversation* in particular:

> [*The Conversation*] is concerned with its own textuality, engaged
> in an ongoing drive to constitute itself as narrative yet haunted
> by a memory of a divided subject. The hero within the film
> strives to make narrative sense out of nonsense in an attempt to
> ward off the fragmentation and dismemberment he has caused in
> the past. The text itself strives to be a genre film at the same time
> that its origins are in a fractured past of the fantasy tale and the
> Continental art-film. The spectator auditor in the theater experi-
> ences unpleasure to the extent that the ruptured narratives and

the unreadable soundtrack fail to provide that discursive ribbon of specularity in which he has learned to constitute himself in a comfortably integral subjectivity. (Turner, 5)

Like Skirrow and Caughie on *Cutter's Way*, so here Turner reads Coppola's film in terms of a drive toward coherence obstructed by a troubled, anxious self-reflexivity. Perhaps more to the point, the triple registers of character-text-spectator in Turner's analysis, where each term is said to reflect the activity of the other, is parallel to the link Skirrow and Caughie establish between the cult-film status of *Cutter's Way* and the film's effort to ground its genre conventions in the "correlative" of post-Vietnam social dissolution: "The excess, ambivalence, and anxiety of *film noir* . . . provide the generic correlative of an America once again post-war and uncertain" (55).

Masochism and New Hollywood Spectatorship

In spite of what I have posited as the more secure connection of *Cutter's Way* to a perceived "mainstream" in its own textual self-definition, what the film registers more powerfully and more explicitly than other neo-noirs is a sense of the irrevocable erosion of that very "mainstream." The traumatized subjectivity at the movie's core, readable as the film's most decisive post-Vietnam signifier, is at the same time shown to be the product of a confrontation with more immediate forms of social change, such as overt racial conflict, themselves implicitly rooted in the experience of the war. The question of shifting terms in New Hollywood spectatorship, of what kind of spectator the film imagines for itself, finds its logical extension in the question the film's diegesis implies so persistently: Who is now the subject of social discourse? To frame the question this way, of course, implies the fragmentation and dispersal of a previously whole, coherent social subject—say, the white heterosexual American middle class, or the "general population" projected as the imagined audience of Classical Hollywood cinema. In an ambitious essay, "White Spectatorship and Genre Mixing," Judith Mayne draws a connection between the genre hybridity of contemporary Hollywood cinema and a growing awareness in Hollywood filmmaking of racial difference within the audience. Even if this awareness amounts to little more than a series of white fantasies about black subjectivity, as Mayne implies, its result is still a distinct loss of confidence in the stability of generic structures formerly called on to confer validity upon the mythologies underlying them and to produce the impression of a unified audience (Mayne, 142–56). If New Hollywood genre-mixing is itself the sign of a wavering faith in these hegemonic functions of the classical model, its connection to questions of race further clarifies how an internalized perception of cultural dispersal shapes New Hollywood discourse.

In this regard, it is striking to note that the introduction of the figure of Cutter at the beginning of the film immediately foregrounds the character's own classification of himself as a social subject. Drunkenly taunting two black men in a bar, Cutter insults them with a racist slur, then justifies himself with cynical irony by claiming not to know the currently acceptable terms of address: "What are we white well-intentioned liberals supposed to call you guys these days, anyway? Negro? Black?" Cutter's tirade ironically encapsulates or reflects shifting social divisions of post-Vietnam America, invoking a centralized category—the "we" of white liberalism—and a marginalized one thenceforth taken as the *object* of the former's discourse. Even as Cutter mocks such rhetoric in a crude parody of liberal discourse, he underlines the actual racism that upholds it—as well as venting his own racism—by implicating Bone, reporting racist epithets he claims Bone routinely uses. Thereupon, Bone attempts to mediate the conflict, excusing Cutter's calculated outrageousness by muttering, "The war, y'know . . . ." Though the men accept this explanation—"I can understand that"—Cutter off-handedly and enigmatically denies it: "I wasn't in any war." The scene condenses a key thematic pattern of the entire film that figures Cutter as the monstrous id of a newly unstable liberal social discourse. Compulsively breaching decorum, Cutter relentlessly exposes the hypocrisy of a symbolic order that arrogates power to the white liberal position, as Cutter sees it, by repressing alternative discourses that nonetheless are seen to assail or beset the "mainstream" one. It is important to note here that Cutter positions himself as identifying with neither the "mainstream" nor the marginalized position. His aggression is directed most violently at the bourgeois even though he is himself capable of passing as petty-bourgeois, as in the scene where he destroys his neighbor's car in a rage, then passes himself off as a good citizen, a remorseful and level-headed veteran, when the police arrive. Yet he directs nearly equal derision at the groups he recognizes as challenging the hegemony of the mainstream. The bileful racism of his introductory scene returns in his minstrel-show parody on seeing Mo in their first scene together or in the scene of the visit to Cord's office, where Cutter contemptuously characterizes the black guard as "Mr. Stepin Fetchit." Elsewhere he refers to picking up two hitchhikers as "a sociological experiment":

"An Afro-American homosexual and two Mestizas with a domesticated simian." Thus Cutter articulates something of his own trauma in fantasized encounters with racial, ethnic, and sexual otherness, while denying the source of that trauma (or the fantasies themselves) in "the war."

In spite of the virulently choric function Cutter frequently serves in the narrative, he is not an entirely dependable spokesperson for the film's point-of-view, especially since it directs a measure of its modulated irony at him. On the one hand, Cutter stands in for the film's perspective with his saturnine vision of the ruptured coherence of the social sphere. At the "Spanish Fiesta Days" parade where Bone recognizes Cord, for instance, Cutter's abrasive sideline commentary sneeringly directs the viewer's attention to the evident hypocrisy and kitschiness of the festival: "Our glorious past . . . Pioneers, Indians, Mexicans . . . the white man's blessing." Implicit in Cutter's scorn is a recognition that the festival's pageantry represses real historical violence, real social trauma, by representing it in the terms of a populist spectacle of cultural difference. Again, significantly, such recognition is presented in relation to Cutter's own self-definition of his position as "white man." Cutter's racist diatribes self-consciously perform the bigotry of a still-centralized whiteness that yet sees itself under siege by the onset of racial otherness, while at the same time refusing to mourn nostalgically the perceived loss of centrality for the *white man* as a—or *the*—social subject. The scene at the parade is crucial narratively, because of Bone's recognition of Cord, but it is more important thematically, as an emblem of altered terms of spectatorship before the spectacle of newly acknowledged cultural difference, with Cutter guiding the responses of the film's viewers, *seeing through* the spectacle's insulating pageantry to the actual social trauma it conceals.

This celebration of "alternative" cultures may, in the terms of the film, confront the "white man" with the threat of dispossession of control of the social sphere, but it is a canny irony that the roles of Mexicans in the parade are enacted mostly by whites, a sign at once of the parade's egalitarian posture and its repression of the very cultural diversity it claims to celebrate. In the disquieting credit sequence, the audience sees the murdered girl dancing in the parade in spectral slow-motion, a WASP-ish cheerleader playing the role of a Hispanic bride. In the parade sequence, Cord appears on a white steed as the festival's "Honorary Presidente." Despite such obvious neutralization of cultural difference, the film repeatedly makes clear that a very literal fear of racial difference underlies the "Spanish Fiesta." For example, Bone refers to the civic unrest that attends the festival—"Buildings trashed, cars burnt"—while the police finally write off the girl's murder as a by-product of the social chaos the festival is seen to produce. The festival thus engenders here the half-spoken threat of aggressively mobilized ethnicities, a fantasy of congregating races coming together in the social sphere to destabilize it irreparably. Playing out its quasi-Oedipalized confrontation between white men within this sphere of cultural difference, the film thus registers the displacement of guilt for white violence—Cord's act of murder—onto imagined scenarios of racial uprising, repeating the very cycle that, as Cutter notes, the parade itself fails to commemorate.

Cutter is both a spectator before this ceaseless procession of social hypocrisy, commenting on it with detached irony, and himself a spectacle of post-Vietnam social trauma, bearing its visible marks on his body. The film's last scene makes Cutter's status as spectacle explicit by connection to the earlier scene by placing him on the same steed Cord rides in the parade. But that status is registered throughout the film as well, as for example in the lingering shot of Mrs. Cord looking at Cutter with a strange mixture of pity and revulsion when he invades Cord's club. Indeed, just as Cutter simultaneously deconstructs the white-male subject-position and asserts his own inevitable participation in it, so—in these terms, a literally split subject—is he divided between obsessively remarking a generalized social trauma and compulsively enacting his own "personal" trauma. Significantly, Bone characterizes the latter in terms of a lost wholeness. Before their final siege upon Cord's estate, Bone tells Cutter, "It's not going to bring [Mo] back, or take away our guilt, or make you whole again." Cutter's scarred and traumatized body, defining an important symbolic register in the film's structure, is called upon to emblematize the fragmentation of the social sphere in the film's most literal register.

The symbolization of Cutter's body is achieved in part by way of the presentation of his body through an explicitly, self-consciously mythic lens, particularly by association with the archetype of Melville's Ahab. (This level of mythic self-consciousness positions the film in a line of descent with the films discussed in the previous chapter.) In the introductory encounter between Cutter and Bone, Cutter greets Bone as his "Ishmael," while the later journey to the Cord office is ironically linked to the whale hunts in *Moby-Dick*: "Thar she blows!" Cutter shouts as the Cord building looms imposingly into view, an insistent low-angle emphasizing its leviathanlike aspect. Despite both the irony of the association and Cutter's own knowingly explicit references to it, this link to classical archetype has the effect of disembodying Cutter's injury, displacing it from the level of physical disability to that of symbolic barometer.

It is interesting in this regard to compare the film's representation of Cutter to analogous previous representations of disabled veterans in cinema from Classical Hollywood to New Hollywood cinema—say, Harold Russell in *The Best Years of Our Lives* (Wyler, 1946) or Jon Voight in *Coming Home* (Ashby, 1978). In all three cases, the veteran's status as social spectacle, object of a generalized, public gaze, derives from his fate as a gauge, by virture of his disability, of postwar social trauma. Unlike Cutter, who revels in disrupting social complacency, both Russell and Voight in key scenes in their respective films react with shame or anger to invasive public stares, vehemently rejecting their relegation to the realm of spectacle. Moreover, both figures are ultimately rehabilitated, repositioned within a nominally normative masculinity through renewed sexuality. In *The Best Years of Our Lives*, Russell's marriage to his prewar sweetheart signals his final, restorative acceptance of his disability. Though the case of *Coming Home* is more complicated, in that film too an intense moment of heterosexual union presages the Voight character's growing acceptance of his paraplegic condition, conceived in the film as a necessary step toward rehabilitation. In both cases, the male figure's acceptance of lack—of, indeed, what both films initially present in fairly explicit terms as a symbolic castration—is predicated on a successful reentry into a sexual symbolic-order. Significantly, in the case of *Coming Home*, this moment depends upon the revelation and thorough examination by the camera of the Voight character's body. The film's need to reintegrate the disabled body into a reconstituted conception of normality requires a full scrutiny of that body, revealing the presumed normality behind the appearance of bodily difference and, by implication, disavowing the stigma of castration by displaying the character's sexual performance, albeit with a rhetoric that nonetheless declares itself free of prurience or voyeurism. In narrative terms, this moment of bodily revelation heralds not only the character's acceptance of lack but, as its paradoxical corollary, the ultimate disavowal of his status as spectacle. Thereafter in the plot, he is not shown to be further troubled by the repulsed or pitying stares of others, and the signifiers of mitigated freakishness through which the character had been introduced are considerably minimized. The character's movement from a condition of emotional paralysis to renewal, from embittered veteran to reintegrated citizen, is correlated with a very literal movement from sexual dysfunction to sexual activity. The reliance of this narrative trajectory upon a fully detailed and extremely physical, thus apparently *literalized*, representation of the body raises, to be sure, an important paradox. In the very moment the character is presumably liberated from the realm of spectacle, his body is subjected to the camera's most relentless gaze. Indeed, in the film's paradoxical terms, the latter must occur so that the former—an absolute requirement of the narrative's goal—can be achieved.

In these cases, then, the characters' bodies initially function symbolically, like Cutter's, as visual emblems of historical trauma, and the gradual literalization in these films of the male body coincides with a thematic of social reintegration. Given the link here between spectacle and narrative movement, it is interesting to contextualize this dynamic in relation to standard treatments of gendered constructions of spectacle and spectatorship in film, such as Laura Mulvey's "Visual Pleasure and Narrative Cinema." As Mulvey's title itself implies, her theory presupposes a dual register in film's symbolic structure, split between a scopophilic level organized around the drive toward pleasurable spectacle and a diegetic level aspiring to narrative mastery through such standard classical devices as conventional linearity, stabilized protagonists, and assured closure. These two registers function as formative mechanisms, as Mulvey argues: "[O]ne implies a separation of the erotic identity of the subject from the object on the screen (active scopophilia), the other demands identification of the ego with the object on the screen through the spectator's fascination with and recognition of his like" (61). The unconscious alignment of woman with the position of passive spectacle and man with active force in propelling narrative, in Mulvey's terms, gives rise to a tension between these registers: "The presence of woman is an indispensible element of spectacle in normal narrative film, yet her visual presence tends to work against the development of a story line, to freeze the flow of action in moments of erotic contemplation" (62).

In the anomalous instances of *male* spectacle surveyed above, this tension is explicitly dramatized, so that the male body's status as spectacle is framed precisely around the narrative goal to divest it of that very condition, to return the male figure to his "proper" position as *subject* of narrative, active force, bearer of the look rather than its object. Indeed, Mulvey reads the overdetermination of the dyad male/active/subject/gazer versus female/passive/object/spectacle as a function of the castration complex, whereby such anxiety is disavowed by "turning the represented figure itself [woman as signifier of castration] into a fetish so that it becomes reassuring rather than dangerous" (64).

Connoting a deeply *un*pleasurable *to-be-looked-at-ness*, the image of the disabled veteran in these instances is initially seen as "feminized," as a visual signifier of potential castration. But this image cannot be fully recuperated through eroticisation or fetishism, in spite of its status as spectacle, since to do so would obviously compromise the overarching structure of male spectatorship—which, of course, cannot permit such transgression in the first place. Thus, in these films, the literalization of the disabled body in visual terms is tightly coordinated with the restoration of a potent masculine subjectivity in narrative terms. This rhetoric of restoration can be achieved in each of these cases, however, only in the terms of an explicit logic of masochism. In order to be reintegrated into the social order, in these narratives, the veteran must learn to take a certain pleasure in his loss, disavowing the permanently disabling character that the social order continues to assign to that loss. Kaja Silverman's influential discussion of masochism is relevant here, though Silverman overemphasizes the supposed *origin* of male masochism and underemphasizes its dimensions of pleasure per se: "The male masochist magnifies the losses and divisions upon which cultural identity is based, refusing to be sutured or recompensed. In short, he radiates a negativity inimical to the social order" (Silverman, 206). In the cases under discussion here, masochistic *pleasure* derives from the possibility of assimilation into the "social order."[8]

Unlike either *The Best Years of Our Lives* or *Coming Home*, *Cutter's Way* is not a parable of social reintegration or rehabilitation, and its aesthetic of masochism is visible in the characters' self-conscious refusal of social integration (despite their status nonetheless as "middle-class"), which is remarked in a number of bitterly masochistic jokes in the film, and which results in an atmosphere of suspension or deferral—of waiting around for something awful to happen—that is characteristic of the masochistic aesthetic.[9] The representation of Cutter's body as spectacle, conversely to the representations of the earlier films, is retained in part precisely by *denial* to the viewer of visual access to Cutter's body. Its relegation to a *symbolic* register of spectacle, where it remains paralyzed as the marker of a historical trauma that must therefore be seen as ongoing, is a function of the film's generic connection to the "buddy" movie. Interestingly, Mulvey sees the "buddy" movie as a generic formation that circumvents the narrative disruption of woman-as-spectacle, "in which the active homosexual eroticism of the central male figures can carry the story without distraction" (62).[10] Yet the symbolization of Cutter's body relies upon clear visual contrasts of the bodies of the two male figures in the film, so that in effect Cutter emerges as a spectacle of trauma through his systematic positioning as an unpleasurable object of Bone's masochistic gaze. If Cutter's status as quadruplegic renders him the signifier of a not-yet-disavowed castration, in the terms of the narrative, it is Bone who—*through* his relation to Cutter—must either disavow or master that condition. The film's melodramatics of male power work themselves out quite systematically around the image of the phallus and the threat of castration. The clear phallic connotations of the film's original title, "Cutter and Bone," aptly suggest the overdetermination of this dynamic in the film's symbolic economy, with "Cutter" evoking an aggressive threat to the "Bone" of phallic normativity. To be sure, Cutter is positioned in the film as both castrated male, exiled from normative masculinity, and castrating avenger, crusading to strip away Cord's social power and, in the same gesture, to initiate Bone into social commitment.

Bone's body functions initially as spectacle in conventional cinematic terms. In the film's opening scenes, he is presented, denuded, as a figure of conventional male beauty and, implicitly, an object of female desire. An extreme close-up of Bone naked at a mirror, shaving after a one-night stand, suggests a quality of narcissism amplified by two later reverse-shots that show the unacknowledged, desiring looks of women as Bone passes. To be sure, despite the visual association of Bone's body with conventional constructions of male beauty, his female sex-partner, even as she gazes at him with longing, expresses off-handedly lacerating sexual dissatisfaction, advising him to "try some Vitamin E." Thus, Bone's apparent emblematism of normative masculinity is itself immediately associated with connotations of lack. The first scenes display the character's complacency and self-absorption, and Cutter later attacks him explicitly for a lack of commitment represented, in Cutter's surprisingly bourgeois terms, by his avoidance of the war, marriage, and career. Yet the presentation of Bone's body, even as it is a compulsive object of narrative revelation—in the opening scene and in the sex scene with Mo—undergoes a process of literalization much as in the representations of Russell or Voight. Moreover, Bone's body is presented in images of wholeness, as in the emphasis on its classical proportions in the opening shots, where the mirror functions to yield a rounded and holistic view of Bone. Similarly, the quality of tranquility the film's narration imparts to the boating scene with Valerie derives from its conception of this scene as the measure of a healthy sexuality. Although the narration largely legitimates Cutter's attacks on Bone's lack of commitment, Bone continues to function in the film as a gauge of normative masculinity. Cutter himself recognizes this when he all but goads Bone into sleeping with Mo. Not only does the film contrast Bone's bodily "wholeness" with Cutter's "physical" lack, but it draws attention to Bone's function as a kind of substitute prosthetic for Cutter, as when Bone literally carries Cutter from place to place.

The film's last scene is worth examining in some detail as a site of the convergence of the film's contradictory energies. The sequence is heavily marked by a rhetoric of ironic indeterminacy characteristic of art-cinema practices at the same time that it aspires to the scenario of redemption Caughie and Skirrow perceive as crucial to the film's operations. Central to this issue is the representation of Cord himself in the sequence. As Caughie and Skirrow argue, the figure of Cord readily lends itself to Oedipal reframing because "his place in the film seems symbolic rather than diegetic" (56). Throughout the film, Cord's appearances are left ephemeral enough to be taken as sites of projection on the part of the film's characters. In the parade sequence, for instance, he is shown in an uncanny slow-motion montage that parallels the representation of his victim in the credit sequence. His image is eclipsed within the composition, rendered inapprehensible, in a manner redolent of Bone's glimpse of him at the murder scene. Yet the character's literal absence from most of the film as a whole, generating a principle of uncertainty in the narrative's structure, also lends itself to condensatory images that give a simultaneous impression of Cord's ubiquity. The low-angle shots of Cord's building, for example, visually condense the sinister aspect the film imputes to the figure of Cord. Cord's appearance in the final scene at once brings together these symbolic and diegetic registers, since the scene is at least rhetorically positioned to provide answers to narrative enigmas, and reveals the film's stake in demonstrating their incompatibility.

The initial encounter in the sequence between Bone and Cord portends the possibility of a thorough delegitimation of Cutter's suspicion of Cord. In spite of the overdetermined irony of the setting, with Cord framed in dim light against a portrait of himself stylized to mock his patriarchal postures, the tenor of the sequence initially grants Cord a disposition of benevolent concern and compassionate understanding. Indeed, Cord becomes the film's most authoritative spokesperson as he states with professed empathy a version of the narrative's events that, by film's end, remains potentially valid: "I understand your friend is pursuing some fantasy of his own that includes me. . . . I've been in a war; I know what it can do to some men. Do you think it would help if I talked to him?" An abrupt cut to the stable where Cutter mounts Cord's steed both enforces the narrative ellipses crucial to the sequence and establishes the unconventional rhythms— at once truncated and oddly languid—that characterize it. The dreamlike sense of unreality attached to Cord's final charge stems from a stylization of the image, as in the painterly long shot of the stable with its artfully molded shafts of light, and an unusual use of point-of-view shots that, by contrast to the conventional effects of point-of-view, function to distance the viewer from the action. The latter effect is achieved not only by the style of the shots themselves, with the camera positioned on the horse's back as Cutter approaches Cord's library, pivoting slowly with a curious floating effect, negating any sense of the immediacy of the action. Also important is the context of the shots in the montage of the sequence, intercut with cutaway shots from a distanced perspective that emphasizes the incongruity and extremity of Cutter's actions. Thus, whatever sense of triumph attends Cutter's last stand is fully ironized, as is clear as well in the sudden cut from Cutter's vainglorious slow-motion charge through Cord's window to his bathetic fall, coming to rest on the floor with a calculatedly anti-climactic thud.

Thus, the film's relation to questions of narrative indeterminacy reveals a crucial link between its mitigated art-cinema poetics and its New Hollywood genre dynamics. The buddy-movie structure of the film enacts a seemingly irreconcilable tension between competing narratives, worked out through the figures of Cutter and Bone, even as it strives for a semblance of narrative closure, thus exposing the genre's potential to problematize normative viewer identification. The conventional treatment of male intersubjectivity in the 1970s buddy movie relied heavily upon a representation of intense identification between the male figures in the diegesis, as in *Scarecrow* (Schatzberg, 1973) or *California Split* (Altman, 1975), which functioned to reconsolidate viewer identification that might otherwise have been split between the principal characters. Though similarly concerned with a thematic of male intersubjectivity in its diegesis, *Cutter's Way* continually foregrounds the incompatibility of the Cutter and Bone positions, even as it registers their intense *desire* for a *lost* identification. Even in the final shots of the film, when the previously skeptical Bone accuses Cord of the murder and shoots him with Cutter's gun, a stylized attention to intricacies of gesture and nuance works to undermine any final validation of Cutter's conviction. Reverse-shots showing Cord ludicrously donning ineffectually protective sunglasses and Bone clumsily aiming the gun still clasped in Cutter's hand undercut the potential rhetoric of reparation by way of an absurdist counterlogic. Moreover, the elision of a prior conversation between Cord and Bone renders unaccountable Bone's change of heart, his new-found belief in Cord's guilt, making the scene readable not as the triumph of Cutter's conviction but as Bone's ultimate, destructive entry into his dead friend's fantasy. In the

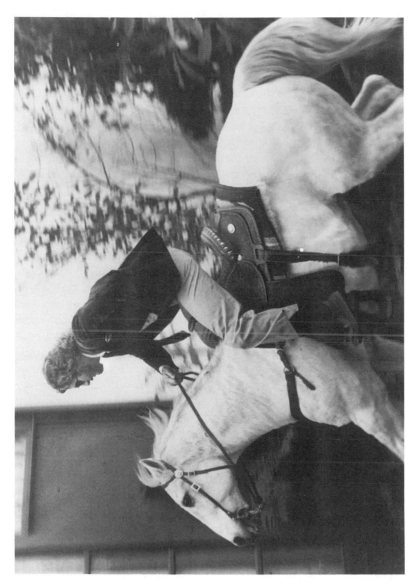

FIGURE 14. Cutter's ironic last charge in *Cutter's Way*. Courtesy Museum of Modern Art, New York.

largest terms, the final shot works out visually the thematics of masochism that so trouble viewer identification throughout the film, in which Cutter's effort to force Bone out of passivity, into some form of ideological or emotional commitment, is seen not as an impulse to rebirth but as tantamount to yet another form of castration. The final shot can be read as a redemptive tableau—Cutter and Bone, holding the gun together, at last joined in previously denied phallic power to confront Cord—only by ignoring the deeply *un*pleasurable implications of Cutter's death and Bone's guilt. To be sure, Bone's final gesture is readable either as Bone's tributary completion of Cutter's quest by propping up his dead hand, or as Bone's decision to kill Cord without implicating himself, imputing the deed to Cutter. In either case, this charged, truncated tableau ultimately realizes the film's construction of a masochistic intersubjectivity that reflects dispersed possibilities of identification.

The split identifications between Cutter and Bone in the narrative of *Cutter's Way* figure in local terms the altered character of New Hollywood spectatorship and the reconfigured mainstream the film heralds more generally. In the cultural politics of this movie, the recognition of male "lack" registers challenges to the edicts of phallocentrism, while at the same time allowing the film to remain centered on the thematics of male subjectivity. Politically speaking, the film's allegiances could not be clearer. The vision of post-Vietnam cultural crisis on view in *Cutter's Way*, a vision fundamentally inflected as anti-Vietnam, anti-corporate, and pro–art-cinema, is that of the very "white liberal" whose beset position the film articulates. In the context of such cultural politics, it is desirable that this "white-liberal" position lose or relinquish its centrality, in the name of greater cultural pluralism after Vietnam. Thus it is that the film itself registers a certain pleasure in this "loss" of centrality, even as this therefore masochistic registration of the loss of white privilege continues simultaneously to enable the almost exclusive representation of white people.

The two phases of *Cutter's Way*'s textual identity—mainstream thriller and art-house *succès d'estime*—represent poles of New Hollywood textuality that, consolidated here in a single film, illuminate altered possibilities of spectator pleasure. As a mainstream thriller, *Cutter's Way* fails to provide the forms of pleasure associated with Classical Hollywood as such, an infantile gratification predicated on immediate identification with the spectacle. While retaining elements of mainstream textuality, the text positions the spectator in a distanced position that balances cinematic pleasure against unpleasure.[11] Rooted in the painful loss of infantile gratification but yielding the compensatory pleasure of symbolic mastery, predicated on the fetishism of ambiguity, incoherence, and lack, New Hollywood spectatorship subsumes potentially masochistic energies. Jacques Lacan's well-known metaphor for subjectivity is the image of a paralytic being carried by a blind man. Though drawn from fifteenth-century iconography, this image of a dialectic between immediate sensation and the perceptual subjectivity always necessarily alienated from that sensation, finds a resonant analogue in the relationship between the paralytic Cutter and the figurally myopic Bone in *Cutter's Way*, illuminating strikingly what makes the film so telling a gauge of New Hollywood textuality and spectatorship.

Coda

Cutter's Way comes at the beginning of a decade during which the New Hollywood no longer seems so new. Many film historians date the ascension of New Hollywood filmmaking in a very delimited way, from the late 1960s to the mid-to-late 1970s. The changes registered by a film like *Cutter's Way* mark it, to be sure, as a gauge of historical change—from "New Hollywood" to *post*-"New Hollywood" or *post*-postclassical cinema? The shifting patterns of production, distribution, audience-address, commodity-differentiation, and reception that this case study of *Cutter's Way* details, in any case, continue to define Hollywood in the 1980s and 1990s. Such factors as the corporate fragmentation of Hollywood, the dramatic rise in independent American filmmaking during the 1980s, and multinational buyouts of studio interests, at the level of production, and the rise of mall cinemas and cable television at the level of exhibition and reception, have altered the bases of Hollywood production considerably during the last fifteen years. These factors have produced a field of representation defined, at least in formal terms, by a certain heterogeneity: an influx of images and images-about-images that no longer boasts the monolithic (and implicitly reassuring) sameness of Classical Hollywood but trumpets its own diversity, puts itself forward as an exhilarating assemblage of multiplicitous fragments.

Because of such fundamental changes during the 1980s in Hollywood as an institution, I have chosen to end my inquiry at the outset of the decade, with the case study of a film that heralds many of the changes to come. Several points must be noted in conclusion, however. Hollywood representation may now be characterized more by an allegedly triumphant fragmentation (of the audience into "taste" segments and variously defined cultural-identity positions, of the studios into splintered production companies) than by a securely hegemonic totality, and this shift may culminate the challenges to various cultural boundaries and hierarchies throughout the history of Hollywood that I have tried to identify in this study. But if it is true that a given institutional structure produces a specific type of representation, it does not follow that changes in the institution's structure will inevitably alter the character of the representation. The period of late capitalism, with its wildly complex circuitries and hyperrealities, has taught us to suspect the direct relationship of base to superstructure predicated in classical Marxism: it is now clear that the base of any economy—psychic, social, institutional—may alter fundamentally while the superstructure, the system of signs and representations built upon it, remains essentially unchanged. By the 1990s, distribution and exhibition practices of Hollywood movies had altered so completely from the time of its monopolistic period that one could discover so challenging an example of European art-cinema as *The Cook, the Thief, His Wife and Her Lover* (Greenaway, 1989) playing side-by-side at the multiplex with the Disney cartoon *The Little Mermaid* (1989). Do such phenomena portend the logical end of commodity differentiation in a final blur of indeterminacy—liberating or otherwise—or do they suggest that such differentiation is understood to be so deeply internalized in consumers that they have no need of the institutional structures of differentiation that formerly enforced it? Do such phenomena imply the end of fixed spectatorial identities or ideological mystification, which a stabilized and monolithic institution could readily promote to serve its own interests, or do they suggest the migration of such capacities to some microlevel of representation, where they will simply be more difficult to locate? Classical Hollywood projected a homogeneous audience for its products; if contemporary Hollywood projects a *heterogeneous* augience, might it not still be the process of projection itself, rather than its alleged, actual or fantasized objects, that requires investigation?

Meanwhile, European filmmakers continue to contribute significantly to the production of Hollywood representations. During the last several years, European directors such as Paul Verhoeven, George Sluizer, Stephen Frears, Agniezska Holland, Wolfgang Peterson, Luc Besson, and Lasse Hallstrom have made significant and influential films in Hollywood. Continued study of European directors in the Hollywood system during this period might address the question of the extent to which these directors' films signal textually, or are received extratextually, in terms of identity or difference from the Hollywood norm, but it would also be obliged to consider whether the structural fragmentation of Hollywood as an institution of representation has altered the terms of differential textuality itself. Moreover, the European art-cinema/Hollywood-movie binarism has lost some of its shaping force as directors from non-European national cinemas have migrated to Hollywood in the last decades. As I have suggested at various points throughout this study, Hollywood representation often projected itself in an ancestral relation to European nationality, so that the potentially differential force of European national cultures as they were articulated in the Hollywood system was thereby neutralized. The Eurocentrism of Hollywood's channeling of European directors has been undermined in recent years by periodic (and often unfulfilled or abbreviated) emigrations of directors from Asian cinemas, such as the Chinese John Woo or the Taiwanese Ang Lee. Also interesting to consider in this regard would be the crucial influx of Australian directors in Hollywood during the 1980s and 1990s, such as Peter Weir, Fred Schepisi, Jocelyn Moorhouse, Bruce Beresford, Gillian Armstrong, or Philip Noyce. To what extent do the national cultures expressed by these directors' works in Australia, during the period of the "Australian New Wave" beginning in the mid-1970s, count as "European"? How might the representations they produce upon their immigration to Hollywood express the triple registers of national/cultural-identity through which they might be mediated? How might their work, in turn, challenge the binary relationship of Hollywood to the European art-cinema that has shaped both institutions for so long?

The challenges registered and the resistances forwarded by and to the work of European directors in Hollywood cinema during the classical and postclassical period of production have no doubt been instrumental in charting the course that brings Hollywood cinema to its present state, where formerly secure boundaries, symbolic or literal, are often questioned and traditional unities abandoned. The countermovement of challenges to and reassertions of hegemony so characteristic of postmodern culture, however, remains constant. In relation to the present topic, this is perhaps nowhere more in evidence than in the popular press. In 1976, *The New York Times* ran an article on European directors in Hollywood. Comparing emigrés during the classical period such as Douglas Sirk, Fritz Lang, and Max Ophuls to more recent emigrés such as Roman Polanski and Milos Forman, the writer concluded that the first group found it easier to assimilate to Hollywood's demands because of the tight organization of the Classical Hollywood system. Because of the rigidity of that organization, the institution's needs were clearer, the writer implies, and therefore the emigrés made better movies within the system. After the breakdown of the studio system, according to the article, films by emigrés often registered the same confusion and loss of cultural authority seen in other contemporary products of the New Hollywood. The implicitly nationalist assumption that "assimilation" is the desired goal of such transactions acts as a defense against the threats to stable definitions of nationhood such transactions continue to pose. Such nostalgic longing for national/cultural coherence (thereby projected as lost) is similarly expressed more recently in a *New Yorker* article on the buyout of Columbia Pictures and related production companies by Sony of Japan. After decrying the racism of American efforts to resist Japanese "invasion," the writer goes on to reassert the category of "foreignness" and reassure American audiences of the unassailable nationalism of their own cultural heritage:

> The Japanese and other foreigners may have proved themselves masters of American manufacturing and marketing, from automobiles to appliances, but these are essentially commodity businesses. Moviemaking, television production, and book publishing—the "software" businesses that Sony coveted—are about as far from commodity operations as they can be. They are creative endeavors—almost entirely dependent on human capital and peculiarly rooted in American culture and an American sensibility—for which no one has devised a surefire formula for success. (*The New Yorker*, 11/25/96, p. 91)

There may be some hope in that "peculiarly," but although twenty years separates these two reports, they signify the same complacent acceptance of traditional (though ill-defined) cultural/national categories. Thus, at the end of this study, which has been so concerned with the ideology and possibility of challenges to such categories, it may be fitting to close with a phrase, "originating" in European culture but often heard in Hollywood—a "foreign" cliché: *Plus ça change, plus ça même.*

Notes

Introduction. Resident Aliens:
Hollywood Films, European Directors

1. This meeting has been recounted by René Clair in his own account of his time in Hollywood during World War II. See Clair, 195.

2. Like many European modernists, Dali professed to see a surrealist bent in Hollywood film, though he limited this perception to "comic films with an irrational tendency" (quoted in Ades, 201), such as those of the Marx Brothers. Indeed, Dali embarked on an unfulfilled collaboration in Hollywood in 1937 on a film with Harpo Marx. Interestingly, another European intellectual of the same era though of a different aesthetic tradition, Antonin Artaud, also discovered a Euro-modernist valence in these films, on which he commented with an explicit contrast of "American" and "European" sensibility: "If Americans, to whose spirit this genre of films belongs, wish to take these films in a merely humorous sense, confining the material of humor to the easy comic margins of the meaning of the word, so much the worse for them; but that will not prevent us from considering the conclusion of *Monkey Business* as a hymn to anarchy and wholehearted revolt" (Artaud, 144). Dali's negotiations of art and commerce, "high" art and "popular" art, is often taken as a leitmotif of his career, and earned him the reputation of sell-out and the nickname of "Avida Dollars" among some of his surrealist colleagues. See the standard biography by Secrest, esp. 195–217; this biography, it should be noted, does not even mention Dali's work on *Spellbound*. For an account of DeMille's concerns about the cultural devaluation of his films and his efforts to legitimize them as "art," see Higashi, 181–98.

3. I should take this opportunity to clarify an implication of this point. Obviously, the basis of the study is a certain causal relationship between directors' national/cultural identities and aspects of the particular films they directed in Hollywood. Two points should be clear, however, in the analyses of the films themselves: this causal relationship is by no means a simple one, and my approaches are by no means dictated by assumptions of traditonal "auteurist" analysis. For one thing, the "identities" of the directors are defined in largely institutional terms, as functions of the particular institutions in which they worked (the studios, the national cinemas, and so forth) or those through which their work has been understood (journalistic media, various types of film criticism, and so forth). At the same time, I agree with recent

claims in film study that the status of the "auteur" demands continued thought and study, and in practice, this book is at one level an effort to contribute to that study. For examples of these recent claims, see especially Andrew, "The Unauthorized Auteur Today," and Naremore, "Authorship and the Cultural Politics of Film Criticism."

4. This point should not be taken to deny the importance of "popular" European cinemas, though it should be noted that work on such cinema in film studies has tended to focus on fascist cinemas, perhaps because of the historical association of the "national-popular" with fascist regimes in Europe (see Forgacs, 179–89). Perhaps for this reason, these studies tend not to discuss the relation between popular national cinemas and the "esoteric" or "coterie" cinemas that produced the films most often exported. See Rentschler, especially his discussion of the relation of Hollywood and Nazi popular cinemas, 99–124, or Hay, espcially his discussion of contested paradigms of the "popular" (such as the "rural" popular), 132–49. The paradigm of "Classical Hollywood cinema" was already in place by the time it was catalogued exhaustively in Bordwell/Staiger/Thompson's *The Classical Hollywood Cinema* (1985). That book has influenced most discussions that follow it. See also Gaines, *Classical Hollywood Narrative*, especially 1–49.

5. The cross-national transactions of pre-Hollywood cinema noted here are traced in detail in Jacobs, 38–41; Sadoul, 424–29; and most extensively, Sopocy.

6. For such anecdotal accounts, including some useful history, see the works by Taylor and Baxter on the subject. These works, it should be noted, exemplify some of the standard narratives of "exile" discussed above, reproducing traditional sociocultural hierarchies instead of responding to the challenges to these hierarchies the cultural politics of the European-in-Hollywood present.

7. This discussion of "symbolic economies" has been influenced fundamentally by the work of Jean-Joseph Goux. Goux theorizes commodity identity and differentiation in relation to the conept of "symbolic economy" as follows: "One of the commodities expresses its value in the *body* of the other, which thus serves as *matter* (mother, material, matrix) for this expression. . . . Thus the commodity that serves as equivalent does not express its own value through this relationship but rather 'merely serves as a means for expressing the value of the other commodity.' Now this dual relationship . . . has precisely the same structure as *the specular relationship with the other*" (Goux, 13). The embedded citation is a quotation from Marx's *Capital*.

8. Graham Petrie's *Hollywood Destinies: European Directors in America, 1922–1931* was the first major scholarly treatment of the topic. Though excellent, and a source of much fundamental research on the transactions between European and Hollywood cinemas, it is limited to a small number of key directors over a tightly defined historical period, and the directors' works are

treated in survey form. More recently, Peter Lev in *The Euro-American Cinema* examines cross-cultural transactions of the cinematic tradition of the postwar international co-production. Though his work raises many issues parallel to those considered here, therefore, it treats an essentially different subject in terms of the institutional politics of representation. In fact, Lev regards the emigré directors working in Hollywood, for the most part, especially those who are "well established" there, "to be primarily American filmmakers" (34). However, the historical detail of that book's first half provides an extremely useful backdrop for the topic. Readers who find the historical dimension of the subject insufficiently or idiosyncratically emphasized here are encouraged to consult those works; see also Norman Kagan's *Greenhorns*, which examines more recent immigrations.

9. In the introduction to a recent number of *Quarterly Review of Film and Video* on the question of the "national" in cinema, Marcia Butzel and Ana M. Lopez argue, "To pursue the question of canon formation in relation to national cinema demands examination . . . of historically changing institutional relations. . . . Study of any national cinema should include distribution and exhibition as well as production within the nation-state" (3). Later, they challenge E. J. Hobsbawm's and Homi Bhabha's "postmodern" questioning of "the pertinence of national categories in our present historical moment" (3). Such questioning, they argue, might reduce historical/political realities to "just another episode in postmodernity's inevitable transnationalizing of cultural differences and identities" (6). On the face of it, I agree with these claims, and hope my study enacts the critical practices they call for to some extent. Despite the subtlety of their conceptions of national/cultural representation, however, the authors risk, in their call for emphasis on empirical research, equating the "poltical" with the "historical," and therefore risk negating the psychocultural processes that always influence both.

Chapter One. Hollywood as Modernism's Other: The Case of *Sunrise*

1. Graham Petrie's excellent study of the first "invasion" of European emigration to Hollywood, in the years 1922–31, shows that European directors were offered Hollywood contracts in order to bring novelty to Hollywood films, but some directors, however successful their European films might have been in America, were regarded as *too* alien to adapt themselves to Hollywood's methods. The result, as Petrie points out, "was often cruelly paradoxical, on the one hand welcoming the Europeans as promising to bring something artistically adventurous and thematically daring to American cinema, and then all too often berating and condemning them for attempting just that" (4). Petrie's study contains a thorough survey of Murnau's career, comparing his German style to the style of his films in Hollywood.

2. Michael Rogin links questions of national culture to the specifically modern image of the country-in-the-city: "Modernization produced both the mass-media means for creating new national identities and nostalgia for lost folk worlds, a longing for the country in the city" (*Blackface, White Noise*, 47).

3. Ideologies of objectivity/subjectivity figure prominently in many important treatments of the visual regimes of modernity. Jonathan Crary characterizes modern visuality in these terms: "The monadic viewpoint of the individual is legitimized . . . but his or her sensory experience is subordinated to an external and pre-given world of objective truth" (*Vision and Visuality*, 33). A more general connection of the experience of urbanness to objectivity/subjectivity occurs in Georg Simmel's classic discussion of the city and modern consciousness: "The most profound reason . . . why the metropolis conduces to the urge for the most individual personal existence—no matter whether justified and successful—appears to me to be the following: the development of modern culture is characterized by the preponderance of what one may call the 'objective spirit' over the 'subjective spirit'" (Simmel, 421).

4. The association of melodrama with a deeply embedded rhetoric of subjectivity is a basic assumption in the scholarship. For instance, although Robert Lang sees critique of the social structure of patriarchy as melodrama's guiding impulse, he emphasizes the inward dimensions of the genre: "There, in the family, apart from the world of action, production and rational order, the melodrama of passion explores a familial world of subjectivity, of emotion and feeling, of problems of identity and desire" (Lang, 5).

5. The association of the medium shot, a constant figure in any cinematic representation, with specifically national dimensions of film style only further illustrates a kind of nationalist unconscious at work in so much film theoretical discourse. Further, it suggests the ingrained association of the American style with qualities of proportion and balance, since the medium shot is a figure of regulated scale, as opposed to the extremes of scale associated with the close-up or the long shot. See the discussion of shot scale, with specific reference to "plan americain" composition, in Aumont et al., 26–31.

6. Theorists of early cinema and the rise of the classical model of filmmaking have often found connections between those topics and modernity itself by arguing that the rhetoric of balance and continuity is a response to the fragmentation of space and time characteristic of modernity. Richard DeCordova finds that "the break-up of perspectival space" in modernity gives rise to a compensatory "production of referential contiguity" (DeCordova, 84) in early film language. Other theorists, such as Eileen Bowser, Tom Gunning, Noel Burch, and Miriam Hansen, have seen the conflation between alternate editing and point-of-view structures as the key moment in the emergence of classical narration. See especially Bowser's analysis of *Old Isaacs*, where she finds that this conflation leads to a new narrative objectivity, displacing character subjectivity: "[It] is no longer necessarily the point-of-view of one of the

characters: it may be a *privileged* point-of-view, that of the 'narrator' or the film's spectators" (Bowser, 261). See also Gunning's analysis of Griffith's *Redman and the Child* (1908), where Gunning finds in similar formal structures "the process of transition from a cinema of attractions to one of narrative integration" (Gunning, 72)—for example, the classical model. For both Bowser and Hansen, such moments herald a more "modern" mode of film narration: "Neither a primeval paradise of viewer participation nor merely a site for the consumption of standardized products, the cinema rehearsed new, specifically modern forms of subjectivity and intersubjectivity" (Hansen, 105). For Bowser, the slippage between literal points-of-view and less clearly determined "eyeline matches" (or "sight links," as Hansen calls them) marks the "beginnings of a more *modern* kind of scene dissection" (Bowser, 262, emphasis mine).

7. In addition to the scholars whose work is discussed in the previous note, this association of classical editing with multiplied viewpoints has an important precedent in a text such as *Aesthetics of Film*, a book that has influenced my own readings of the ideological ramifications of film form greatly, since the authors argue, as I do here, that the forms of classical style themselves contain their own potential subversion: "The multiplicity of points of view, which founds the classical editing of the film scene, is undoubtedly the fundamental base of these microcircuits of identification in the surface text" (Aumont et al., 226).

8. The dynamic here is very close to what Miriam Hansen identifies as that of the "triangulated look" in *Intolerance* (Griffith, 1916): "By emphasizing this triangularity in patterns of looking, the film puts the viewer in a peculiar bind. On the most rudimentary level, the viewer is asked to identify with the legitimate couple. At the same time, he or she is excluded from that relationship by the very fact of spectatorship and occupies a position structurally analogous to that of the envious third, figured in *Intolerance* as evil eye, old maid, and hysteric. With this configuration of spectatorship, *Intolerance* spells out a basic contradiction of classical cinema, if not cinema *tout court* . . . that the mobilization of voyeuristic mechanisms harbors the risk of latent displeasure, of jealousy feelings potentially arising with the spectator's structural exclusion" (Hansen, 160).

9. Petrie, for example, speaks of the "artifice" of the epilogue, finding the ending "out of key" with the rest of the narrative. See Petrie, 38–41.

10. *CloseUp* 1.4: 6. Subsequent references to material from *CloseUp* will be given with volume, number, and page in parentheses after the first quotation from a given article, with the page number only cited in each reference thereafter.

11. The critique of cinema in modernist philosophy is represented, in both explicit and implicit form, in the work of Henri Bergson and Maurice Merleau-Ponty; for Bergson, in particular, film was a failed effort to reconstitute movement in the wake of its modern fragmentation. See Bergson, 298–314, and Merleau-Ponty, 252–86.

12. For discussion of the unusually lucrative terms of Murnau's Hollywood contract, which included the promise of nearly total artistic freedom, see Petrie, 41–42. For discussion of economic investment of Hollywood studios in German film production, and of subsequent emigration of German filmmakers to Hollywood, see Saunders, especially 68–73 and 209–12.

13. In a representative article on German response to *Sunrise*, the *New York Times* approvingly quotes one reviewer: "The narrow thread of the story is overloaded with show . . ." (*New York Times*, 29 January 1928, 6:2).

Chapter Two. Representation and Form: Representing Nationality in *This Land Is Mine*

1. Several important treatments of Hollywood cinema see such problematics as central to Hollywood representation in general. On the problem of "commitment" in American film, see Robert Ray's analysis of "Classic Hollywood's most representative film" (89), *Casablanca*, in *A Certain Tendency of the Hollywood Cinema*. Ray argues that the film's ideological project is representative in its thematic of "the avoidance of choice between autonomy and commitment," even as, paradoxically, the film trades compulsively in the rhetoric of choice. A similar dynamic is treated in Bernard Dick's analysis of the World War II film in a chapter on the paradoxical issue of "neutral intervention": see Dick, 65–100.

2. Related problems of historical placement are treated in theoretical terms by Marc Ferro, though Ferro's emphasis is more on shifting responses to texts over time: Ferro observes, following Eisenstein, that "every society receives its images in function of its own culture. . . . The same is true of a work's content and meaning, which may be read in varying and contrary ways at two different points in history" (18–19). Significantly, Ferro draws on Renoir's work to illustrate the point: "[*Grand Illusion*], which attempted to be pacifist, left-wing and internationalist and was greeted as such in 1938, was reconsidered in 1946 . . . and seen as a profoundly ambiguous work" (19).

3. Leo Braudy, for instance, sees Renoir's work as the embodiment of "open" style in *The World in a Frame*, 218–25. Among standard critical treatments of Renoir, see also André Bazin on the "improvisatory" element in Renoir's style in *Jean Renoir*, 80–81; on ideological openness, see Durgnat, 400–405.

4. Thomas Doherty argues that the basic ideological function of Hollywood's wartime narratives is the channeling of communal hostility, the production of "properly directed hatred"; see Doherty, 122–48.

5. The best discussion of Renoir's relation to the Popular Front is Faulkner, 71–105; see also Bazin, 36–52. A notorious contemporary antifascist melodrama that explicitly endorses Communism, illustrating the ideological

strategy most such films seek problematically to avoid, is *Mission to Moscow* (Curtiz, 1943). See the detailed introduction by David Culbert in the published screenplay, 11–41.

6. See Sesonske, 290–98.

7. Key influential theories of Classical Hollywood's models of representation see the exclusionist aspect of the constitution of the couple as fundamental. As Raymond Bellour states, "[T]he film gradually leads to a final solution which allows the more or less conflicting terms posed at the beginning to be resolved, and which in the majority of cases takes the form of a marriage. I've gradually come to think this pattern organizes—indeed, constitutes—the classical American cinema as a whole" (Bergstrom, 187). The point here is not that *This Land Is Mine* defies this pattern but that it modifies the specifically exclusionist cast of the pattern. See also Wexman, 3–36.

8. *This Land Is Mine* script, 54; further references cited in the text. Unless followed by parenthetical citation, however, quotations from the film are not from the published version of the script but are transcribed from the text of the film itself.

9. A representative contemporary review chiding the film for its allegorized nationalism is James Agee's; see *Agee on Film*, 36.

10. For a treatment of the relation of U.S. foreign policy to Vichy France, providing analysis of how this topic is represented in the war film and *Casablanca* in particular, see Raskin, 153–64.

11. Leo Braudy makes a similar point about Renoir's deployment of the stylization of studio shooting when he notes that the film's studio-sets become "an image of confinement" (Braudy, 41).

12. Significantly, Bazin's discussion of the "realism" of Renoir's pre-Hollywood soundtracks turns on a comparison of location to studio shooting: "The soundtrack of *La Chienne* (1932) is consistently excellent thanks to the on-location recording. . . . Even in the scenes consisting completely of dialogue, which are shot in the studio, the sound is realistic" (28). For Bazin, Renoir's Hollywood period is marked by a decline in "realistic" sound, a point with which I concur for different reasons and with different conclusions. See Bazin, 93.

13. See *Children of the Earth*, 184. On the French Revolution as a "triumph of bourgeois individualism," with specific reference to the "Declaration of the Rights of Man and Citizen," see Solé, *Questions of the French Revolution*, 54–56.

14. The conflation of the Rights of Man with the Bill of Rights is so complete that many critics have wrongly assumed the document read in the last scene is the Bill of Rights. In his book on Laughton, Simon Callow repeats James Agate's earlier misidentification of the Rights of Man read in this scene of the film as the American Bill of Rights; see Callow, 161–63.

15. For elaboration on the concept of the "star text," see Dyer, 99–181, or Butler, 7–16.

16. James Naremore's treatment of "expressive coherence" in film performance relies relevantly upon a distinction between persona and performance in order to achieve continuity in the "acted image." See *Acting in the Cinema*, 68–82.

17. Lee Strasberg names Laughton as an important precursor of post–World War II Method acting in "A Dream of Passion: The Development of the Method"; see *Star Texts*, 42. Without discussing Laughton, Marianne Conroy suggestively links Method acting to questions of cultural hierarchy and national identity; see "Method Acting, the National Culture, and the Middlebrow Disposition in Cold War America."

Chapter Three. Masscult Modernism, Modernist Masscult: Cultural Hierarchy in *Scarlet Street*

1. An implicit distinction between modernist and realist conventions shapes much of the discourse surrounding film noir. Paul Schrader's standard survey of noir notes the possibility of the genre's grounding in social reality, but emphasizes its modernist self-consciousness: "Because *film noir* was first of all a style, because it worked out its conflicts visually rather than thematically, because it was aware of its own identity, it was able to create artistic solutions to sociological problems" (Schrader, 182). More recently, Brian Neve comments, "Certainly the emphasis on fate and despair as themes in the literature on *film noir* can be cited as . . . evidence that social interpretations of such films are generally misplaced" (Neve, 145). Yet this comment occurs at the outset of a chapter in *Film and Politics in America* called "*Film Noir* and Society."

2. For a representative treatment of the "legend" of Lang in Hollywood, presenting Lang through the prism of many stereotypes of foreignness, see Otis Ferguson's 1941 profile of the director: "he came over with a full-grown European reputation seven years ago. . . . He was a Prussian with a monocle; he treated his actors like a Prussian with a monocle, and he had tantrums" (Ferguson, 374).

3. In a reading of the film that constructs it as a site of endlessly ramifying hieroglyphic play, synthesizing Derridean free-play and the psychoanalytic unconscious, Tom Conley sees such excremental imagery as Chris's reference to the portrait as "mud" as a key organizing principle of the film; see *Film Hieroglyphs*, 36–45. Adele's consignment of Chris's flower to the toilet is also suggestive in this context.

4. Relevant here is the by now standard work on the relation of cultural value to social organization, Pierre Bourdieu's *Distinction*, where Bourdieu

argues that the class basis of cultural hierarchy is sustained in clear social distinctions within aesthetic realms. For example, high culture is associated with creation, middlebrow culture with consumption; middlebrow culture is perceived as an extension of everyday life, highbrow culture as distinct from it.

5. It is perhaps here that Kaja Silverman's discussion of male lack in postwar Hollywood cinema is most relevant to my argument: "A number of films made in Hollywood between 1944 and 1947 attest with unusual candor to the castrations through which the male subject is constituted—the pound of flesh which is his price of entry into the symbolic order. . . . Not surprisingly, given their preoccupation with male lack, these films are also characterized by a loss of faith in the familiar and self-evident. The hero no longer feels 'at home' in the house or town where he grew up, and resists cultural (re)assimilation" (*Male Subjectivity at the Margins*, 52–53). The explicit link of male lack to the aesthetics of "exile" is especially significant. I should point out here that my later references to the "restorative" impulse of film noir should not be taken to undermine my concurrence with Silverman's reading here of postwar Hollywood, especially since that restorative impulse is often a rhetorical gesture, insufficient to counteract the alienation to which the films so eloquently testify.

6. For an extended treatment of gender in film noir, see Krutnik; it is worth noting that even though Krutnik's work follows tradition in seeing film noir as a "progressive" genre, allowing critique of conventional gender constructions, it simultaneously emphasizes the "restitution of order" (145) and the "closure of the narrative of transgression" (145) characteristic of the genre, thus approximating in this regard the analysis of film noir here.

7. The direct impetus of Rose's essay is to challenge Raymond Bellour's theory of Hollywood film as Oedipal narrative. Bellour argues that the drive of Hollywood film narrative is toward resolved Oedipal scenarios. Rose counters that Bellour overstates the success of those resolutions and understates the extent to which they are sought at the expense of female subjectivity. The immediate context of her discussion is a close analysis of the construction of the female look in Hitchcock's *The Birds* (1963). In these terms, the horror plot of the film relies on a reversal: our "feathered friends" are really violent agents of seemingly causeless aggression. This fact itself breeds a kind of paranoia in the text, but according to Rose, such paranoia is rooted in the unconscious psychic mechanisms of sexual difference: "In *The Birds*, the woman is object and cause of the attack" (145)—a dual register that further animates the threatening reversals on which such paranoia relies. Rose's analysis is a sustained close reading of this individual film, but the ideas are generally suggestive for larger structures of filmic representation, as I employ them here.

8. Dana Polan makes this point persuasively in his reading of the film in the context of 1940s Hollywood ideology: "Chris Cross's paintings remain visually the same [in *Scarlet Street*] but change their possible significations

with each change in the narrative story; the characters' debate about the artistic merits or not of each painting is repeated in the spectator for whom the art comes to have no univocal sense. The twists and turns that the characters undergo—their criss-crossings—echo in the spectator who must continually revise his/her own estimation of the value of the images" (Polan, 229). In a perceptive article that appeared after the initial periodical appearance of this chapter, Jeanne Hall amplifies a number of points regarding spectatorship and cultural hierarchy that overlap both Polan's and my own. See Hall, 34–47.

9. Interestingly, Lee Edelman sees a self-reflexive patina in the film's rhetorical deployment of the realist painting: "[D]istancing itself from the merely photographic, [*Laura*] envisions the idealized portrait as its imaginary double. In part this self-presentation responds to the anxious aesthetic politics of film as a cultural practice in America. Identifying itself with the painting, the film seeks to appropriate the cachet of 'art' for a medium conceived as popular entertainment" (239–40). Not only does Edelman situate the film explicitly within postwar cultural hierarchies, but he remarks passingly in a footnote that this is "especially significant among those films produced by emigré directors in America during World War II" (274). See "Imagining the Homosexual: *Laura* and the Other Faces of Gender" in *Homographesis*.

10. The idea is that of Paul Mallon, a columnist for Hearst, as quoted in the art column of *Time*, 25 February 1946, p. 40.

11. Freud's discussions of introjection tend to link the concept to the specifically libidinal economies of individual psyches, but the concept's amenability to cultural generalization is as suggestive as that of other Freudian concepts that have been so generalized. The striking point is that the rejection of the object is paradoxically seen to entail "a setting up of the object inside the ego": "It may be that by this introjection, which is a kind of regression to the mechanism of the oral phase, the ego makes it easier for the object to be given up or renders that process possible. It may be that this identification is the sole condition under which the id can give up its objects" (*The Ego and the Id*).

Chapter Four. Un-American Activities in 1950s Hollywood: Hollywood Reading Europe/Europe Reading Hollywood

1. At the 1995 conference of the Society for Cinema Studies, a panel on "The Other '50s" reexamined traditional conceptions of Hollywood representation during this period in approximately the terms described here. Recent work in the field that similarly reconceives the period includes Ed Sikov's *Laughing Hysterically* and Barbara Klinger's *Melodrama and Meaning*. Studies such as these are to be distinguished from cultural histories that try to "correct" misconstructions of the era, such as Miller and Nowak's *The Fifties: The Way We Really Were* (New York: Doubleday, 1977), which succeeds only in replacing one simplified and monolithic projection of the period with another.

2. The example of *Crossfire* is a particularly instructive one. The tale of an anti-Semitic murder on an army base, the film was directed and produced by two of the "Hollywood Ten," Edward Dmytryk and Adrian Scott, and it was released concurrent with the initial hearings of the HCUA. The complexities of this example are treated in Daryl Fox, "*Crossfire* and HUAC." Dmytryk's post–Hollywood Ten career, interestingly, reveals little of the "liberal humanist" ideology that was often read by the HCUA as evidence of subversive intent. Films such as *The Caine Mutiny* (1954) or *The Carpetbaggers* (1964), especially, read almost like gestures of recantation of a prior liberalism.

3. For more extended commentary on Hollywood's reaction to the influx into America of Italian neorealist films, see Lev, especially 39–42. One of these films, of course, *The Miracle* (Rossellini, 1947), was crucial in the loosening of legal censorship of movies during the 1950s. Initially banned in the United States, the film was later the subject of a Supreme Court decision of 1952 that extended First Amendment protection to films for the first time.

4. *Scarlet Street* is also an example, despite its release through a Hollywood studio, of the rise in independent production in postwar Hollywood. The film is a product of a production company consisting of Fritz Lang, Walter Wanger, and Joan Bennett, "Diana Films." For an excellent treatment of the film's "adult" aspirations and the censorship difficulties they caused, see Bernstein, 27–52.

5. For a representative treatment of Lang's *M* as a "progressive" text, see Lotte Eisner's curious Marxist interpretation of the film: "What [Lang] really wanted to say was that the ultimate reason for the murders is the unequal distribution of wealth" (Eisner, 128).

6. The reviewer in *The New Yorker* finds that in Losey's version, as compared to Lang's, "the piece is no longer as starkly horrifying as it was" because of "too much exposition designed to demonstrate that people with twisted personalities got that way through no fault of their own" (*New Yorker*, 91). The reviewer for *Time*, meanwhile, notes that in spite of Losey's flagrant "imitations" of Lang's style, his changes in the story are "almost always for the worse" (*Time*, 102).

7. Kracauer's "realist" aesthetic is implicitly rejected on such grounds in both Corrigan, 93, and Coates, 156.

8. See Daniel Bell's decidedly partisan yet representative treatment of the Kefauver hearings in *The End of Ideology*, 115–36. Writing in 1960, Bell notes the frustrated quality of the search, but concludes that the quest itself was therefore invalid, associating a quality of paranoia with the hearings themselves: "Unfortunately for a good story—and the existence of the Mafia would be a whale of a story—neither the Senate Crime Committee in its testimony, nor Kefauver in his book, presented any real evidence that the Mafia exists as a functioning organization" (Bell, 126).

9. Andersen discusses the parallels between crime and business as a crucial aspect of *film gris*, with particular reference to connections between theft and property. See Andersen, 186–87.

10. It is instructive to compare this aspect of Losey's remake with Lang's 1950s Hollywood melodrama, *While the City Sleeps* (1956), a film that appears to have been influenced at crucial points by the 1951 version of *M*. In Lang's later film, the serial killer is presented in terms of a strikingly similar profile, even down to suggestions of a parallel foot-fetish; yet despite such psychologizing effects, Lang remains completely uninterested in traditional depth-models of rendering character. Indeed, as especially Jacques Rivette and François Truffaut noted, the film is among Lang's bitterest and most desolate, opting to focus on the complicity of the institutions of law and media in fetishizing the killer's crimes.

11. Brian Henderson cautions against reading Godard's criticism through his films, arguing that such interpretation falsifies Godard's earlier work by imposing just such a false teleology on them. See Henderson, 104.

12. Godard's essay "Defence and Illustration of Classical Construction" not only illustrates Godard's ambivalent response to "modern" cinema, since Godard there favors the "classical" over the "modern," but clarifies his sense of Hollywood cinema as the place where the two forms engage in dialogue (Godard, 26–30). It is worth noting here, too, that Godard refers throughout the essay to "American cinema" where he usually discusses *Hollywood* film, implying a distinction between a specifically *national* American film and a transnational Hollywood.

13. This tendency is noted by Jim Hillier in his excellent introduction to the portfolio on American cinema in *Cahiers du Cinéma*, 73. Rob Kroes makes a parallel point in the chapter on the "New Wave" in his discussion of cross-cultural transactions between European and American cultures (Kroes, 148).

14. For a critical treatment of *Contempt* in a "Euro-American" context, see Lev, 83–89.

15. Given Godard's emphasis on an aesthetic of degeneration and death in *No Sad Songs for Me*, it seems right to argue, as Catherine Russell does in a book I read after this chapter was complete, that the auteurist response to Hollywood cinema is parallel to Walter Benjamin's conception of mortification in photography, referring to "the discursive rendering of death as a sign of historical transience" (Russell, 32). In general, Russell's treatment of the issue parallels my own: "The modernity of American cinema for the *Cahiers* critics of the 1950s consisted in formal stylization and an excess of representation, which was a departure from the limited codification of Hollywood illusionism" (Russell, 35).

16. It should be obvious, however, that this claim oversimplifies Godard's reading of Hollywood, since he is fully attuned to the retrograde

nature of dominant Hollywood ideology. His claims for the superiority of American storytelling, for instance, find their corrollary in his assertion that this superiority results from a cultural naiveté about the structure of history itself. See *Un Vrai Histoire du Cinema*, 157.

Chapter Five. Reinventing Otherness:
Petulia, Art-Cinema, and the New Hollywood

1. In a wide-ranging discussion of reflexivity in film and literature, Robert Stam denies reflexivity any inherently political valence; see Stam, 13–17.

2. See Dennis Turner, "*Breathless*: Mirror Stage of the Nouvelle Vague," especially 52–53.

3. For biographical treatment of Lester's career in England, see Sinyard, 85.

4. Even in simpler terms, this argument seems to be inaccurate on the face of it. Though the unannounced flashback appeared for a number of years in nominally "commercial" Hollywood films, its ultimate fate was to migrate to such curiously unplaceable films as *Don't Look Now* (Roeg, 1973) or *Wild at Heart* (Lynch, 1989). Throughout the '70s, to be sure, the device was perhaps most closely associated with the films of Nicolas Roeg, who had been cine-matographer on *Petulia*. The self-conscious hybridity of Roeg's films makes them notoriously difficult to situate, even nationally; in her analysis of *Bad Timing* (Roeg, 1980), Teresa de Lauretis finds, precisely because of the film's dazzling (and explicitly neo-*Petulia*-esque) formal patterns, she can locate it comfortably in neither the Hollywood nor European art-cinema traditions, and opts instead to contextualize it in relation to the emergent category of "third cinema." See de Lauretis, 88. On the category of "third cinema" as an alternative to the Hollywood/art-cinema binarism, see Willemin.

5. Such parallels between the screwball comedy and the '40s melodrama are not merely incidental. The narrative parallels between *Petulia* and an ear-lier Hollywood melodrama by an emigré director, *Caught* (Ophuls, 1948), are quite striking, though thematics of class differ greatly between the two films. In both cases, a nominally "independent" woman—the '40s career-woman in the Ophuls film and the '60s "women's-libber" in *Petulia*—is "caught" between the romantic alternatives of a humane doctor and a crazed million-aire. In both cases, the structure of the narrative figures a strangely static back-and-forth movement between these alternatives. Stanley Cavell has noted affinities between the 1930s screwball comedy and the '40s melodrama (which he calls in tribute to another Ophuls film the "melodrama of the Unknown Woman") in Classical Hollywood; see "Psychoanalysis and Cinema: The Melodrama of the Unknown Woman," 11–13.

6. Because my edition of Debord is numbered not according to pages but to notes or aphorisms, citations will appear in parenthesis with reference to the number of the note. For this reference, see Debord, note 30.

7. On this point, see Baudrillard's *Symbolic Exchange and Death*: "The hyperreal represents a much more advanced phase [than realism or surrealism] insofar as it effaces the contradiction of the real and the imaginary. Irreality no longer belongs to the dream or the phantasm, to a beyond or hidden interiority, but to *the hallucinatory resemblance of the real to itself*" (72).

8. Julie Christie's star text figures importantly here, since Christie herself, especially after her star-making role in *Darling* (Schlesinger, 1965), was inevitably associated with the discourse of fashion. Baudrillard's meditation on fashion positions it not only as the ultimate form of commodity fetishism but a key formation of the logic of the simulacra: "Today, every principle of identity is affected by fashion, precisely because of its potential to revert all forms to non-origin and recurrence. Fashion is always *retro*, but always on the basis of the abolition of the passe. . . . Paradoxically, fashion is the *inactual* (the 'out-of-date,' the 'irrelevant'). . . . The aesthetic of renewal: fashion draws triviality from the death and modernity of the *déjà vu*" (*Symbolic Exchange and Death*, 88).

Chapter Six. Mythic Self-Consciousness and Homosexual Panic in the New Hollywood: *One Flew over the Cuckoo's Nest* and *Deliverance*

1. Irving Massey introduces the concept of "mythic self-consciousness" in a discussion of Lévi-Strauss's ideas of history in the context of post-colonial theory; see Massey, 55.

2. Clearly, the dominant approach in film studies is to view New Hollywood filmmaking simply as an extension of the Classical model of Hollywood filmmaking, disguising its continued false-consciousness, presumably, by creating the illusion of difference: "The New Hollywood can explore ambiguous narrational possibilities but those explorations remain within classical boundaries" (*Classical Hollywood Cinema*, 377). More recently, however, Jon Lewis proposes a multitude of New Hollywoods, emphasizing change from one film "generation" to the next; see Lewis, 165.

3. The *locus classicus* of such constructions is probably Richard Slotkin's *Regeneration through Violence*, an important influence on, for instance, Ray's reading of Hollywood; my intention here, however, is not to rehearse these mythologies yet again, demonstrating their continued prevalence, but to examine the structure of the mythologies and their interaction with demystifying forces within the text.

4. See also Eckert, "The English Cine-Structuralists," 46–51.

5. I am proposing here, obviously, a structural parallel of mythic narratives. It would be interesting to pursue the parallels even further in American film: Alenka Zupancic's reading of *Dead Poets' Society* (Weir, 1990) suggests interesting parallels in its observations about how the regulated quality of disciplinary spaces—in that case, a boys' school—undergoes a "loss of innocence" when it is invaded by what it projects as threateningly differential elements. That narrative, too, bears striking parallels to those under discussion here, suggesting the pervasiveness of such myths in Hollywood ideology. See Zupancic, 98–103.

6. Buzzoni and Humphries offer an explicitly post-Freudian reading of the film's imagery; see Buzzoni and Humphries, 23–24.

7. Mary Douglas similarly emphasizes the self-contained, microcosmic structure of institutional economy: "[Institutions] start with rules of thumb and norms; eventually, they can end by storing all the useful information. When everything is institutionalized, no history or other storage devices are necessary" (Douglas, 48). Douglas also argues that institutions "naturalize" themselves by setting themselves up analogously to larger structures in "nature," by essentially declaring themselves miniworlds that gain their authority by replicating the natural world in miniature (Douglas, 51–52).

8. Goux finds in the experience of sexual difference the very genesis of symbol, idealism, and myth itself: "Exploring the mythical division of male and female roles in procreation makes it possible, as we shall see, to reconstruct the archeology of idealism" (213). Later, Goux meditates on how such mythic conceptions of sexual difference might be demystified: "Production and maintenance of the 'idea' in this very ancient sense owe less to the refinement of abstraction than to a frame like that used by the mason building an earthen wall. Nevertheless this winding path may be the way to pin down and debunk the mysterious congruence of the positions of father, logos, and phallus, as a relation to something of vital essence which they signify in their respective domains. If sexuality exceeds all procreative ends, it is perhaps more because *human reproduction is not simply sexual* than because sexuality is not procreative" (226).

9. John Simon notes Forman's rejection of Kesey's archetype in his review of the film; see Simon, 206–8. In a more extended treatment of the issue, Elaine B. Safer sees the "comic realism" of Forman clashing markedly with Kesey's idiosyncratic archetype; see Safer, 132–41.

10. For Linda Ruth Williams, despite this trajectory of individuation, the text's subject of *collective* disavowal is what leads directly to its qualities of self-consciousness, its properties of textual "openness": In the aftermath of the rape, she argues, the men try to master their violation by reconstructing fantasized versions of masculinity, but "these images do not add up to a redeemed, sovereign sexual identity which only sits on *one* side of the great sexual divide, and nor do

290 PASSPORT TO HOLLYWOOD

they testify to a past dead and gone, but one which continues to be reworked.... [I]t is the men's desperate need to forget the awful things they have experienced which means, paradoxically, that nothing here is ever entirely finished with. This is an open text, not simply because of its inconclusiveness, its 'failure' to resolve meanings, but in the way it keeps anxiously returning to its own past" (*Critical Desire*, 144). This point is germane as well to the later discussion in this chapter of the collective nature the film attributes to Bobby's violation.

Chapter Seven. *Cutter's Way* and New Hollywood Spectatorship

1. The quotation serves as part of a telling epigraph from Jean Baudrillard to the first chapter of Timothy Corrigan's study of shifting patterns of production and reception in the New Hollywood. The full quotation follows: "The best example is the Vietnam war.... What sense did that war make if not that its unfolding sealed the end of history in the culminating and decisive event of our age?" (quoted in Corrigan, 11).

2. Such a narrative has been propagated by Stephen Bach, a former executive at United Artists, in his detailed production history of the Cimino film, which he presents as a function of studio conglomeration and budgetary inflation. Bach characterizes the film as a blockbuster-out-of-control, betraying the values of the classical model: "Character and story were sacrificed to the filmmaker's love of visual effect and production for their own sakes. The 'look' of the thing subsumed the sense of the thing and implied a callous or uncaring quality about characters for whom the audience was asked to care more than the film seemed to" (*Final Cut*, 416). In these terms, Bach's narrative approximates Justin Wyatt's notion of the "high concept" film as a key category of contemporary Hollywood production, subordinating classical edicts to postmodern spectacle; see *High Concept*, 75–76.

3. Robin Wood, for instance, mounts a comparison of *E.T.* and *Blade Runner* to illustrate crises in contemporary Hollywood; see Wood, 175–80.

4. For a brief production history of the film illuminating its origin as a studio picture, see Jameson, 21–22.

5. This standard division of these two "waves" is exemplarily recited in Willoquet-Maricondi, 6.

6. Though he does not accept the implications of this narrative, Robert Ray recites it in a representative fashion in *Certain Tendency of the Hollywood Cinema*; see Ray, 287–95.

7. In spite of its typical marginalization, Robin Wood sees the "buddy" movie as essentially formative of the ethos of 1970s Hollywood; see Wood, 227–44.

8. For a discussion of masochism as rooted in a tension between subject positions as spectacle and spectator, see Neale, "Masculinity as Spectacle," 10–16.

9. This is the case at least as masochism has been most influentially defined in the field of film studies, in the work of Gaylyn Studlar, who suggests that the masochistic aesthetic replaces psychic disavowal, which might at least provide a sense of resolution, with a condition of anxious, paralyzed suspense, and often takes shape around characters' humorous recognition of their own self-imposed misery (Studlar, 62). It remains a question whether Gilles Deleuze's anatomy of masochism can be so easily translated to the experience of film, given Deleuze's claim that masochism always and only functions in directly and literally sexual situations (Deleuze, 90–91).

10. D. N. Rodowick has most persuasively taken Mulvey to task in this regard: "Because Mulvey considers the look to be essentially active in its aims, identification with the male protagonist is only considered from a point of view that associates it with a sense of omnipotence and of assuming control in the narrative. She makes no distinction between identification and object-choice where active sexual aims may be directed towards the male figure nor does she consider the significance of authority in the male figure from the point of view of an economy of masochism" (Rodowick, 11).

11. The balance achieved here is parallel to that which Thomas Kavanagh defines as the "two imaginaries" of film theory: "As a spectator viewing a film, I am, to the extent that I take pleasure in it and am fascinated by it, participating in a dimension of my imaginary evoked and prolonged by the film as object. But to the extent that I go on to represent that experience within a properly symbolic discourse, I do so through calling into play and appealing to a second allegiance, a second imaginary identification. Here, however, my identification is not with the film as object, but with my own status as theorist. . . . Rich with my pleasure as spectator, I insist that pleasure become the material and support of a second, apparently symbolizing movement whereby what is consolidated is my identification with a second narcissistic imaginary" (Kavanagh, 214–15).

Bibliography

Ades, Dawn. *Dali*. London: Thames and Hudson, 1982.

Adorno, T. W. *Aesthetic Theory*. London: Routledge and Kegan Paul, 1984.

———. *The Culture Industry*. New York: Routledge, 1991.

———. "The Form of the Phonograph Record." *October* 55 (Winter 1990).

Agee, James. *Agee on Film*. New York: Grosset and Dunlap, 1958.

Allen, Robert C. and Douglas Gomery. *Film History: Theory and Practice*. New York: McGraw-Hill, 1985.

Anderegg, Michael. "Hollywood and Vietnam: John Wayne and Jane Fonda as Discourse." In *Inventing Vietnam: The War in Film and Television*. Anderegg, ed. Philadelphia: Temple University Press, 1991.

Anderson, Benedict. *Imagined Communities: Reflections on the Spread of Nationalism*. London: Verso, 1983.

Andersen, Thom. "Red Hollywood." In *Literature and the Visual Arts in Contemporary Society*. Suzanne Ferguson and Barbara Groseclose, eds. Columbus: Ohio State University Press, 1985.

Andrew, Dudley. *André Bazin*. New York: Oxford University Press, 1978.

———. "The Gravity of *Sunrise*." *Quarterly Review of Film Studies* 2.3 (1977): 356–79.

———. "The Unauthorized Auteur Today." In *Film Theory Goes to the Movies*. Jim Collins, Hilary Radner, and Ava Preacher Collins, eds. New York: Routledge, 1993.

Anon. "Cinema." *Time* 57 (19 June 1951): 102–4.

———. "Select Audiences for *Cutter's*." *Variety*, 29 April 1981.

Artaud, Antonin. *The Theater and Its Double*. Mary Caroline Richards, trans. New York: Grove, 1958.

Aumont, Jacques, Alain Bergala, Michael Marie, and Marc Vernet. *Aesthetics of Film*. Richard Neupert, trans. Austin: University of Texas Press, 1992.

Bach, Stephen. *Final Cut: Dreams and Disaster in the Making of* Heaven's Gate. London: Jonathan Cape, 1985.

Baudrillard, Jean. *Symbolic Exchange and Death*. Iain Hamilton Grant, trans. London: Sage, 1993.

———. *Selected Writings*. Mark Poster, ed. Cambridge: Polity Press, 1988.

Baxter, John. *The Hollywood Exiles*. London: Taplinger, 1976.

Bazin, André. *Jean Renoir*. Francois Truffaut, ed. W. W. Halsey II and William H. Simon, trans. New York: Simon and Schuster, 1973.

Bell, Daniel. *The End of Ideology: On the Exhaustion of Political Ideas in the Fifties*. Glencoe, Ill.: Free Press, 1960.

Bellour, Raymond. "To Alternate/To Narrate." In *Early Cinema*. Elsaesser, ed.

Benjamin, Walter. "The Work of Art in the Age of Mechanical Reproduction." In *Illuminations*. Hannah Arendt, ed. Schocken, 1969.

Bergstrom, Janet. "Alternation, Segmentation, Hypnosis: An Interview with Raymond Bellour." In *Feminism and Film Theory*. Penley, ed.

———. "Sexuality at a Loss: The Films of F. W. Murnau." *Poetics Today* 6.1–2 (1985): 185–204.

Bergson, Henri. *Creative Evolution*. Arthur Miller, trans. New York: Henry Holt, 1911.

Berman, Marshall. *All That Is Solid Melts into Air: The Experience of Modernity*. New York: Viking Penguin, 1988.

Bernstein, Matthew. "A Tale of Three Cities: The Banning of *Scarlet Street*." *Cinema Journal* 35.1 (Fall 1995): 27–52.

Biskind, Peter. *Seeing is Believing, or How Hollywood Taught Us to Stop Worrying and Love the Fifties*. New York: Pantheon, 1983.

Borde, Raymond and Etienne Chaumeton. *Panorama du Film Noir Americain*. Paris: Editions d'Aujourdhui, 1976.

Bordwell, David. *Narration in the Fiction Film*. Madison: University of Wisconsin Press, 1985.

Bordwell, David, Janet Staiger, and Kristin Thompson. *The Classical Hollywood Cinema*. New York: Columbia University Press, 1985.

Bourdieu, Pierre. *Distinction: Social Critique of the Judgment of Taste*. Cambridge, Mass.: Harvard University Press, 1984.

Bowser, Eileen. *The Transformation of Cinema, 1907–1915*. New York: Scribner's, 1990.

Braudy, Leo. *The World in a Frame*. New York: Doubleday, 1976.

———. *Jean Renoir: The World of His Films*. New York: Doubleday, 1972.

Burch, Noel. *Life to Those Shadows*. Berkeley: University of California Press, 1990.

Butzel, Marcia and Ana M. Lopez. "Mediating the National." *Quarterly Review of Film and Video* 14.3 (1993): 1–8.

Buzzoni, Genevieve and Reynold Humphries. "'One Flew Over the Cuckoo's Nest.'" *Framework* 2.5 (Winter 1976–1977): 23–24.

Calinescu, Matei. *Five Faces of Modernity*. Durham: Duke University Press, 1987.

Callow, Simon. *Charles Laughton: A Difficult Actor*. London: Methuen, 1987.

Cavell, Stanley. "Psychoanalysis and Cinema: The Melodrama of the Unknown Woman." In *Images in Our Souls: Cavell, Psychoanalysis and Cinema*. Baltimore: Johns Hopkins University Press, 1987.

———. *Pursuits of Happiness: The Hollywood Comedy of Remarriage*. Cambridge, Mass.: Harvard University Press, 1981.

Ciment, Michel. *Conversations with Losey*. New York: Methuen, 1985.

Clair, René. *Cinema Yesterday and Today*. New York: Dover, 1972.

CloseUp. Territet, Switzerland. Volume 1 (July 1927)—10 (December 1933).

Clover, Carol. *Men, Women and Chainsaws: Gender in the Modern Horror Film*. Princeton, N.J.: Princeton University Press, 1992.

Coates, Paul. *The Gorgon's Gaze: German Cinema, Expressionism, and the Image of Horror*. London: Cambridge University Press, 1991.

Conley, Tom. *Film Hieroglyphs: Ruptures in Classical Cinema*. Minneapolis: University of Minnesota Press, 1993.

Cormack, Mike. *Ideology and Cinematography in Hollywood, 1930–1939*. New York: St. Martin's Press, 1994.

Corrigan, Timothy. *A Cinema without Walls: Movies and Culture after Vietnam*. New Brunswick, N.J.: Rutgers University Press, 1991.

Crary, Jonathan. "Modernizing Vision." In *Vision and Visuality*. Hal Foster, ed. Seattle: Bay Press, 1988.

Debord, Guy. *Society of the Spectacle*. Detroit: Black and Red, 1983.

DeCordova, Richard. "From Lumiere to Pathe: The Breakup of Perspectival Space." In *Early Cinema*. Elsaesser, ed.

De Lauretis, Teresa. *Alice Doesn't: Feminism, Semiotics, Cinema*. Bloomington: Indiana University Press, 1984.

Deleuze, Gilles, *Sacher-Masoch: An Interpretation*. Trans. Jean McNeil. London: Faber and Faber, 1971.

Dick, Bernard F. *Star-Spangled Screen: American World War Two Film*. Lexington: University of Kentucky Press, 1985.

Doane, Mary Ann. "Desire in *Sunrise*." *Film Reader* 2 (January 1977): 71–77.

———. *Femmes Fatales*. New York: Routledge, 1991.

Douglas, Mary. *How Institutions Think*. Syracuse, N.Y.: Syracuse University Press, 1986.

Dyer, Richard. *Stars*. London: British Film Institute, 1979.

Durgnat, Raymond. *Jean Renoir*. Berkeley: University of California Press, 1974.

Eckert, Charles. "The English Cine-Structuralists." *Film Comment* 9.3 (May/June 1973): 46–51.

Edelman, Lee. *Homographesis: Essays in Gay Literary and Cultural Theory*. New York: Routledge, 1994.

Eisenstein, Sergei. *Film Form*. Jay Leyda, ed. and trans. New York: Harcourt, Brace and World, 1949.

Eisner, Lotte. *Murnau*. London: Secker and Warburg, 1973.

———. *Fritz Lang*. New York: Oxford University Press, 1977.

Eliade, Mircea. *Cosmos and History*. Willard R. Trask, trans. New York: Harper & Row, 1959.

Elsaesser, Thomas. *Early Cinema: Space/Frame/Narrative*. London: British Film Institute, 1990.

———. "Secret Affinities." *Sight and Sound* 58.1 (Winter 1988/1989): 33–39.

Eliot, T. S. *Selected Prose*. New York: Farrar, Straus and Giroux, 1975.

Eysteinsson, Astradur. *The Concept of Modernism*. Ithaca, N.Y.: Cornell University Press, 1990.

Falkenberg, Pamela. "'Hollywood' and the 'Art-Cinema' as a Bipolar Modeling System." *Wide Angle* 7.3 (1985): 44–53.

Farber, Stephen. "Americana Sweet and Sour." *Hudson Review* 29.2 (Spring 1976): 95–102.

Faulkner, Christopher. *The Social Cinema of Jean Renoir*. Princeton, N.J.: Princeton University Press, 1986.

Ferguson, Otis. *The Film Criticism of Otis Ferguson*. Philadelphia: Temple University Press, 1971.

Ferro, Marc. *Cinema and History*. Naomi Greene, trans. Detroit: Wayne State University Press, 1988.

Forgacs, Daniel. "National-Popular: Genealogy of a Concept." In *The Cultural Studies Reader*. Simon During, ed. New York: Routledge, 1993.

Foster, Hal. "The 'Primitive' Unconscious of Modern Art." *October* 34 (Fall 1985).

Freud, Sigmund. *Complete Psychological Works*, vol. 19. James Strachey, ed. London: Hogarth, 1961.

Friedberg, Anne. *Window Shopping: Cinema and the Postmodern*. Berkeley: University of California Press, 1993.

Frisby, David. *Fragments of Modernity: Theories of Modernity in the Work of Simmel, Kracauer and Benjamin*. Cambridge, Mass.: MIT Press, 1986.

Gaines, Jane, ed. *Classical Hollywood Narrative: The Paradigm Wars*. Durham: Duke University Press, 1992.

Gassner, John and Dudley Nichols, eds. *Twenty Best Film Plays*. New York: Crown, 1943.

Gellner, Ernest. *Nations and Nationalism*. Ithaca, N.Y.: Cornell University Press, 1983

Godard, Jean-Luc. *Godard on Godard*. Tom Milne and Jean Narboni, eds. New York: Viking Press, 1972.

———. *Un Vrai Histoire du Cinéma*. Paris: Albatross, 1980.

Goulding, Daniel J., ed. *Five Filmmakers: Tarkovsky, Forman, Polanski, Szabo, Makavaev*. Bloomington: Indiana University Press, 1994.

Goux, Jean-Joseph. *Symbolic Economies: After Marx and Freud*. Jennifer Curtis Gage, trans. Ithaca, N.Y.: Cornell University Press, 1990.

Gunning, Tom. *D. W. Griffith and the Origins of American Narrative Film*. Urbana: University of Illinois Press, 1991.

Hall, Jeanne. "'A Little Problem with Perspective': Art and Authorship in Fritz Lang's *Scarlet Street*." *Film Criticism* 21.1 (Fall 1996): 34–47.

Hames, Peter. "Forman." In *Five Filmmakers*. Goulding, ed.

Hartung, Philip T. Review of *Scarlet Street*. *Commonweal*. 22 February 1946.

Hatch, Robert. Review of *Petulia*. *Nation* (8 July 1968): 29.

Hansen, Miriam. *Babel and Babylon: Spectatorship in American Silent Film.* Cambridge, Mass.: Harvard University Press, 1991.

Hay, James. *Popular Film Culture in Fascist Italy: The Passing of the Rex.* Bloomington: Indiana University Press, 1987.

Hellman, John. *American Myth and the Legacy of Vietnam.* New York: Columbia University Press, 1986.

Henderson, Brian. *A Critique of Film Theory.* New York: Dutton, 1981.

Herring, Robert. "Synthetic Dawn." In *CloseUp* 2.3 (1928): 43.

Higashi, S. "DeMille and Lasky: Legitimizing Film as Art." *Film History* 4.4 (1990): 181–98.

Hillier, Jim, ed. *Cahiers du Cinéma: The 1950s; Neo-Realism, Hollywood, New Wave.* Cambridge, Mass.: Harvard University Press, 1985.

Hoberman, J. "Passer Cuts to the Bone." *Village Voice,* 25–31 March 1981.

Hobsbawm, E. J. *Nations and Nationalism since 1780: Programme, Myth, Reality.* Cambridge: Cambridge University Press, 1990.

Hofstadter, Richard. *The Paranoid Style in American Politics.* New York: Knopf, 1965.

Huyssen, Andreas. *After the Great Divide: Modernism, Mass Culture, Post-modernism.* Bloomington: Indiana University Press, 1986.

Jacobs, Lewis. *The Rise of the American Film.* New York: Harcourt, Brace, 1939.

Jameson, Fredric. "Postmodernism, or the Cultural Logic of Late Capitalism." *New Left Review* 146 (July/August 1984): 53–92.

———. "Periodizing the '60s." In *The '60s without Apology. Social Text* Collective, eds. Minneapolis: University of Minnesota Press, 1984.

Jameson, Richard T. "Passer's Way." *Film Comment* 17.4 (July/August 1981): 18–21.

Jay, Martin. *Permanent Exiles: Essays in the Intellectual Migration from Germany to America.* New York: Columbia University Press, 1986.

Jeffords, Susan. *The Remasculinization of America: Gender and the Vietnam War.* Bloomington: Indiana University Press, 1989.

Kagan, Norman. *Greenhorns: Foreign Filmmakers Interpret America.* Ann Arbor, Mich.: Pierian Press, 1982.

Kaplan, E. Ann. "Patterns of Violence toward Women in Fritz Lang's *While the City Sleeps." Wide Angle* 3.4 (1980).

——— . "Ideology and Cinematic Practice in Lang's *Scarlet Street* and Renoir's *La Chienne.*" *Wide Angle* 5.3 (1983).

Kavanagh, Thomas M. "Film Theory and the Two Imaginaries." In *The Limits of Theory*. Kavanagh, ed. Stanford, Calif.: Stanford University Press, 1988.

Klinger, Barbara. *Melodrama and Meaning: History, Culture and the Films of Douglas Sirk*. Bloomington: Indiana University Press, 1994.

Koch, Howard. *Mission to Moscow*. David Culbert, ed. Madison: University of Wisconsin Press, 1980.

Kozloff, Max. *The Privileged Eye: Essays on Photography*. Albuquerque, N.M.: University of New Mexico, 1987.

Kracauer, Siegfried. *From Caligari to Hitler*. Princeton, N.J.: Princeton University Press, 1947.

——— . "National Types as Hollywood Presents Them." In *Mass Culture: The Popular Arts in America*. Bernard Rosenberg, ed. Glencoe, Ill.: Free Press, 1957.

Kroes, Rob. *If You've Seen One You've Seen the Mall*. Urbana: University of Illinois Press, 1996.

Krupnick, Mark, ed. *Displacement: Derrida and After*. Bloomington: Indiana University Press, 1983.

Krutnick, Frank. *In a Lonely Street: Film Noir, Genre, Masculinity*. New York: Routledge, 1991.

Lang, Robert. *American Film Melodrama: Griffith, Vidor, Minnelli*. Princeton, N.J.: Princeton University Press, 1989.

Lev, Peter. *The Euro-American Cinema*. Austin: University of Texas Press, 1993.

Lévi-Strauss, Claude. *The Savage Mind*. Chicago: University of Chicago Press, 1968.

Lewis, Jon. *Whom God Wishes to Destroy: Francis Coppola and the New Hollywood*. Durham, N.C.: Duke University Press, 1995.

Leydon, Joe. "Interview with Ivan Passer and Jeffrey Alan Fiskin." *Film Comment* 17.4 (July/August 1981): 21–23.

McCarten, John. "The Current Cinema." *New Yorker* 27 (16 June 1951): 90–91.

Macdonald, Dwight. "A Theory of Mass Culture." *Diogenes* 3 (Summer 1953).

Manvell, Roger. *New Cinema in the USA*. New York: Dutton, 1968.

Massey, Irving. *Identity and Community*. Detroit: Wayne State University Press, 1994.

Mayne, Judith. *Cinema and Spectatorship*. New York: Routledge, 1993.

Merleau-Ponty, Maurice. *Essential Writings of Merleau-Ponty*. Alden L. Fisher, ed. New York: Harcourt, Brace and World, 1969.

Metz, Christian. *The Imaginary Signifier*. Ben Brewster, Celia Britton, Alfred Guzzetti, and Annwyl Williams, trans. Bloomington: Indiana University Press, 1982.

Mulvey, Laura. "Visual Pleasure and Narrative Cinema." In *Feminism and Film Theory*. Penley, ed.

Naremore, James. "Authorship and the Cultural Politics of Film Criticism." *Film Quarterly* 44.1 (Fall 1990).

Neale, Steve. "Art-Cinema as Institution." *Screen* 22.1 (1981): 11–39.

———. "Masculinity as Spectacle." *Screen* 24.6 (November/December 1983): 2–16.

———. "New Hollywood Cinema." *Screen* 17.2 (Summer 1976): 117–22.

Neve, Brian. *Film and Politics in America: A Social Tradition*. New York: Routledge, 1992.

Nichols, Dudley. *This Land Is Mine*. New York: Ungar, 1970.

———. "The Writer and the Film." In *Twenty Best Film Plays*. Gassner and Nichols, eds.

Orr, John. *Cinema and Modernity*. Cambridge: Polity Press, 1993.

"Our Country and Our Culture." *Partisan Review* 19.3 (May/June 1953).

Penley, Constance, ed. *Feminism and Film Theory*. New York: Routledge, 1988.

Petrie, Graham. *Hollywood Destinies: European Directors in America, 1922–1931*. New York: Routledge, 1985.

Polan, Dana. *Power and Paranoia: History, Narrative, and the American Cinema, 1940–1950*. New York: Columbia University Press, 1986.

Raskin, Richard. "*Casablanca* and United States Foreign Policy." *Film History* 4.2 (1990): 153–64.

Ray, Robert. *A Certain Tendency of the Hollywood Cinema, 1930–1980*. Princeton, N.J.: Princeton University Press, 1985.

Rentschler, Eric. *The Ministry of Illusion: Nazi Cinema and Its Afterlife*. Cambridge, Mass. Harvard University Press, 1996.

Review of *Sunrise*. *New York Times*. 29 January 1928, 6:2.

Rodowick, D. N. *The Crisis of Political Modernism*. Urbana: University of Illinois Press, 1988.

———. *The Difficulty of Difference: Psychoanalysis, Sexual Difference, and Film Theory*. New York: Routledge, 1991.

Rogin, Michael. *Blackface, White Noise: Jewish Immigrants in the Hollywood Melting Pot*. Berkeley: University of California Press, 1996.

———. *Ronald Reagan, the Movie, and Other Episodes in Political Demonology*. Berkeley: University of California Press, 1987.

Rose, Jacqueline. "Paranoia and the Film System." In *Feminism and Film Theory*. Penley, ed.

Ross, Andrew. *No Respect: Intellectuals and Popular Culture*. New York: Routledge, 1989.

Russell, Catherine. *Narrative Mortality: Death, Closure and New Wave Cinemas*. Minneapolis: University of Minnesota Press, 1995.

Sadoul, Georges. *Les Pionniers du Cinema*. Paris: Editions Denoel, 1947.

Safer, Elaine B. "'It's the Truth Even if It Didn't Happen': Ken Kesey's *One Flew over the Cuckoo's Nest*." *Literature/Film Quarterly* 5.2 (Spring 1977): 132–41.

Schatz, Thomas. *Hollywood Genres: Formulas, Filmmaking and the Studio System*. Philadelphia: Temple University Press, 1981.

———. "The New Hollywood." In *Film Theory Goes to the Movies*. Ava Collins, Jim Collins, and Hilary Radner, eds. New York: Routledge, 1993.

Schickel, Richard. Review of *Petulia*. *Life* (31 May 1968): 12.

Schrader, Paul. "Notes on *Film Noir*." In *Film Genre Reader*. Barry K. Grant, ed. Austin: University of Texas Press, 1986.

Secrest, Meryle. *Salvador Dali*. New York: Dutton, 1986.

Sedgwick, Eve Kosofsky. *Between Men: English Literature and Male Homosocial Desire*. New York: Columbia University Press, 1985.

Sesonske, Alexander. *Jean Renoir: The French Films*. Cambridge, Mass.: Harvard University Press, 1980.

Shell, Marc. *Children of the Earth: Literature, Politics and Nationhood*. New York: Oxford University Press, 1993.

Sikov, Ed. *Laughing Hysterically*. New York: Columbia University Press, 1994.

Silverman, Kaja. *Male Subjectivity at the Margins*. New York: Routledge, 1992.

Simmel, Georg. *Sociology of Georg Simmel*. Kurt H. Wolff, ed. and trans. Glencoe, Ill.: Free Press, 1950.

Simon, John. "Unholy Writ." In *Reverse Angle: A Decade of American Film*. New York: Clarkson N. Potter, 1982.

Slotkin, Richard. *Regeneration through Violence: The Mythology of the American Frontier, 1600–1860*. Wesleyan, Conn.: Wesleyan University Press, 1973.

Solé, Jacques. *Questions of the French Revolution*. Shelley Temchin, trans. New York: Pantheon, 1989.

Sopocy, Martin. "French and British Influences on Porter's *Life of an American Fireman*." *Film History* 1.2 (1987): 137–48.

Sorlin, Pierre. *European Cinemas, European Societies, 1939–1990*. New York: Routledge, 1991.

Staiger, Janet. *Interpreting Films*. Princeton, N.J.: Princeton University Press, 1993.

———. "The Politics of Film Canons." *Cinema Journal* 24.3 (Spring 1985): 4–23.

Studlar, Gaylyn. *In the Realm of Pleasure: von Sternberg, Dietrich and the Masochistic Aesthetic*. Urbana: University of Illinois Press, 1988.

Taylor, John Russell. *Strangers in Paradise: The Hollywood Emigrés, 1933–1950*. New York: Holt, Rinehart, and Winston, 1983.

Thompson, Jon. *Fiction, Crime and Empire: Clues to Modernity and Postmodernism*. Urbana: University of Illinois Press, 1993.

Torgovnick, Marianna. *Gone Primitive: Savage Intellects, Modern Lives*. Chicago: University of Chicago Press, 1991.

Turim, Maureen. *Flashbacks in Film: Memory and History*. New York: Routledge, 1989.

Turner, Dennis. "*Breathless*: Mirror Stage of the Nouvelle Vague." *SubStance* 12.4 (1983): 50–63.

———. "The Subject of *The Conversation*." *Cinema Journal* 24.4 (Summer 1985): 4–22.

Tyler, Parker. *Classics of the Foreign Film*. New York: Citadel, 1962.

Waldman, Diane. "The Childish, the Insane and the Ugly: The Representation of Modern Art in Popular Films and Fiction of the Forties." *Wide Angle* 5.2 (1982).

Warner, Marina. *L'Atalante*. London: British Film Institute, 1993.

Wexman, Virginia Wright. *Creating the Couple: Love, Marriage and Hollywood Performance*. Princeton, N.J.: Princeton University Press, 1993.

Whyte, William. *The Organization Man*. New York: Simon and Schuster, 1956.

Willemin, Paul. *Questions of "Third Cinema."* Bloomington: Indiana University Press, 1981.

Williams, Linda Ruth. *Critical Desire: Psychoanalysis and the Literary Subject*. London: Edward Arnold, 1995.

Williams, Raymond. "The Metropolis and the Emergence of Modernism." In *Unreal City: Urban Experience in Modern European Literature and Art*. David Kelly and Edward Timms, eds. Manchester, U.K.: Manchester University Press, 1985.

———. "When Was Modernism?" In *The Politics of Modernism*. London: Verso, 1989.

Willoquet-Maricondi, Paula. "Full-Metal Jacketing, or Masculinity in the Making." *Cinema Journal* 33.2 (Winter 1994): 5–21.

Wilson, Edmund. *Axel's Castle*. New York: Scribner's, 1931.

Wollen, Peter. *Signs and Meaning in the Cinema*. Bloomington: Indiana University Press, 1972.

Wood, Robin. *Hollywood from Vietnam to Reagan*. New York: Columbia University Press, 1986.

Wyatt, Justin. *High Concept: Movies and Marketing in Hollywood*. Austin: University of Texas Press, 1996.

Zupancic, Alenka. "A Perfect Place to Die." In Slavoj Zizek, ed. *Everything You Always Wanted to Know about Lacan (But Were Afraid to Ask Hitchcock)*. London: Verso, 1992.

Index